Read this book online today:

With SAP PRESS BooksOnline we offer you online access to knowledge from the leading SAP experts. Whether you use it as a beneficial supplement or as an alternative to the printed book, with SAP PRESS BooksOnline you can:

- Access your book anywhere, at any time. All you need is an Internet connection.
- Perform full text searches on your book and on the entire SAP PRESS library.
- Build your own personalized SAP library.

The SAP PRESS customer advantage:

Register this book today at www.sap-press.com and obtain exclusive free trial access to its online version. If you like it (and we think you will), you can choose to purchase permanent, unrestricted access to the online edition at a very special price!

Here's how to get started:

1. Visit www.sap-press.com.
2. Click on the link for SAP PRESS BooksOnline and login (or create an account).
3. Enter your free trial license key, shown below in the corner of the page.
4. Try out your online book with full, unrestricted access for a limited time!

Your personal free trial **license key** for this online book is:

`5he7-qxda-p3b8-fysg`

Inside SAP® BusinessObjects Advanced Analysis

# PRESS

SAP PRESS is a joint initiative of SAP and Galileo Press. The know-how offered by SAP specialists combined with the expertise of the Galileo Press publishing house offers the reader expert books in the field. SAP PRESS features first-hand information and expert advice, and provides useful skills for professional decision-making.

SAP PRESS offers a variety of books on technical and business related topics for the SAP user. For further information, please visit our website: *www.sap-press.com*.

Ingo Hilgefort
Reporting & Analytics Using SAP BusinessObjects
2009, 655 pp.
978-1-59229-310-0

Ingo Hilgefort
Integrating SAP BusinessObjects XI 3.1 Tools with SAP NetWeaver
2009, 258 pp.
978-1-59229-274-5

Ray Li, Evan DeLodder
Creating Dashboards with Xcelsius - Practical Guide
2010, 587 pp.
978-1-59229-335-3

Jim Brogden, Mac Holden, Heather Sinkwitz
SAP BusinessObjects Web Intelligence
2010, app. 550 pp.
978-1-59229-322-3

Ingo Hilgefort

Inside SAP® BusinessObjects Advanced Analysis

Bonn • Boston

Galileo Press is named after the Italian physicist, mathematician and philosopher Galileo Galilei (1564–1642). He is known as one of the founders of modern science and an advocate of our contemporary, heliocentric worldview. His words *Eppur se muove* (And yet it moves) have become legendary. The Galileo Press logo depicts Jupiter orbited by the four Galilean moons, which were discovered by Galileo in 1610.

Editor Erik Herman
Copyeditor Mike Beady
Cover Design Graham Geary
Photo Credit iStockphoto.com/janrysavy
Layout Design Vera Brauner
Production Manager Kelly O'Callaghan
Production Editor Graham Geary
Typesetting Publishers' Design and Production Services, Inc.
Printed and bound in Canada

ISBN 978-1-59229-371-1

© 2011 by Galileo Press Inc., Boston (MA)
1st Edition 2011

Library of Congress Cataloging-in-Publication Data
Hilgefort, Ingo.
  Inside SAP Businessobjects advanced analysis / Ingo Hilgefort. — 1st ed.
    p. cm.
  ISBN-13: 978-1-59229-371-1
  ISBN-10: 1-59229-371-9
 1. BusinessObjects. 2. SAP NetWeaver BW. 3. SAP ERP. 4. Management information systems. 5. Business intelligence—Data processing. I. Title.
  HF5548.4.B875H548 2010
  658.4'038028553—dc22
                               2010032223

All rights reserved. Neither this publication nor any part of it may be copied or reproduced in any form or by any means or translated into another language, without the prior consent of Galileo Press GmbH, Rheinwerkallee 4, 53227 Bonn, Germany.

Galileo Press makes no warranties or representations with respect to the content hereof and specifically disclaims any implied warranties of merchantability or fitness for any particular purpose. Galileo Press assumes no responsibility for any errors that may appear in this publication.

"Galileo Press" and the Galileo Press logo are registered trademarks of Galileo Press GmbH, Bonn, Germany. SAP PRESS is an imprint of Galileo Press.

All of the screenshots and graphics reproduced in this book are subject to copyright © SAP AG, Dietmar-Hopp-Allee 16, 69190 Walldorf, Germany.

SAP, the SAP-Logo, mySAP, mySAP.com, mySAP Business Suite, SAP NetWeaver, SAP R/3, SAP R/2, SAP B2B, SAPtronic, SAPscript, SAP BW, SAP CRM, SAP Early Watch, SAP ArchiveLink, SAP GUI, SAP Business Workflow, SAP Business Engineer, SAP Business Navigator, SAP Business Framework, SAP Business Information Warehouse, SAP inter-enterprise solutions, SAP APO, AcceleratedSAP, InterSAP, SAPoffice, SAPfind, SAPfile, SAPtime, SAPmail, SAPaccess, SAP-EDI, R/3 Retail, Accelerated HR, Accelerated HiTech, Accelerated Consumer Products, ABAP, ABAP/4, ALE/WEB, Alloy, BAPI, Business Framework, BW Explorer, Duet, Enjoy-SAP, mySAP.com e-business platform, mySAP Enterprise Portals, RIVA, SAPPHIRE, TeamSAP, Webflow and SAP PRESS are registered or unregistered trademarks of SAP AG, Walldorf, Germany.

All other products mentioned in this book are registered or unregistered trademarks of their respective companies.

Contents at a Glance

1 SAP BusinessObjects Advanced Analysis, Edition for Microsoft Office – Your New Business Explorer (BEx) Analyzer 19

2 Installation, Deployment and Configuration of Advanced Analysis Office 49

3 Advanced Analysis Office — Data Connectivity and Metadata Reuse 87

4 Advanced Analysis Office — Basic Functions 99

5 Advanced Analysis Office — Advanced Functions 187

6 Advanced Analysis Office and BEx Analyzer — a Comparison ... 255

7 Advanced Analysis Office Integrated with SAP BusinessObjects Enterprise 265

8 Advanced Analysis Office — Usage Scenarios 285

9 Advanced Analysis — Product Outlook 323

Dear Reader,

In your hands is Galileo/SAP PRESS' latest book from Ingo Hilgefort, *Inside SAP BusinessObjects Advanced Analysis, edition for Microsoft Office*. Ingo possess a level of product knowledge and passion for the SAP BusinessObjects business intelligence (BI) tools that is unsurpassed in the industry. Ingo combines his deep technical knowledge with an ability to write concise, focused, and actionable content. What this means to you as a reader and SAP professional, is that by reading this book, you'll obtain information that makes you more knowledgeable, more efficient, and a more valuable resource in your professional endeavors. Throughout the pages of this book, you'll be presented with a comprehensive review of the product features and functionalities, as well as targeted guidance on installation, deployment, data connectivity, and usage scenarios. You'll also benefit from a side-by-side comparison of SAP Advanced Analysis Office with SAP BEx Analyzer, and an outline of the main topics in the SAP BI roadmap for the Advanced Analysis Office version and the Web version. Without a doubt, that's a lot of material to cover in 350 pages and Ingo has done a masterful job.

It's been a unique pleasure working with Ingo to bring this book to the market. Enjoy!

Erik Herman
Editor, SAP PRESS

Galileo Press
Boston, MA

erik.herman@galileo-press.com
www.sap-press.com

Contents

Foreword 11
Acknowledgments 13
Preface 15

1 SAP BusinessObjects Advanced Analysis, Edition for Microsoft Office – Your New Business Explorer (BEx) Analyzer 19

1.1 SAP BusinessObjects Advanced Analysis, Edition for Microsoft Office – a Short Introduction 19
  1.1.1 A Brief Introduction to Voyager 20
  1.1.2 A Brief Introduction to SAP BEx 21
  1.1.3 Pioneer — Combining Voyager and SAP BEx 23
1.2 Introduction to the Complete SAP BusinessObjects BI Client Portfolio 25
  1.2.1 Enterprise Reporting 27
  1.2.2 Ad Hoc Query and Reporting 29
  1.2.3 Advanced Analysis 31
  1.2.4 Dashboarding and Data Visualization 33
  1.2.5 Search, Discovery, and Exploration 34
1.3 SAP Advanced Analysis — One Part of the Overall BI Puzzle 36
1.4 User Requirements for Advanced Analysis Office 40
1.5 Summary 48

2 Installation, Deployment and Configuration of Advanced Analysis Office 49

2.1 Installation of SAP Advanced Analysis Office 49
  2.1.1 Technical Prerequisites 49
2.2 Deployment Options for SAP Advanced Analysis Office ... 53
  2.2.1 Advanced Analysis Office Architecture 54
  2.2.2 Deploying Advanced Analysis without SAP BusinessObjects Enterprise 55
  2.2.3 Deploying Advanced Analysis Combined with SAP BusinessObjects Enterprise 57

	2.2.4	Summary and Conclusions	58
	2.2.5	Setting Up Connections in SAP BusinessObjects Enterprise	62
	2.2.6	Configuring Microsoft Excel and Microsoft PowerPoint Settings	66
	2.2.7	Configuring Connections to SAP BusinessObjects Enterprise	68
	2.2.8	Enabling or Disabling Advanced Analysis Office Plug-In	73
	2.2.9	Multi-Lingual Behavior of Advanced Analysis Office	75
	2.2.10	Setting Up User Authorizations and Rights	76
	2.2.11	User Authentication	83
2.3	Summary		84

3 Advanced Analysis Office — Data Connectivity and Metadata Reuse 87

3.1	Data Connectivity Options	85
3.2	Leveraging SAP NetWeaver BW Metadata	87
	3.2.1 BEx Query versus InfoProvider	95
3.3	Summary	97

4 Advanced Analysis Office — Basic Functions 99

4.1	Advanced Analysis Office — Microsoft Excel	101
	4.1.1 Establishing Data Connectivity	102
	4.1.2 Open and Saving Workbooks	110
	4.1.3 Insert Your First Crosstab	111
	4.1.4 Navigation Options	114
	4.1.5 Formatting Data	121
	4.1.6 Sorting and Filtering	126
	4.1.7 Charting	140
	4.1.8 Conditional Formatting	142
	4.1.9 Ranking, Conditions, and Filter by Measures	152
	4.1.10 Totals and Subtotals	161
	4.1.11 Prompting and Variables	164
	4.1.12 Displaying Information about the Data	167
4.2	Advanced Analysis Office — Microsoft PowerPoint	170

		4.2.1	Advanced Analysis Office — Microsoft Excel versus Microsoft PowerPoint	173
		4.2.2	Advanced Analysis Office for Microsoft PowerPoint — Basic Steps	174
	4.3	Summary		186

5 Advanced Analysis Office — Advanced Functions 187

	5.1	Advanced Functionality in Advanced Analysis Office for Microsoft Excel		187
		5.1.1	Using Hierarchies	187
		5.1.2	Displaying Characteristics as Hierarchy	203
		5.1.3	Creating Calculations	206
		5.1.4	Using Data as a "Formula"	211
		5.1.5	Adding a Filter Panel	228
		5.1.6	Creating a Microsoft PowerPoint Slide	230
		5.1.7	Using Additional Information and Settings	234
		5.1.8	Working with Styles	242
	5.2	Advanced Functionality in Advanced Analysis Office for Microsoft PowerPoint		247
	5.3	Summary		253

6 Advanced Analysis Office and BEx Analyzer — a Comparison ... 255

	6.1	Supported Functionality	255
	6.2	Missing Functionality	257
	6.3	Summary and Conclusion	259

7 Advanced Analysis Office Integrated with SAP BusinessObjects Enterprise 265

	7.1	Lifecycle Management		261
	7.2	Object-Level and Data-Level Security		269
		7.2.1	Data-Level Security	270
		7.2.2	Object-Level Security	270
	7.3	Sharing of Common Objects		271
		7.3.1	Sharing Connections	271
		7.3.2	Sharing Workbooks and Presentations	276

	7.4	User Authentication and SSO	278
	7.5	Integration with InfoView	280
	7.6	Summary	283

8 Advanced Analysis Office — Usage Scenarios ... 285

	8.1	Advanced Analysis Office and Customer Support	285
	8.2	Advanced Analysis Office and Product Profitability	296
	8.3	Advanced Analysis Office and Sales Planning	307
	8.4	Advanced Analysis Office and Procurement	315
	8.5	Summary	321

9 Advanced Analysis — Product Outlook ... 323

	9.1	Advanced Analysis, Edition for Microsoft Office	323
	9.2	Advanced Analysis, Web Edition	325
	9.3	Integration with SAP BusinessObjects XI 4.0	330
	9.4	Beyond SAP BusinessObjects XI 4.0	332
	9.5	Summary	334

The Author	335
Index	337

Foreword

Every software user wants 'it.' 'It' — that is the right information, at the right time, targeted at the consumer of the information. The right information: All the information that is relevant in the business context of an inquiry. Not more information than necessary, not missing out on essential information. The right time: meaning access to information before the reason for an inquiry, maybe a minor issue becomes a major problem. The consumer: Increasingly we are going to a self-service world, where business users pursue inquiries on data and information themselves, not relying on IT or few, selected expert users.

Users expect to find answers via a simple search, preferably using common business terms, not abstract names of data fields. Lines of business heads expect answers to business questions instantly, to be preventive, not reactionary. Companies and users nowadays expect bits and bytes of information to be connected and related. In other words, information consumers and information providers are looking for contextualized information which is related and/or embedded in a business context. And users expect instant gratification, which is an answer to their questions and thus information at their fingertips. Users are accustomed to finding answers to their queries in the Internet within seconds and expect the same instant response time in their working life, be it intra-company, between companies, or business-to-consumer. Ultimately, it's about business analytics for the masses, information for the masses within a very short response time.

SAP, with its market-leading business intelligence solutions, and its avant-garde research and development in in-memory technology, and its application of this technology to cutting edge business solutions, is well positioned to transform business intelligence and business analytics. The application of contextualized, instantly available information to business analytics will put users into a position to ask in laymen's terms, question upon question and get instant answers to these business inquiries. Imagine the future of business interactions under these changed boundary conditions. Advanced analytics and predictive analytics cease to be a discipline for the few and becomes a common denominator for decision making. SAP's vision is to make business intelligence available to everyone in a business transaction — within and beyond the enterprise. SAP is well positioned to spearhead this business transformation — as a leader in business applications as well as in business intelligence.

It has been my pleasure to work with Ingo Hilgefort over the past couple of years, enjoying his creative approaches to solving customers' business questions. Ingo pioneered an approach where he profiles customers into business intelligence patterns providing real-life, practical recommendations as to what solutions and growth paths are applicable to their system landscape. Ingo has directly or indirectly interacted with thousands of customers providing answers to their inquiries via various channels, be it speaking engagements, blogs, his books, or online engagement. Ingo is a veteran at integrating SAP BusinessObjects with SAP applications, and has worked in this field since 2000. I am very pleased that Ingo dedicates his passion for business intelligence by sharing his knowledge in this book, providing thoughtful insights and effective recommendations. This book is a delightful and essential read for any SAP customer or business intelligence aficionado seeking to make the most out of SAP's business intelligence solutions. This book will expedite readers' ability to maximize the value they and their organizations get from SAP solutions.

Elvira Wallis
SVP, Customer Insight & Action
SAP Labs, Palo Alto, US

Acknowledgments

I will keep this short, but I definitely want to say many, many thanks to several people. First, thanks to the team at Galileo/SAP PRESS, and especially Erik Herman, for making this a great and smooth experience. In addition, I want to give a tremendous thanks to the following great people for their input, feedback, and support:

- Katie Newlon, Timken Company (retired) & ASUG BI Community
- Tammy Powlas, Fairfax Water & ASUG BI Community
- Joyce Butler, Cameron International & ASUG BI Community
- Rajeev Kapur, Newell Rubbermaid & ASUG BI Community
- Yatkwai Kee, Newell Rubbermaid & ASUG BI Community
- Eric Schemer, SAP AG
- Alexander Peter, SAP AG
- Daniel Haecker, SAP AG

A great thank-you to all of these people, it is great to know and work with you.

And last but not least, I can't forget my manager, Juergen Lindner, and the managers of my team — Isabell Petzelt and Elvira Wallis. I would not be here without your help, support, and encouragement. It is a great honor to be a part of such a great team with such leadership.

Ingo Hilgefort

Preface

Well, this is part four of my journey as an author. I started off with a book on installation and deployment guidance; moved on to SAP BusinessObjects Business Intelligence (BI) client tools to answer the question, "Which BI Tool to use"; and then covered SAP BusinessObjects Explorer. Now you are holding book four in your hands — *SAP BusinessObjects Advanced Analysis, Edition for Microsoft Office*. After the success and the overwhelming feedback from customers and partners on the first three books, it felt like the next logical step was to provide a guide for Advanced Analysis Office.

The goal of this book — which is similar to the previous books — is to give you a simple step-by-step guide to this great new product so that you can leverage Advanced Analysis Office as part of your overall SAP BusinessObjects BI portfolio.

Target Group

The main audience for this book is twofold. First, I hope that BI team leads, BI project managers, and BI decision makers can use this book to understand the functionality and capabilities of Advanced Analysis, Microsoft Office edition. The book provides guidance on installation and deployment and also on the support of metadata from SAP NetWeaver Business Warehouse (BW) and when to use Advanced Analysis Office as part of an overall portfolio.

In addition, this book contains a step-by-step overview on how to use Advanced Analysis Office, starting with some simple steps and then moving into its more advanced capabilities.

The focus here is not to make you an expert on the installation, deployment, and configuration of Advanced Analysis Office. The focus is to provide you with a

Preface

simple, step-by-step introduction to the product and provide you great examples and scenarios so that you can leverage the product as part of your BI offering.

To fully benefit from this book, you should have some previous knowledge of SAP NetWeaver BW. With regard to SAP BusinessObjects, we kept the need for previous knowledge at a minimum, so you should be able to follow along with this book even without any SAP BusinessObjects knowledge.

Technical Prerequisites

All of the steps and examples in the book are based on the initial release of Advanced Analysis Office on an SAP NetWeaver BW 7.01 system. I used SAP BusinessObjects XI 3.1 Service Pack 02 as my BI platform and will indicate upcoming changes with the SAP BusinessObjects XI 4.0 platform in the product outlook chapter.

Please note that Advanced Analysis Office can work on top of an SAP BusinessObjects XI 3.1 platform and an SAP BusinessObjects XI 4.0 platform. Advanced Analysis Office should support both versions of your BI platform and therefore everything that you learn in this book is applicable to both releases.

All of the SAP BusinessObjects software can be downloaded from the service marketplace and you can receive temporary license keys from *http://service.sap.com/licensekeys*. The book is practically oriented, so if you do not have the software we highly recommend that you download the following components to follow all of the outlined steps:

- SAP BusinessObjects Enterprise XI 3.1 Service Pack 01 and Service Pack 02
- SAP BusinessObjects Integration for SAP Solutions XI 3.1 Service Pack 01 and Service Pack 02
- SAP BusinessObjects Advanced Analysis, edition for Microsoft Office

Service Pack 02 is an installation on top of Service Pack 01, therefore, you need to install the Service Pack 01 downloads before updating your landscape with Service Pack 02. You can also install Service Pack 03 for the listed products as Service Pack 03 is a full installation.

Preface

You should also have access to an SAP NetWeaver BW system so that you can follow the examples. If you can't access an existing system, you can also download a trial version from SAP NetWeaver via the Download section in the SAP Developer Network (SDN).

Structure of the Book

Here is a short overview on the content of the chapters:

Chapter 1 — SAP BusinessObjects Advanced Analysis, Microsoft Office Edition — Introduction

In this chapter you will receive an introduction to SAP BusinessObjects Advanced Analysis, edition for Microsoft Office and learn how different BI tools have helped it evolve into the tool as it exists today. In addition, you will learn about the role SAP BusinessObjects Advanced Analysis, edition for Microsoft Office plays in an overall BI portfolio, when you might use it, and what tools you can use with it.

Chapter 2 — Installation and Deployment

In the second chapter we will look at typical deployment scenarios for SAP BusinessObjects Advanced Analysis, edition for Microsoft Office, and learn more about the installation and configuration as part of the overall landscape.

Chapter 3 — Data Connectivity

In chapter 3 we take a look at the options for connecting to your corporate data in SAP NetWeaver BW and how the tool can leverage existing SAP NetWeaver BW queries and metadata for your workbooks.

Chapter 4 — Basic Functionality

In chapter 4 we will show you the basic functionalities of SAP BusinessObjects Advanced Analysis, edition for Microsoft Office, with a simple, step-by-step guide.

17

Chapter 5 — Advanced Features

Chapter 5 is an introduction to the more advanced capabilities of SAP BusinessObjects Advanced Analysis, edition for Microsoft Office, for Microsoft Excel® and Microsoft PowerPoint®. We will review several functionalities and provide you with a step-by-step guide that you can follow.

Chapter 6 — Business Explorer (BEx) Analyzer vs. Advanced Analysis

Chapter 6 compares the BEx Analyzer functionality to the SAP BusinessObjects Advanced Analysis, edition for Microsoft Office functionality.

Chapter 7 — Platform Integration

Chapter 7 provides you with an overview of how SAP BusinessObjects Advanced Analysis, edition for Microsoft Office, integrates into your SAP BusinessObjects Enterprise platform for Release XI 3.1 and Release XI 4.0.

Chapter 8 — Usage Scenario

Chapter 8 provides you with a set of typical business scenarios and business problems and shows you how you can use SAP BusinessObjects Advanced Analysis, edition for Microsoft Office to solve problems and provide answers to your business.

Chapter 9 — Product Outlook

Chapter 9 contains a brief outlook into upcoming enhancements to the product roadmap.

With SAP BusinessObjects Advanced Analysis, edition for Microsoft Office, you now have a complete Business Intelligence (BI) portfolio for an SAP NetWeaver and SAP BusinessObjects integrated landscape.

1 SAP BusinessObjects Advanced Analysis, Edition for Microsoft Office – Your New Business Explorer (BEx) Analyzer

In this chapter, we will start with a short introduction to SAP BusinessObjects Advanced Analysis, edition for Microsoft Office, and look at how you can integrate it into your BI offerings for your users.

1.1 SAP BusinessObjects Advanced Analysis, Edition for Microsoft Office – a Short Introduction

When SAP acquired BusinessObjects both companies were competing against each other for an Online Analytical Processing (OLAP)–style client tool for their customers. In SAP-based deployments, customer were (and still are) using SAP BEx as either a plug-in for Microsoft Office (known as SAP BEx Analyzer) or as a Web reporting tool. With BusinessObjects, Voyager was created to compete with BEx and offer customers an alternative BI client tool for their SAP NetWeaver Business Information Warehouse (BW)–based reporting, but to also offer customers using Microsoft Analysis Services a great analysis tool. History changed the roadmap of these tools in early 2008 and they are now combined to provide you — the customer — with the best possible BI client tool for advanced analysis with combined functionality from SAP BEx and Voyager. Before we continue with the details of SAP BusinessObjects Advanced Analysis, edition for Microsoft Office, let's take a quick look at Voyager and SAP BEx.

1 | SAP BusinessObjects Advanced Analysis, Edition for Microsoft Office

> **SAP BusinessObjects Advanced Analysis, Edition for Microsoft Office**
>
> Purely for simplicity, we will refer to SAP BusinessObjects Advanced Analysis, Edition for Microsoft Office, as Advanced Analysis Office and to SAP BusinessObjects Advanced Analysis, Web Edition, as Advanced Analysis Web. Please note that only Advanced Analysis Office is being released on the SAP BusinessObjects XI 3.1 platform. Both versions for Advanced Analysis are scheduled for release with the XI 4.0 platform.

1.1.1 A Brief Introduction to Voyager

BusinessObjects has a long history of creating a BI client tool for the typical power user with OLAP-style workflows. BusinessObjects acquired Crystal Decisions, and with that acquisition also obtained a product called Crystal Analysis, which then later became OLAP Intelligence. OLAP Intelligence was the predecessor of Voyager. When the planning of Voyager started the focus was twofold — to compete with BEx and to focus on an easy-to-use, purely web-based solution that gave a great user experience.

As Figure 1.1 shows, Voyager was created with a focus on SAP NetWeaver BW, Microsoft Analysis Service, and Hyperion Essbase as underlying OLAP data sources and had the ability to use multiple data sources in a single Voyager workspace.

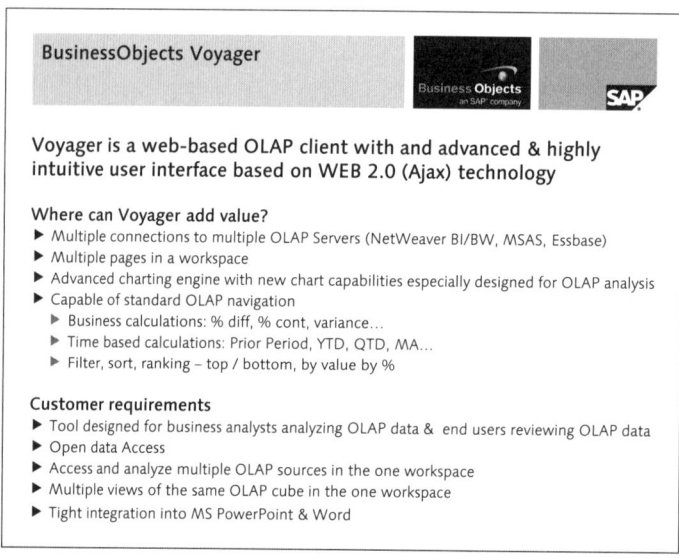

Figure 1.1 BusinessObjects Voyager

Voyager also had an excellent user interface (UI) and user experience, and advanced charting (see Figure 1.2).

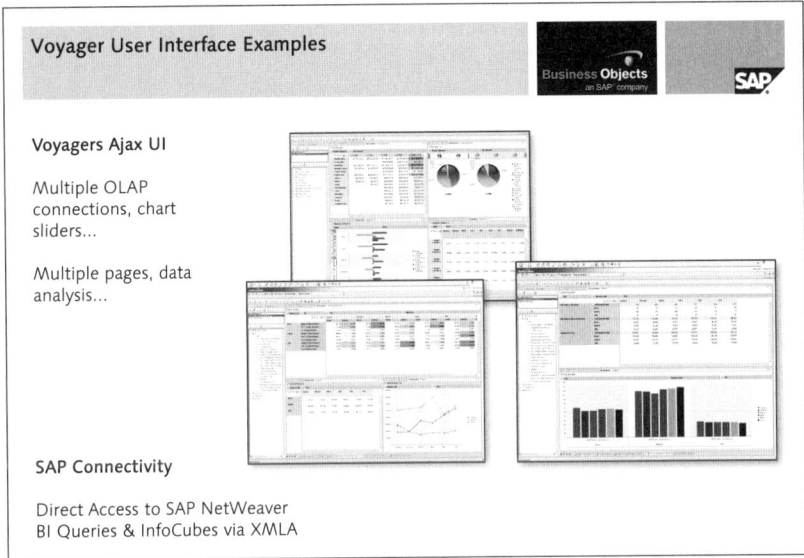

Figure 1.2 BusinessObjects Voyager UI Examples

Overall, Voyager was the counterpart to BEx Web Reporting from BusinessObjects.

1.1.2 A Brief Introduction to SAP BEx

Over the years, SAP developed two distinct flavors of their BEx reporting tool. BEx is a suite of tools, including the Web Application Designer (WAD), but the two main tools are the BEx Analyzer and the BEx Web Analyzer.

BEx Analyzer is a plug-in for Microsoft Excel that lets customers analyze their SAP NetWeaver BW data in a common and well-known environment (see Figure 1.3).

BEx Analyzer offers customers typical OLAP-type workflows and functionalities in a common environment by working as a plug-in inside Microsoft Excel, however, one of the shortcomings of BEx Analyzer is that it is not able to report on any other datasource than SAP NetWeaver BW.

1 | SAP BusinessObjects Advanced Analysis, Edition for Microsoft Office

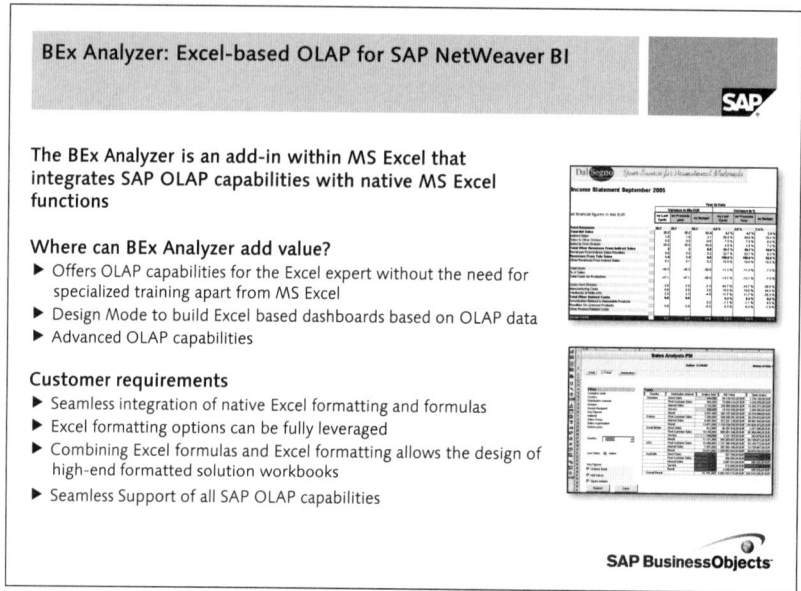

Figure 1.3 BusinessExplorer Analyzer

BEx Web Analyzer (see Figure 1.4) is the BEx Analyzer counterpart in a web environment and provides similar functionality for a browser-based deployment.

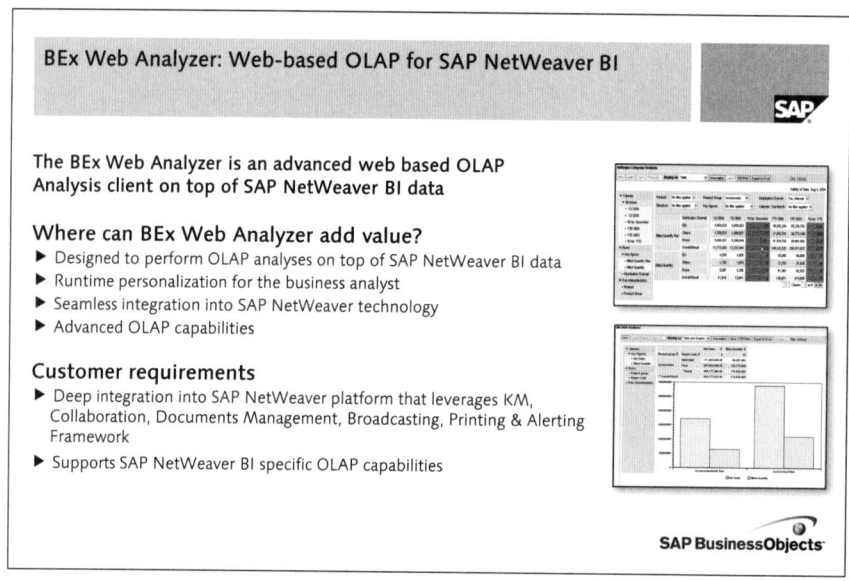

Figure 1.4 BusinessExplorer Web Reporting

Both BI clients — BEx Analyzer and BEx Web Analyzer — provide an environment for advanced analysis but, compared to Voyager, there was room for improvement with regards to the user experience and the fact that BEx tools were only focused on SAP NetWeaver BW — most customers have the need for other datasources.

1.1.3 Pioneer — Combining Voyager and SAP BEx

With the acquisition of BusinessObjects, SAP also acquired Voyager as one of the BI client tools from BusinessObjects. Shortly after the acquisition, teams from both companies quickly created a combined roadmap (see Figure 1.5).

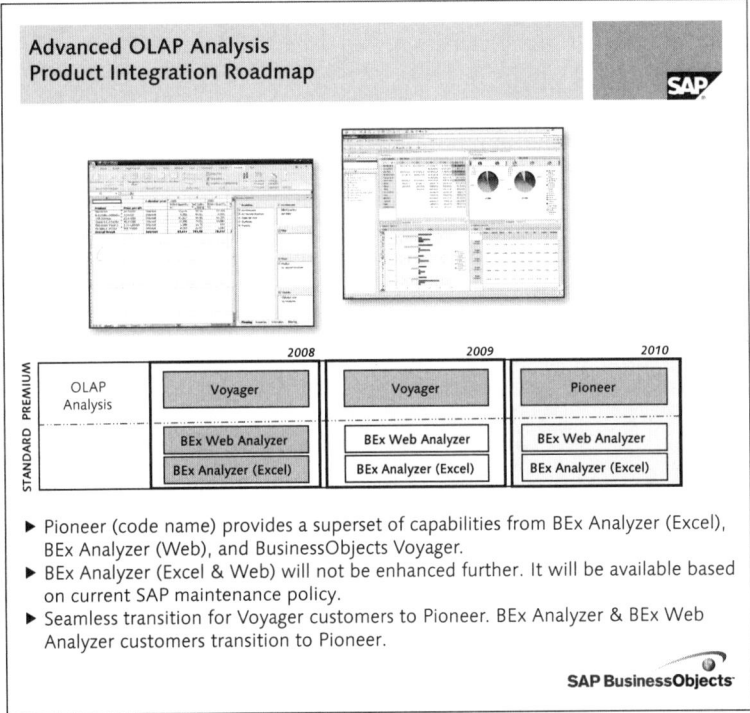

Figure 1.5 Advanced OLAP Analysis Product Roadmap

This combined roadmap clearly shows that the Pioneer project will combine Voyager, BEx Analyzer, and BEx Web Analyzer. SAP BusinessObjects Advanced Analysis is the official product name for the Pioneer project (see Figure 1.6).

1 | SAP BusinessObjects Advanced Analysis, Edition for Microsoft Office

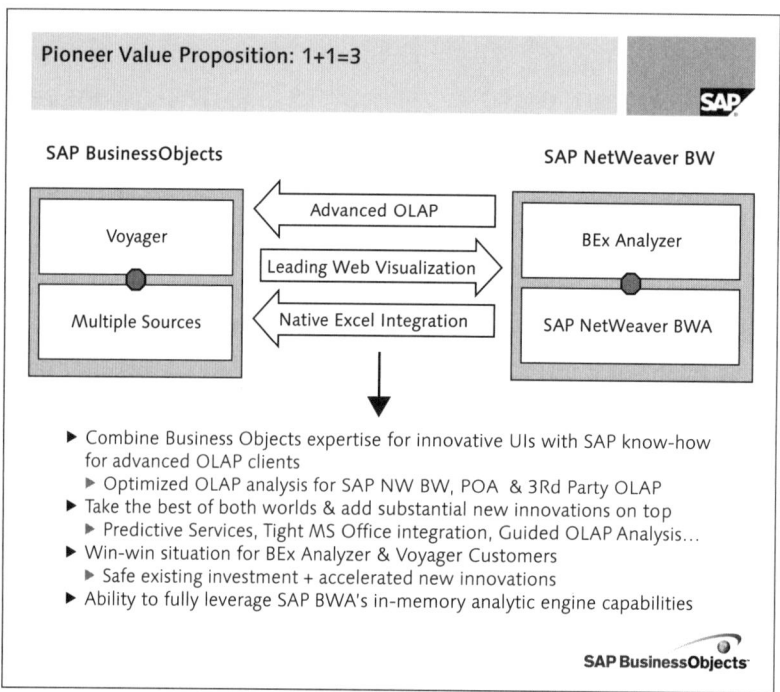

Figure 1.6 Pioneer

SAP BusinessObjects Advanced Analysis (former Project Pioneer) is using the best of both worlds – SAP and BusinessObjects – by leveraging the great integration with Microsoft Excel and the advanced analysis functionality from the BEx suite with the leading visualizations from Voyager.

As you can see in Figure 1.7 SAP BusinessObjects Advanced Analysis will come in two versions, one version for the Microsoft Office edition and a web edition. Please note, that for the SAP BusinessObjects XI 3.1 platform SAP BusinessObjects Advanced Analysis will only be released for the Microsoft Office edition and the web edition will be released as the next major release of the SAP BusinessObjects platform.

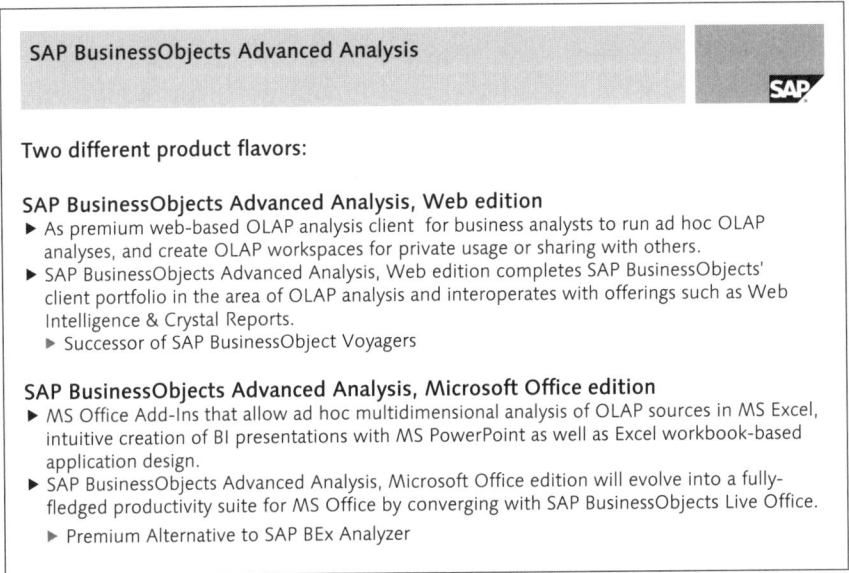

Figure 1.7 SAP BusinessObjects Advanced Analysis

1.2 Introduction to the Complete SAP BusinessObjects BI Client Portfolio

In this section, we will look at the SAP BusinessObjects portfolio of BI tools and provide a quick introduction to each tool and their main use.

During the integration of SAP and SAP BusinessObjects (former BusinessObjects), reporting and analysis product portfolios were grouped into usage scenarios, and we will use these scenarios to look at the product portfolios and the typical customer requirements for these areas (see Figure 1.8).

As you can see in Figure 1.8, with the exception of the Ad-hoc Reporting & Analysis area, SAP and SAP BusinessObjects both offered products to serve similar customer requirements. Now, as a single company, these tools will merge over time. Figure 1.9 shows the decisions that have been made for combining SAP and SAP BusinessObjects products.

1 | SAP BusinessObjects Advanced Analysis, Edition for Microsoft Office

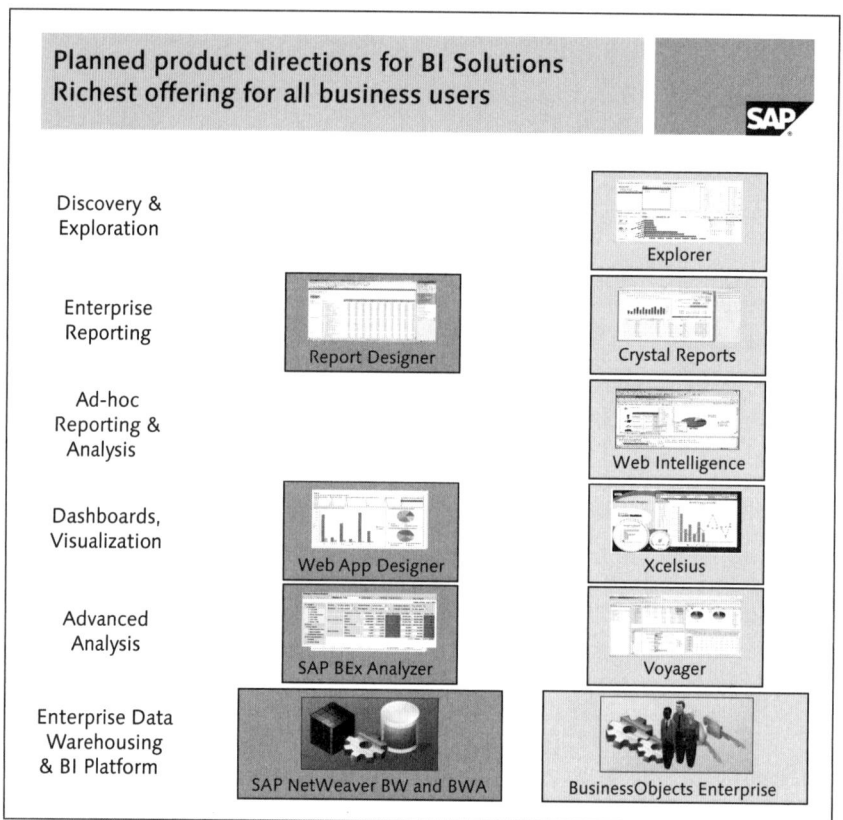

Figure 1.8 SAP BusinessObjects Roadmap

The most important information that Figure 1.9 provides is the clarity about which of the product offerings are taking the lead in the BI tools categories. All of the products listed are either already available today, such as Crystal Reports, Xcelsius, and Web Intelligence, or will be shortly, such as Advanced Analysis. Advanced Analysis Office is now available in combination with SAP BusinessObjects XI 3.1 and Advanced Analysis Web will be available with the next major release of the SAP BusinessObjects BI platform.

In the next couple of sections we will use the BI tools categories to see which SAP BusinessObjects products are being offered and take a look at their use.

Introduction to the Complete SAP BusinessObjects BI Client Portfolio | **1.2**

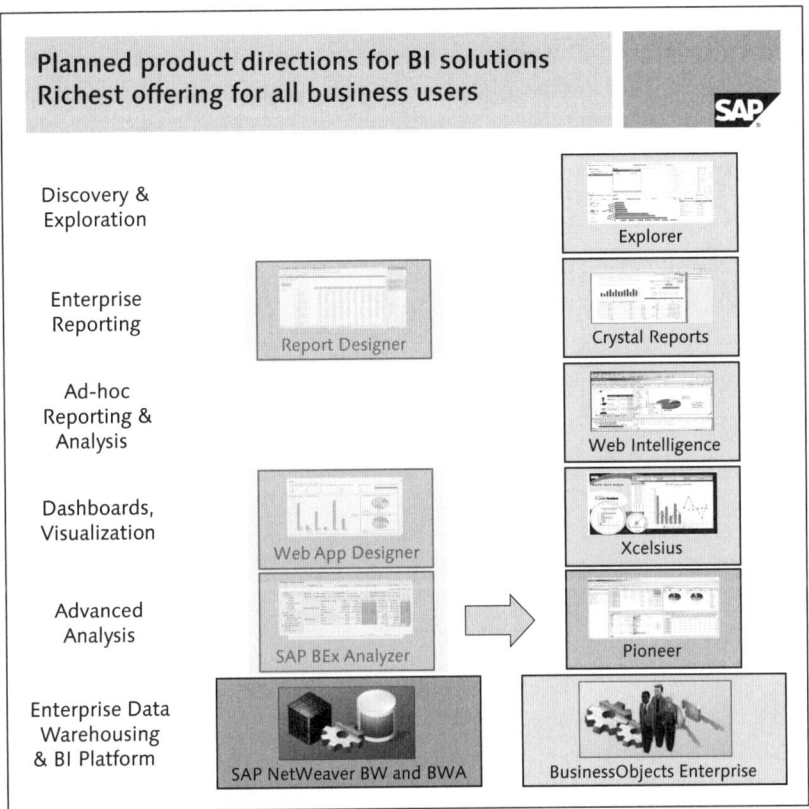

Figure 1.9 SAP BusinessObjects Roadmap

1.2.1 Enterprise Reporting

Crystal Reports is the de facto standard reporting tool for Enterprise Reporting. In this category, Crystal Reports will replace BEx Report Designer and provide the following reporting capabilities:

- Highly formatted and print optimized reporting
- Layout-focused reporting
- Static reporting
- Parameterized reporting

27

Based on the preceding capabilities, you may think Crystal Reports is only capable of creating well-formatted, pixel-perfect invoices; purchase orders; or account balance statements (see Figure 1.10), but Crystal Reports has evolved into a reporting tool that is capable of creating reports that include very sophisticated user interactivity — including integrating Xcelsius data visualizations as part of your report (see Figure 1.11).

Crystal Reports is a tool that is very easy to use and learn. It lets you access any kind of data sources and create a wide variety of reports and navigations within those reports. Nevertheless, the main focus and purpose of Crystal Reports is to provide you with the functionality to create content while you have complete control over the layout, font, positioning of objects and the rendering and printing on all different types of clients.

Account Number	G/L Account	Balance Carryforward	Balance Previous	Cum. Balance Previous	Debit Total	Credit Total	Cumulated Debit Balance	Cumulated Credit Balance	Cumulated Balance
INT/1000	Real estate and similar rights	-26,273.54	0.00	-26,273.54	225,216.24	939,007.93	0.00	-740,065.23	-740,065.23
INT/100000	Petty cash	-7,000.00	0.00	-7,000.00	0.00	0.00	0.00	-7,000.00	-7,000.00
INT/1010	Accumltd. Deprctn - Real Estate and Similar Rights	-644,077.00	0.00	-644,077.00	0.00	268,565.00	0.00	-912,642.00	-912,642.00
INT/11000	Machinery and equipment	2,000.00	0.00	2,000.00	2,000.00	0.00	4,000.00	0.00	4,000.00
INT/11010	Accumulated depreciation-plant and machinery	-493,188.00	0.00	-493,188.00	0.00	204,074.00	0.00	-697,262.00	-697,262.00
INT/113100	G.L Account	-3,322.00	0.00	-3,322.00	1,300.00	1,000.00	0.00	-3,022.00	-3,022.00
INT/113105	Bank 1 (other interim postings)	0.00	0.00	0.00	1,000.00	1,000.00	0.00	0.00	0.00
INT/140000	Customers - Domestic Receivables 1	0.00	0.00	0.00	2,100.00	1,100.00	1,000.00	0.00	1,000.00
INT/154000	Input tax	43.90	0.00	43.90	689.65	0.00	733.55	0.00	733.55
INT/160000	Accounts payable-domestic	-318.25	0.00	-318.25	0.00	7,300.00	0.00	-7,618.25	-7,618.25
INT/175000	Output tax	0.00	0.00	0.00	13.79	0.00	13.79	0.00	13.79
INT/191000	GR/IR clearing - own production	0.00	0.00	0.00	0.00	0.00	0.00	0.00	0.00

Figure 1.10 Crystal Reports Report

Introduction to the Complete SAP BusinessObjects BI Client Portfolio | **1.2**

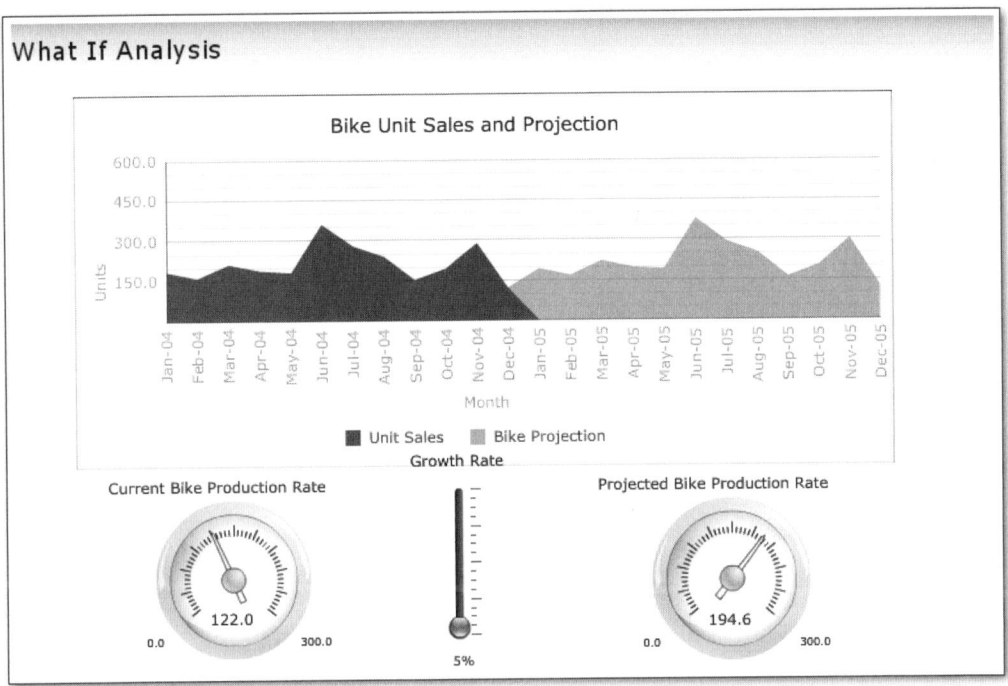

Figure 1.11 Crystal Reports – Interactive Report

1.2.2 Ad Hoc Query and Reporting

In the ad hoc query and reporting category, Web Intelligence takes the lead and provides you with the functionality to establish a self-service environment for end users to easily create, edit, and share reports based on any data source. Web Intelligence is a very simple and intuitive reporting tool that lets you create and edit reports in a web-based environment.

You can leverage Web Intelligence to consume and analyze information in a self-service-oriented environment so that there is no need for you to rely on your information technology (IT) department to specify and create a new report for you. You can easily specify the data you want to leverage in your report using the Web Intelligence query panel (see Figure 1.12).

1   SAP BusinessObjects Advanced Analysis, Edition for Microsoft Office

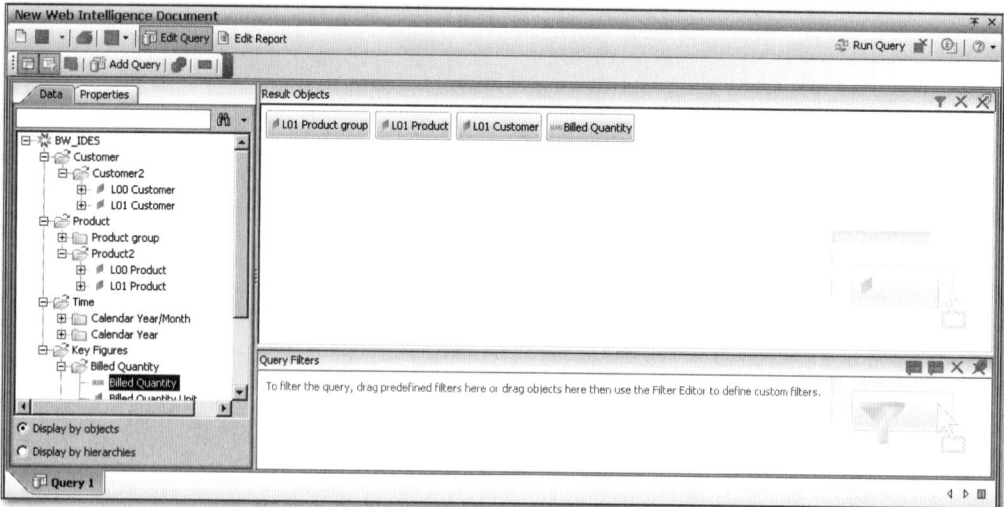

Figure 1.12   Web Intelligence Query Panel

You can easily leverage Web Intelligence to either create a new report or use an existing report, like the one shown in Figure 1.13, and change the report based on your needs. With some very simple steps you can change the report to not only provide a different layout, but also to show different information, as shown in Figure 1.14.

L01 Product group	L01 Product	L01 Customer	Billed Quantity	Net Sales
Office	Lamy Pencil	9999 Hotel Ltd	502	2,535
Office	Lamy Pencil	Abbey Coffee & Tea Group Inc	1,760	8,873
Office	Lamy Pencil	Abbey Co Inc	1,446	7,288
Office	Lamy Pencil	Abbey Enterprises Group Inc	502	2,535
Office	Lamy Pencil	Abbey Fine Foods Inc	502	2,535
Office	Lamy Pencil	Abbey Foods Ltd	660	3,327
Office	Lamy Pencil	Abbey Group Inc	1,917	9,665
Office	Lamy Pencil	Abbey Ltd	4,651	23,449
Office	Lamy Pencil	Abbey Lumber Co Inc	1,288	6,496
Office	Lamy Pencil	Abbey Motor Group Inc	1,131	5,704
Office	Lamy Pencil	Abbey Services Co Inc	502	2,535
Office	Lamy Pencil	Abbey Solutions Group Inc	345	1,743

Figure 1.13   Web Intelligence Report

Introduction to the Complete SAP BusinessObjects BI Client Portfolio | **1.2**

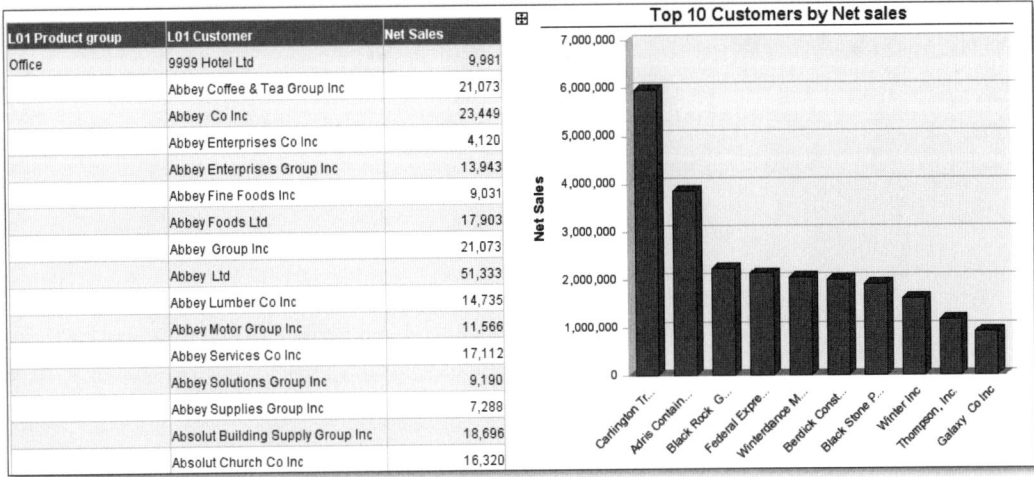

Figure 1.14 Web Intelligence Report

In addition, Web Intelligence gives you the choice of a fully web-based solution or a rich client solution for your ad hoc reporting needs.

1.2.3 Advanced Analysis

A key area in the overall BI tools portfolio is the functionality of an in-depth OLAP analysis client that provides you with the capability to create predefined workbooks that include guided navigations and the option to leverage the tool for an ad hoc OLAP analysis.

As you can see in Figure 1.8 and Figure 1.9, this area was covered by the BEx Analyzer for SAP and by Voyager for SAP BusinessObjects. Advanced Analysis, which will combine the best of both offerings (BEx and Voyager), will have a Microsoft Office version (see Figure 1.15) and a web-based version (see Figure 1.16).

31

1 | SAP BusinessObjects Advanced Analysis, Edition for Microsoft Office

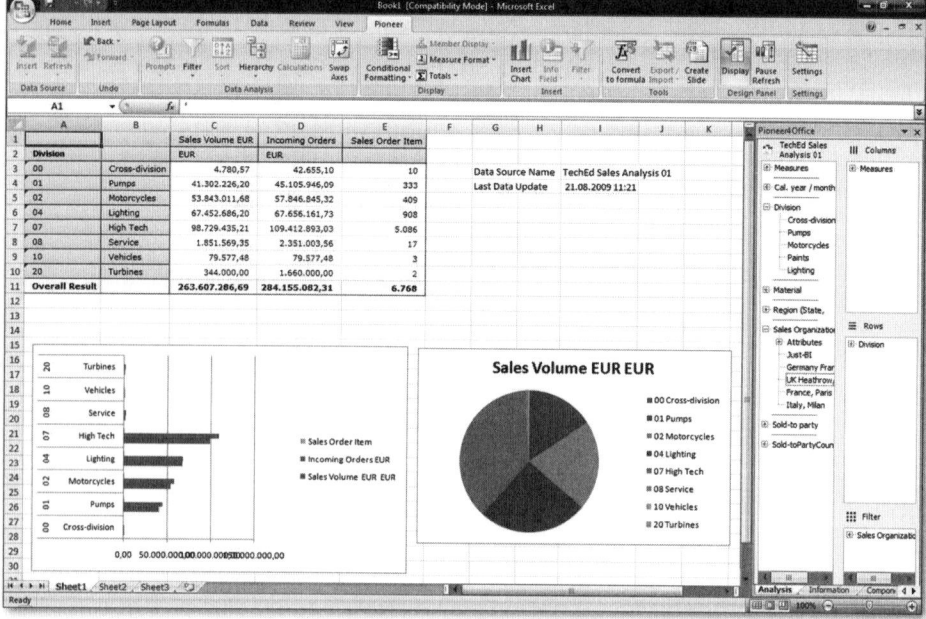

Figure 1.15 Advanced Analysis Office

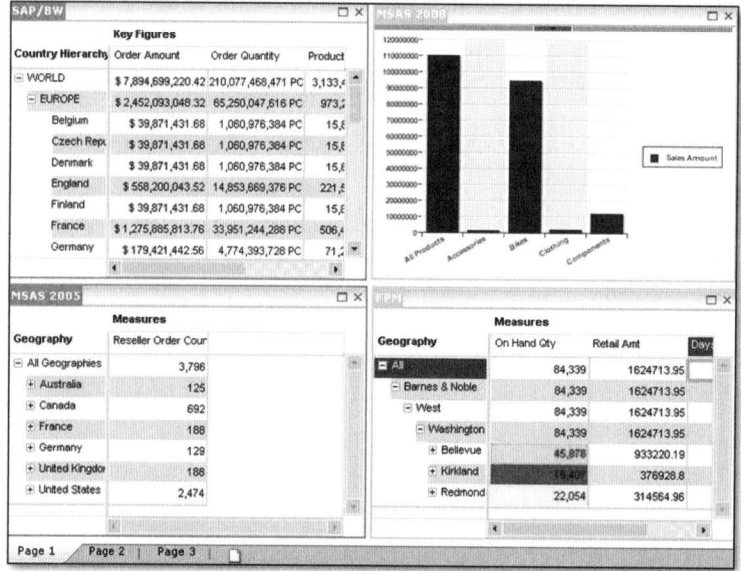

Figure 1.16 Advanced Analysis Web

32

1.2.4 Dashboarding and Data Visualization

Xcelsius is becoming the leading tool for dashboarding and data visualization, and is being positioned as the environment to create dashboard-style reports and analytics. Xcelsius is a very simple and intuitive tool that lets you create a broad range of data visualizations; starting from a very simple chart (see Figure 1.17) up to very complex interactive dashboards (see Figure 1.18).

Xcelsius uses a spreadsheet as part of its design environment and lets you set up conditions and logic for your dashboards in a simple manner. You can easily leverage all of the components that are delivered as part of the Xcelsius 2008 design environment, but you can also extend the environment by using the Xcelsius SDK and create your own visualization components using Adobe Flex.

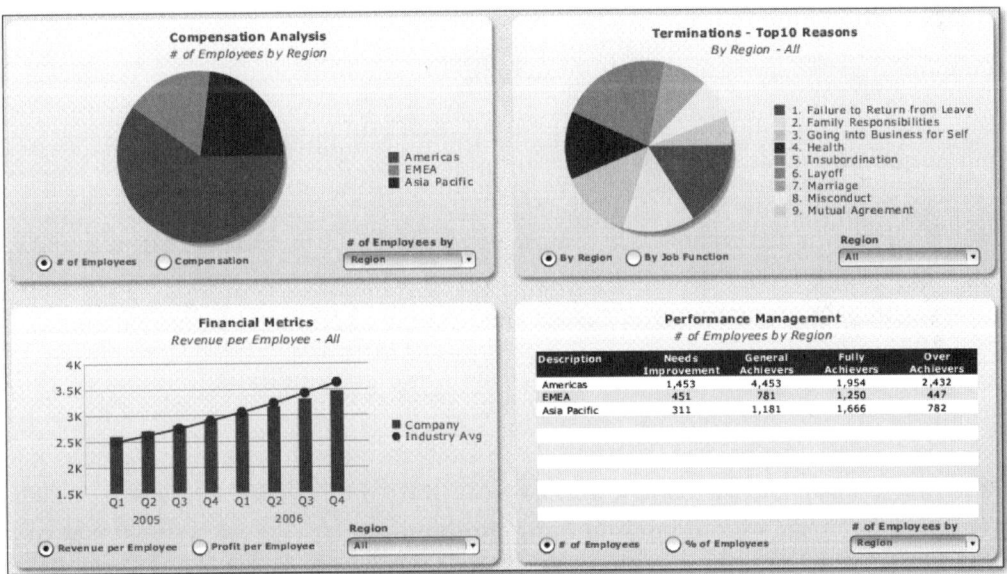

Figure 1.17 Xcelsius Dashboard

1 | SAP BusinessObjects Advanced Analysis, Edition for Microsoft Office

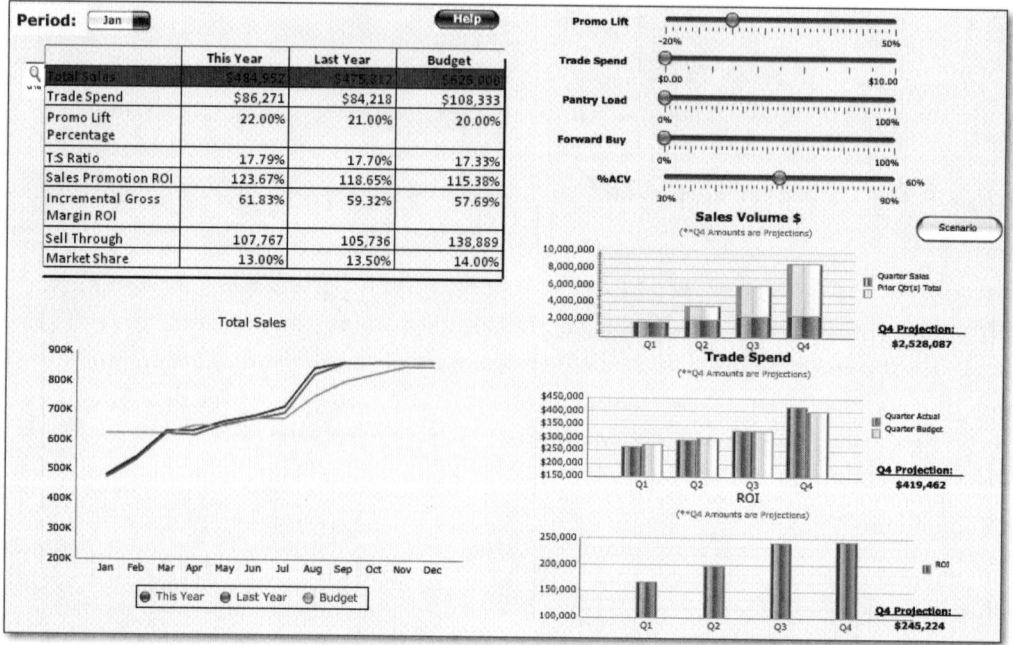

Figure 1.18 Xcelsius Dashboard

Xcelsius has the capability of leveraging several different datasources in a single dashboard. The most common options for your SAP datasources are to use a combination of Live Office with Crystal Reports or Web Intelligence, or to use Query as a Web Service in combination with a Universe, or to use the new connectivity providing direct access to SAP NetWeaver BW InfoProvider.

1.2.5 Search, Discovery, and Exploration

With the addition of SAP BusinessObjects Explorer (not to be confused with SAP BEx), you now have a very different but intuitive tool as part of your BI portfolio. SAP BusinessObjects Explorer provides you with the functionality to use a search interface on top of your data set. You can then use SAP BusinessObjects Explorer to navigate and explore the data further (see Figure 1.19).

Introduction to the Complete SAP BusinessObjects BI Client Portfolio | **1.2**

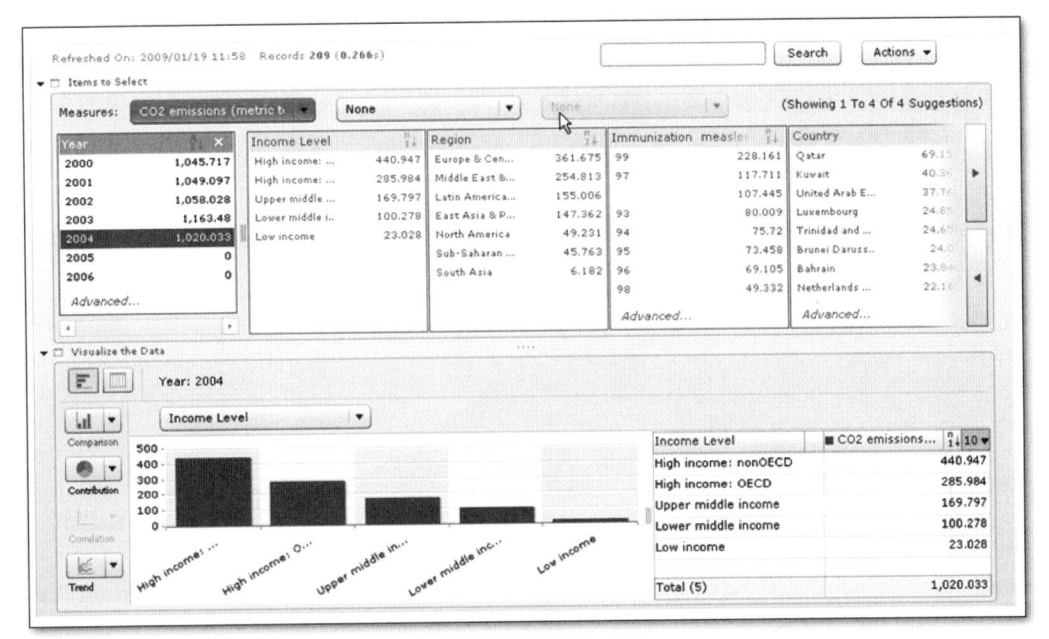

Figure 1.19 SAP BusinessObjects Explorer

SAP BusinessObjects Explorer is a tool that provides access to a large volume of data, and when used in combination with SAP NetWeaver BW Accelerator, does so at a high performance. SAP BusinessObjects Explorer can leverage the semantic layer of SAP BusinessObjects and create indexes of the available data via the semantic layer.

With the integration of SAP BusinessObjects Explorer and Web Intelligence, users can use SAP BusinessObjects Explorer to start analyzing data and then use Web Intelligence to share the results and for formatting purposes (see Figure 1.20).

In this section, we looked at the current and upcoming offerings in the BI portfolio from SAP and SAP BusinessObjects. In the next section, we will take a look how Advanced Analysis Office fits into the overall BI offering and see which types of requirements it can fulfill.

1 | SAP BusinessObjects Advanced Analysis, Edition for Microsoft Office

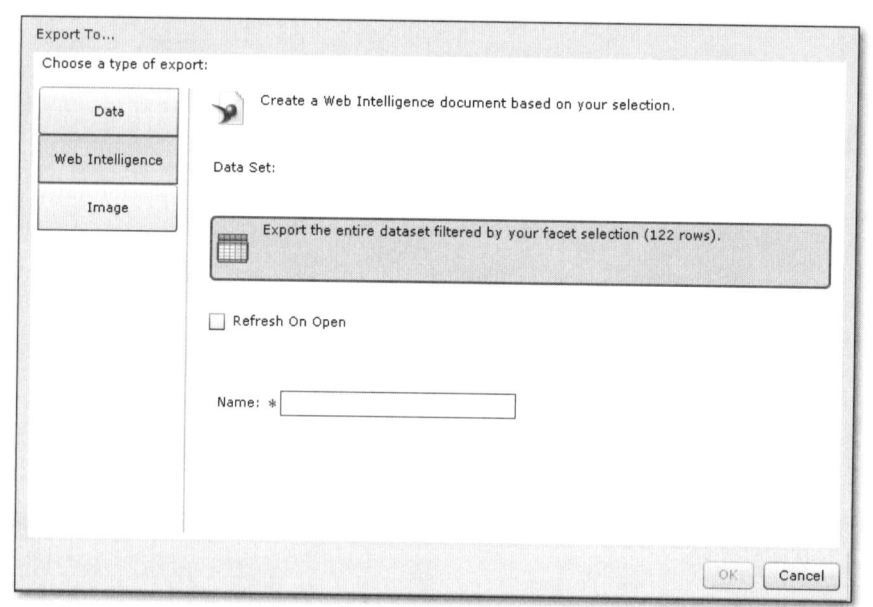

Figure 1.20 BusinessObjects Explorer - Export

1.3 SAP Advanced Analysis — One Part of the Overall BI Puzzle

In this section, we will look at how Advanced Analysis Office fits into the overall BI client tools and determine which requirements may be best suited for Advanced Analysis.

Figure 1.21 lists the different BI client tools from the SAP BusinessObjects BI portfolio along with the skill set required to use the tool for consuming the content, not necessarily for creating the content. Note that Advanced Analysis Office and Advanced Analysis Web are on the far right-hand side, but Advanced Analysis Office can also address the Information Consumer and Business Analyst as a user audience.

Figure 1.22 shows you the BI clients from the portfolio along with a set of common requirements, and visualizes how the tools are able to fulfill these requirements. Advanced Analysis provides you with a tool that allows for advanced functionality in hierarchical awareness, guided navigation, and data visualization.

1.3 SAP Advanced Analysis — One Part of the Overall BI Puzzle

SAP BusinessObjects Explorer	Crystal Reports	Xcelsius	Web Intelligence	Advanced Analysis Office	Advanced Analysis Web
▶ Search and explore data ▶ Common "Google" style user experience ▶ Limited analysis functionality	▶ Pre-built report from static to parameterized layouts ▶ Operational reporting	▶ Easy to use data visualizations ▶ Compelling interactive dashboarding type of analytics	▶ Online and offline reporting capabilities ▶ Powerful ad hoc reporting capabilities ▶ Limited advanced analysis capabilities	▶ Ad hoc OLAP analysis ▶ Content creation and consumption in Microsoft Office ▶ Hierarchy awareness	▶ Advanced analysis capabilities ▶ Trend analysis and Outlier

User Skill Set

Information Consumer

Executive/Management

Business Analyst

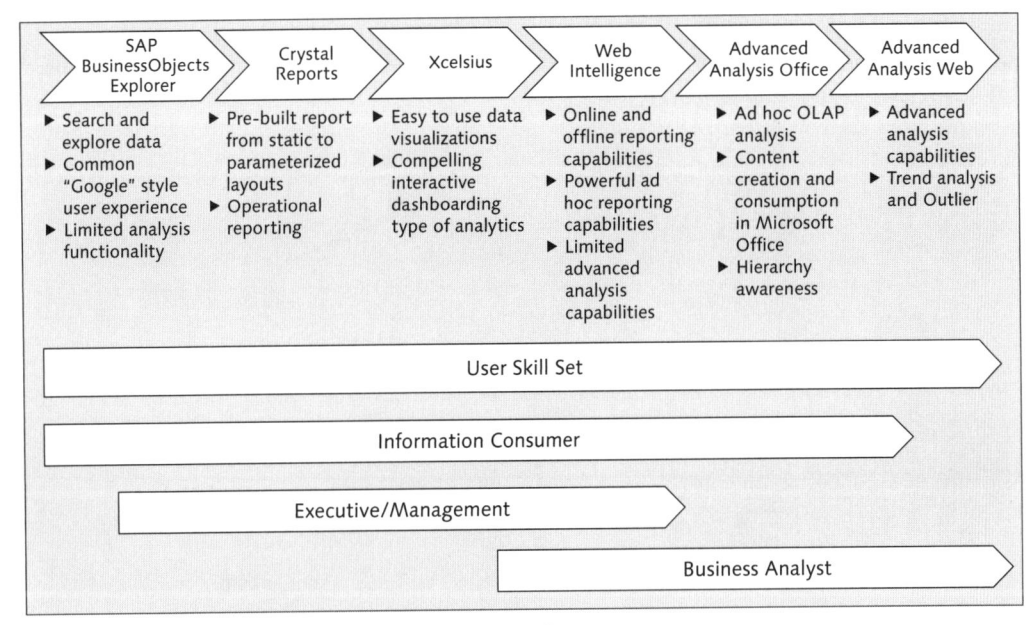

Figure 1.21 SAP BusinessObjects BI Tools and User Skill Set

	Crystal Reports	Web Intelligence	Xcelsius	Business-Objects Explorer	Advanced Analysis
Highly Formatted Layout (print focused)	●	◐	◔	◔	◔
Parameterized/ Dynamic Layout	●	◕	◕	◐	◐
Self Service/ Free Form Layout	◔	◐	○	◑	◐
Hierarchical Awareness	◐	◐	◐	◕	◕
Dashboarding & Visualization	◔	◔	●	◔	◕
Interoperability	●	◐	◐	◔	◕
Guided Navigation	◔	◔	◕	◔	●

Figure 1.22 Capability Matrix

37

1 | SAP BusinessObjects Advanced Analysis, Edition for Microsoft Office

Figure 1.23 shows the typical user personas for Advanced Analysis Office. Advanced Analysis Office was designed with the Business Analyst and the Information Consumer as the target audience.

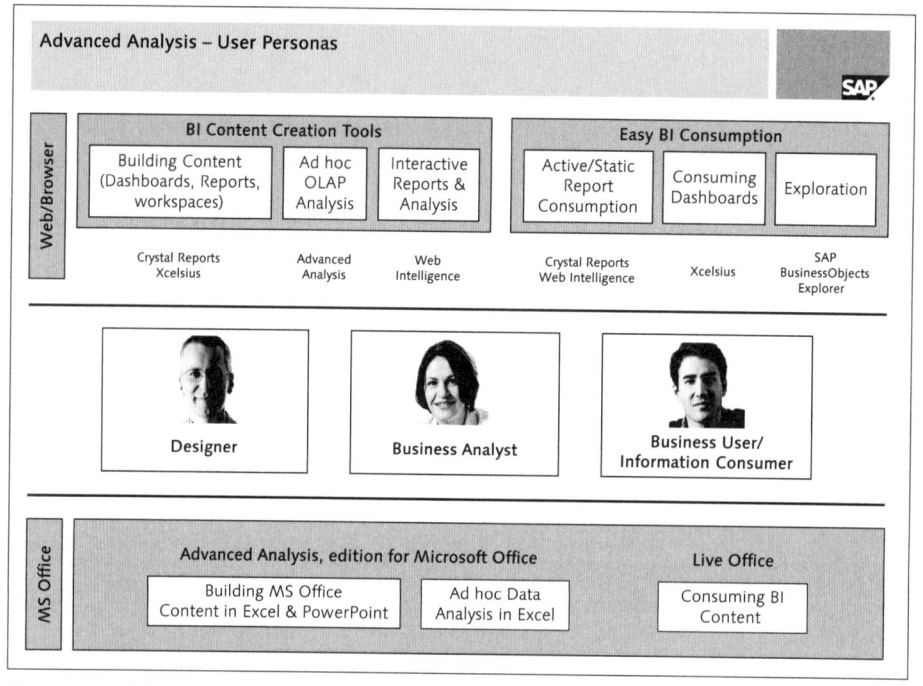

Figure 1.23 Advanced Analysis Office - Personas

Advanced Analysis Office is the tool best suited for BI content in a Microsoft Office–based environment and can be used in combination with Live Office. Live Office is needed for Crystal Reports or Web Intelligence–based content in a Microsoft Office environment. In Figure 1.24, you can see the different tasks per persona. Advanced Analysis Office is leveraged by three different user types:

▶ A Designer, who creates Microsoft Excel–based workbooks or Microsoft PowerPoint presentations combined with data from your SAP NetWeaver BW system.

1.3 SAP Advanced Analysis — One Part of the Overall BI Puzzle

- A Business Analyst, who performs ad hoc data analysis in Microsoft Excel and also prepares presentations by placing embedded data from your SAP NetWeaver BW system into Microsoft PowerPoint–based presentations.
- An Information Consumer, who will leverage Advanced Analysis Office to open and view prepared content and, if required, make minor modifications.

Use Cases for Advanced Analysis, edition for MS Office & Live Office

- Centralized creation of Advanced Analysis content (workbooks & PowerPoints)
- Sophisticated workbook design (VBA, APIs, etc.)

- Ad hoc data access and data analysis, slicing & dicing, and so on, in Excel
- Ad hoc embedding of BI data into PowerPoint presentations

- Consumes predefined BI content in Excel, PowerPoint & MS Word

Designer | Business Analyst | Business User/ Information Consumer

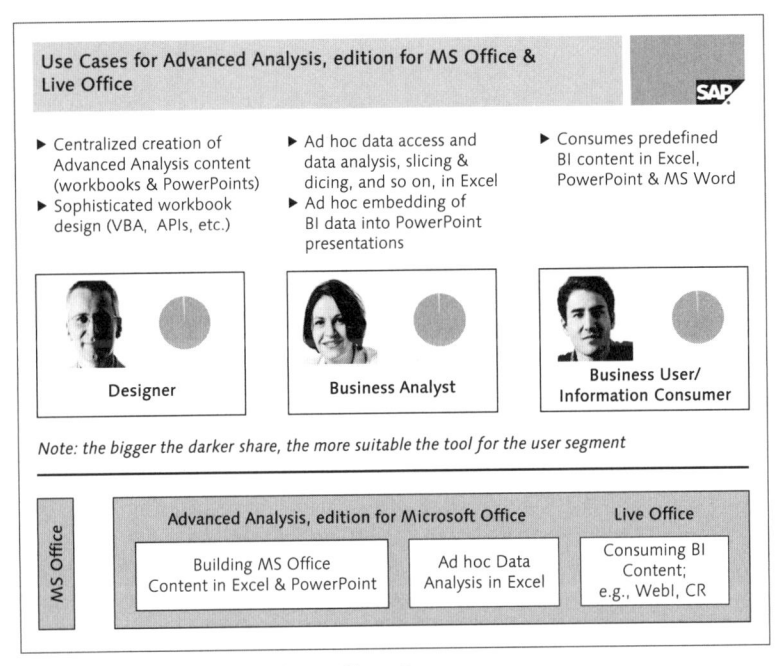

Note: the bigger the darker share, the more suitable the tool for the user segment

MS Office:
- Advanced Analysis, edition for Microsoft Office
  - Building MS Office Content in Excel & PowerPoint
  - Ad hoc Data Analysis in Excel
- Live Office
  - Consuming BI Content; e.g., WebI, CR

Figure 1.24 Advanced Analysis Office - Personas

Figure 1.25 shows you all of the SAP BusinessObjects BI client tools, including Advanced Analysis Office, along with the three different users.

As you can see in Figure 1.25, Advanced Analysis Office targets the Information Consumer and the Business Analyst. Especially for the Business Analyst, as of Release XI 3.1, Advanced Analysis Office provides the best option for delivering BI content to a user audience. For the Information Consumer, all of the BI client tools are targeted for the Information Consumer. Figure 1.26 contains a simple decision tree.

1 | SAP BusinessObjects Advanced Analysis, Edition for Microsoft Office

	Enterprise Reporting	Ad Hoc Query & Analysis	Advanced Analysis Office	Dashboarding & Data Visualization	Discovery & Exploration
Information Consumers	Crystal Reports	Web Intelligence	Advanced Analysis Office	Xcelsius	SAP Business Objects Explorer
Executive & Managers					
Business Analysts			Advanced Analysis Office		

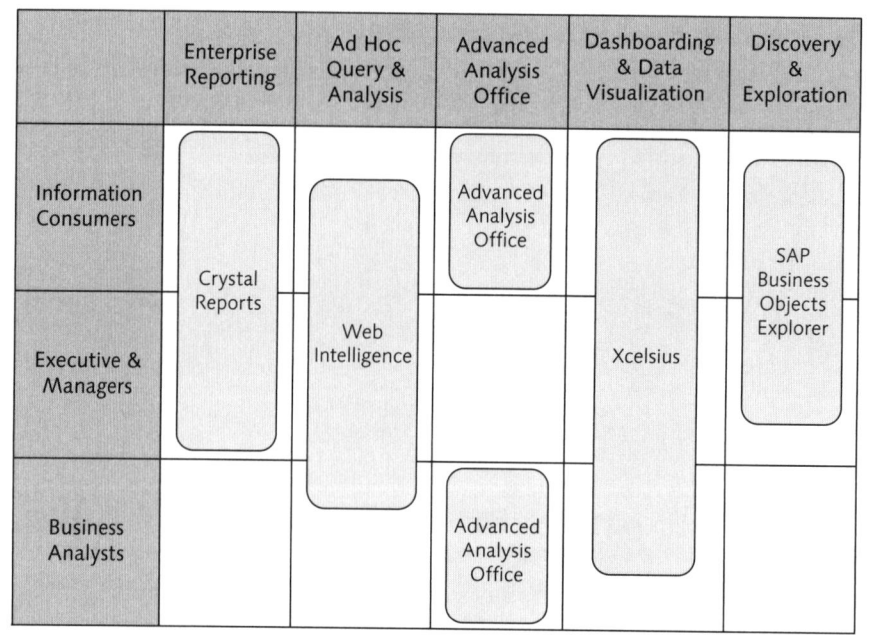

Figure 1.25 SAP BusinessObjects BI Clients

You can use the decision tree in Figure 1.26 to evaluate which of the SAP BusinessObjects BI client tools you should leverage based on user requirements. We will go into more details on this in the next section and take a look at a list of requirements and evaluate which tools would be a better fit if Advanced Analysis Office cannot fulfill the requirement.

1.4 User Requirements for Advanced Analysis Office

In this section, we will use a set of common user requirements from different departments and to see if Advanced Analysis Office is the best choice to fulfill the requirement or if one of the other SAP BusinessObjects BI client tools might be a better option. In the following paragraphs, we will outline the requirements from different areas of our virtual company and then evaluate which of those we can fulfill with Advanced Analysis Office.

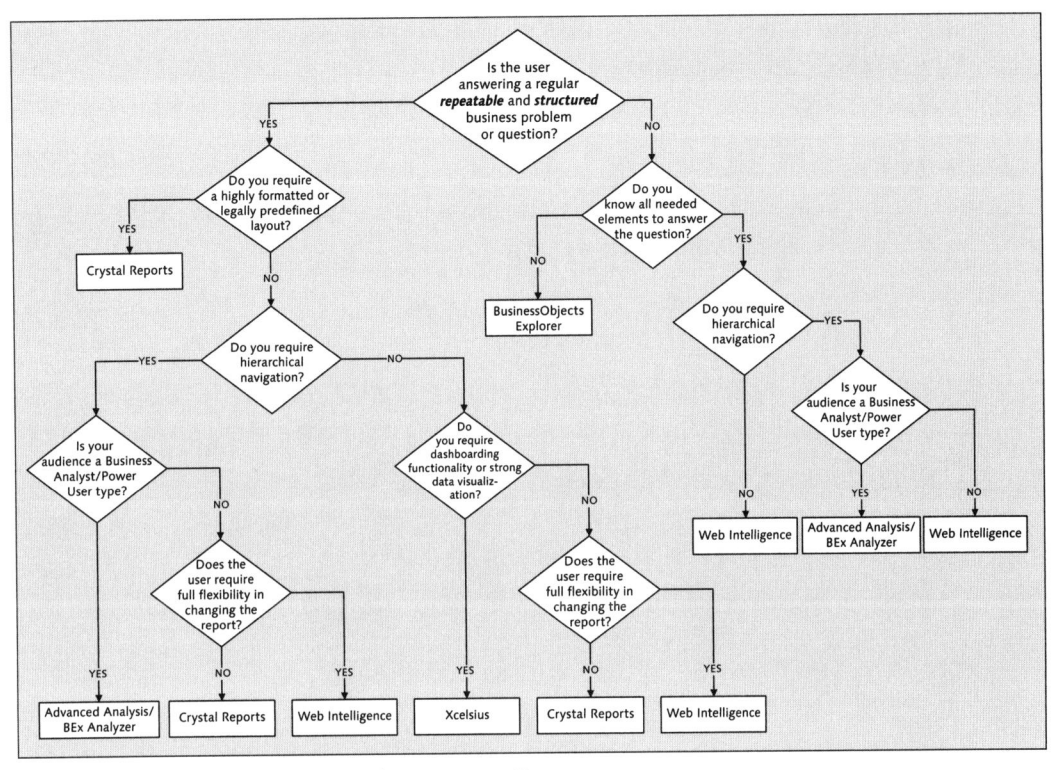

Figure 1.26 SAP BusinessObjects BI Client Decision Tree

Financial Reporting and Analysis Requirements

- The content must be available in a web-based environment and in a Microsoft Office environment (especially Microsoft Excel).

- For specific content (like an income statement or a balance sheet) that is being created, the design needs to be layout focused with the actual print of the report being a very high priority.

- The reporting and analysis tools need to let the user create new calculations and formulas and share those with other consumers of the content.

- The reporting and analysis tools need to allow the use of hierarchies and allow navigation along those hierarchies in the actual content.

- The reporting and analysis tools need to leverage custom structures that have been defined on a BW query layer.

- The content needs to resolve the time dependency defined for the financial cost and profit center hierarchies.

- Some of the content can leverage precalculated data but the user needs to refresh all of the content on-demand, if needed.

- The user needs to navigate from aggregated data to more detailed items. For example: navigating from a cost center aggregated value to the actual line items per cost element.

- In some of the content it is necessary to navigate into the actual SAP transaction to retrieve further details.

Sales Reporting and Analysis Requirements

- Content must be available online and offline (for sales representatives on the road).

- Email distribution of content may be required.

- Users need the capability to change the view of the actual content. For example: changing a weekly sales statistics broken down by country into a weekly sales statistics broken down by sales region and quarter.

- The content often needs to show data comparisons along different time series.

- Ideally, users should be able to modify existing reports or create new reports ad hoc.

- Users should be able to perform a scenario-based analysis, where the user can see and can also influence certain factors and see the impact on the overall numbers. For example: a what-if analysis in a sales planning workflow.

Human Resource (HR) Reporting and Analysis Requirements

- The content needs to leverage data from several different sources (SAP and non-SAP) and present it in a single report.

- The content needs to present highly textual information in a layout-focused format.

- Some of the content (such as employee appraisals or performance reviews) will be used as actual official documents and therefore needs to follow strict layout rules.
- The tools leveraged for the content need to leverage specific features, such as date-specific aggregation to show the correct numbers for items like a headcount statistic or a salary at a given date for an employee. Resolving these time-dependent key figures is very important for the content.

Executive Leadership and Management Reporting and Analysis Requirements

- The content needs to present highly aggregated information with the necessary alerting for important key performance indicators (KPI).
- The data needs to be shown in a highly visualized manner and the main KPIs need to be presented in a single dashboard.
- The reports and analytics need to allow for further navigation to either more detail-oriented reports or for further analysis of the summarized data.
- The reports and analytics need to be very simple and easy to use and critical information needs to be identifiable right away.
- Response time for this audience is critical and information needs to be presented on a dashboard within a 5 - 10 second response time (otherwise people might navigate away from the page).

Next, we will use these requirements to see if Advanced Analysis Office would be the best possible choice out of the SAP BusinessObjects BI portfolio to fulfill the requirement.

Fulfilled and Unfulfilled Financial Reporting and Analysis Requirements

Note that only one requirement from our financial area is not fulfilled using Advanced Analysis. The requirement to offer a web-based and Microsoft Office–based environment is half fulfilled, as Advanced Analysis is not available as a Web Edition for SAP BusinessObjects XI 3.1. The Advanced Analysis Web Edition is planned for the next major release of SAP BusinessObjects XI 4.0.

> **Unfulfilled Financial Area Requirements**
>
> - For specific content (like an income statement or a balance sheet) that is being created, the design needs to be layout focused with the actual print being a very high priority.
> - The content must be available in a web-based environment.

For the two requirements from the financial area that cannot be fulfilled using Advanced Analysis, let's look at which of the BI client tools would fulfill the requirement.

- The requirement to have layout-focused reports and analytics can be fulfilled using Web Intelligence and Crystal Reports. The choice for one or the other depends on the complexity of the layout and how important the printing requirement is in the given situation. For simple printing requirements, Web Intelligence is a good choice, but when the printing and layout become more complex with stronger requirements, then Crystal Reports is the better choice.

- A web-based environment cannot be fulfilled by Advanced Analysis and which BI client tool to use depends on all of the other requirements that need to be fulfilled. Therefore, there is no best option based solely on the requirement to have the reports and analytics surfaced in a web-based environment.

> **Fulfilled Financial Area Requirements**
>
> - The content must be available in a Microsoft Office environment (especially Microsoft Excel).
> - The reporting and analysis tools need to let the user create new calculations and formulas and share those with other consumers of the content.
> - The reporting and analysis tools need to allow the use of hierarchies and allow navigation along those hierarchies in the actual content.
> - The reporting and analysis tools need to leverage custom structures that have been defined on a BW query layer.
> - The content needs to resolve the time dependency defined for the financial cost and profit center hierarchies.
> - Some of the content can leverage precalculated data but the user needs to refresh all of the content on-demand, if needed.

> - The user needs to navigate from aggregated data to more detailed items. For example: navigating from a cost center aggregated value to the actual line items per cost element.
> - In some of the content it is necessary to navigate into the actual SAP transaction to retrieve further details.

It should be no surprise that Advanced Analysis Office fulfills nearly all of the requirements for the financial area, as financial reporting often requires the functionality described previously and both tools —BEx and Voyager — have been strong in those areas for some time now.

Fulfilled and Unfulfilled Sales Reporting and Analysis Requirements

For sales, the situation is similar to the financial area where Advanced Analysis was able to fulfill most of our requirements.

> **Unfulfilled Sales Area Requirements**
> - Users should be able to perform a scenario-based analysis, where the user can see the data and can also can influence certain factors and see the impact on the overall numbers. For example: a what-if analysis in a sales planning workflow.
> - Email distribution of content may be required.

For the unfulfilled requirements, let's look at which BI client tools can fulfill the requirement and would be a good choice.

- To create a what-if analysis, the recommendation clearly goes to Xcelsius. None of the BI client tools offers such functionality with the exception of Xcelsius, where you can easily create a compelling dashboard with what-if analysis capabilities integrated into your dashboard.
- To distribute the reports and analytics via email to your users, we need to decide on either Crystal Reports or Web Intelligence. Such functionality is planned for Advanced Analysis as well, but it is not available in the Advanced Analysis release based on SAP BusinessObjects Enterprise XI 3.1.

1 | SAP BusinessObjects Advanced Analysis, Edition for Microsoft Office

> **Fulfilled Sales Area Requirements**
> - Content must be available online and offline (for sales representatives on the road).
> - Users need the capability to change the view of the actual content. For example: changing a weekly sales statistics broken down by country into a weekly sales statistics broken down by sales region and quarter.
> - The content often needs to show data comparisons along different time series.
> - Ideally, users should be able to modify existing reports or create new reports ad hoc.

Especially for providing offline access (for example, for people on the road), Advanced Analysis Office, with the capability of integrating data from your SAP NetWeaver BW system into a Microsoft PowerPoint presentation, can be a great option to fulfill these requirements.

Fulfilled and Unfulfilled HR Reporting and Analysis Requirements

The following represents the fulfilled and unfulfilled requirements from the HR area. It should be no surprise that most of the requirements are not fulfilled with Advanced Analysis Office, especially those asking for highly textual information.

> **Unfulfilled HR Area Requirements**
> - The content needs to present highly textual information in a layout-focused format.
> - Some of the content (such as employee appraisals or performance reviews) will be used as actual official documents and therefore needs to follow strict layout rules.
> - The content needs to leverage data from several different sources (SAP and non-SAP) and present it in a single report.

For the unfulfilled requirements, you can see that two of them are about highly textual reports with a strong focus on the actual layout of the report itself. For these types of reports, Crystal Reports is the recommended BI client tool. To show SAP and non-SAP data in a single report, you can leverage all of the BI client tools, except Advanced Analysis Office in the first release. Advanced Analysis Office for Release XI 3.1 of the SAP BusinessObjects platform can only access data from your SAP NetWeaver BW system.

Fulfilled HR Area Requirements

- The tools leveraged for the content need to leverage specific features, such as date-specific aggregation to show the correct numbers for items like a headcount statistic or a salary at a given date for an employee. Resolving these time-dependent key figures is very important for the content.

Fulfilled and Unfulfilled Executive and Leadership Reporting and Analysis Requirements

Now we'll look at the requirements from our Executives and Leadership team and evaluate how Advanced Analysis Office can help us fulfill these requirements.

Unfulfilled Executive and Leadership Area Requirements

- The data needs to be shown in a highly visualized manner and the main KPIs need to be presented in a single dashboard.
- The reports and analytics need to be very simple and easy to use and critical information needs to be identifiable right away.

On the list of unfulfilled requirements it might be somewhat surprising that the requirement asking for an easy-to-consume type of reporting is listed here as unfulfilled. Advanced Analysis Office is a product with great user experience and was designed especially with the end user in mind and leverages large portions of the user experience of Voyager, but Advanced Analysis Office is not necessarily a product targeting the executive level for corporate KPIs. In such a situation, a dashboard created with Xcelsius might be a better choice.

Fulfilled Executive and Leadership Area requirements

- The content needs to present highly aggregated information with the necessary alerting for important KPIs.
- The reports and analytics need to allow for further navigation to either more detail-oriented reports or for further analysis of the summarized data.
- Response time for this audience is critical and the information needs to be presented on a dashboard within 5 - 10 second response time (otherwise people might navigate away from the page).

As you can see, the list of fulfilled requirements from our executive and leadership team includes requirements to show highly aggregated KPIs and the navigation from higher aggregated numbers to more detailed numbers. All of these items are typical requirements, which you will learn to fulfill using Advanced Analysis Office in the next couple of chapters.

1.5 Summary

In this chapter, we gave a brief overview on the complete SAP BusinessObjects BI client tools portfolio and explained how Advanced Analysis Office fits into the overall BI portfolio. In addition, we reviewed a set of requirements from several different areas and evaluated how Advanced Analysis Office can help us fulfill those requirements and identify those that might need an alternative BI client tool.

In the next chapter, we will install Advanced Analysis Office as part of our SAP BusinessObjects XI 3.1 landscape and take a look at the steps necessary to get Advanced Analysis Office installed and configured as part of our overall SAP landscape.

In this chapter, you will learn the necessary steps to install, deploy, and configure Advanced Analysis Office as part of your overall Business Intelligence (BI) landscape.

2 Installation, Deployment and Configuration of Advanced Analysis Office

In this chapter, we will learn about the components necessary for a successful deployment of Advanced Analysis Office and learn the steps to install and configure Advanced Analysis Office as part of our BI landscape. We will also look at the different ways to deploy Advanced Analysis Office and how they vary in their functionality.

2.1 Installation of SAP Advanced Analysis Office

In this section, we will look at the technical prerequisites for installing Advanced Analysis Office and go through the actual installation routine.

2.1.1 Technical Prerequisites

The following is a list of the technical prerequisites for deploying Advanced Analysis Office. The list is divided into requirements for your client computer and requirements for your backend systems.

Client Computer

- Microsoft Office 2003 or higher must be installed. Please note, the plug-in to Microsoft PowerPoint for Advanced Analysis Office is only available for Microsoft Office 2007.

- SAP Frontend 7.x must be installed.
- Your must run Microsoft Windows XP or a later Microsoft Windows–based operating system.

Backend Systems

- You need at least SAP NetWeaver Business Information Warehouse (BW) Release 7.0. The recommended release for integrating SAP NetWeaver BW and SAP BusinessObjects is SAP NetWeaver BW 7.01 SP05. That way, you can leverage other benefits, such as performance improvement with Web Intelligence and direct connectivity for Xcelsius.
- Advanced Analysis Office can integrate with your SAP BusinessObjects Enterprise Release XI 3.1. It is recommended that Release XI 3.1 be at least on Service Pack 02.
- Advanced Analysis Office can also integrate with SAP BusinessObjects Enterprise Release XI 4.0.
- SAP NetWeaver BW queries created or edited with SAP BEx Query Designer 3.5 or SAP BEx Query Designer 7.x are accessible with Advanced Analysis Office, assuming that the SAP NetWeaver BW system is Release 7.0 or higher.

> **BI ABAP versus BI Java**
>
> As you will learn in the next chapter, you do not need to have the BI Java parts deployed to leverage Advanced Analysis Office. The relevant interfaces — the BI Consumer Services — are part of the actual client-side installation of Advanced Analysis Office, so it is not required to have BI Java deployed as part of your SAP NetWeaver BW system.

After you verify that your system landscape meets the listed requirements we can start with the installation of Advanced Analysis Office on our client system.

> **Advanced Analysis Office, Software Download**
>
> You can download Advanced Analysis Office from the SAP Service Marketplace at *http://service.sap.com/swdc*.

After you download the software you can start the actual installation routine.

Installation of SAP Advanced Analysis Office | **2.1**

1. Start the installation routine by double-clicking on SAPAAOSetup.exe in the folder you placed the software.

2. The SAP NetWeaver Frontend Installer will start (see Figure 2.1).

Figure 2.1 SAP NetWeaver Front-End Installer

3. Click NEXT (see Figure 2.2).

Figure 2.2 Available Components

51

4. Make sure you select the component ADVANCED ANALYSIS, EDITION FOR MICROSOFT OFFICE.

5. Click NEXT (see Figure 2.3).

Figure 2.3 Target Directory

6. Now you can define the target directory for the installation of Advanced Analysis by clicking the BROWSE button. Define the target directory and click NEXT. The actual installation routine will start.

7. After a short period of time the installation routine will finish (see Figure 2.4).

Figure 2.4 Installation Finished

Deployment Options for SAP Advanced Analysis Office | 2.2

8. Click DONE to exit the installation routine.

Assuming your client has Microsoft Office 2007 installed, you should now have both programs — Advanced Analysis Office for Microsoft Excel and Microsoft PowerPoint — in a folder that you can find via the menu path START • PROGRAMS • SAP BUSINESSOBJECTS (see Figure 2.5).

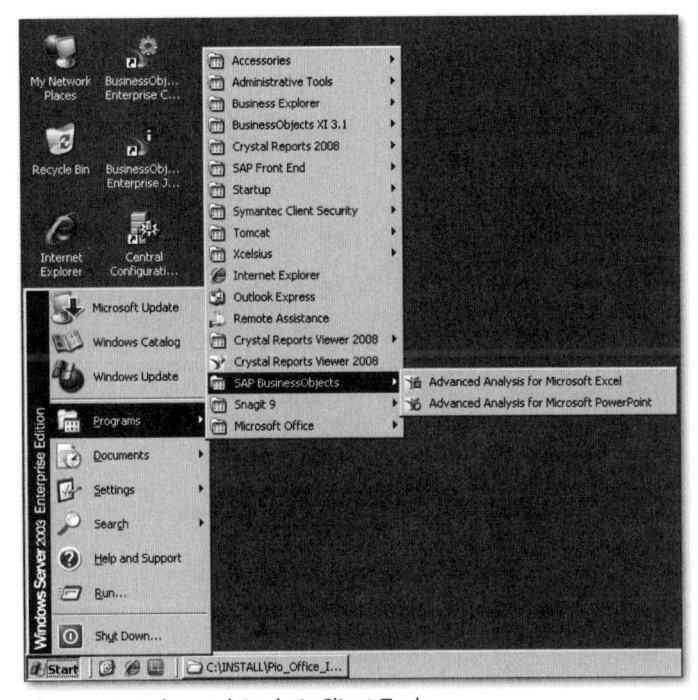

Figure 2.5 Advanced Analysis Client Tools

This completes the installation routine for Advanced Analysis Office on the client computer. Before we move on to more detailed configuration steps, let's take a look at the different deployment options for Advanced Analysis Office as part of your overall SAP and SAP BusinessObjects landscape.

2.2 Deployment Options for SAP Advanced Analysis Office

In this section, we will review the deployment options of Advanced Analysis Office as part of your SAP and SAP BusinessObjects landscape. In particular, we

53

will review the functional differences of deploying Advanced Analysis Office with SAP BusinessObjects Enterprise.

2.2.1 Advanced Analysis Office Architecture

Advanced Analysis, in combination with SAP BusinessObjects Enterprise XI 3.1, can be deployed two different ways. As shown in Figure 2.6, you have the option of using Advanced Analysis Office in combination with SAP BusinessObjects Enterprise connected to your SAP NetWeaver BW system. The second deployment option, which is only recommended for smaller deployments, is a pure client-side deployment of Advanced Analysis Office connected directly to your SAP NetWeaver BW system.

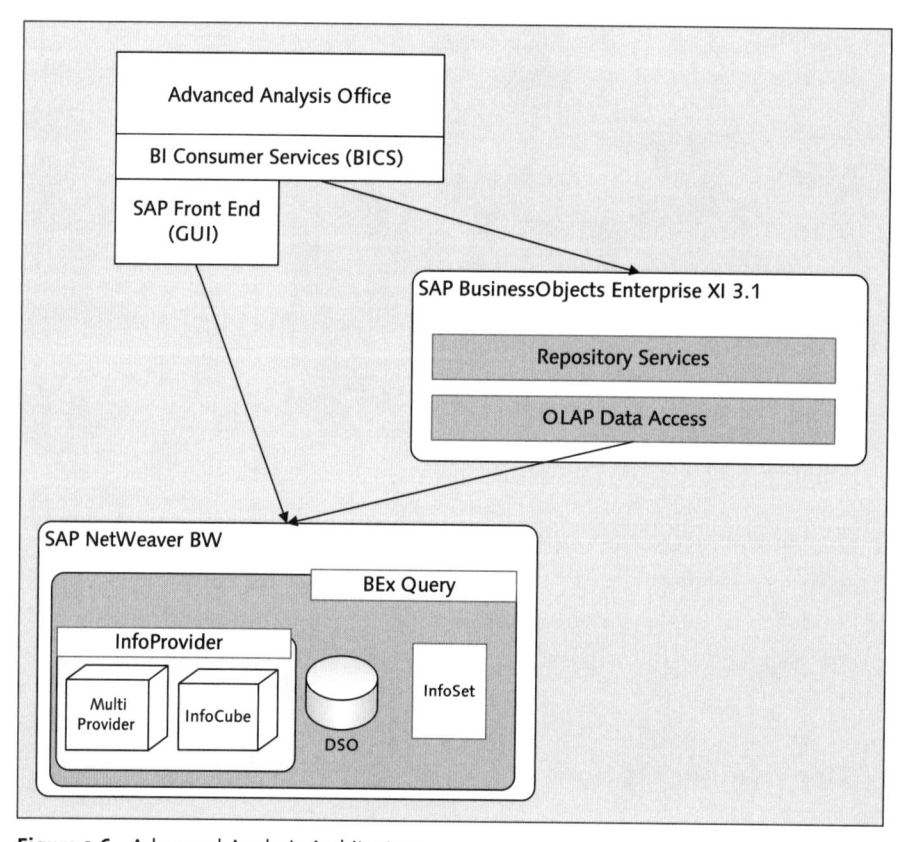

Figure 2.6 Advanced Analysis Architecture

In the following two sections, we will look at what the technical pre-requisites are for these two deployment options and what the functional differences are between them. In the summary for this section, we will compare the two deployment options and provide a recommended approach.

2.2.2 Deploying Advanced Analysis without SAP BusinessObjects Enterprise

In general, deploying Advanced Analysis without deploying SAP BusinessObjects Enterprise is only recommended for smaller deployments, because you will miss some crucial functionality, such as sharing connections to your SAP NetWeaver BW system.

Figure 2.7 shows an overview of an Advanced Analysis Office deployment without an SAP BusinessObjects Enterprise system. In terms of technical requirements, all you need is an SAP Front-End 7.x deployed on each client system that will use Advanced Analysis Office.

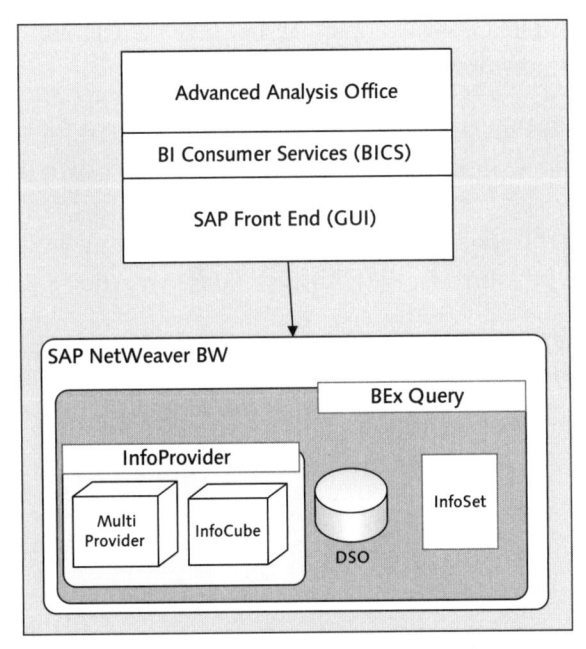

Figure 2.7 Advanced Analysis Office Lean Deployment

In such a deployment, the user can leverage Advanced Analysis Office as a plug-in for Microsoft Excel and PowerPoint and connect directly to the SAP NetWeaver BW system. However, such a deployment does have some consequences for the user workflows:

- All connections towards any SAP NetWeaver BW system will have to be created on each client computer as part of the SAP Front End.
- Microsoft Excel and PowerPoint documents can only be shared on some form of central shared folder as there is no central repository.

For the administrator of such a deployment, the following items will have to be considered as well:

- SAP Front End has to be deployed on each client computer that will leverage Advanced Analysis Office.
- Such a deployment does not offer any form of administration services around access to Microsoft Excel and PowerPoint documents.
- Such a deployment does not leverage any form of a central lifecycle mechanism, which means there is no automated way of populating shared documents from development to a QA or production environment.

As you can see, such a lean deployment of Advanced Analysis Office without SAP BusinessObjects Enterprise provides all of the functionality of Advanced Analysis Office to your users, but it comes with some implications for the administrative workflows. In the next section, we will take a look at the benefits of deploying SAP BusinessObjects Enterprise as part of your Advanced Analysis Office workflows.

2.2.3 Deploying Advanced Analysis Combined with SAP BusinessObjects Enterprise

If you are looking for a deployment option that also provides functionality for sharing documents and connections, you should consider an SAP BusinessObjects Enterprise deployment as part of your overall landscape.

Figure 2.8 shows the overall options for leveraging Advanced Analysis Office in combination with SAP BusinessObjects Enterprise. By adding SAP BusinessObjects Enterprise to your landscape you are adding a central repository, which lets you share connections and Microsoft Excel and PowerPoint documents with all of your users.

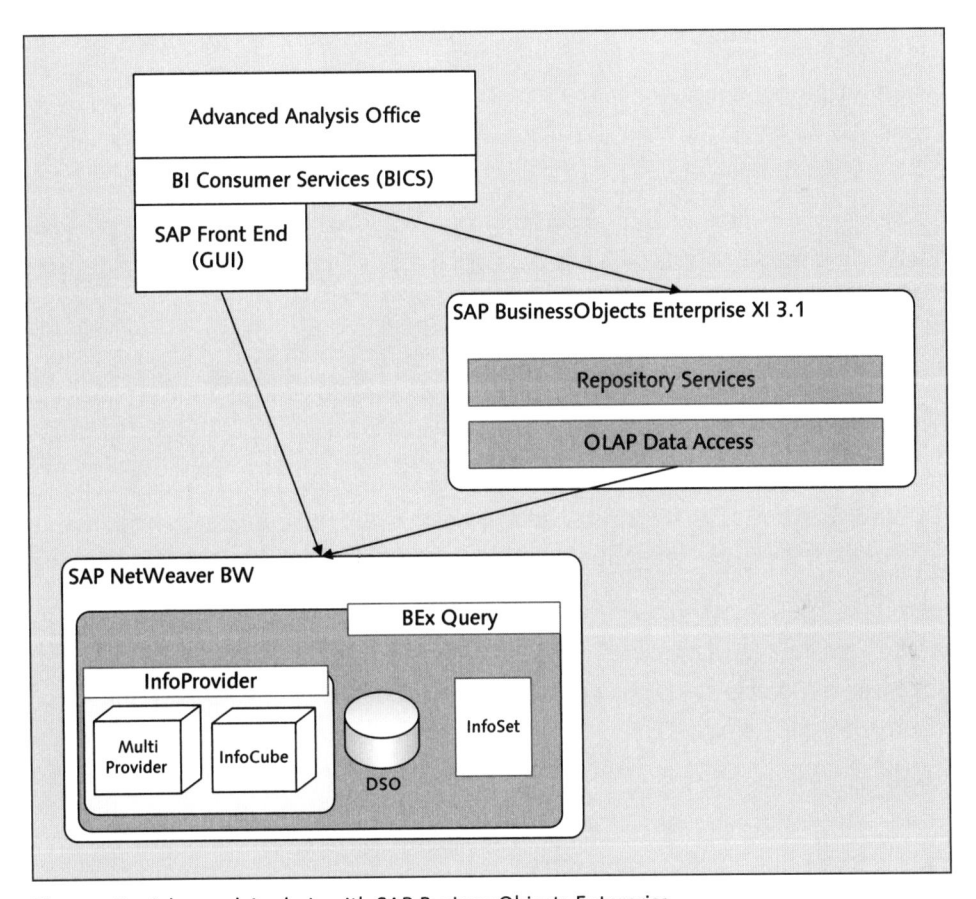

Figure 2.8 Advanced Analysis with SAP BusinessObjects Enterprise

For your end users, leveraging SAP BusinessObjects Enterprise services has the following benefits:

- Users can centrally save, open, and share documents created with Advanced Analysis Office by storing them via the SAP BusinessObjects Enterprise system.

For administrators, deploying Advanced Analysis Office in combination with SAP BusinessObjects Enterprise results in the following changes in workflows:

- Administrators can now create connections to the SAP NetWeaver BW system centrally and control access to those connections in the SAP BusinessObjects Enterprise system.

- Administrators can assign authorizations to centrally stored documents created with Advanced Analysis Office and control access to these documents on a user and group level.

- Administrators can leverage the SAP BusinessObjects LifeCycle Manager to follow documents and connections from development, to QA, to a production environment.

- When Advanced Analysis Office is deployed combined with SAP BusinessObjects Enterprise, there is no need to have the SAP Front End deployed on the client, because users can share connections via the SAP BusinessObjects Enterprise system.

As you can see, the combined deployment of Advanced Analysis Office with SAP BusinessObjects Enterprise has a lot of advantages for your users and your information technology (IT) department. In the next section, we will review both deployment options and provide recommendations on possible scenarios.

2.2.4 Summary and Conclusions

Based on the information from the previous two sections, let's compare the two deployment options in several categories (see Table 2.1).

Deployment Options for SAP Advanced Analysis Office | 2.2

	Advanced Analysis Office without SAP BusinessObjects Enterprise XI 3.1	Advanced Analysis Office combined with SAP BusinessObjects Enterprise XI 3.1
Client Software Deployment	Microsoft Office and SAP Front-End 7.x for all users required	Only Microsoft Office required
Server Software Deployment	No server software required	SAP BusinessObjects Enterprise XI 3.1
Sharing workbooks and PPTs	No central location for sharing workbooks and PPTs	Central repository as part of SAP BusinessObjects Enterprise
Creating Connections	Connections to SAP NetWeaver BW need to be created on each client computer	Connections are created in the Central Management Console of SAP BusinessObjects Enterprise
Sharing Connections	Connections cannot be shared among users	Connections are centrally created, stored, and can be shared via SAP BusinessObjects Enterprise
Lifecycle Management	No real Life Cycle Management possible, because objects are stored locally	Connections, workbooks, and PPTs can be transported using SAP BusinessObjects Life Cycle Manager
Single Sign-On (SSO)	Only client SSO possible, no server-side SSO Client SSO does require the configuration of a client Secure Network Communication (SNC) software component	Only client SSO possible, no server-side SSO Client SSO does require the configuration of a client SNC software component

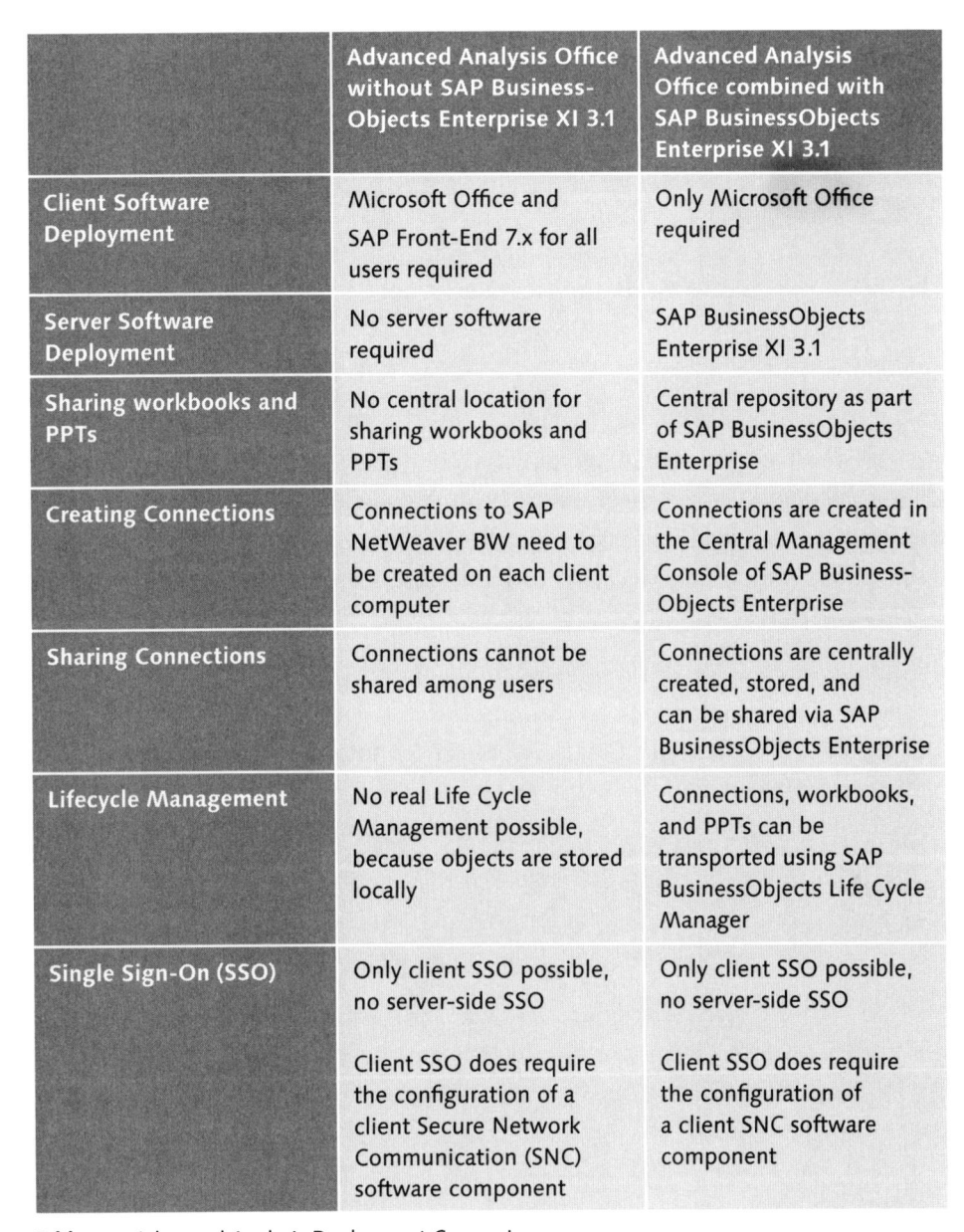

Table 2.1 Advanced Analysis Deployment Comparison

59

As you can see, the combination of SAP BusinessObjects Enterprise with Advanced Analysis Office provides several benefits, such as sharing connections to your SAP NetWeaver BW system and being able to transport your connections, workbooks, and PPTs from your development landscape to your QA or production landscape.

For the SSO, it is important to note, that in both deployment options only a client-side SSO is possible. Even in a deployment scenario with SAP BusinessObjects Enterprise XI 3.1 a server-based SSO is not possible. The client-side SSO does require the use and configuration of an SNC software component.

Overall, the recommended approach for deploying Advanced Analysis Office with or without SAP BusinessObjects Enterprise XI 3.1 depends on your overall reporting and analytics requirement and your existing reporting and analytics landscape. You can also see a small decision tree shown in Figure 2.9 which helps you to decide, if you should leverage SAP BusinessObjects Enterprise as BI platform for your Advanced Analysis Office deployment.

- An Advanced Analysis Office deployment combined with SAP BusinessObjects Enterprise is recommended for customers that are already using SAP BusinessObjects BI client tools like Crystal Reports, Web Intelligence, Xcelsius, and SAP BusinessObjects Explorer.

- An Advanced Analysis Office deployment without SAP BusinessObjects Enterprise is recommended for those customers that are planning to deploy Advanced Analysis Office as a replacement for SAP Business Explorer Analyzer (BEx Analyzer) and are not planning to deploy any other SAP BusinessObjects BI client tools for now.

In a situation where Advanced Analysis Office is the only BI client tool from the SAP BusinessObjects BI portfolio, a lean deployment can reduce the overall total cost of ownership (TCO) of your IT landscape, but you should still consider the benefits an SAP BusinessObjects Enterprise deployment can add to your landscape. In a situation where you are using multiple BI client tools from the SAP Business-

Objects portfolio, an SAP BusinessObjects Enterprise deployment is highly recommended, because you can then leverage the full benefits of SAP BusinessObjects Enterprise as a central BI platform.

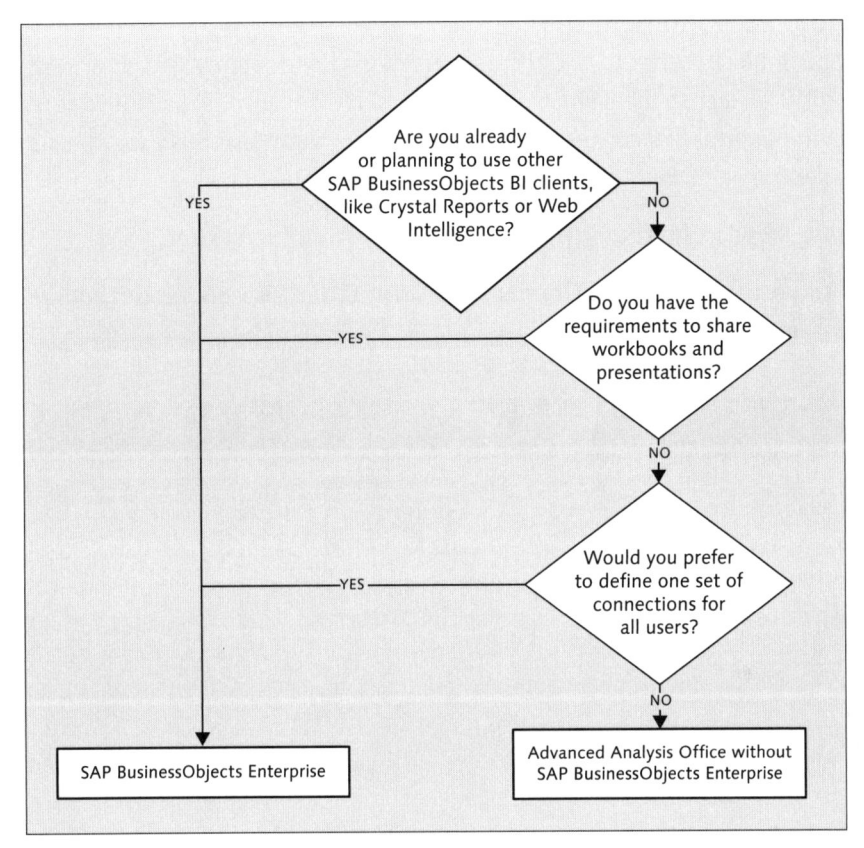

Figure 2.9 Advanced Analysis Office Decision Tree

In this section, we reviewed the different options for deploying Advanced Analysis Office with or without SAP BusinessObjects Enterprise. In the next section, we will take a look at a set of configuration steps that are necessary to get started with Advanced Analysis Office.

2.2.5 Setting Up Connections in SAP BusinessObjects Enterprise

In this section, we will look at several configuration steps that are necessary to get started with Advanced Analysis Office.

You have two options for setting up connections for your SAP NetWeaver BW system. The simplest way is to use the SAP Front End and simply add your SAP NetWeaver BW system to the SAP Logon Pad. The second option is to create a connection via the Central Management Console (CMC) of your SAP BusinessObjects Enterprise system.

The following steps show you how to create a connection in the CMC:

1. Log on to your SAP BusinessObjects Enterprise CMC with an administrative account (see Figure 2.10).

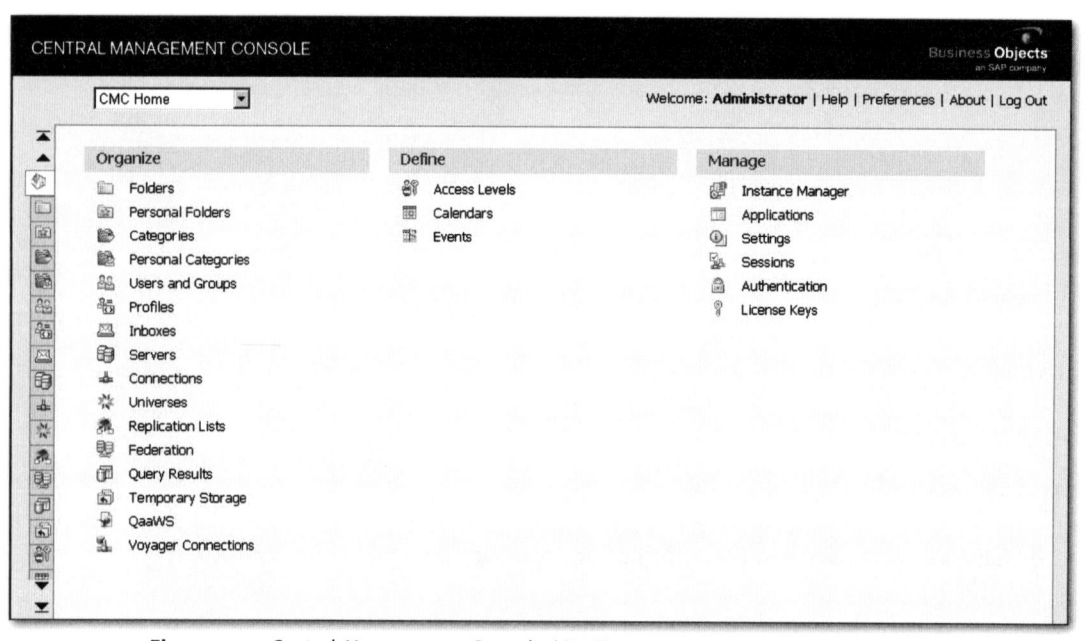

Figure 2.10 Central Management Console (CMC)

2. Select the VOYAGER CONNECTIONS option. Advanced Analysis Office with SAP BusinessObjects XI 3.1 shares the connection definitions with Voyager (see Figure 2.11).

Deployment Options for SAP Advanced Analysis Office | **2.2**

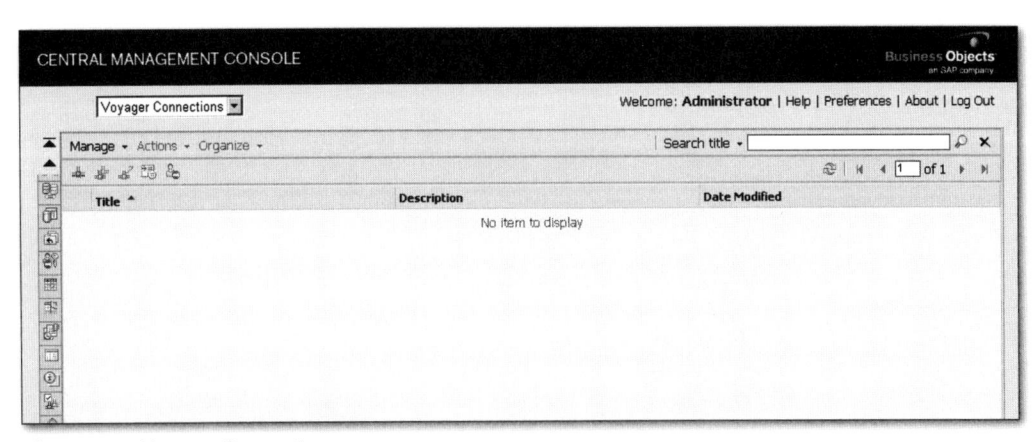

Figure 2.11 Voyager Connections

3. Use the ![icon] icon to create a new connection (see Figure 2.12).

Figure 2.12 New Voyager Connection

63

4. Enter the necessary details for your SAP NetWeaver BW system. You can see some of the more common details in Table 2.2.

Name	Description
Name	This is the name of the connection the user will see in Advanced Analysis Office.
Description (optional)	This is the description for the connection. The value is optional.
Provider	This is the type of connection. For Advanced Analysis connecting to SAP NetWeaver BW, you need to select the SAP BUSINESS INFORMATION WAREHOUSE provider.
Server Type	Here you can select between a connection based on an application server (SERVER) or a message server with a logon group (GROUP).
System	This is the System ID of your SAP NetWeaver BW system.
Server	This is either the full qualified name of your application server or your message server, depending on the SERVER-TYPE you selected.
System Number	This is the System Number of your SAP NetWeaver BW system.
Client	This is the Client number you would like to connect to from your SAP NetWeaver BW system.
Language	The two-digit letter code for the language.
Save Language	You can use this option to save the language, so that the setting in the user profile does not overwrite the setting in the connection. If you leave this setting unchecked, each user can configure the language in his own user profile as part of SAP BusinessObjects Enterprise.
Authentication	Here you can select one of three options: PROMPT, SSO, or USER SPECIFIED. Remember that, in combination with SAP BusinessObjects XI 3.1, there is no server-based SSO, so the safest way is to use the PROMPT option.

Table 2.2 Connection Details

Deployment Options for SAP Advanced Analysis Office | 2.2

5. After you enter the details of your SAP NetWeaver BW system, click on the CONNECT button (see Figure 2.13).

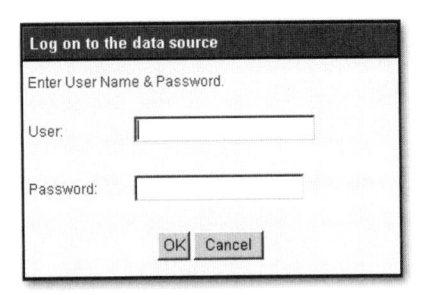

Figure 2.13 Log on Screen

6. Enter the USER and PASSWORD to connect to the SAP NetWeaver BW system.

7. Click OK.

8. You will see the CUBE BROWSER (see Figure 2.14), which lets you select an InfoProvider or a BW Query based on the CAPTION or the NAME.

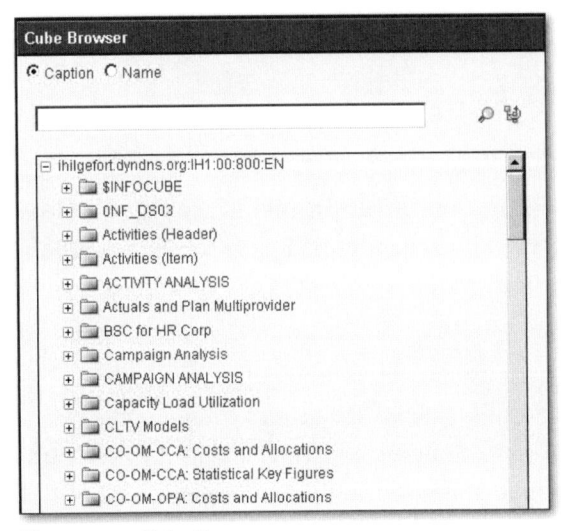

Figure 2.14 Cube Browser

9. Select any BW query from your SAP NetWeaver BW system for now and click SELECT.

10. Click SAVE to save your connection.

You have now created a connection, which your users can use to connect from Advanced Analysis Office to your SAP NetWeaver BW system. In the next section, we will prepare Microsoft Excel and PowerPoint for using Advanced Analysis Office.

2.2.6 Configuring Microsoft Excel and Microsoft PowerPoint Settings

Before we use Advanced Analysis Office as part of Microsoft Excel or PowerPoint, let's first configure several generic settings, which can influence the behavior of Advanced Analysis Office.

1. Start Advanced Analysis Office for Microsoft Excel via the menu path START • PROGRAMS • SAP BUSINESSOBJECTS • ADVANCED ANALYSIS FOR MICROSOFT EXCEL.

2. Select the ADVANCED ANALYSIS tab (see Figure 2.15).

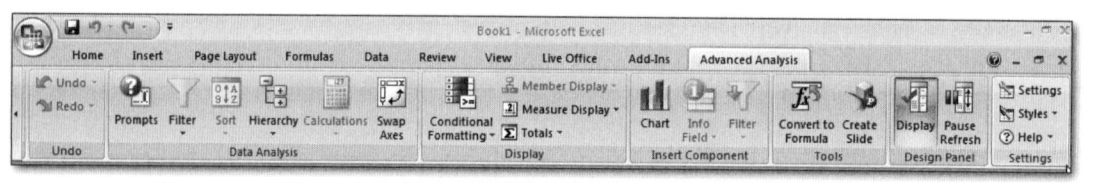

Figure 2.15 Advanced Analysis Ribbon

3. Select the SETTINGS option in the Advanced Analysis ribbon (see Figure 2.16). The option SETTINGS might not be visible depending on your screen resolution and therefore you might have to scroll to the right end of the Advanced Analysis ribbon.

The USER SETTINGS are based on each user's preference configured on the client computer. The RECENTLY USED LIST option allows the user to configure the number of data sources shown in the connections history. The NUMBER OF MEMBERS DISPLAYED IN FILTER DIALOG option lets the user limit the amount of members shown when filtering characteristics in the workbook.

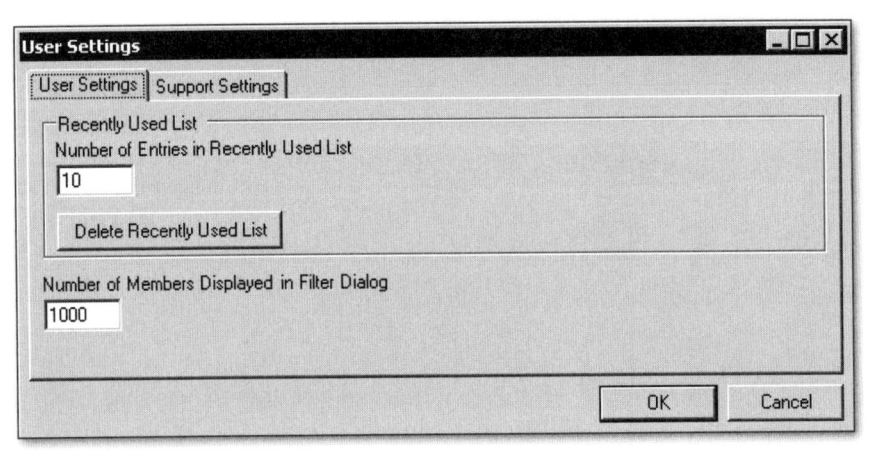

Figure 2.16 User Settings

4. Navigate to the SUPPORT SETTINGS tab (see Figure 2.17).

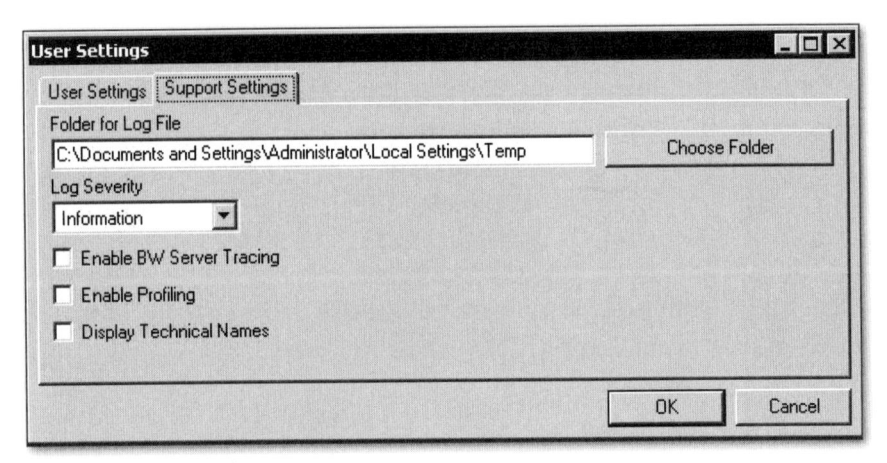

Figure 2.17 Support Settings

The SUPPORT SETTINGS provide users with a very simple way of creating log files, if they're needed, or if technical support needs further details.

These settings are stored as part of the local installation of Advanced Analysis and therefore depend on each client computer. In the next section, we will take a look at how you can configure a connection to your SAP NetWeaver BW system as part of your SAP BusinessObjects Enterprise development.

2.2.7 Configuring Connections to SAP BusinessObjects Enterprise

In this section we will configure the connection to your SAP BusinessObjects Enterprise for Advanced Analysis Office for Microsoft Excel and Microsoft PowerPoint.

When you insert a crosstab the first time based on a connection towards your SAP NetWeaver BW system, Advanced Analysis Office will ask you to establish a connection towards your SAP BusinessObjects Enterprise system as well. You can also skip this step as you can deploy Advanced Analysis Office in combination with SAP BusinessObjects Enterprise, but you can also deploy Advanced Analysis Office for smaller groups without SAP BusinessObjects Enterprise and therefore you can skip the step of establishing a connection to the SAP BusinessObjects Enterprise system.

In case you did skip this step in Advanced Analysis Office you won't be able to Open or Save a workbook or PowerPoint from your SAP BusinessObjects Enterprise system and because of that we will learn how to configure your client computer with a connection towards your SAP BusinessObjects Enterprise system.

In the case that you have never established a connection to your SAP BusinessObjects Enterprise system from Advanced Analysis Office you basically have two options to establish the connection settings.

Option 1

1. Start Advanced Analysis Office with Microsoft Excel by selecting the menu START • PROGRAMS • SAP BUSINESSOBJECTS • ADVANCED ANALYSIS FOR MICROSOFT EXCEL.

2. Select the option INSERT • SELECT DATA SOURCE from the Advanced Analysis ribbon. You will be presented with the logon dialog to SAP BusinessObjects Enterprise (see Figure 2.18).

Deployment Options for SAP Advanced Analysis Office | 2.2

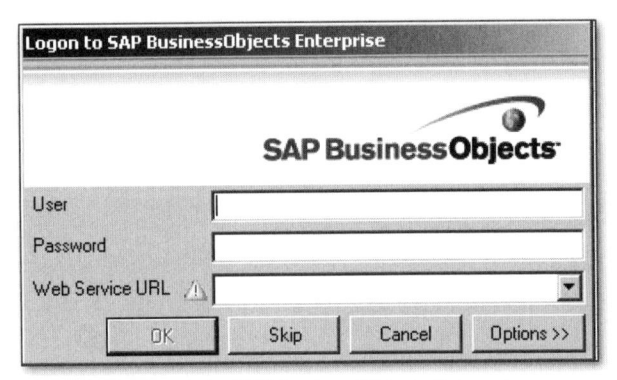

Figure 2.18 Logon to SAP BusinessObjects Enterprise

3. In case it is the first time you are using Advanced Analysis Office, you will need to enter the Web Service URL, which follows the syntax

   http://<Application Server>:<Port>/dswsbobje/services/session.

4. Click OPTIONS (see Figure 2.19).

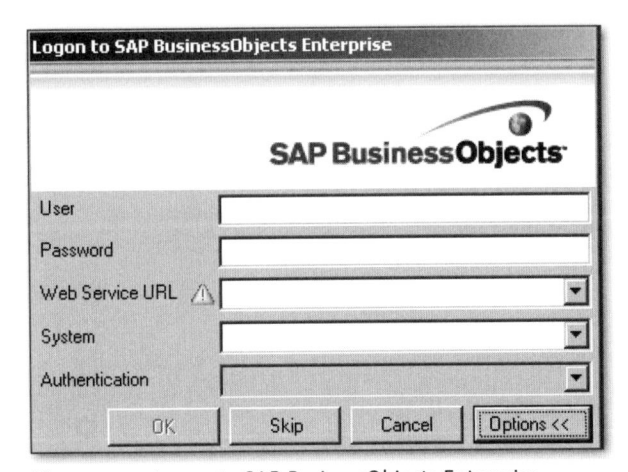

Figure 2.19 Logon to SAP BusinessObjects Enterprise

5. Select the AUTHENTICATION type for your SAP BusinessObjects Enterprise system.

6. For the SYSTEM value you need to enter the name of your Central Management System (CMS) of your SAP BusinessObjects Enterprise system.

69

7. Enter the USER and PASSWORD to logon to your SAP BusinessObjects Enterprise system.

   In case you configured your SAP BusinessObjects Enterprise system with the SAP authentication, please note, that the logon screen does not allow us to enter the client number, system ID and user as separate fields and therefore we will have to enter the user name in the following syntax:
   <System ID>~<Client Number>/<User ID>, for example:
   IH1~800/DEMO for user Demo in system IH1 with the client number 800.

8. Click OK.

9. Now you are able to leverage the shared connection and connect to the defined systems, or still leverage the local connections from the SAP Frontend (see Figure 2.20).

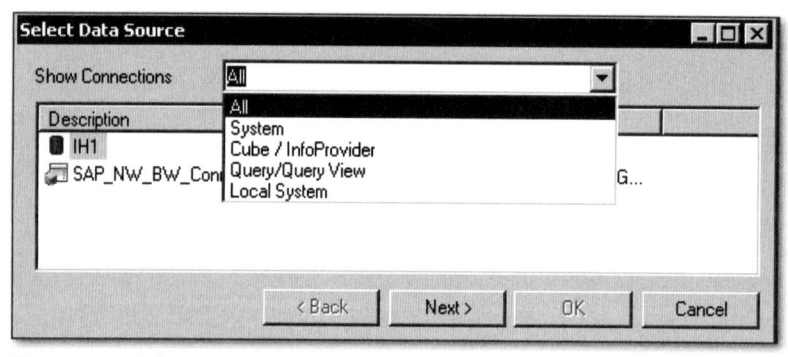

Figure 2.20 Select Data Source

At this point the settings have been written to your local computer and you will be able to leverage them for future connections.

10. Click CANCEL.

11. Close Advanced Analysis Office for Microsoft Excel.

12. Start Advanced Analysis Office with Microsoft Excel by selecting the menu START • PROGRAMS • SAP BUSINESSOBJECTS • ADVANCED ANALYSIS FOR MICROSOFT EXCEL.

13. Click the Microsoft Office button in Microsoft Excel.

14. Now the OPEN WORKBOOK and SAVE WORKBOOK menu items should be activated and when using them the configuration from the previous steps is shown allowing you to connect towards your SAP BusinessObjects Enterprise system.

Option 2

In case you are in the role of an IT administrator you can also leverage this approach and in that way prepare the setting for all users. You can create a simple XML file similar to the one shown below.

```
<?xml version="1.0"?>
<BOESystems scope="user" type="complex" fullpath="/Settings/
BOESettings/BOESystems">
<![CDATA[<?xml version="1.0" encoding="utf-16"?>
<ArrayOfCoBoeSystemInfo xmlns:xsi="http://www.w3.org/2001/XMLSchema-
instance" xmlns:xsd="http://www.w3.org/2001/XMLSchema">
<CoBoeSystemInfo>
<SystemId>  %SYSTEM_ID%  </SystemId>
<ContextId>Default</ContextId>
<SystemName>  %SYSTEM_NAME%  </SystemName>
<Hostname>  %HOSTNAME%  </Hostname>
<Scheme>  %PROTOCOL%  </Scheme>
<Port>  %PORT%  </Port>
<SessionServiceUrl>  %URL%  </SessionServiceUrl>
<Active>true</Active>
<BoeVersion>3.1</BoeVersion>
<CMSNames><string>  %CMS%  </string></CMSNames>
</CoBoeSystemInfo>
</ArrayOfCoBoeSystemInfo>]]>
</BOESystems>
```

Table 2.3 shows the placeholders in the XML file and the type of value that is expected.

Placeholder	Description	Example
%SYSTEM_ID%	Here you need to enter a name for your System.	BusinessObjects_Server_1
%SYSTEM_NAME%	Here you need to enter a name for your System.	BusinessObjects_Server_1

Table 2.3 XML File Placeholders

Placeholder	Description	Example
%HOSTNAME%	Here you need to enter the hostname of the application server of your SAP BusinessObjects Enterprise system.	DEMO
%PROTOCOL%	Here you need to enter the protocol you are going to use.	HTTP or HTTS
%PORT%	Here you need to enter the port of your application server	8080
%URL%	Here you need to enter the relative path to the web services of your SAP BusinessObjects Enterprise system.	In a default deployment: /dswsbobje/services/session
%CMS%	Here you need to enter the name of your CMS of your SAP BusinessObjects Enterprise system	BOE_DEMO

Table 2.3 XML File Placeholders (Cont.)

The XML file needs to be named BOESettings.xml and needs to be placed into the folder \Application Data\SAP AG\SAP BusinessObjects Advanced Analysis\Settings\ for each user on the local computer.

> **Multiple SAP BusinessObjects Enterprise Systems**
>
> Both options – a manual entry or the XML file – provide you the option to add multiple SAP BusinessObjects Enterprise system definitions to the list. In case you define multiple systems the user will have the option to select one system from the list of available entries.

In this section we reviewed the options to configure the connection to your SAP BusinessObjects Enterprise system for Advanced Analysis Office. In the next section we will learn to enable or disable the Advanced Analysis Plug-In for Microsoft Office.

2.2.8 Enabling or Disabling Advanced Analysis Office Plug-In

Advanced Analysis Office cannot be activated at the same time, together with BusinessExplorer (BEx) Analyzer inside of Microsoft Excel. In a normal situation, when you start Advanced Analysis Office for Microsoft Excel, BEx Analyzer will be de-activated and when starting BEx Analyzer, Advanced Analysis Office for Microsoft Excel will be de-activated. But there might be situations where you manually have to enable or disable the Advanced Analysis Office plug-in inside of Microsoft Excel, therefore we will go through the steps to enable or disable the plug-in. In the following steps we will assume you are using Microsoft Excel 2007.

1. Start Microsoft Excel 2007.
2. Click the Microsoft Office button.
3. Select the menu EXCEL OPTIONS (see Figure 2.21).

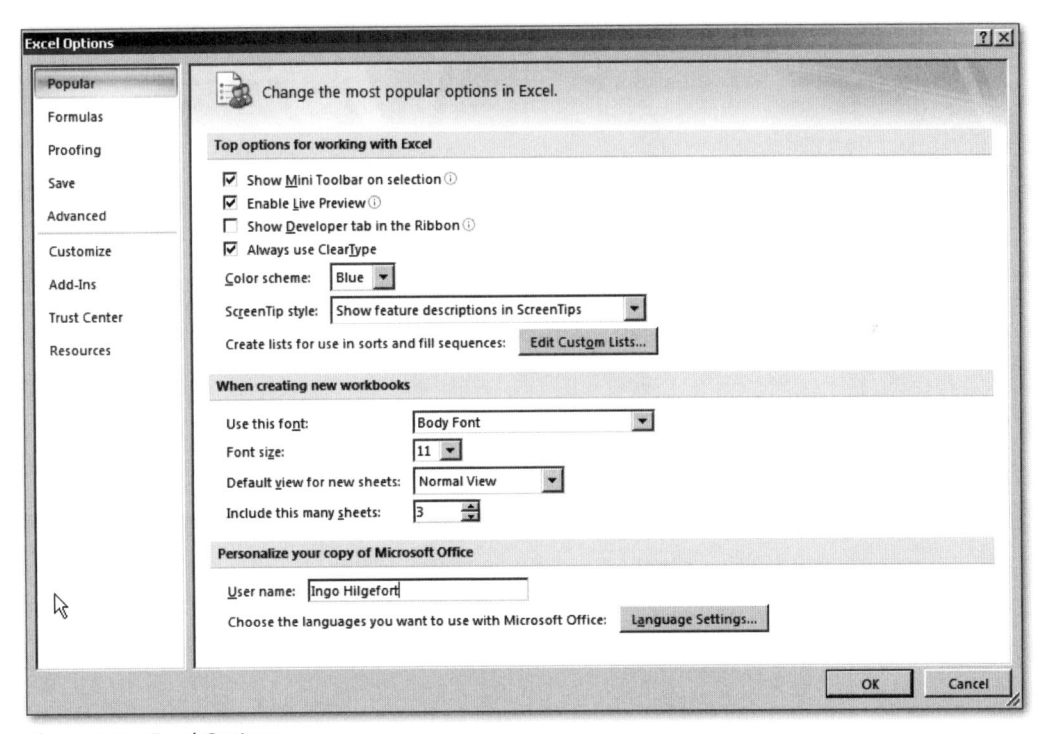

Figure 2.21 Excel Options

4. Select the entry ADD-INS (see Figure 2.22).

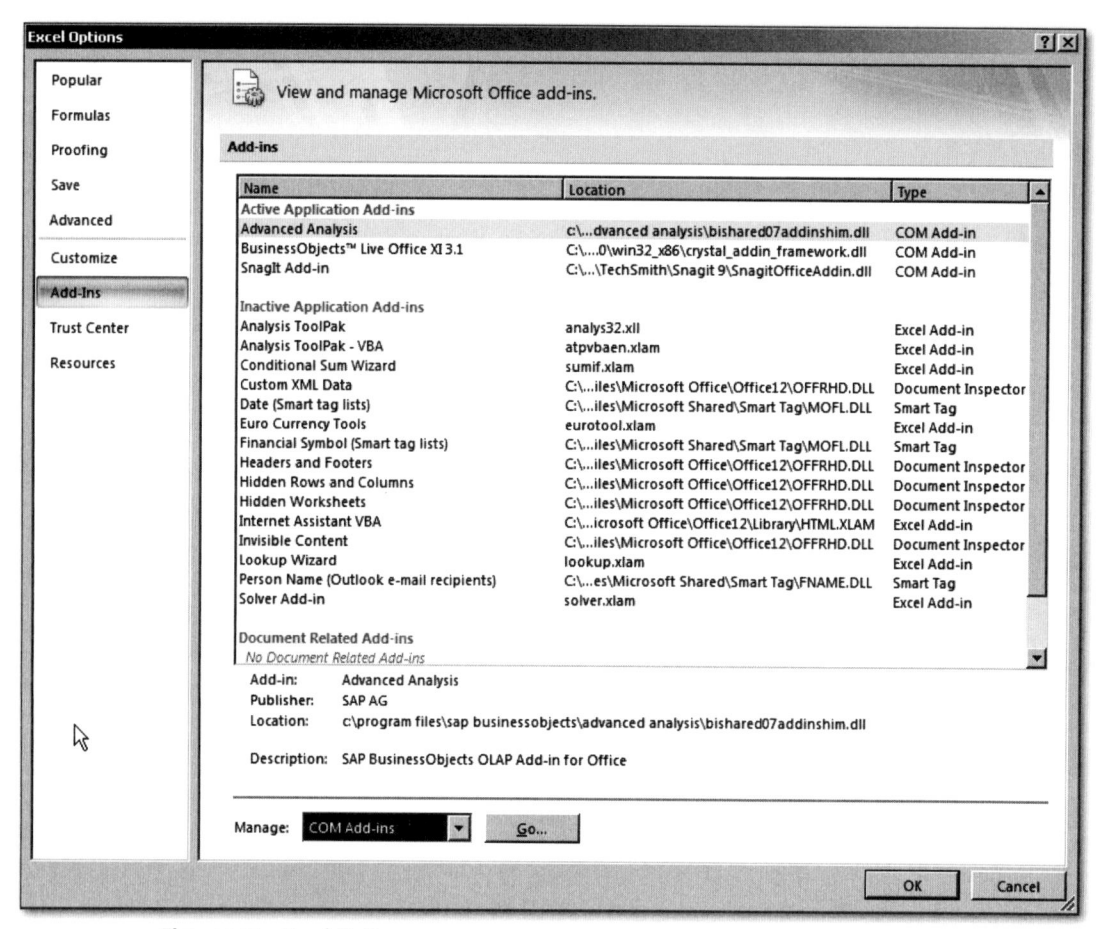

Figure 2.22 Excel Options

5. In the listbox MANAGE select the entry COM ADD-INS.
6. Click GO (see Figure 2.23).

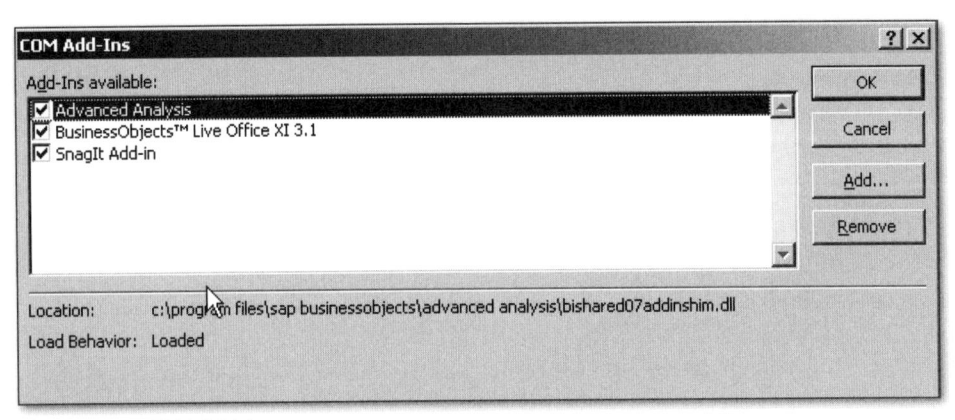

Figure 2.23 COM Add-Ins

Here you can use the checkboxes next to the Advanced Analysis Office plug-in and enable or disable the plug-in.

In Microsoft PowerPoint you will find the option to enable or disable the plug-in using this approach as well.

> **Advanced Analysis Office LoadBehavior**
>
> You can configure the load behavior of the Advanced Analysis Office Add-In by configuring the following registry setting `LoadBehavior` in the registry branch `HKEY_LOCAL_MACHINE\SOFTWARE\Microsoft\Office\Excel\AddIns\SBOP.AdvancedAnalysis.Addin.1` to the value 3 for enabling and to the value 2 for disabling the Add-In.

In this section, we reviewed how to enable or disable the plug-in for Advanced Analysis Office. In the next section we will look at multi-lingual behavior of Advanced Analysis Office.

2.2.9 Multi-Lingual Behavior of Advanced Analysis Office

In this section we will quickly review the behavior of Advanced Analysis Office in regards to multi-lingual data and multi-lingual UI (User Interface).

When you are using Advanced Analysis Office in combination with your SAP NetWeaver BW system, you are logging on with a specific logon language to the SAP NetWeaver BW system. The logon language used decides which data will be returned for those cases where you might have language dependent master data. The logon language does not decide which language is being used for labels being used in the workbook or slide deck. Items like labels for Info Fields or the menu language of the Advanced Analysis Office ribbon are based on the language of your Microsoft Office installation.

In short:

- The logon language for SAP NetWeaver BW sets the language for the data and language dependent master data retrieved from SAP NetWeaver BW.

- The language from Microsoft Office sets the language for the menus in the Advanced Analysis Office ribbon and for labels being used as part of the workbook or presentation.

In this short section we learned how Advanced Analysis Office is leveraging the language of the Microsoft Office installation and the logon language to the SAP NetWeaver BW system. In the next section we will take a look at the required authorizations to use Advanced Analysis Office with SAP NetWeaver BW based data.

2.2.10 Setting Up User Authorizations and Rights

To use Advanced Analysis Office in combination with SAP BusinessObjects Enterprise, a user needs to have the proper authorizations and rights on both the SAP NetWeaver BW system and the SAP BusinessObjects Enterprise system.

Table 2.4 shows the necessary authorizations for SAP NetWeaver BW.

Authorization Objects	Authorization Field	Authorization Value
S_RFC	RFC_TYPE	FUGR
	RFC_NAME	SYST, SYSU, RSBOLAP_BICS_CONSUMER, RFC1, SDIFRUNTIME, RSBOLAP_BICS, RSOBJS_RFC_INTERFACE, RSBOLAP_BICS_PROVIDER RSBOLAP_BICS_PROVIDER_VAR RZX0 RZX2
	ACTVT	16
S_USER_AGR	ACT_GROUP	If you want to limit access to a specific role, then you need to enter the technical name of the roles here. You can enter multiple names.
	ACTVT	01, 02, 03
S_RS_COMP	RSINFOAREA	If you want to limit access to a specific InfoArea, then you need to enter the technical name of the InfoArea here. You can enter multiple names.
	RSINFOCUBE	If you would like to limit access to a specific InfoProvider, then you need to enter the technical name of the InfoProvider here. You can enter multiple names.
	RSZCOMPTP	REP CKF RKF QVW SOB STR VAR

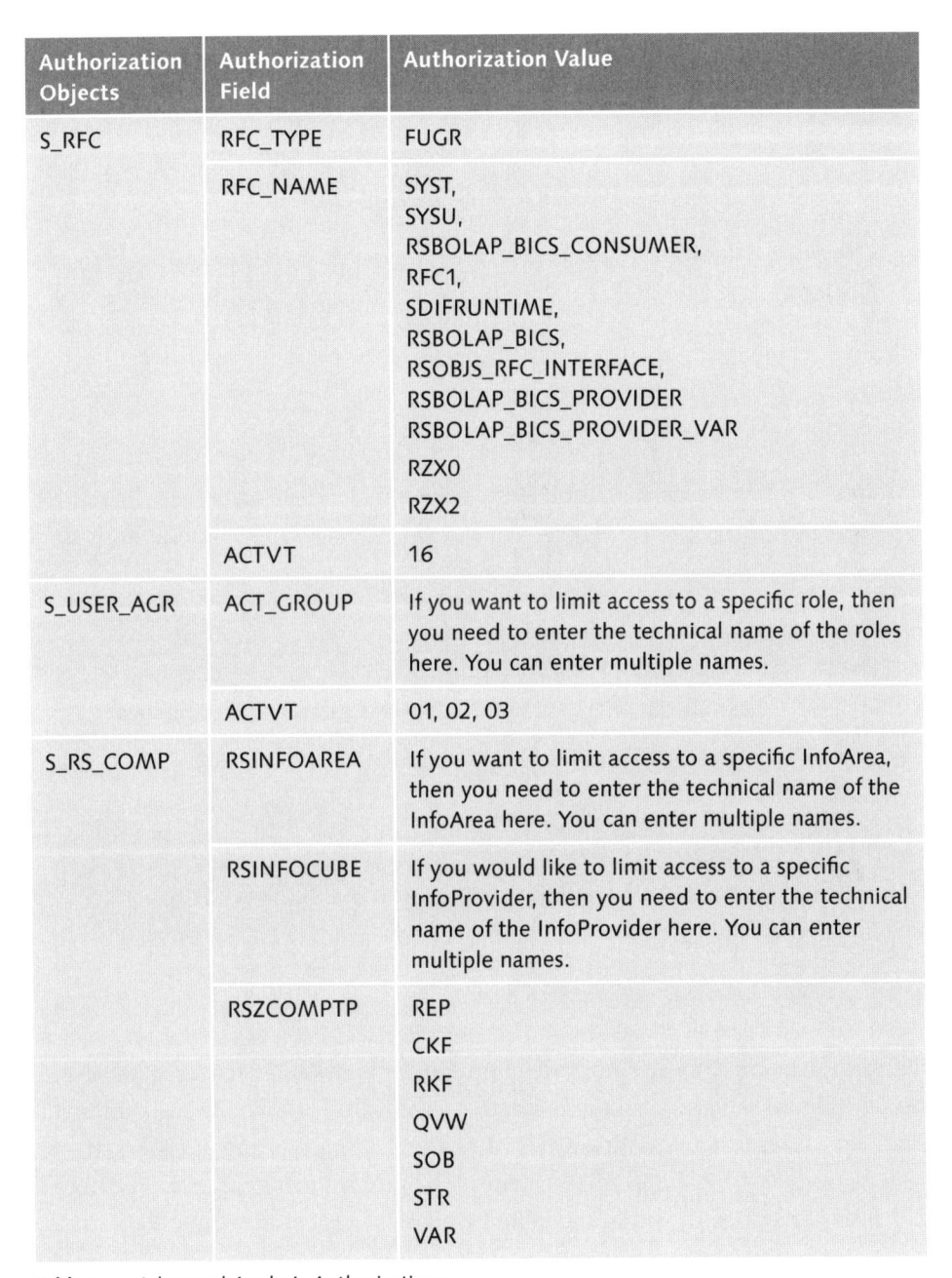

Table 2.4 Advanced Analysis Authorizations

Authorization Objects	Authorization Field	Authorization Value
S_RS_COMP1	RSZCOMPID	If you want to limit access to a specific BW Query, then you need to enter the technical name of the BW Query here. You can enter multiple names.
	ACTVT	03, 16
	RSZCOMPID	If you want to limit access to a specific BW Query, then you need to enter the technical name of the BW Query here. You can enter multiple names.
	RSZCOMPTP	REP CKF RKF QVW SOB STR VAR
	RSZOWNER	If you want to limit access to a specific BW Query based on the owner, then you need to enter the user ID of the owner here. You can enter multiple IDs.
	ACTVT	03, 16
S_RS_AUTH	BIAUTH	Here you need to enter the authorization object for your configured data level security.
S_CTS_ADMI	CTS_ADMFCT	TABL

Table 2.4 Advanced Analysis Authorizations (Cont.)

The Authorization Objects, Authorization Fields, and Values listed in Table 2.4 should only be seen as a recommendation. The values shown in the table will allow your users to work with Advanced Analysis Office and successfully retrieve the data from SAP NetWeaver BW Queries. The settings for your landscape might vary from the values shown in the table based on your requirements.

With SAP BusinessObjects Enterprise, you have two options for setting up rights for your users:

- You can limit access to the Voyager Connections that are being reused by Advanced Analysis Office.
- You can limit access to the workbooks and PPTs that are being stored in the SAP BusinessObjects Enterprise repository.

To set up security for the Voyager connections, you can follow these steps:

1. Log on to the CMC of your SAP BusinessObjects Enterprise system with an administrative account.
2. Select VOYAGER CONNECTIONS on the main page.
3. Select the connection you want to secure.
4. Right-click on the connection to open the context menu, or follow the menu path MANAGE • USER SECURITY (see Figure 2.24).

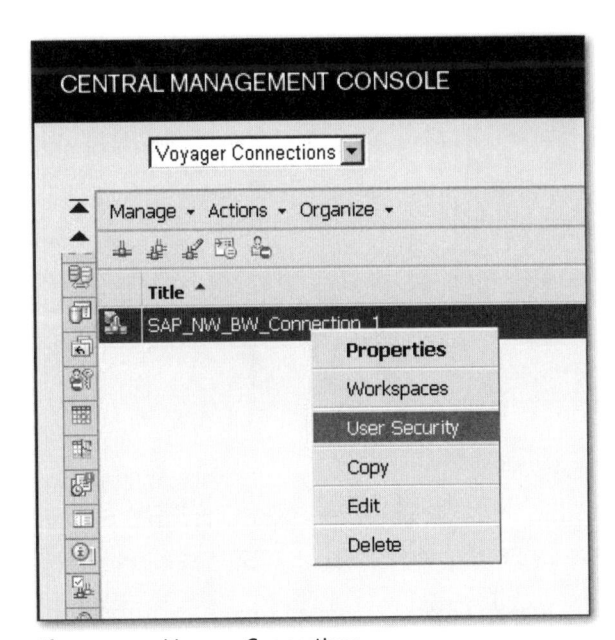

Figure 2.24 Voyager Connections

5. In the next screen, click the ADD PRINCIPALS button to add new users or user groups to the list of authorized users (see Figure 2.25).

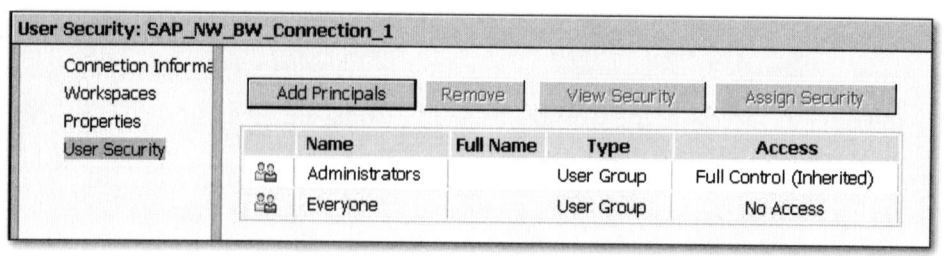

2 | Installation, Deployment and Configuration of Advanced Analysis Office

Figure 2.25 Add Principals

6. The list of available user and user groups appears and you can add the required users or user groups to the list of SELECTED USERS/GROUPS (see Figure 2.26).

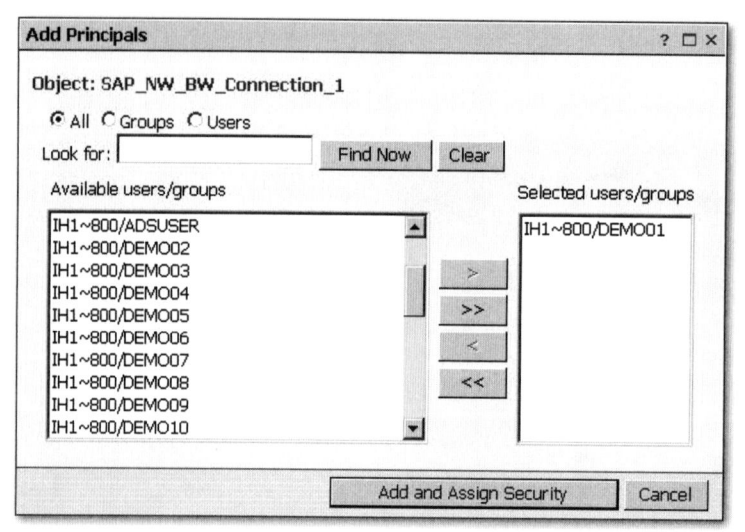

Figure 2.26 Selected Users/Groups

7. Add the users or user groups from your system to the list of SELECTED USERS/ GROUPS and click ADD AND ASSIGN SECURITY (see Figure 2.27).

8. Now you can select a preconfigured ACCESS LEVEL and assign one of them to your user/user group or you can navigate to the ADVANCED tab to assign or deny individual rights.

9. Click on the ADVANCED tab.

80

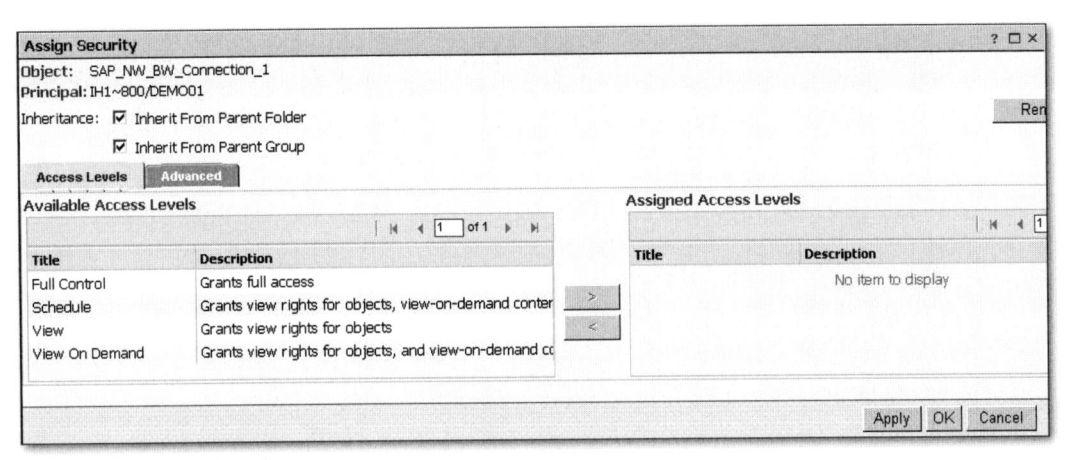

2.2 Deployment Options for SAP Advanced Analysis Office

Figure 2.27 Assign Security

10. Click on ADD/REMOVE RIGHTS (see Figure 2.28).

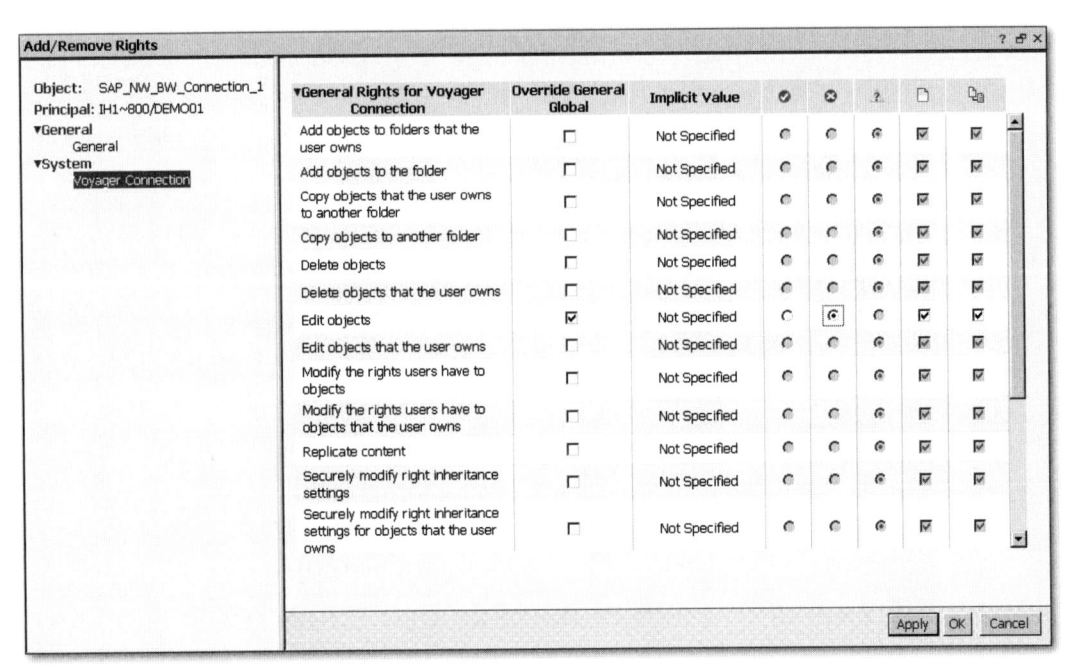

Figure 2.28 Add/Remove Rights

81

Here you can override the individual rights and configure the rights for the selected user, or user group, for the Voyager Connections. Please note that there is a GENERAL area of rights and a specific VOYAGER CONNECTION entry in the folder SYSTEM.

To set up folder-level security in the SAP BusinessObjects XI 3.1 Enterprise system, you can follow these steps:

1. Log on to the CMC of your SAP BusinessObjects Enterprise system with an administrative account.
2. Select the FOLDERS entry on the main page.
3. Select the folder that you want to use to store Advanced Analysis objects and that you want to secure.
4. Right-click on the folder to open the context menu, or follow the MANAGE • USER SECURITY menu path.
5. In the next screen, click the ADD PRINCIPALS button to add new users or user groups to the list of authorized users.
6. The list of available users and user groups appears and you can add the necessary users or user groups to the list of SELECTED USERS/GROUPS.
7. Add the users or user groups from your system to the list of SELECTED USERS/GROUPS and click ADD AND ASSIGN SECURITY.
8. Now you can select a preconfigured ACCESS LEVEL and assign one of them to your users/user groups or you can navigate to the ADVANCED tab to assign or deny individual rights.
9. Click on the ADVANCED tab.
10. Click on ADD/REMOVE RIGHTS (see Figure 2.29).

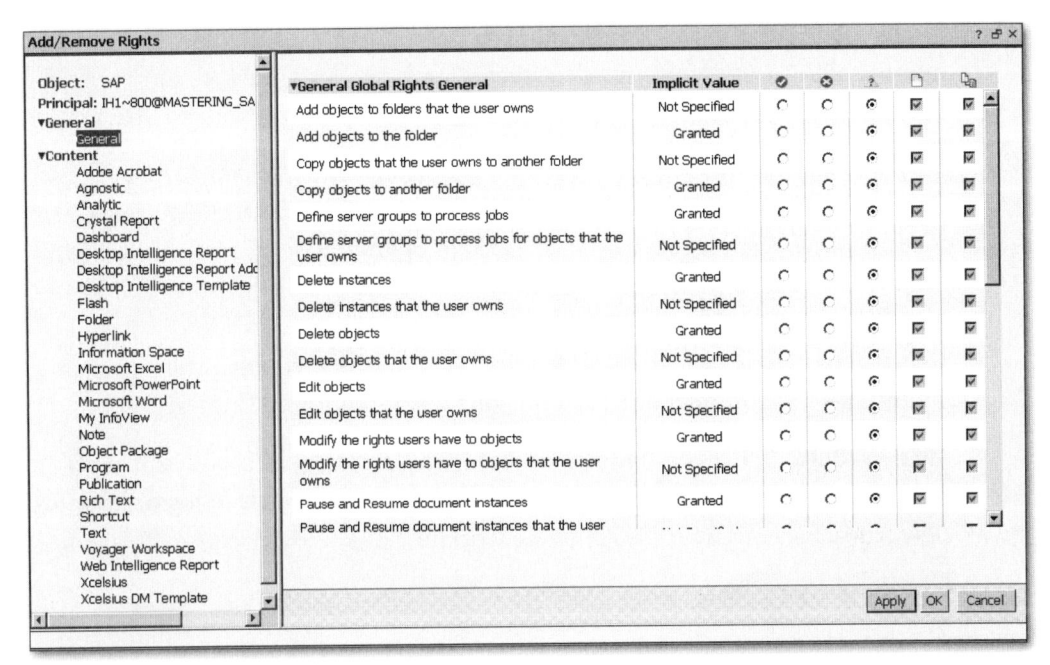

Figure 2.29 Add/Remove Rights

Here you can override the individual rights and configure the rights for the selected users or user groups for the folder. Please note that there is a GENERAL area of rights and a specific CONTENT entry, which lets you specify rights based on content type.

> **Advanced Analysis Office Content Type**
>
> For deploying Advanced Analysis Office in combination with SAP BusinessObjects Enterprise XI 3.1, the relevant content types for Advanced Analysis Office are Microsoft Excel and PowerPoint.

2.2.11 User Authentication

If you are deploying Advanced Analysis Office in combination with SAP BusinessObjects Enterprise XI 3.1, you can leverage all of the configured authentication options when authenticating users in Advanced Analysis Office. It is important to remember that Advanced Analysis Office combined with SAP BusinessObjects Enterprise XI 3.1 does not provide server side– based SSO solution; only a client-side SSO solution is provided, which does require integration with an SNC.

Based on this you can configure the SAP authentication as part of your SAP BusinessObjects Enterprise system, but even though you can leverage the SAP credentials to authenticate against the SAP BusinessObjects Enterprise system, you will still be asked to authenticate against the underlying source system by Advanced Analysis Office. The benefit of using SAP authentication as part of your SAP BusinessObjects Enterprise is that you can then reuse your SAP credentials for the shared connections and for opening or saving your Advanced Analysis workbooks.

For SAP BusinessObjects Enterprise XI 4.0 integration, a server-side SSO is planned, which will then let you leverage your SAP Credentials to log on to InfoView and achieve SSO for the complete workflow of an Advanced Analysis Office document.

2.3 Summary

In this chapter, we reviewed the technical prerequisites for deploying Advanced Analysis Office and continued with the installation and configuration steps on the SAP NetWeaver BW and SAP BusinessObjects Enterprise systems. In the next chapter, we will review the connection options and how Advanced Analysis Office can leverage existing metadata from your SAP NetWeaver BW system.

In this chapter, we will review the options for connecting to your SAP corporate data using Advanced Analysis Office.

3 Advanced Analysis Office — Data Connectivity and Metadata Reuse

In this chapter, we will take a look at the connectivity options Advanced Analysis Office provides on top of our SAP NetWeaver Business Information Warehouse (BW) system. In addition, we will see how Advanced Analysis Office can leverage existing metadata from SAP NetWeaver BW.

3.1 Data Connectivity Options

Before we look at how Advanced Analysis Office can leverage metadata from your SAP NetWeaver BW system, let's take a look at the data connectivity options for Advanced Analysis Office.

Figure 3.1 shows the different options for leveraging your corporate data from the SAP NetWeaver BW system. Advanced Analysis Office can leverage the Business Explorer (BEx) queries as a source and it can leverage the InfoProvider directly without using a BEx Query. We will highlight the differences between connecting to a BEx Query or an InfoProvider in Section 3.2.1, BEx Query vs. InfoProvider.

In addition to SAP NetWeaver BW connectivity, you can also leverage the Transient Provider, which lets you connect, via a BEx Query, in the local Business Intelligence (BI) client of your SAP ERP system, to a classic InfoSet and provide real-time ERP data to your end users. Please note that using Transient Provider requires SAP ERP 6.0 Enhancement Package 05 (SAP BusinessSuite Innovation 2010).

3 | Advanced Analysis Office — Data Connectivity and Metadata Reuse

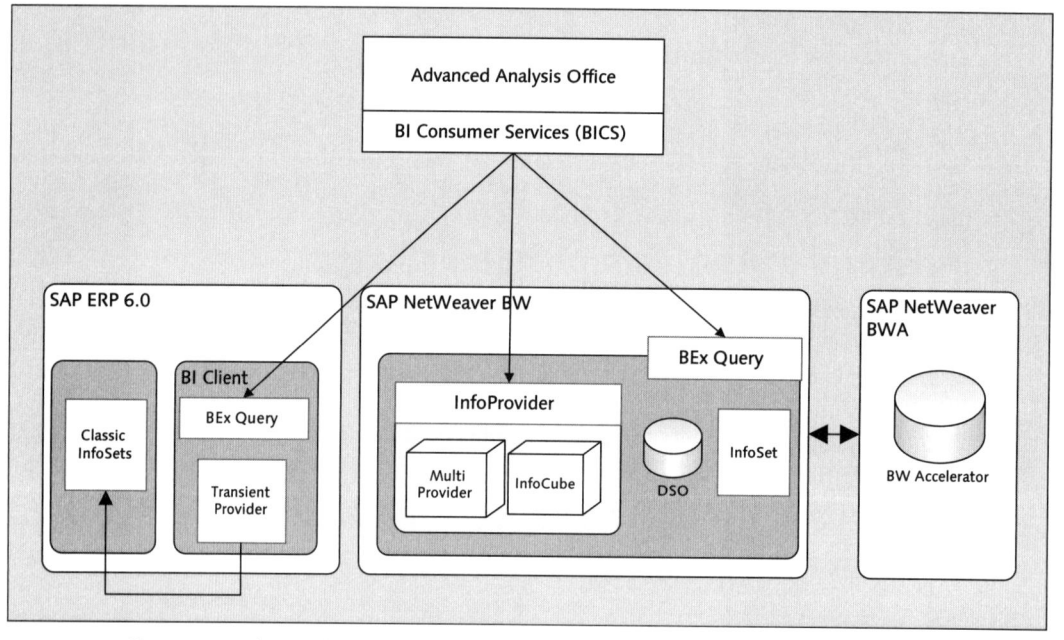

Figure 3.1 Advanced Analysis Data Connectivity

By using the BEx query, Advanced Analysis Office can connect to:

- BEx Query Views
- InfoCubes
- MultiProviders
- Remote Cubes
- Virtual InfoCubes
- Data Store Objects (DSOs)
- BW InfoSets
- Classic InfoSets (via Transient Provider and a local BI client)

If you want to leverage BEx Query Views as a source for Advanced Analysis Office, they are listed as a subordinate of the actual BEx Query. When you use a BEx Query View as a source, Advanced Analysis Office leverages all filter and navigation settings from the BEx Query View and provides an equivalent workbook.

Without using a BEx Query, Advanced Analysis Office can connect to:

- InfoCubes
- MultiProviders
- DSO Objects
- SAP NetWeaver BW InfoSets

So far, we reviewed the different options for connecting to SAP NetWeaver BW as a data source. In the next section, we will take a look at how Advanced Analysis Office can leverage existing BEx queries and their metadata and what the major differences are between a connection via a BEx query and a direct connection via the InfoProvider.

3.2 Leveraging SAP NetWeaver BW Metadata

In this section, we will take a more detailed look at how Advanced Analysis Office can leverage existing metadata in your SAP NetWeaver BW system. For this section we will use Advanced Analysis as a Microsoft Excel plug-in (the metadata support in Microsoft PowerPoint is identical).

To start, we will use a BEx query (see Figure 3.2) based on the SAP NetWeaver Demo model cube Actuals and Plan MultiProvider (0D_NW_M01).

The BEx Query contains the characteristics COUNTRY and REGION in the ROWS, the characteristics SOLD-TO-PARTY, PRODUCT CATEGORY, PRODUCT GROUP, and CALENDAR YEAR/MONTH in the FREE CHARACTERISTICS. In addition, we have several KEY FIGURES as part of our BEx Query.

In the FILTER area (see Figure 3.3) of our BEx Query we have a variable for CALENDAR YEAR and we defined a default value for REGION.

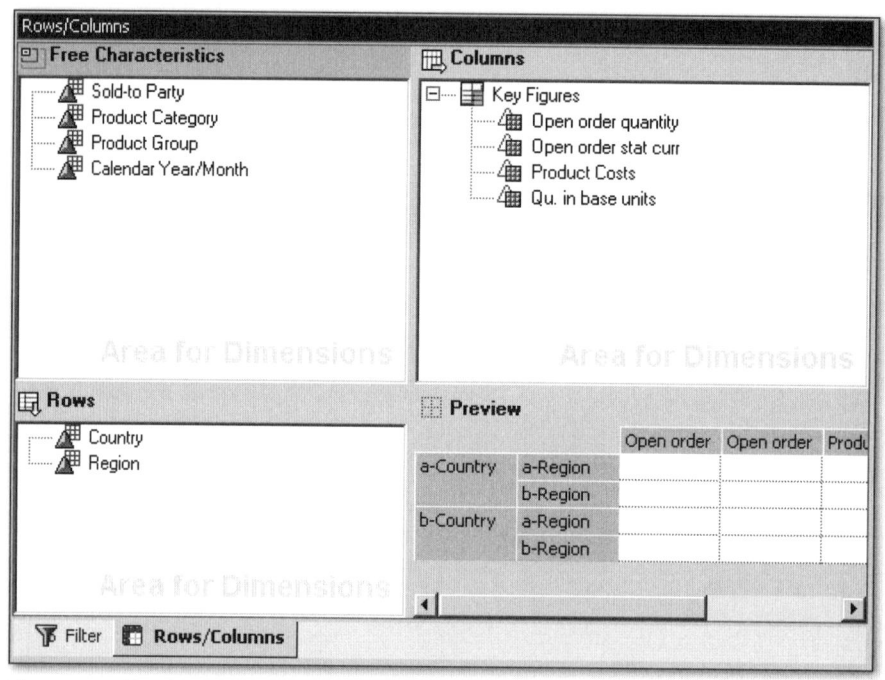

Figure 3.2 BEx Query

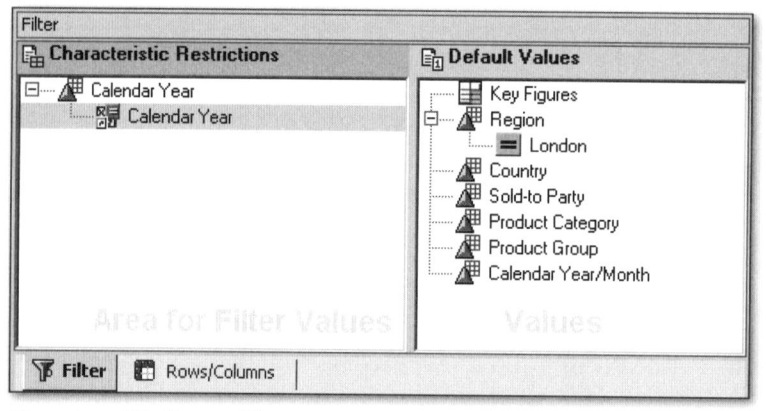

Figure 3.3 BEx Query - Filter

Now when we use Advanced Analysis Office in Microsoft Excel we can identify the elements of our BEx Query in the ADVANCED ANALYSIS PANEL (see Figure 3.4).

Leveraging SAP NetWeaver BW Metadata | 3.2

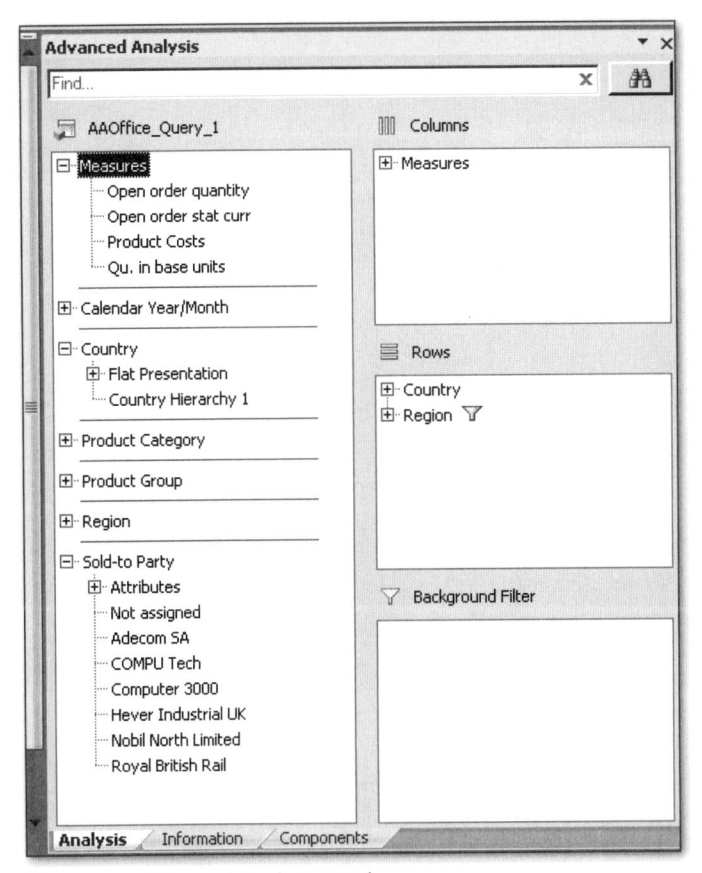

Figure 3.4 Advanced Analysis Panel

The ADVANCED ANALYSIS PANEL provides you with an overview of all available elements. In the next chapter we will learn in more details how to establish a connection to our SAP NetWeaver BW system. For now we will focus on the metadata retrieval and how the elements of the BEx Query are being displayed to you so that we get an understanding on where and how the elements of the BEx query are shown to you in Advanced Analysis Office.

Before we now take a look at the details on how Advanced Analysis Office is leveraging the meta-data from the BEx query I would like to highlight the fact, that Advanced Analysis is not using the well known BEx query terms anymore and therefore you can see the new terms compared to the old terms in Table 3.1.

89

BEx Query	Advanced Analysis Office
Keyfigure	Measure
Characteristic	Dimension
Variable	Prompt
Characteristic Values	Member

Table 3.1 Terms in Advanced Analysis Office

Terms that are not listed in Table 3.1 are identical in Advanced Analysis Office compared to the BEx query, unless they are explained in a later chapter such as the Conditional Formatting being the equivalent functionality to Exceptions in the BEx query.

For the following chapters in this book we will leverage the well known terms from the BEx query so that you do recognize the terms and I hope that the table helps you to learn the new terminology of Advanced Analysis Office quickly.

As shown in Figure 3.4, we can identify the following by leveraging the BEx Query metadata:

- Each characteristic from the ROWS and FREE CHARACTERISTICS in the BEx Query is shown in the ADVANCED ANALYSIS PANEL on the left-hand side as information that is available to Advanced Analysis Office.
  For example: PRODUCT GROUP.

- Each characteristic from the ROWS is also placed into the ROWS of your crosstab.
  For example: REGION and COUNTRY.

- Values defined and configured in DEFAULTS of the BEx Query are leveraged by Advanced Analysis Office and used to define the initial view of your data.
  For example: default value LONDON for REGION.

- Variables defined in the BEx Query are presented as prompts in Advanced Analysis Office. Prompts are not part of the Advanced Analysis Panel and are presented via a separate menu item.

- All key figures from the BEx Query are presented under MEASURES in the ADVANCED ANALYSIS PANEL.

In addition, we can also identify the following behavior of Advanced Analysis Office with regards to metadata retrieval:

- Advanced Analysis Office provides all available hierarchies for each characteristic even if no hierarchies have been selected in the BEx Query. You can find this behavior under COUNTRY in the ADVANCED ANALYSIS PANEL. For COUNTRY, we see the standard flat representation of all countries, but we can also identify COUNTRY HIERARCHY 1 and leverage it in our analysis even though we did not select a hierarchy in the BEx Query.
- In addition to the available hierarchies, Advanced Analysis also provides the available display attributes even though we did not add those display attributes to the underlying BEx Query. You can see this behavior with the SOLD-TO-PARTY characteristic shown in the Advanced Analysis Panel with the list of ATTRIBUTES.

Our second BEx Query makes use of custom structures (see Figure 3.5).

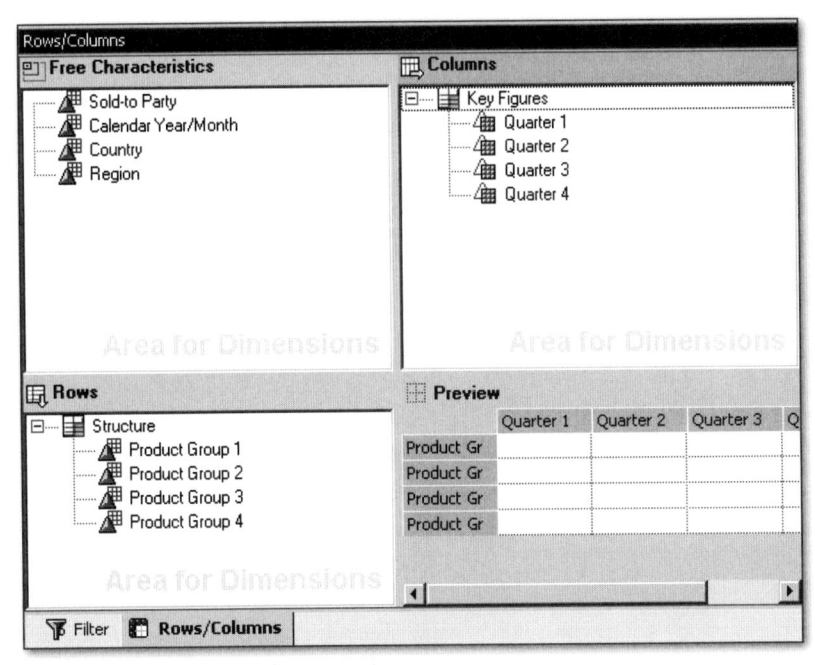

Figure 3.5 BEx Query with Custom Structures

3 | Advanced Analysis Office — Data Connectivity and Metadata Reuse

As you can see, we created a custom structure in the ROWS section. The custom structure is based on the PRODUCT characteristic and groups our products into four groups. In the COLUMNS section we created a custom structure based on a set of four selections combining CALENDAR YEAR/MONTH with the NET SALES REVENUE key figure into the aggregated totals for the four calendar quarters.

This type of BEx Query will provide the complete details of each custom structure in the Advanced Analysis Panel (see Figure 3.6).

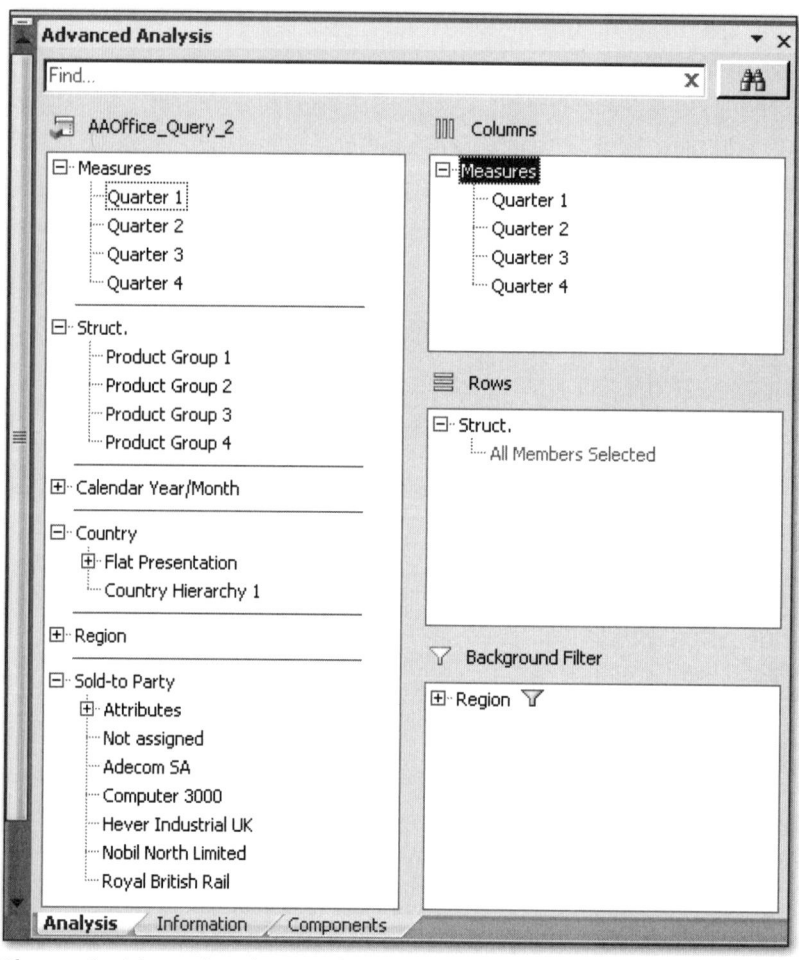

Figure 3.6 Advanced Analysis Panel

Not only are the custom structures available to you in the panel, but you can also select each element of the custom structure individually, which lets you reuse large custom structures so that you don't have to build specific BEx queries with a subset of the structure elements. You can use the Member Selector for a custom structure in the same way you select members from a characteristic or a subset of all available key figures.

The following is a list of settings and elements from the BEx Query, leveraged by Advanced Analysis Office (see also Table 3.2):

- The option for activating Display as Hierarchy for the Rows or Columns is available in Advanced Analysis Office.

- Any display settings for key figures are inherited in Advanced Analysis Office and displayed with the configured decimals and scaling factors. These types of settings can also be changed later on in the workbook.

- Display settings, like the configuration for showing the key or the key and text for a characteristic leveraged by Advanced Analysis Office, can also be changed later on in the workbook.

- Structure elements configured to be hidden or initially hidden will behave the same in Advanced Analysis Office. A hidden object will not be shown at all and a hidden object that can be shown will be interpreted as a Filter and shown as such in the Advanced Analysis Panel.

- For Advanced Analysis Office to leverage BEx Queries as a source, there is no need to configure the Allow External Access property for the BEx query.

BEx Query Element	Advanced Analysis Office Interpretation
Characteristics	Each Characteristic from the Rows, Columns, and Free Characteristic areas are available for navigation purposes.
Display Attributes	All available Display Attributes are shown as subordinates of the corresponding characteristic, even when they are not part of the BEx query.

Table 3.2 Supported SAP NetWeaver BW Metadata

BEx Query Element	Advanced Analysis Office Interpretation
Custom Structures`	The structure and structure elements are shown in Advanced Analysis Office and you can select single structure elements.
Navigational Attributes	Navigational Attributes are treated just like a characteristic.
Key Figures	Each Key Figure is shown in the list of measures.
Variables	All Variables configured as Ready for Input are available in a prompting screen. Other variables, such as Text Variables or EXIT Variables, are leveraged as well.
Restricted Key Figures and Calculated Key Figures	Restricted and Calculated Key Figures are treated just like a Key Figure. Advanced Analysis Office users cannot change the definition of Restricted and Calculated Key Figures without using the BEx Query Designer.
Hierarchies	All available Hierarchies are available for navigation and filtering purposes in Advanced Analysis Office, even if no hierarchies have been activated in the BEx Query.
Key Date Variables	Key Date Variables are supported just like any other variable.
Conditions	Conditions created as part of the BEx query are fully leveraged by Advanced Analysis Office, but the definitions of the Conditions are not visible in Advanced Analysis Office. You can also leverage the new Filter by Measure feature to achieve similar functionality.
Exceptions	Exceptions defined in the BW query are fully leveraged by Advanced Analysis Office and the definitions of the Exceptions are available in a read-only mode. You can also leverage the new Conditional Highlighting feature to achieve similar functionality.
Currency and Unit Conversion	Currency and Unit conversions are fully supported by Advanced Analysis Office and can either be done using variables or performed ad hoc in Advanced Analysis Office.

Table 3.2 Supported SAP NetWeaver BW Metadata (Cont.)

In addition to leveraging all of the metadata from the SAP NetWeaver BW system it is important to remember the following facts on the settings you can influence in the BEx Query:

- Advanced Analysis Office fully leverages all of the display settings in the BEx Query for the Key Figures, such as scaling factors, number of decimals, and the placement of the +/- signs.

- Advanced Analysis Office supports the Display as Hierarchy setting for the Rows and Columns section configured in the BEx Query, which lets you configure standard characteristics for display in a hierarchical/cascading way. In addition to leveraging this option, you can also follow the HIERARCHY • COMPACT DISPLAY IN ROWS menu path to achieve a similar result (see Chapter 5, Advanced Analysis Office — Advanced Functions, for more details).

- Advanced Analysis Office also supports the option for configuring elements of a structure to be hidden. This option is leveraged by Advanced Analysis Office and the hidden elements will not be shown to users in Advanced Analysis Office.

In this section, we reviewed how Advanced Analysis provides you with access to all of the available metadata in your SAP NetWeaver BW system. In the next section, we will compare access to a BEx query to using the InfoProvider directly.

3.2.1 BEx Query versus InfoProvider

The question often comes up, Why should you leverage the BEx Query and not leverage a direct connection to the InfoProvider? In this section, we will compare these two options.

Advanced Analysis Office provides you with access to the InfoProvider level. Table 3.3 shows a list of available metadata elements from SAP NetWeaver BW and indicates which elements are available when using a BEx Query or InfoProvider access with Advanced Analysis Office.

3 | Advanced Analysis Office — Data Connectivity and Metadata Reuse

SAP NetWeaver BW Metadata	Bex Query Access	InfoProvider Access
Characteristics	X	X
Display Attributes	X	X
Custom Structures	X	Not available
Navigational Attributes	X	X
Key Figures	X	X
Variables	X	Not available
Restricted Key Figures and Calculated Key Figures	X	Not available
Hierarchies	X	X
Key Date Variables	X	Not available
Conditions	X	Not available
Exceptions	X	Not available
Currency and Unit Conversion	X	X
Authorization Variables	X	Not available

Table 3.3 BEx Query versus InfoProvider

As shown in Table 3.3, the elements that would not be available with direct InfoProvider access are the Restricted and Calculated Key Figures and the option to resolve time-dependent objects by using Key Date Variables. Most importantly, however, you should note that by connecting to the InfoProvider level you cannot leverage the Authorization variables, which means that the data connection doesn't automatically filter the data based on the defined data level security in your SAP NetWeaver BW system. The BI authorizations in SAP NetWeaver BW don't work as a filter when performing a data retrieval request, and by not leveraging the authorization variables there is no option for you to provide workbooks to your end users to automatically filter the data. Therefore, it is highly recommended to leverage the BEx query as the source for your workbooks with Advanced Analysis Office. This recommendation stands for all of the other SAP BusinessObjects BI client tools.

3.3 Summary

In this chapter, we reviewed the options that Advanced Analysis Office provides for leveraging your corporate data stored in SAP NetWeaver BW. We reviewed the different options for connecting to the data and provided you with details on the supported elements. In the next chapter, we will learn the basic features and functions of Advanced Analysis Office in Microsoft Excel and PowerPoint.

Now that we've installed and configured Advanced Analysis Office, let's learn how to use it to analyze corporate data and make informed decisions.

4   Advanced Analysis Office — Basic Functions

In this chapter, you will use Advanced Analysis Office with Microsoft Excel and PowerPoint to learn how to navigate and leverage its basic functionality in conjunction with your data inside the SAP NetWeaver Business Information Warehouse (BW) data warehouse. We will leverage the SAP NetWeaver Demo model and BW queries based on the InfoProvider from the SAP NetWeaver Demo model for all of our activities in this chapter.

> **SAP NetWeaver Demo Model**
>
> If you want to leverage the SAP NetWeaver Demo model for some simple exercises, you can find more details at *http://www.sdn.sap.com/irj/sdn/nw-demomodel*.

We will use a BW Query (see Figure 4.1), which includes the following characteristics and key figures:

- FREE CHARACTERISTICS

    - COUNTRY

    - REGION

    - DISTRIBUTION CHANNEL

    - SALES ORGANIZATION

    - SOLD-TO PARTY

    - PRODUCT CATEGORY

- ▸ Calendar Year/Month
- ▸ Calendar Year
▸ Rows
- ▸ Product Group
- ▸ Product
▸ Columns
- ▸ Net Value
- ▸ Open Orders Quantity
- ▸ Open Orders Value
- ▸ Product Costs
- ▸ Transport Costs

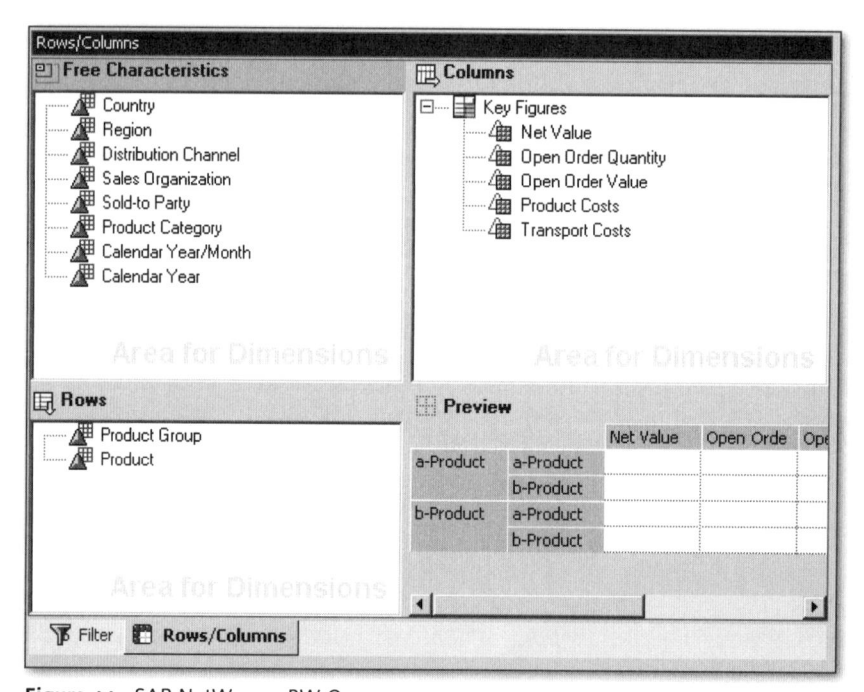

Figure 4.1 SAP NetWeaver BW Query

In addition to the preceding elements, our BW Query also contains variables for prompting and a set of defined default values (see Figure 4.2). We use a mandatory range value variable for the CALENDAR YEAR characteristic and an optional selection option variable for the PRODUCT characteristic; for CALENDAR YEAR/MONTH we also defined the values January 2010 to March 2010 as default values.

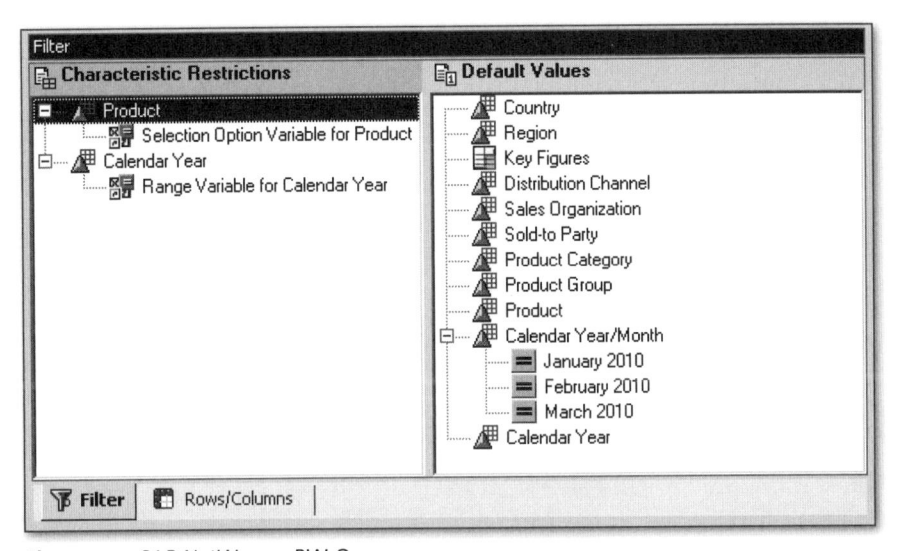

Figure 4.2 SAP NetWeaver BW Query

We will now use this BW Query in conjunction with Advanced Analysis Office to explore its functionality. The chapter is divided into two main parts: a step-by-step introduction to Advanced Analysis Office with Microsoft Excel and one with Microsoft PowerPoint.

4.1 Advanced Analysis Office — Microsoft Excel

In this section, we'll show you how to use the features and functions of Advanced Analysis Office in Microsoft Excel. You will start by learning how to establish a data connection from Advanced Analysis Office to your corporate data inside SAP NetWeaver BW.

4.1.1 Establishing Data Connectivity

Advanced Analysis Office lets you connect to your sources in SAP NetWeaver BW. You have the option of creating a shared connection in SAP BusinessObjects Enterprise, which would be the preferred option, or you can use the configurations of your local SAP Graphical User Interface (GUI) and connect to SAP NetWeaver BW that way. In this section, you will leverage both options to see how you can connect Advanced Analysis Office to your data; however, in the following sections you can use your preferred choice.

Setting Up Connectivity via SAP Frontend

To establish a data connection using SAP Frontend, you can leverage the SAP Logon pad as part of the SAP Frontend and create your system entry just as you created it for tools like Business Explorer (BEx) Query Designer and the BEx Analyzer (see Figure 4.3).

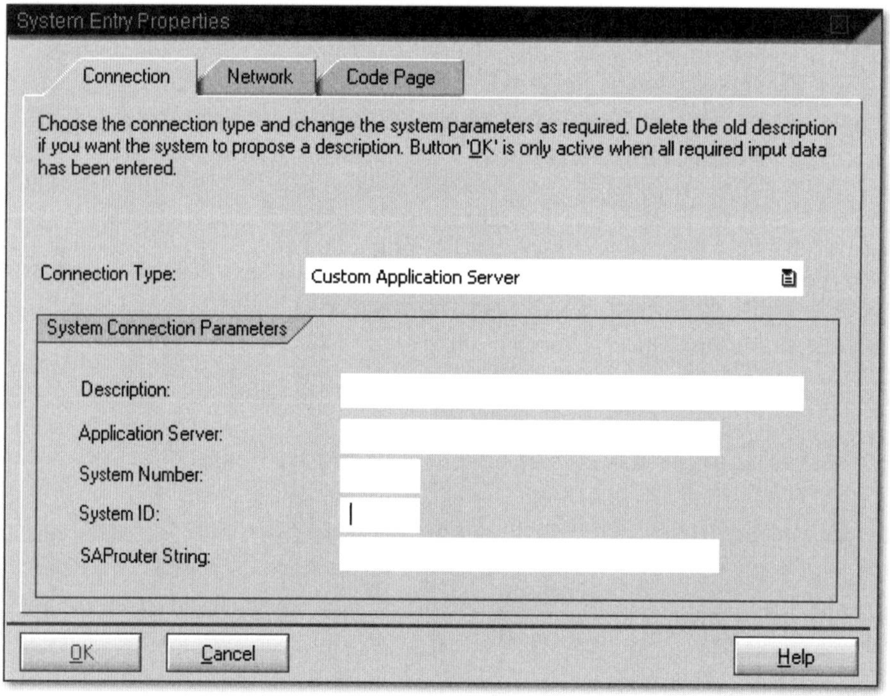

Figure 4.3 SAP Logon System Entries

After you create the system entry for the SAP Logon pad, you can connect to your data using Advanced Analysis Office.

1. Start Advanced Analysis Office with Microsoft Excel via the menu path START • PROGRAMS • SAP BUSINESSOBJECTS • ADVANCED ANALYSIS FOR MICROSOFT EXCEL.

2. Select the INSERT • SELECT DATA SOURCE option from the Advanced Analysis Ribbon (see Figure 4.4).

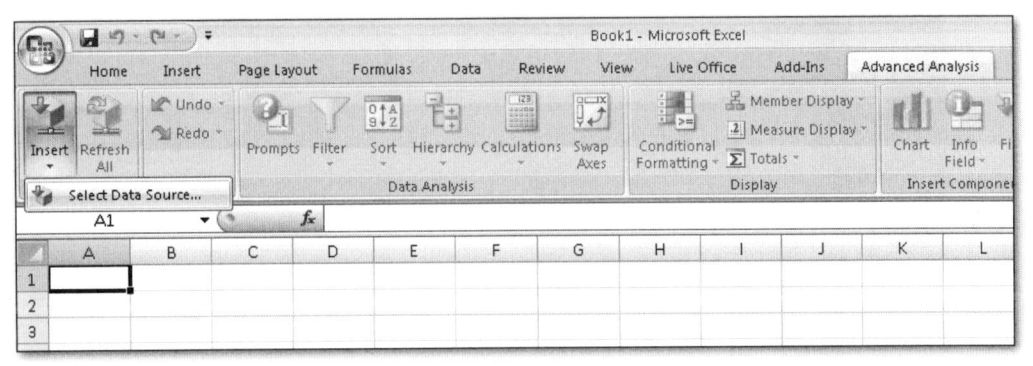

Figure 4.4 Insert Data Source

3. You will see the log-on screen for SAP BusinessObjects Enterprise (see Figure 4.5).

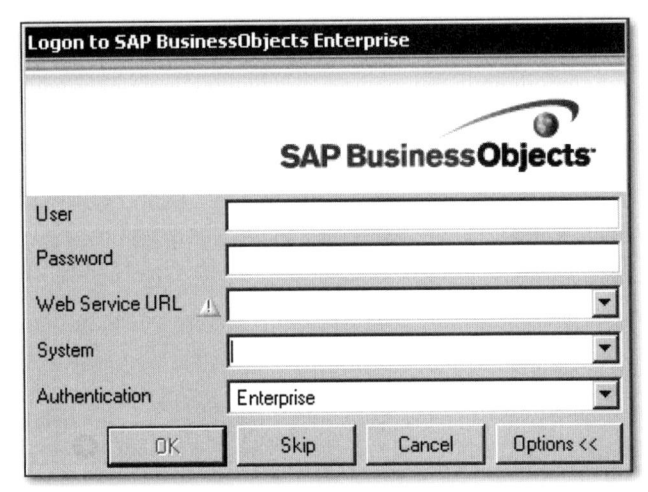

Figure 4.5 Logon Screen

4 | Advanced Analysis Office — Basic Functions

If you don't want to share the workbook with your colleagues, or don't want to use a shared connection, you can click the SKIP button. In our example, we will use the SKIP option for now and come back to this later.

4. Click SKIP.

5. You are now presented with the list of available SAP systems based on the entries of your SAP Logon pad (see Figure 4.6).

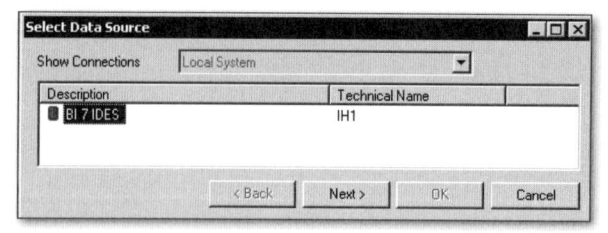

Figure 4.6 Select Data Source

6. Select the entry for your SAP system.

7. Click NEXT.

8. Enter your SAP credentials in the log-on screen and click NEXT.

9. Now you can select from a list of roles or navigate to the list of INFOAREAS that is available to you, based on your authentication (see Figure 4.7).

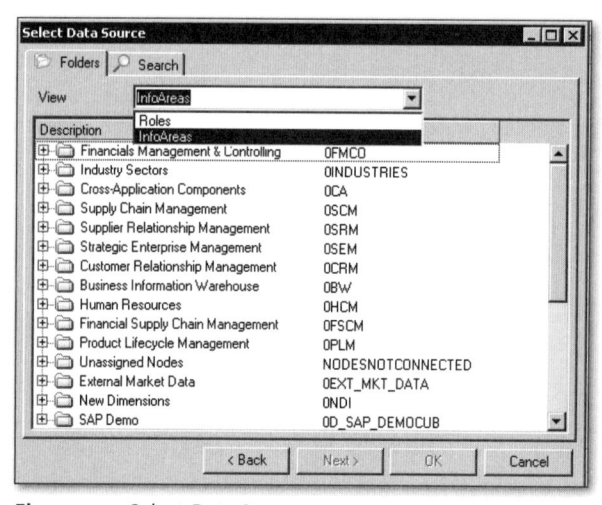

Figure 4.7 Select Data Source

104

Advanced Analysis Office — Microsoft Excel | **4.1**

10. Navigate to the InfoProvider from the SAP NetWeaver Demo Model and open the list of available SAP NetWeaver BW queries (see Figure 4.8).

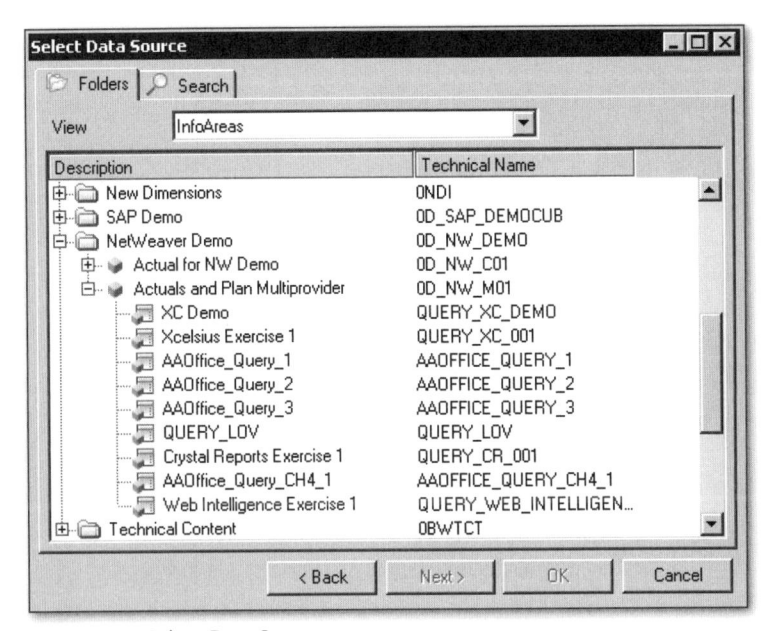

Figure 4.8 Select Data Source

Now you can select a BW Query or you can select the InfoProvider directly.

11. Select the previously created BW Query and click OK (see Figure 4.9).

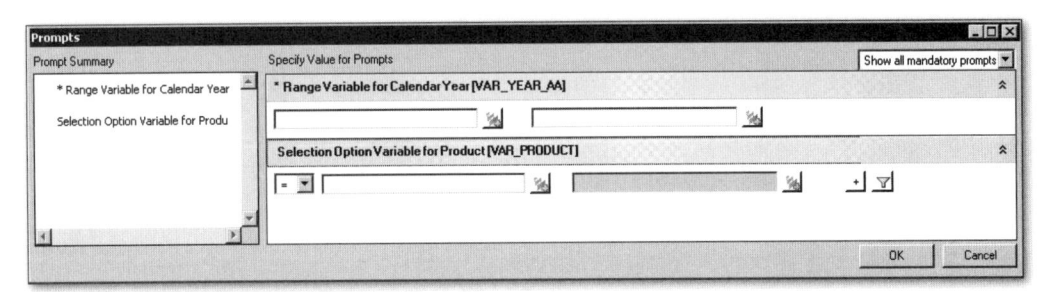

Figure 4.9 Prompts

105

12. Because your BW Query contains two variables, you need to provide values for them. Select the values based on your available data and click OK.

13. You can either enter the values manually or you can click on the icon next to the cells to retrieve a list of possible members.

> **Advanced Analysis Prompting**
>
> We will look at the prompting dialog in more detail in Section 4.1.11 Prompting and Variables. For the following activities we'll just continue entering values for the prompts and learn the details of this functionality later on.

Based on the values for the prompts, Advanced Analysis Office displays the result set and successfully establishes your first Advanced Analysis Office in Microsoft Excel connection and displays your corporate data from SAP NetWeaver BW (see Figure 4.10).

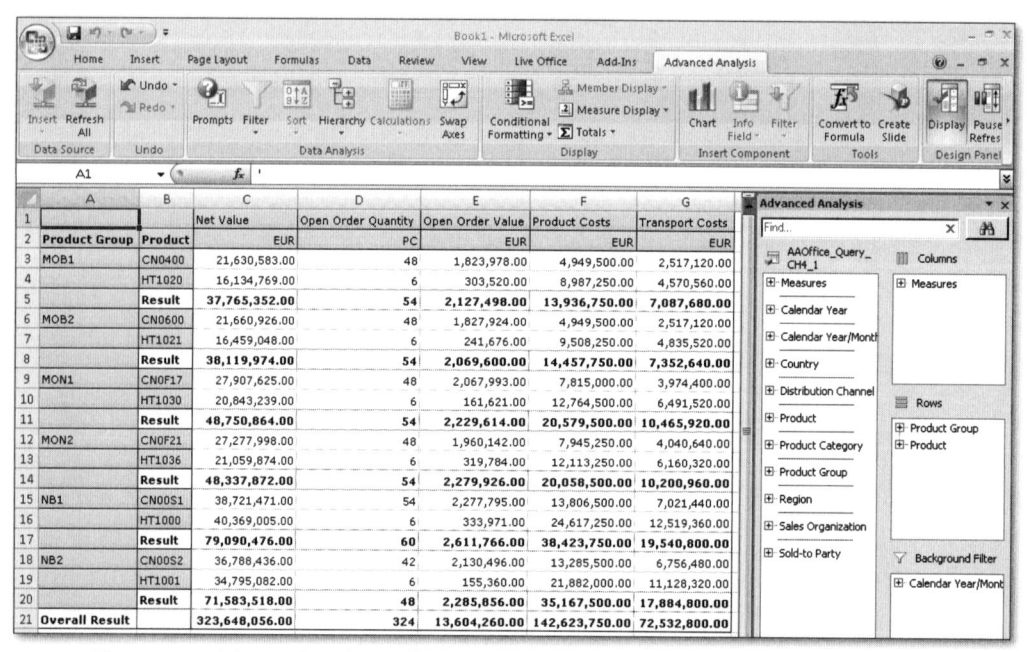

Figure 4.10 Advanced Analysis Office in Microsoft Excel

Advanced Analysis Office — Microsoft Excel | **4.1**

In the second option, you can create a shared connection as part of SAP Business-Objects Enterprise and use it in Advanced Analysis Office.

1. Log on to your SAP BusinessObjects Enterprise Central Management Console (CMC) with an administrative account.

2. Select the VOYAGER CONNECTIONS option. Advanced Analysis Office integrated with SAP BusinessObjects XI 3.1 shares the connection definitions with Voyager (see Figure 4.11).

3. Click on the [icon] icon to create a new connection.

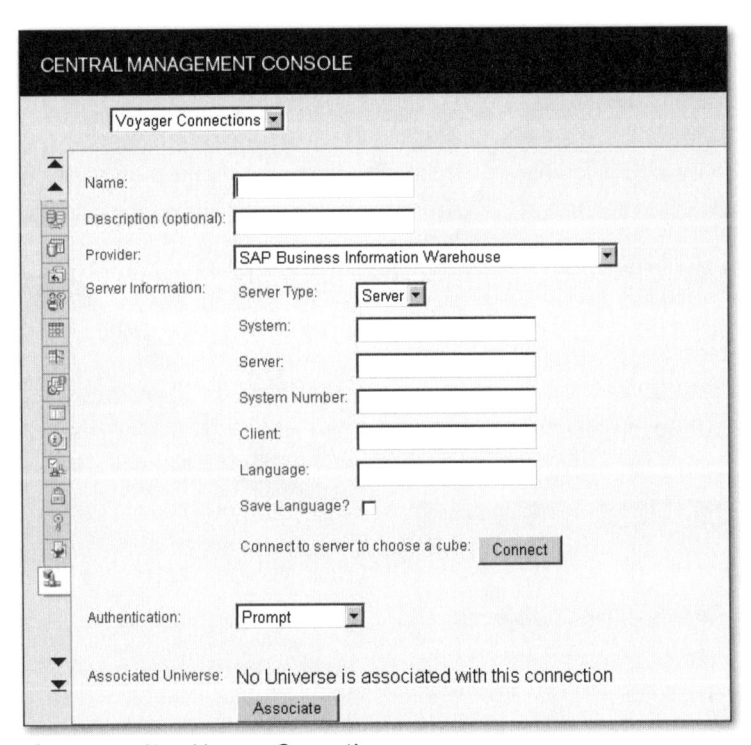

Figure 4.11 New Voyager Connection

4. Enter the necessary details for SAP NetWeaver BW. You can see more details in Chapter 2, Installation, Deployment, and Configuration of Advanced Analysis Office, Table 2.2.

5. After you enter the details, click on the CONNECT button.

107

6. Enter the USER and PASSWORD to connect to SAP NetWeaver BW.

7. Click OK.

8. You will see the CUBE BROWSER, which lets you select an InfoProvider or a BW Query based on the CAPTION or the NAME.

9. Select the previously created BW Query from SAP NetWeaver BW and click SELECT.

10. Set the AUTHENTICATION option to Single Sign-On (SSO) so that you can have SSO with your SAP credentials for this shared connection.

11. Click SAVE to save your connection.

Next, we'll use the newly created shared connection in Advanced Analysis Office in Microsoft Excel:

1. Start Advanced Analysis Office with Microsoft Excel via the menu path START • PROGRAMS • SAP BUSINESSOBJECTS • ADVANCED ANALYSIS FOR MICROSOFT EXCEL.

2. Select the INSERT • SELECT DATA SOURCE option from the Advanced Analysis ribbon.

3. This time, you need to use the shared connection; therefore, you need to authenticate for SAP BusinessObjects Enterprise (see Figure 4.12).

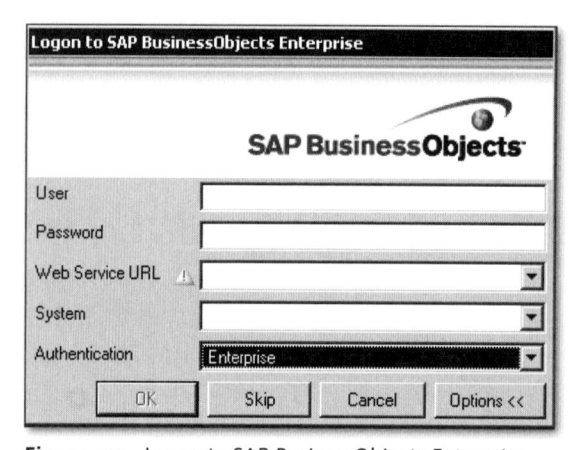

Figure 4.12 Logon to SAP BusinessObjects Enterprise

Advanced Analysis Office — Microsoft Excel | **4.1**

4. If it is your first time using Advanced Analysis Office, you will need to enter the Web Service URL, which follows the syntax
   `http://<Application Server>:<Port>/dswsbobje/services/session`. For the system value, you need to enter the name of your Central Management System (CMS).

5. Please note that the log-on screen won't let you enter the client number, system ID, and user as separate fields; therefore, we have to enter the user name in the following syntax:
   <System ID>~<Client Number>/<User ID>, for example:
   IH1~800/DEMO for user Demo in system IH1 with client number 800.

6. Enter the USER NAME and PASSWORD, the WEB SERVICES URL, the SYSTEM name and set the AUTHENTICATION option to SAP.

7. Now you can leverage the shared connection and connect to the defined systems, or leverage the local connections from the SAP Frontend (see Figure 4.13).

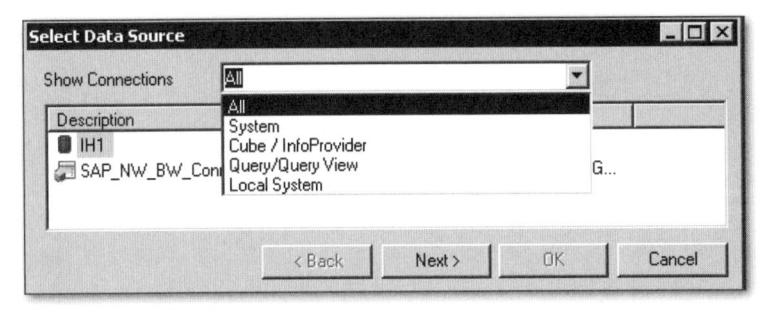

Figure 4.13 Select Data Source

8. Select the shared connection from the QUERY/QUERY VIEW category.

9. Click OK.

10. You will be asked to log on to your SAP system even though you authenticated with your SAP credentials as the integration with SAP BusinessObjects Enterprise XI 3.1 does not provide you with a server-side SSO experience.

11. Provide your SAP credentials and click OK. If your shared connection contains variables from the underlying BW Query, you will be asked to provide input values; otherwise, you will receive the dataset.

In this section, you learned the two options for leveraging connections from Advanced Analysis Office in Microsoft Excel to SAP NetWeaver BW. In the next section, you will learn how to open and save your workbooks to SAP BusinessObjects Enterprise.

4.1.2 Open and Saving Workbooks

When using Advanced Analysis Office, you have two main options for sharing all of your workbooks with other users:

- You can leverage a common shared network location to share the workbooks, which then results in a situation where you need to make sure each user can save and open from the shared network location.
- You can leverage SAP BusinessObjects Enterprise as a repository for storing workbooks.

If you are using SAP BusinessObjects Enterprise as central repository, which is the recommended approach, you can use the Advanced Analysis Office menu items to save and open your workbooks (see Figure 4.14).

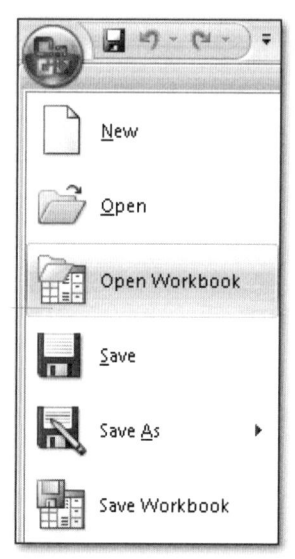

Figure 4.14 Microsoft Office Button Menu

By simply clicking on the MICROSOFT OFFICE button in Microsoft Excel you can leverage these two additional menu items, which are active after the installation of Advanced Analysis Office.

These two additional menu options let you save your workbooks in SAP BusinessObjects Enterprise and share it with other users, who can use the OPEN WORKBOOK option to open the workbooks and use the same workbook design and data.

> **Open and Saving Workbooks**
>
> The OPEN WORKBOOK and SAVE WORKBOOK options work under the assumption that a connection to SAP BusinessObjects Enterprise already exists. If you work with a local connection to SAP NetWeaver BW, you need to follow the INSERT • SELECT DATA SOURCE menu path and log on to SAP BusinessObjects Enterprise so that OPEN WORKBOOK and SAVE Workbook can connect to your SAP BusinessObjects Enterprise system.

4.1.3 Insert Your First Crosstab

Let's build your first workbook with Advanced Analysis Office and leverage the BW Query we created previously.

1. Start Advanced Analysis Office with Microsoft Excel via the menu path START • PROGRAMS • SAP BUSINESSOBJECTS • ADVANCED ANALYSIS FOR MICROSOFT EXCEL. Before you select the connection, make sure that you have an empty spreadsheet in Microsoft Excel and select a cell, otherwise you won't be able to insert the information from your BW system.

2. Select the INSERT • SELECT DATA SOURCE option from the Advanced Analysis ribbon.

3. The next step depends on your preference. You can use a locally defined connection via the SAP Frontend or leverage a shared connection from SAP BusinessObjects Enterprise.

4. After you log on to SAP NetWeaver BW or SAP BusinessObjects Enterprise, select the previously created BW Query or shared connection.

5. Provide the necessary values for the variables you created as part of the BW Query and click OK (see Figure 4.15).

4 | Advanced Analysis Office — Basic Functions

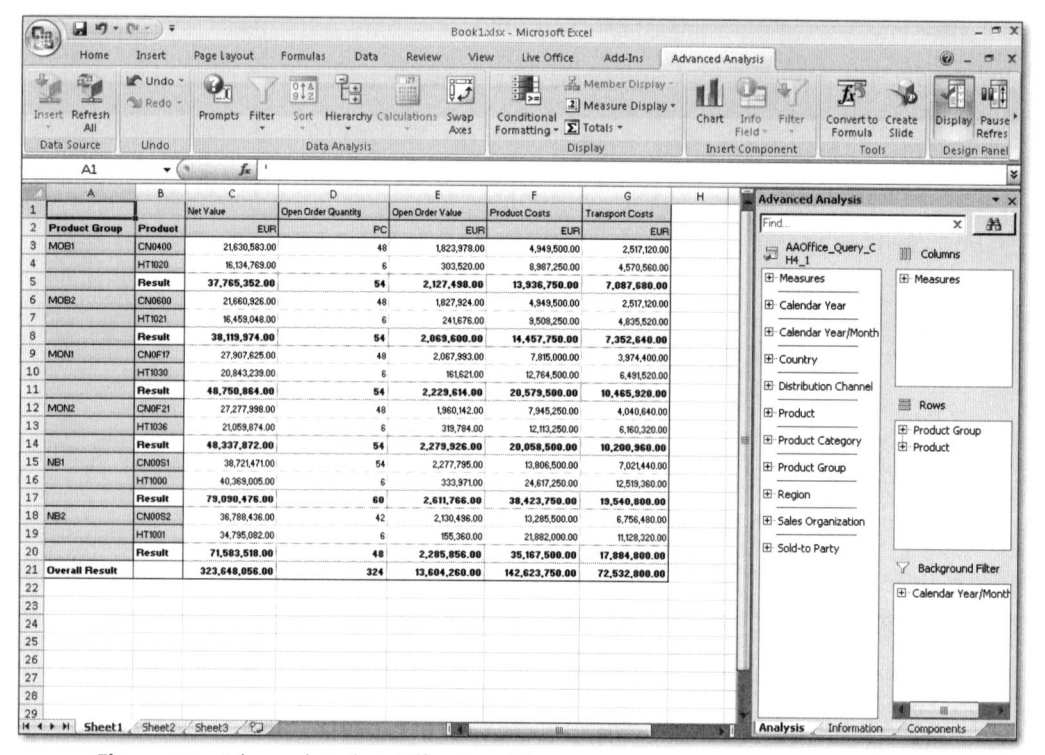

Figure 4.15 Advanced Analysis Office Crosstab

The crosstab, based on the definition in the BW Query, is placed into the spreadsheet and you can start using Advanced Analysis Office.

The initial view of your crosstab is based on the following rules:

- When using a BW Query as a source, the elements used in the rows and columns are placed into the rows and columns of your crosstab. All of the elements placed in the free characteristics area of your BW Query are available in the Advanced Analysis navigation panel and you can leverage them for navigation purposes.

- When connecting directly to an InfoProvider, all key figures are placed into the columns and the initial view provides an aggregated view of all characteristics.

- When using a BW Query view as the starting point for your crosstab, you will receive an exact representation of the BW Query view in your spreadsheet.

After you create your first crosstab you will also see the Advanced Analysis Office panel as part of your spreadsheet (see Figure 4.16).

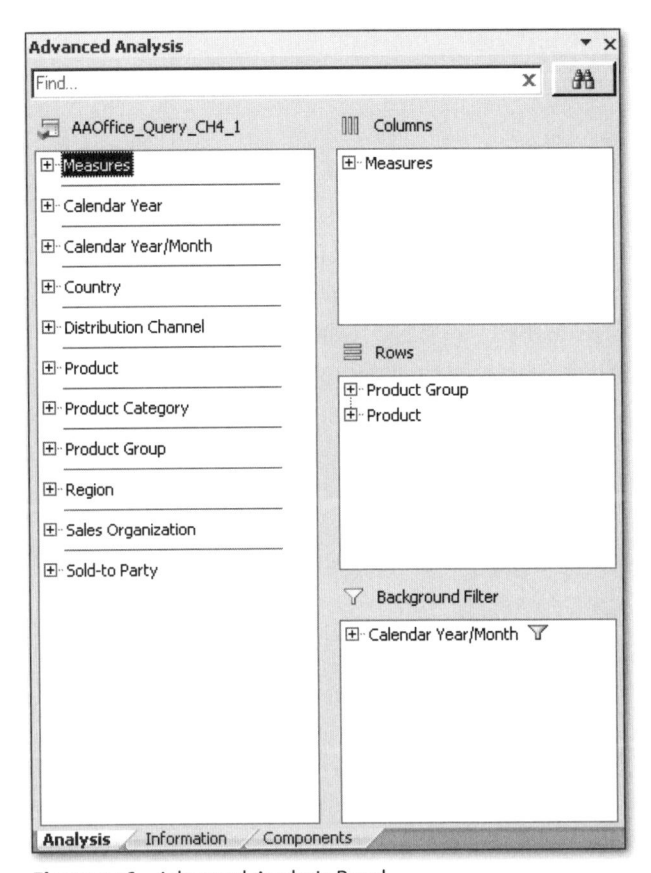

Figure 4.16 Advanced Analysis Panel

The panel provides you with access to all of the characteristics and key figures from your underlying source and you can also use the panel for navigation purposes via drag and drop. For example, you can drag the SOLD-TO PARTY characteristic from the list of available characteristics over to the ROWS area and have SOLD-TO PARTY become part of the crosstab. If you cannot view the Advanced Analysis panel you can click on the DISPLAY icon in the Advanced Analysis Office ribbon to enable (or disable) the panel's display (see Figure 4.17).

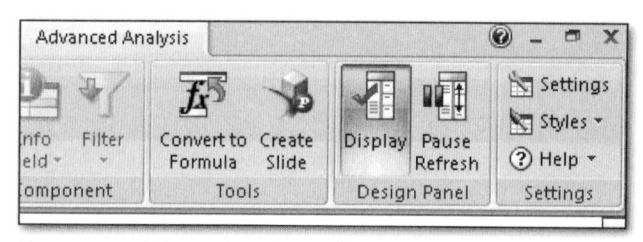

Figure 4.17 Advanced Analysis Office Ribbon

Next to the DISPLAY icon is the PAUSE REFRESH icon. The PAUSE REFRESH option gives you the functionality to design your workbook in an offline mode and pause the online retrieval of data for each navigation step. You can activate the PAUSE REFRESH option (see Figure 4.18) to perform navigation steps on your crosstab. When you finish the navigation and design steps, you can toggle the PAUSE REFRESH option again to refresh your workbook.

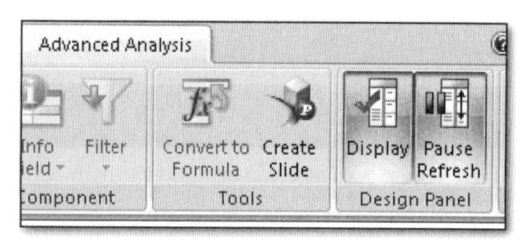

Figure 4.18 Pause Refresh

In this section, we learned the basic steps for inserting data from SAP NetWeaver BW into the spreadsheet for Advanced Analysis Office. In the next step, we'll look at the navigation options for Advanced Analysis Office to arrange the data as required.

4.1.4 Navigation Options

After you insert your initial crosstab you may have to rearrange the information that is displayed and Advanced Analysis Office provides two options to do so. You can leverage a simple drag-and-drop navigation inside the crosstab to change the orientation of the data or you can leverage the navigation panel. Let's use our

Advanced Analysis Office — Microsoft Excel | 4.1

example BW Query to leverage some of these navigation steps and rearrange the data.

1. Start Advanced Analysis Office with Microsoft Excel via the menu path START • PROGRAMS • SAP BUSINESSOBJECTS • ADVANCED ANALYSIS FOR MICROSOFT EXCEL.

2. Select the INSERT • SELECT DATA SOURCE option from the Advanced Analysis ribbon.

3. After you log on to SAP NetWeaver BW or SAP BusinessObjects Enterprise, select the previously created BW Query or shared connection. Based on the definition of the BW Query, you will be presented with the PRODUCT GROUP and PRODUCT characteristics in the rows and the key figures in the columns, which matches the BW Query design (see Figure 4.19).

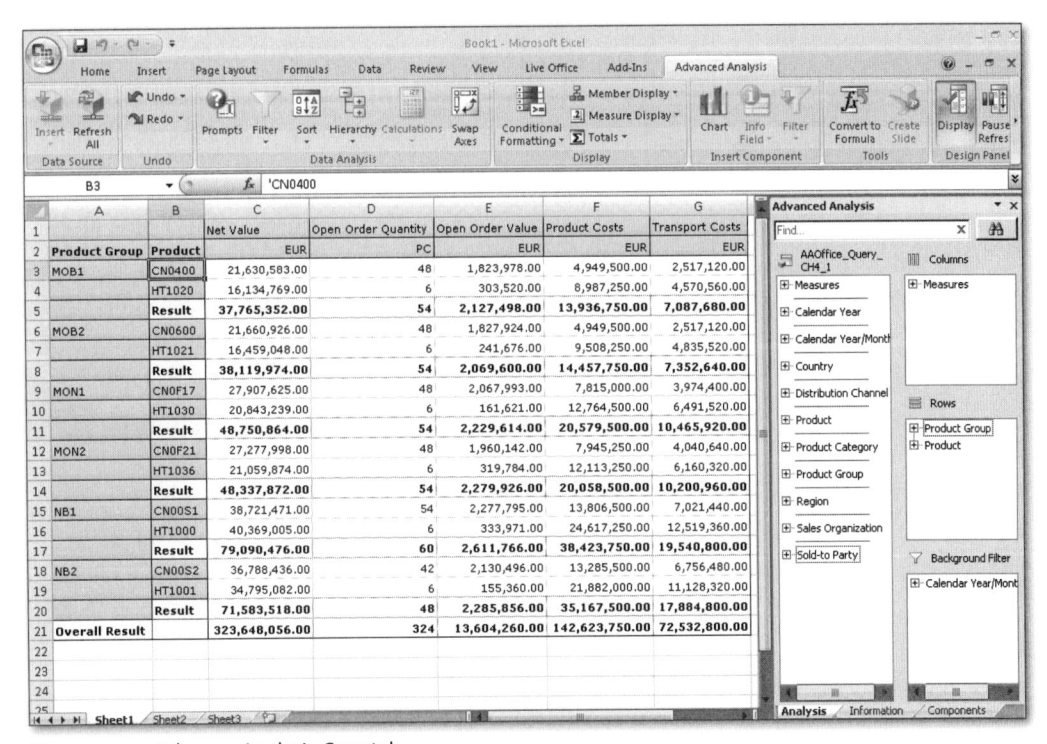

Figure 4.19 Advance Analysis Crosstab

115

4. First, we'll remove the PRODUCT GROUP characteristic from our crosstab. You can select the PRODUCT GROUP characteristic in the ROWS area and drag and drop it into the empty area of the panel (see Figure 4.20).

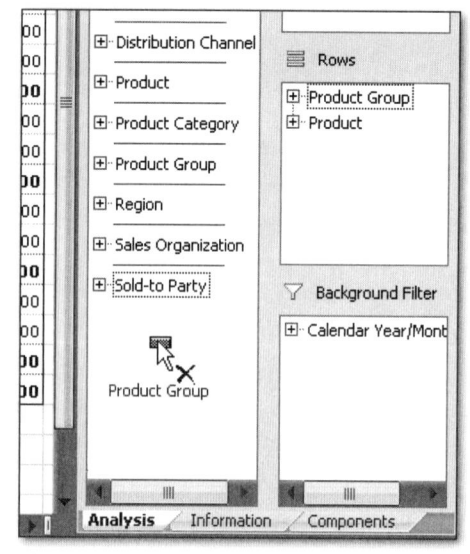

Figure 4.20 Navigation Panel

5. Next, we'll exchange the PRODUCT characteristic with CALENDAR YEAR/MONTH. Select CALENDAR YEAR/MONTH in the navigation panel and move it via drag-and-drop navigation on top of the PRODUCT characteristic (see Figure 4.21).

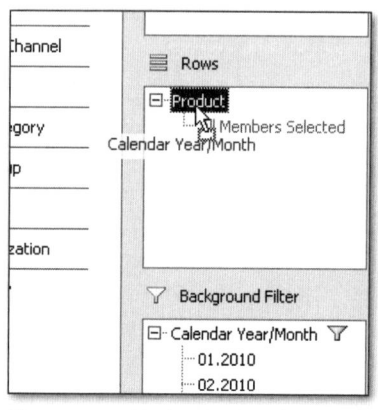

Figure 4.21 Navigation Panel

Make sure that your mouse is pointing to the PRODUCT characteristic to make sure those two characteristics are exchanged.

6. Now select the CALENDAR YEAR/MONTH characteristic in the crosstab and right-click to open the context menu. You will see the FILTER MEMBERS AND SWAP WITH menu (see Figure 4.22). This menu lets you swap, for example, CALENDAR YEAR/MONTH with another characteristic, but the difference is that this step also filters CALENDAR YEAR/MONTH based on your selection in the crosstab.

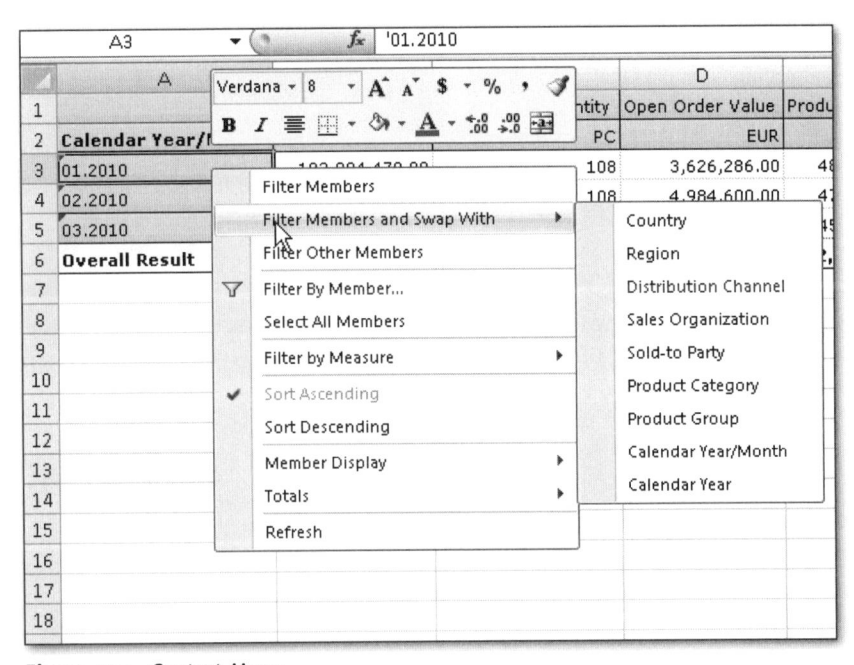

Figure 4.22 Context Menu

7. Your crosstab now shows CALENDAR YEAR/MONTH in the ROWS with all available key figures in the COLUMNS.

8. Select PRODUCT GROUP in the navigation panel and right-click to open the context menu (see Figure 4.23).

117

4 | Advanced Analysis Office — Basic Functions

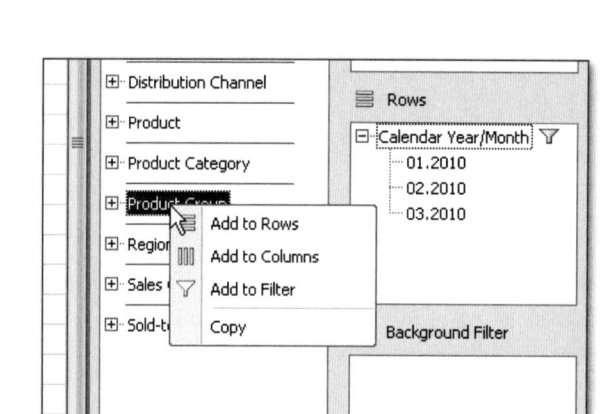

Figure 4.23 Context Menu

9. Select the ADD TO ROWS option. By default, the added characteristic — in this example PRODUCT GROUP — is inserted as an inner group (see Figure 4.24). If you prefer the characteristic be added as an outer group, you can drag and drop the characteristic in the navigation panel on top of an existing entry (see Figure 4.25) or you can drag and drop the characteristic directly into the crosstab (see Figure 4.26).

	A	B	C	D
1			Net Value	Open Order Quantity
2	Calendar Year/Month	Product Group	EUR	PC
3	01.2010	MOB1	11,116,069.00	18
4		MOB2	10,771,003.00	18
5		MON1	17,815,558.00	18
6		MON2	16,704,002.00	18
7		NB1	24,409,966.00	22
8		NB2	22,277,881.00	14
9		Result	103,094,479.00	108
10	02.2010	MOB1	13,612,317.00	18
11		MOB2	14,311,220.00	18
12		MON1	15,062,860.00	18
13		MON2	15,451,069.00	18
14		NB1	27,875,930.00	20
15		NB2	25,229,641.00	16
16		Result	111,543,037.00	108

Figure 4.24 Advanced Analysis Crosstab

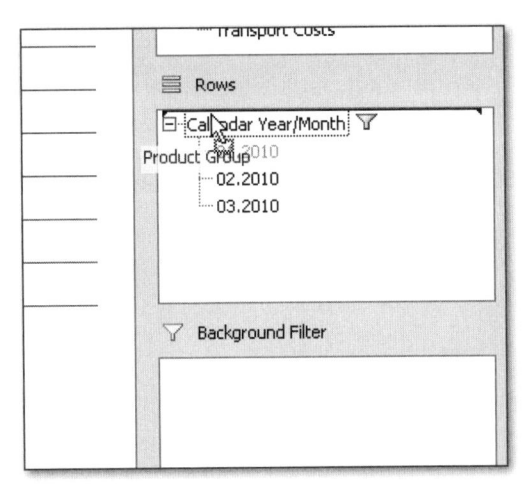

Figure 4.25 Advanced Analysis Navigation Panel

Figure 4.26 Advanced Analysis Crosstab

You can use the navigation panel in conjunction with drag and drop but you can also drag elements from the navigational panel directly into the crosstab as shown in Figure 4.26. For situations where you would like to exchange the rows with the columns, you can use SWAP AXES in the Advanced Analysis ribbon.

4 | Advanced Analysis Office — Basic Functions

> **Drag-and-Drop Navigation**
>
> The typical drag-and-drop navigation is enabled as part of the navigation panel and between the navigation panel and the crosstab, but you cannot use drag-and-drop navigation inside the crosstab itself.

10. Now open the list of elements for the COUNTRY characteristic and open FLAT PRESENTATION (see Figure 4.27).

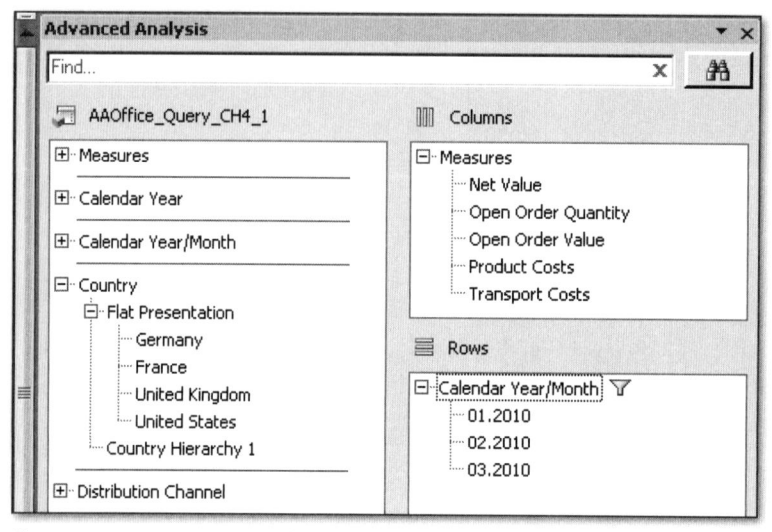

Figure 4.27 Navigation Panel

If a characteristic is configured with active hierarchies, the navigation panel shows the FLAT PRESENTATION of the characteristic and lets you select the available hierarchies, in this example, COUNTRY HIERARCHY 1.

11. Select GERMANY for the COUNTRY and open the context menu with a right-click (see Figure 4.28).

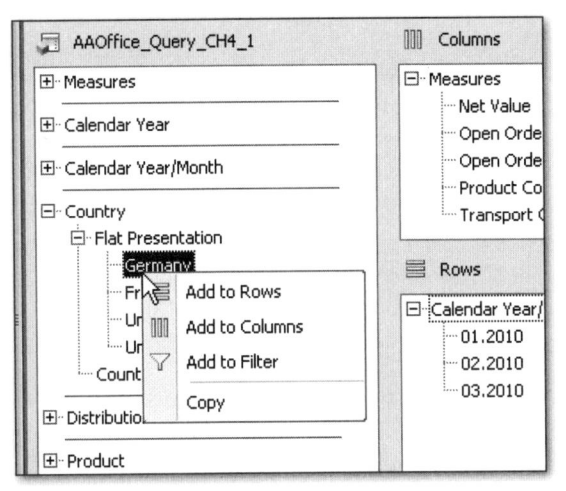

Figure 4.28 Context Menu

Just as you can select a characteristic and add it to the ROWS, COLUMNS, or FILTER area, you can also use a single member or multiple members of the characteristic directly. To select multiple members, simply use `Ctrl` or `Shift` and select multiple members.

In this section, you learned how to navigate as part of the navigation panel or as part of the crosstab, and you learned several ways to leverage the data view. In the next section, we will format the data elements of your crosstab.

4.1.5 Formatting Data

When formatting the actual information that is displayed in your crosstab, there are two main elements: formatting the display of the characteristics and formatting the display of the key figures.

1. Select COUNTRY in the navigation panel and exchange it via drag and drop with CALENDAR YEAR/MONTH in the crosstab.

2. Next, right-click to open the context menu for COUNTRY in the crosstab (see Figure 4.29).

4 | Advanced Analysis Office — Basic Functions

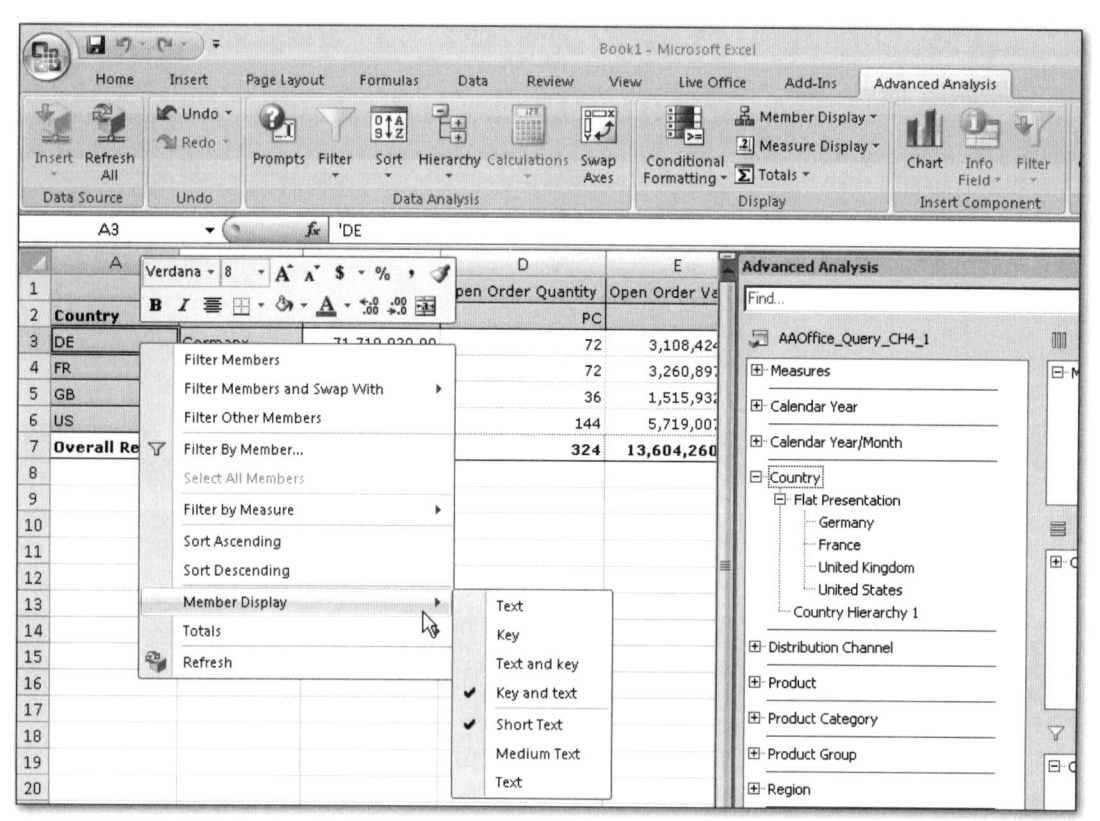

Figure 4.29 Member Display

3. You can use MEMBER DISPLAY to configure the members of each characteristic. The list of options depends on the configuration of the InfoObject in SAP NetWeaver BW.

4. You can also use MEMBER DISPLAY in the Advanced Analysis ribbon (see Figure 4.30).

5. Next, select a number in the column for the key figure NET VALUE (see Figure 4.31) and right-click to open the context menu.

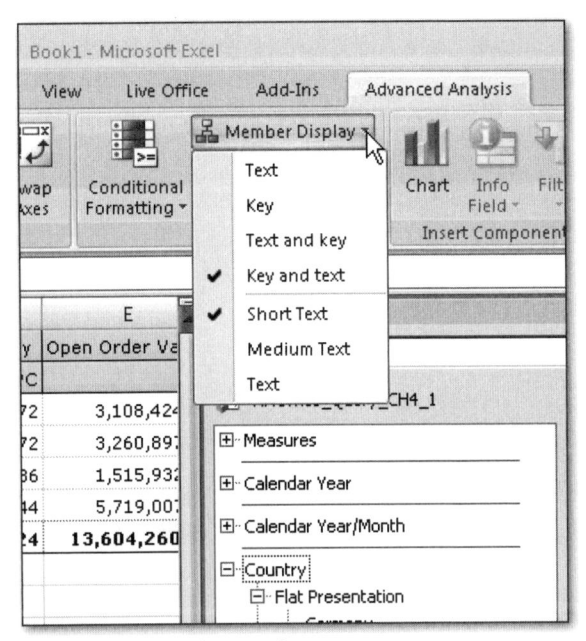

Figure 4.30 Member Display

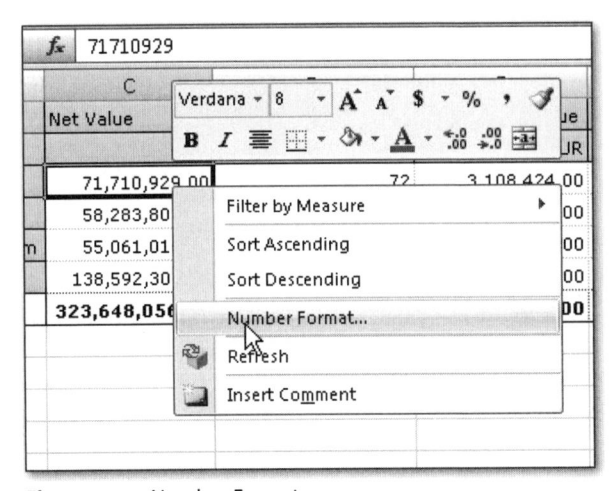

Figure 4.31 Number Format

6. Select NUMBER FORMAT (see Figure 4.32).

4 | Advanced Analysis Office — Basic Functions

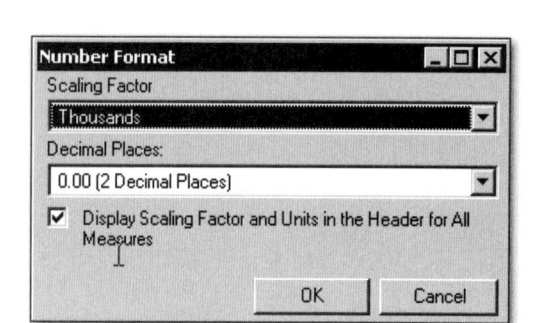

Figure 4.32 Number Format

Here, you can define the NUMBER FORMAT for the selected key figure. You can define the SCALING FACTOR and the number of DECIMAL PLACES. In addition, you can enable or disable the option for displaying the scaling factor as part of your crosstab. The setting is valid for the key figure you selected and gets applied to all values of this key figure.

7. Set SCALING FACTOR to THOUSANDS, set DECIMAL PLACES to the value 2, and check the DISPLAY SCALING FACTOR AND UNITS IN THE HEADER FOR ALL MEASURES checkbox.

8. Click OK (see Figure 4.33).

Figure 4.33 Formatted Key Figure

9. Select NET VALUE by either selecting the column header or selecting a single cell of the NET VALUE column in the crosstab.

10. Select MEASURE DISPLAY from the Advanced Analysis ribbon (see Figure 4.34).

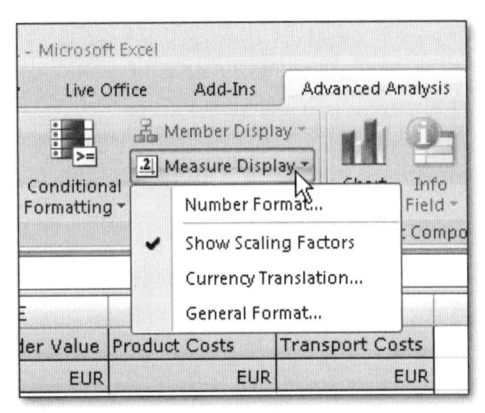

Figure 4.34 Measure Display

In addition to formatting the numeric display with the NUMBER FORMAT option, MEASURE DISPLAY offers the functionality to define a GENERAL FORMAT for all key figures (see Figure 4.35) and to show the scaling factors for all key figures. In addition, MEASURE DISPLAY also provides you with the ability to perform a CURRENCY CONVERSION on the fly (see Figure 4.36).

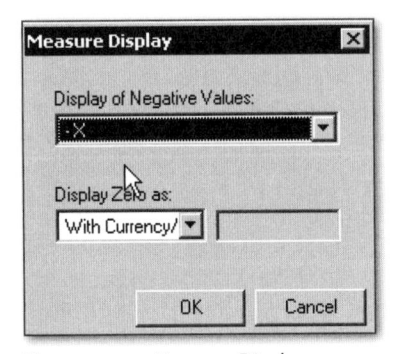

Figure 4.35 Measure Display

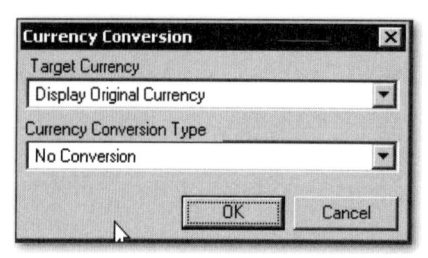

Figure 4.36 Currency Conversion

A currency conversion requires the necessary elements to be defined in the SAP NetWeaver BW backend, such as TARGET CURRENCY, CURRENCY CONVERSION TYPE, and CONVERSION RATES.

In this section, we looked at all of the different options for formatting the characteristics and key figures in the crosstab. In the next section, we will look at the sorting and filtering capabilities of Advanced Analysis Office.

4.1.6 Sorting and Filtering

In this section, we will learn how to sort the information in our crosstab and how to apply filters to our corporate information from SAP NetWeaver BW.

1. Start Advanced Analysis Office with Microsoft Excel via the menu path START • PROGRAMS • SAP BUSINESSOBJECTS • ADVANCED ANALYSIS FOR MICROSOFT EXCEL.

2. Select the INSERT • SELECT DATA SOURCE option from the Advanced Analysis ribbon.

3. Select the connection to our previously created BW Query. The connection should now be listed as part of the SELECT DATA SOURCE menu.

    Based on the definition of the BW Query, you are presented with PRODUCT GROUP and PRODUCT in the rows and the key figures in the columns.

4. Remove the PRODUCT characteristic from the crosstab.

5. Exchange SOLD-TO PARTY with PRODUCT GROUP via drag and drop (see Figure 4.37).

Advanced Analysis Office — Microsoft Excel | **4.1**

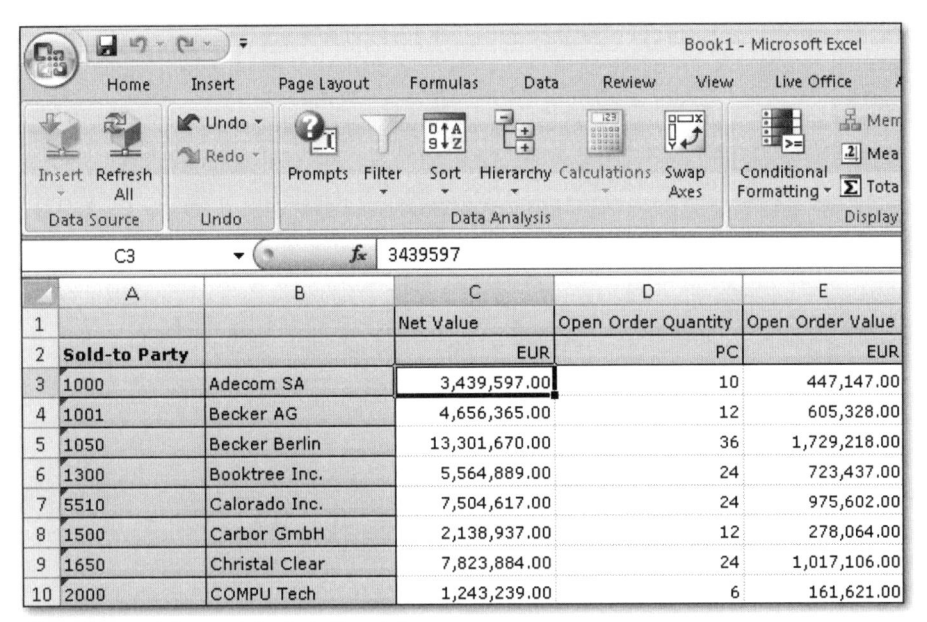

Figure 4.37 Advanced Analysis Crosstab

6. Select SOLD-TO PARTY. Select the column that shows the key value for the characteristic and follow the MEMBER DISPLAY • KEY AND TEXT menu path from the Advanced Analysis Office ribbon (see Figure 4.38).

7. Select the SORT • SORT ASCENDING option.

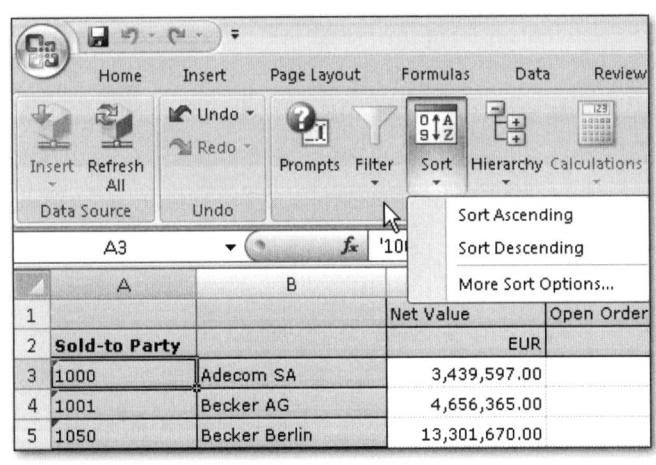

Figure 4.38 Menu Sort

127

4 | Advanced Analysis Office — Basic Functions

Please note that the sort is always applied to the column of your characteristic. In our example we selected the key, therefore, the sort will use the key as the sort criteria.

8. Now select the columns with the names of our customers by selecting the description of the SOLD-TO PARTY and follow the SORT • SORT ASCENDING menu path. Depending on your data, the sort will be different because now the sort is based on the alphabetical order of the customers and not the customer numbers.

9. The menu option for sorting your data is also available via a right-click on the crosstab (see Figure 4.39).

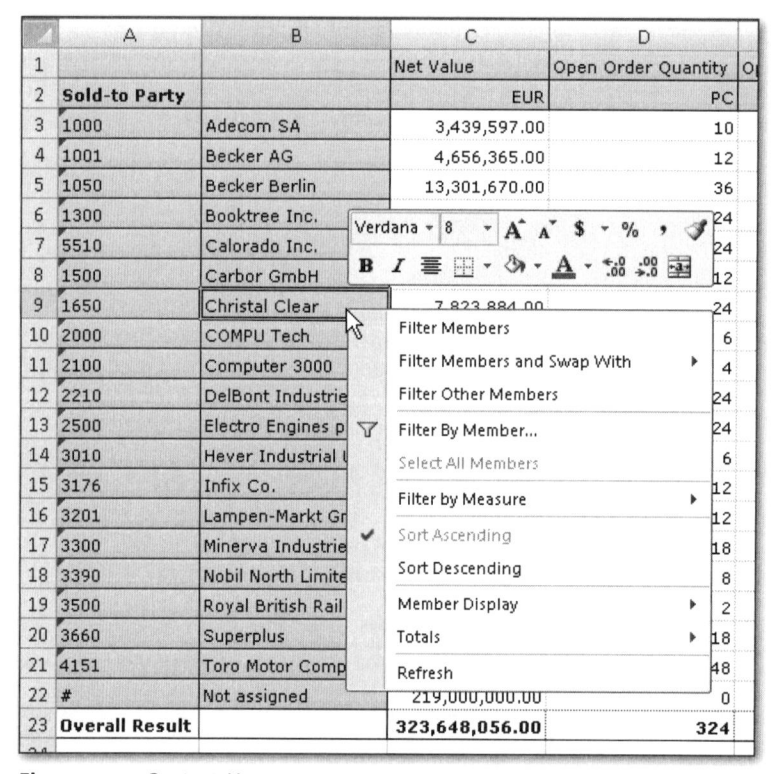

Figure 4.39 Context Menu

128

Advanced Analysis Office — Microsoft Excel | **4.1**

If the column is already sorted, the actual sort will have a checkmark next to it and the menu will be inactive.

10. Next, select an entry for the NET VALUE column and follow the menu path SORT • SORT ASCENDING. You can sort your data based on characteristics or based on key figures (see Figure 4.40).

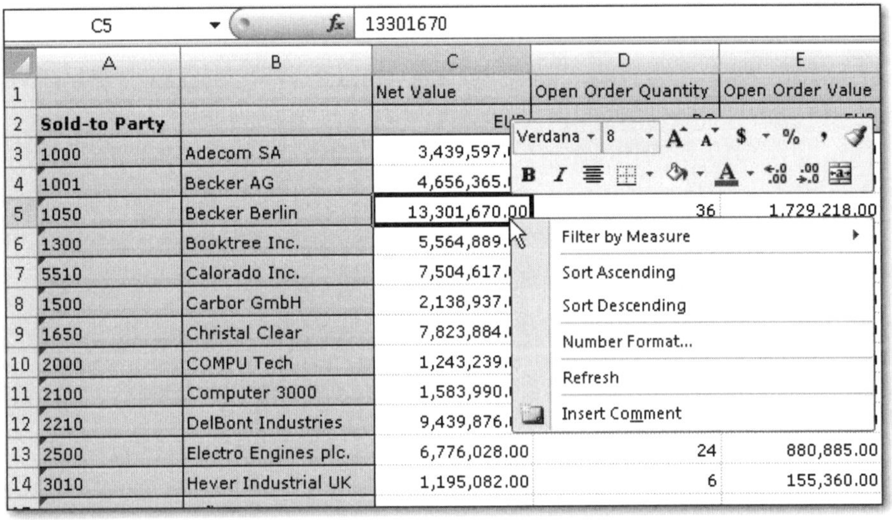

Figure 4.40 Sort by Keyfigure

11. Select the key column of SOLD-TO PARTY in your crosstab and navigate to the SORT menu in the ribbon, but this time use the MORE SORT OPTIONS option (see Figure 4.41).

12. You will see an additional dialog (see Figure 4.42) that lets you specify more complex sort options.

129

4 | Advanced Analysis Office — Basic Functions

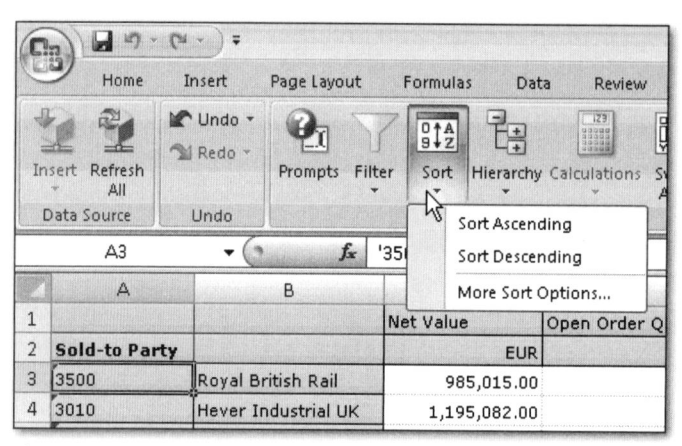

Figure 4.41 More Sort Options

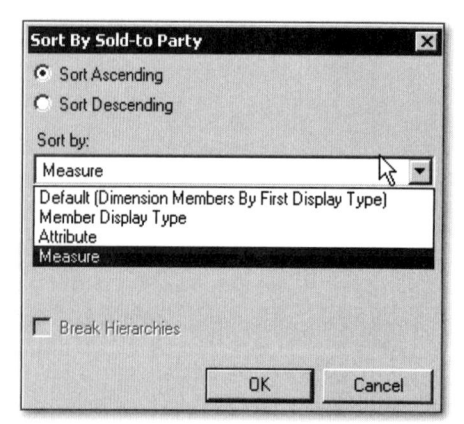

Figure 4.42 Additional Sort Options

The list of options depends on the selected object and the configuration of the object in SAP NetWeaver BW. In our example, we selected SOLD-TO PARTY and are able to sort our data based on MEMBER DISPLAY TYPE, ATTRIBUTES, or MEASURE. The option for defining a sort by ATTRIBUTES depends on whether the InfoObject is configured with Display Attributes or not.

A sort based on the MEMBER DISPLAY TYPE lets you specify which element of the characteristic will drive the actual sorting. Compared to the DEFAULT option, where the display in the crosstab decides how the sort is performed, here you have more control over the configuration (see Figure 4.43).

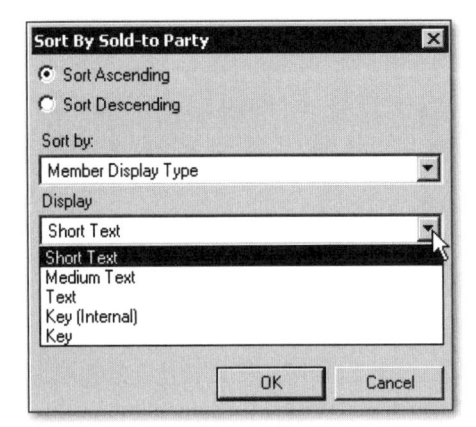

Figure 4.43 Sort by Member Display Type

When sorting by ATTRIBUTE, you can leverage all of the configured DISPLAY ATTRIBUTES and then define which element of the DISPLAY ATTRIBUTE will be the relevant element for the sorting (see Figure 4.44).

Figure 4.44 Sort by Attribute

When sorting by MEASURE, you are presented with a list of key figures and you can select which key figure will be relevant for sorting (see Figure 4.45).

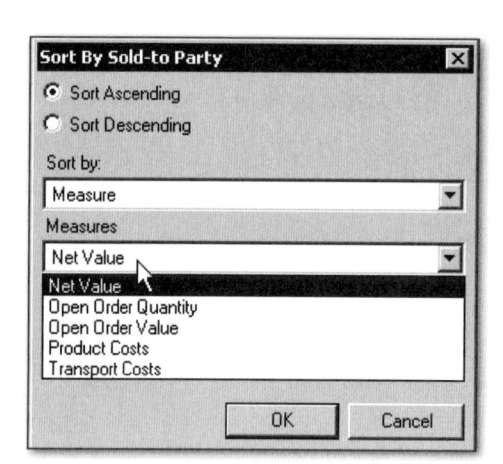

Figure 4.45 Sort by Measure

Now that we've learned how to sort the information in our crosstab, let's move on and take a look at all of the options for filtering the data to our requirements. Advanced Analysis Office provides you with two main filtering options: FILTER BY MEASURE and FILTER BY MEMBER. In this section, we will look at the details for filtering data based on members. The option for filtering information based on measures and key figures is discussed in Section 4.1.9, Ranking, Conditions, and Filter by Measures.

Right now our crosstab shows the SOLD-TO PARTY characteristic in the rows and all available key figures in the columns.

1. Select the key column of SOLD-TO PARTY.

2. There are three options for creating a filter as part of your crosstab:

    ▶ You can use the FILTER menu in the Advanced Analysis Office ribbon and select the FILTER BY MEMBER option (see Figure 4.46).

    ▶ You can right-click on the context menu and use the FILTER BY MEMBER option (see Figure 4.47).

    ▶ You can drag and drop the values you want to use as a filter from the characteristic to the FILTER area in the navigation panel (see Figure 4.48).

Advanced Analysis Office — Microsoft Excel | **4.1**

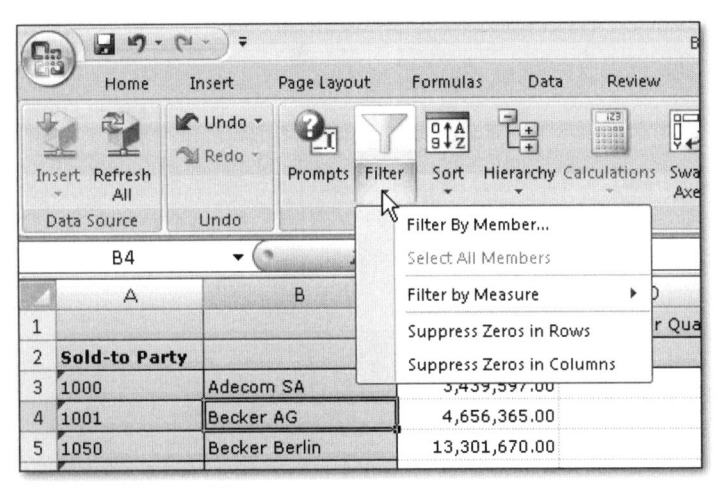

Figure 4.46 Menu Filter

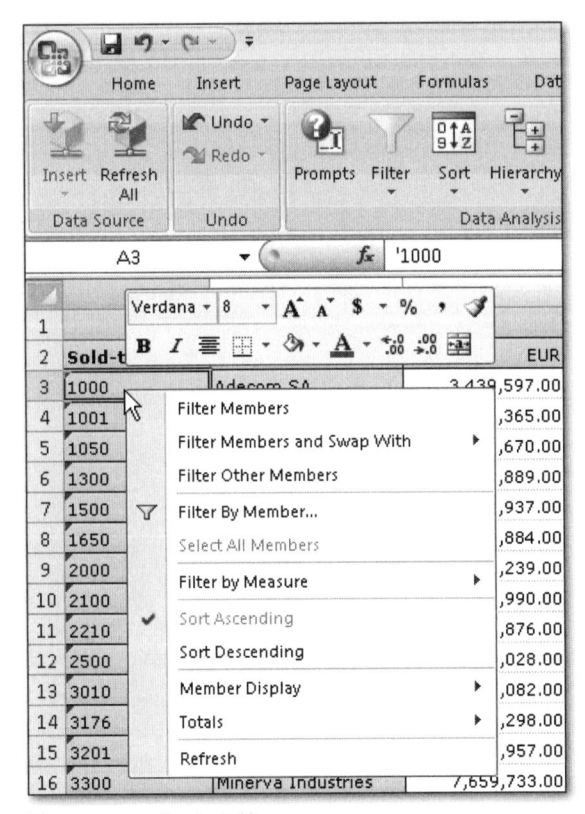

Figure 4.47 Context Menu

133

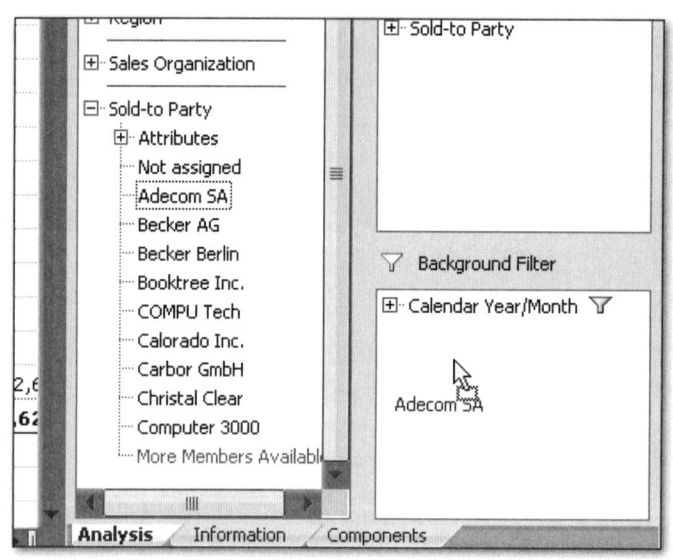

Figure 4.48 Navigation Panel

Note that filtering a selected member can be achieved in all three options very easily, but the context menu (see Figure 4.47) also offers a few additional options that can be very helpful in certain situations:

▶ FILTER OTHER MEMBERS lets you select a set of members and exclude the not selected members from the actual crosstab. You can — for example — select the first five rows of the SOLD-TO PARTY characteristic in your crosstab and use the FILTER OTHER MEMBERS option in the context menu. Now the filter will use all of the members that have not been selected (= OTHER MEMBERS) as a filter for the crosstab. Basically, this option uses the selected members and excludes them from the crosstab.

▶ FILTER MEMBERS uses the selected values and applies them as a filter to your crosstab.

▶ FILTER MEMBERS AND SWAP WITH lets you perform two steps with a single menu call. For example, when selecting the first five rows of the SOLD-TO PARTY characteristic using the FILTER MEMBERS AND SWAP WITH menu, you filter the data based on the first five entries of SOLD-TO PARTY and can then swap SOLD-TO PARTY with another characteristic of your underlying BW Query.

3. Next, select the first row for SOLD-TO PARTY and follow the menu path FILTER • FILTER BY MEMBER from the ribbon.

4. You are presented with the Member Selector from Advanced Analysis Office (see Figure 4.49).

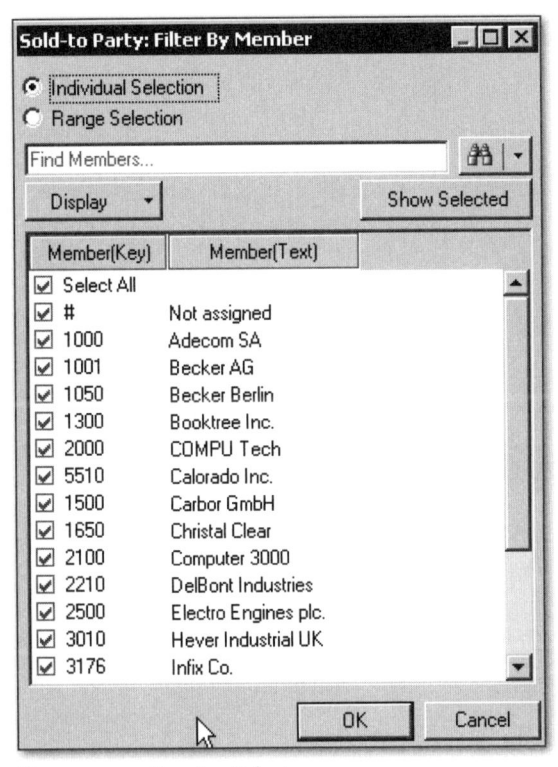

Figure 4.49 Member Selector

The Member Selector lets you select the members of the characteristic you want to leverage as a filter for your crosstab.

Inside the Member Selector you can use the DISPLAY button (see Figure 4.50) to configure which elements of the characteristic you want to see. If the characteristic is configured with ATTRIBUTES, you can use them to decide which values you want to use as a filter.

4 | Advanced Analysis Office — Basic Functions

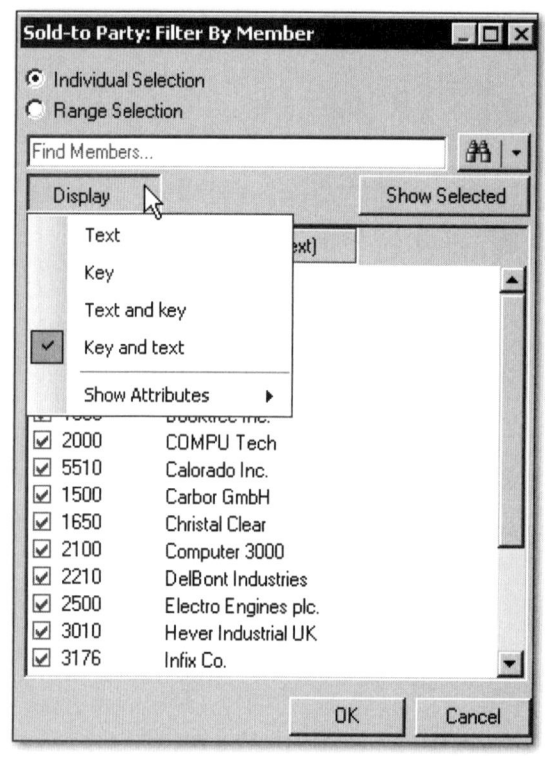

Figure 4.50 Member Selector Display Settings

With the search option (see Figure 4.51), you can decide which characteristic values are used when you perform a search. You can use parts of the key or text of your characteristic as search criteria and then use the matching values as filter values.

When using the option for selecting a well-defined list of values instead of defining a range of values, you can define the operator for the rule (see Figure 4.52) and define the actual values. It is really important to use the ADD RANGE button to make sure the rule that you defined is added to the list of filters. This option also provides you with the capability to have more than a single filter rule for a single characteristic.

Advanced Analysis Office — Microsoft Excel | **4.1**

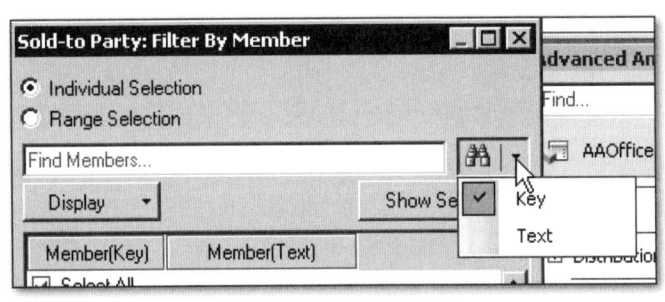

Figure 4.51 Member Selector Search Configuration

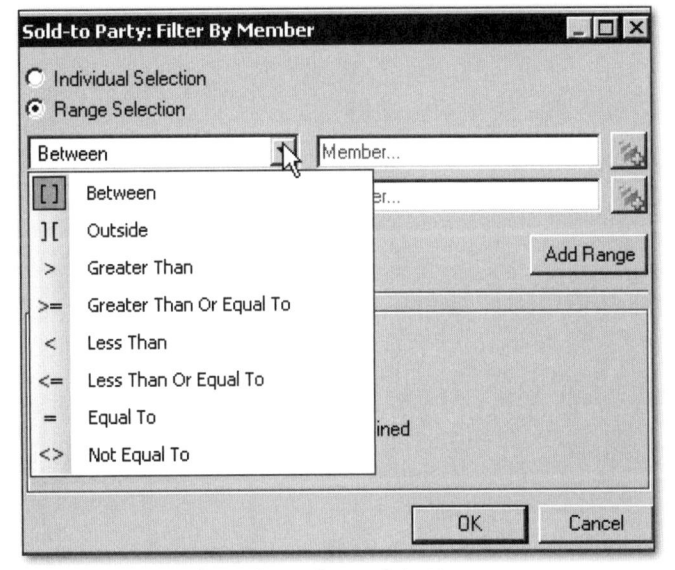

Figure 4.52 Member Selector Range Selection

5. Use the option to define a RANGE SELECTION and click the ![icon] icon to define a range from the key values 1000 to 2000 for SOLD-TO PARTY.

6. Click ADD RANGE (see Figure 4.53).

4 | Advanced Analysis Office — Basic Functions

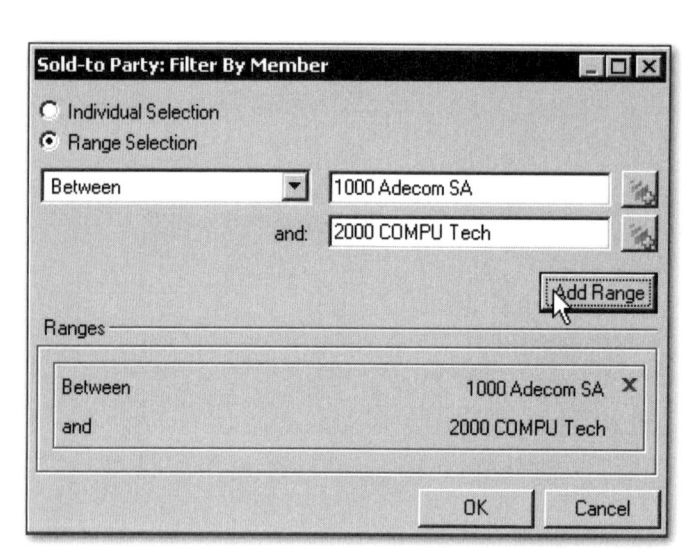

Figure 4.53 Defined Range Selection

7. Click OK.

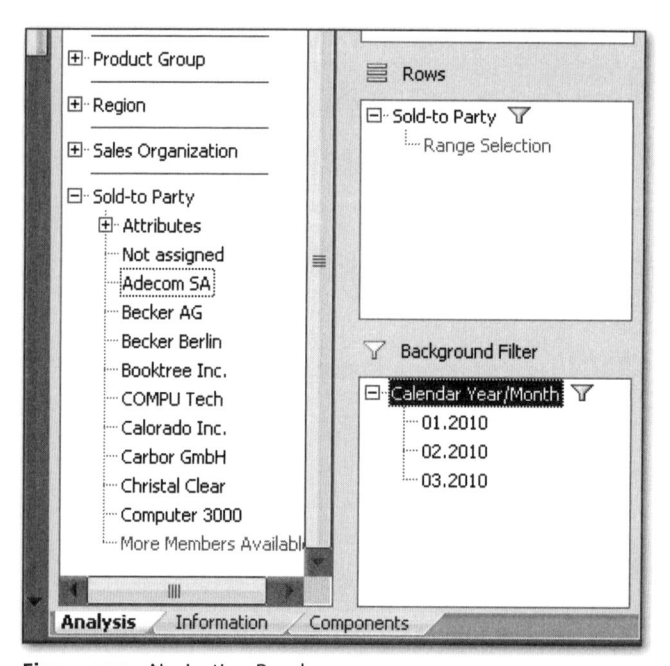

Figure 4.54 Navigation Panel

We've now created an additional filter for our crosstab in the navigation panel represented by the ▽ icon next to SOLD-TO PARTY and RANGE SELECTION. You can use the ▽ icon to open up the defined filter. The difference with the filter for CALENDAR YEAR/MONTH is that those values have been defined in the BW Query directly and therefore the list of selected members is shown.

8. Select the key column for SOLD-TO PARTY in the crosstab and navigate to the FILTER menu in the Advanced Analysis Office ribbon (see Figure 4.55).

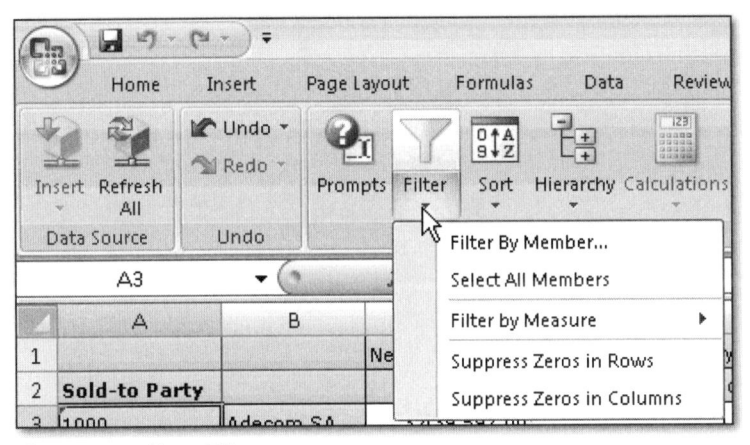

Figure 4.55 Menu Filter

Because we created a filter as part of the crosstab, the FILTER menu now shows the SELECT ALL MEMBERS option. The SELECT ALL MEMBERS option can remove all of our defined filters and return the complete list of members as part of the crosstab. The SELECT ALL MEMBERS option is also available on the context menu (see Figure 4.47, earlier in this chapter).

In addition, the FILTER menu provides you with the option for filtering rows or columns with zero values by using SUPPRESS ZEROS IN ROWS and SUPPRESS ZEROS IN COLUMNS.

Now we can select the right information for our crosstab by creating filtered characteristics. In the next section, we will start to include charts into our workbook with Advanced Analysis Office.

4 | Advanced Analysis Office — Basic Functions

4.1.7 Charting

Advanced Analysis Office is fully integrated with the charting capabilities of Microsoft Excel and doesn't add an additional layer on top of the functionality from Microsoft Excel. As soon as you create a chart via the Advanced Analysis Office menu, you can leverage the full bandwidth of charting capabilities inside Microsoft Excel.

1. Select any cell in the workbook we created in the previous activities.

2. Select CHART in the Advanced Analysis ribbon (see Figure 4.56).

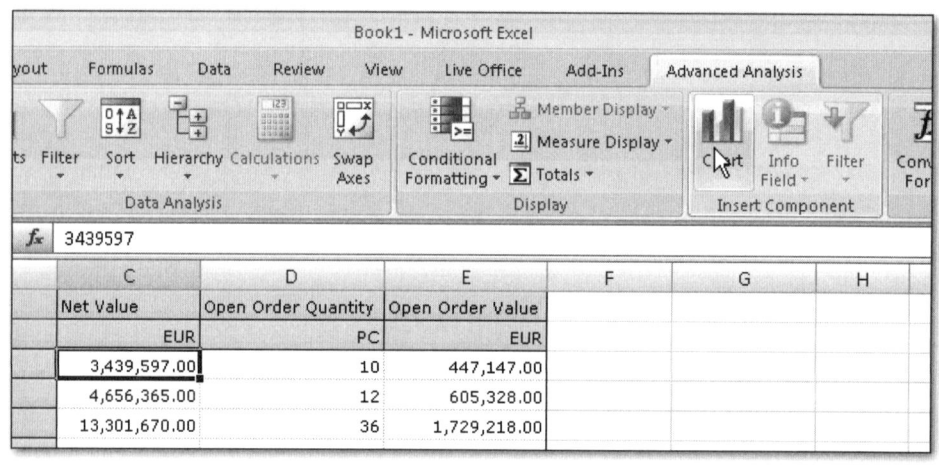

Figure 4.56 Insert Charts

3. As soon as the chart is embedded into your workbook, you can use the standard charting functions and features of Microsoft Excel, such as the DESIGN tab (see Figure 4.57).

Please note that even though Advanced Analysis Office is integrated with all of the charting capabilities of Microsoft Excel, it is very important that you use the Advanced Analysis ribbon to create the initial chart instead of using native Microsoft Excel functions. The reason for this is the link between the chart to the crosstab data and any update that you do in the actual crosstab. If you leverage the native Microsoft Excel features to create the initial view of the chart, you would have to select a range of cells, but when using the Advanced Analysis Office ribbon feature to create a chart, the chart is connected with the crosstab and stays dynamic.

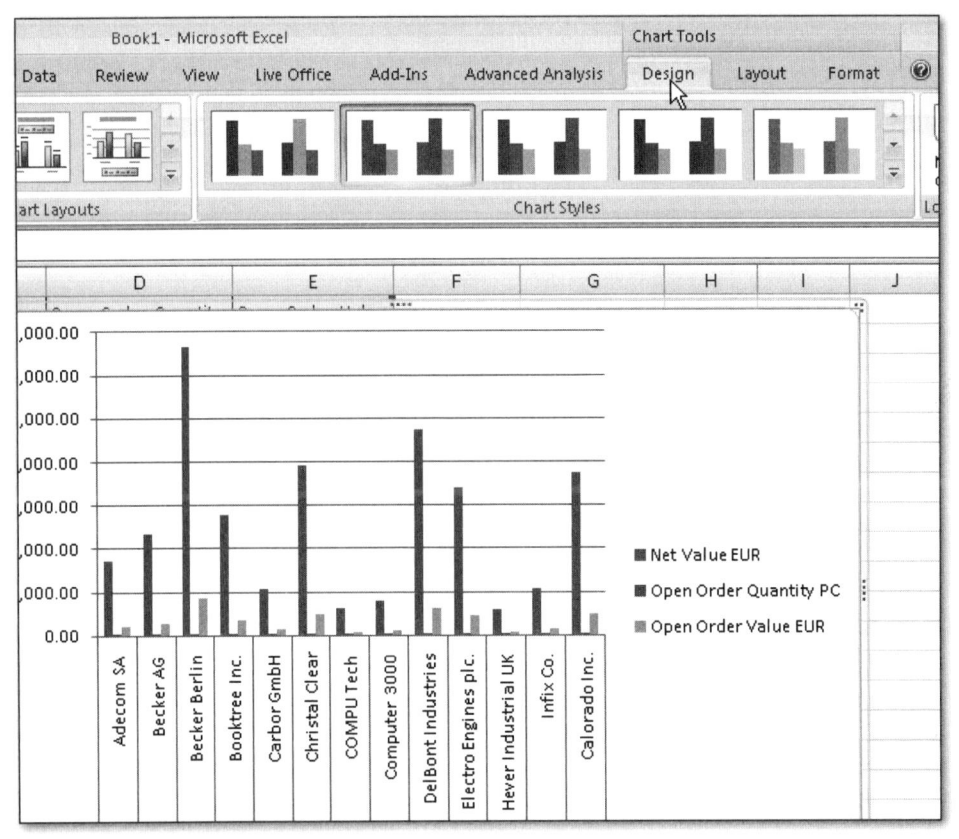

Figure 4.57 Chart Design Options

For example, we created a filter for SOLD-TO PARTY from number 1000 to number 2000. After we create a chart using the CHART option in the ribbon, we can remove the filter and our chart will reflect the changes by showing all values without making any changes. In Microsoft Excel, you have to update the chart manually to leverage the additional rows of data. Figure 4.58 shows two charts in the workbook, the Microsoft Excel chart on the left side shows fewer bars compared to the chart from Advanced Analysis Office on the right, which is leveraging the exact rows of data shown in the crosstab.

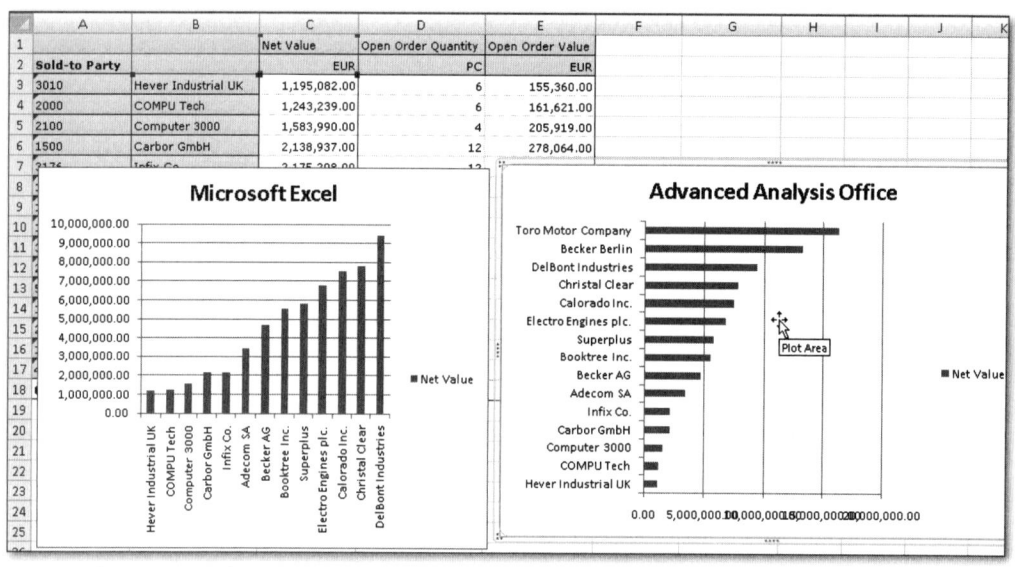

Figure 4.58 Chart Comparison

In this section we reviewed the integration of Advanced Analysis Office with the Microsoft Excel charting capabilities and created our first chart in our workbook. In the next section we will look at the option to create conditional highlighting.

4.1.8 Conditional Formatting

The term *conditional formatting* basically replaces what are known as Exceptions in Business Explorer (BEx) Analyzer. Conditional formatting lets you define rules for highlighting characteristics or key figures as part of your crosstab.

Let's reopen the BW Query we created previously and start a new workbook.

1. Start Advanced Analysis Office with Microsoft Excel via the menu path START • PROGRAMS • SAP BUSINESSOBJECTS • ADVANCED ANALYSIS FOR MICROSOFT EXCEL. If you already started Advanced Analysis for Microsoft Excel, create a new empty spreadsheet.

2. Select the INSERT • SELECT DATA SOURCE option from the Advanced Analysis ribbon.

3. Select the connection to our previously created BW Query. The connection should now be listed as part of the SELECT DATA SOURCE menu.

   Based on the definition of the BW Query, you are presented with the PRODUCT GROUP and PRODUCT characteristics in the rows and in the key figures in the columns.

4. Remove PRODUCT from your crosstab.

5. Exchange CALENDAR YEAR/MONTH with PRODUCT GROUP.

6. Right-click on CALENDAR YEAR/MONTH in the crosstab and use the FILTER BY MEMBER menu.

7. Define a filter that shows all twelve months for 2010.

8. Click OK. Your crosstab should look similar to Figure 4.59.

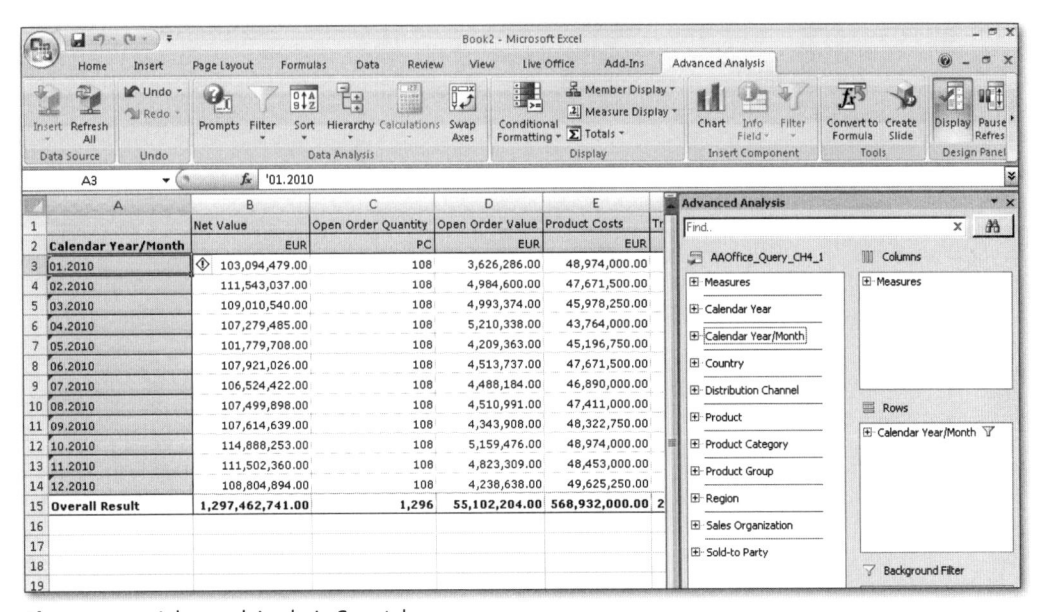

Figure 4.59 Advanced Analysis Crosstab

9. Now follow the CONDITIONAL FORMATTING • NEW menu path from the Advanced Analysis Office ribbon (see Figure 4.60).

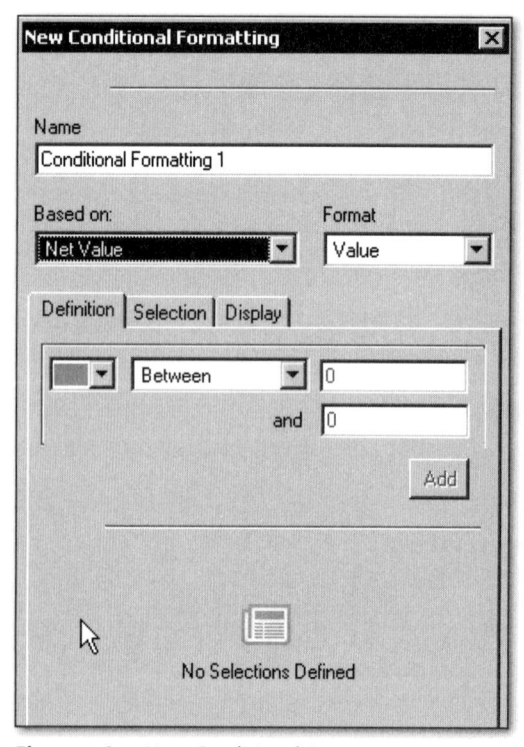

Figure 4.60 New Conditional Formatting

10. You are presented with a new setup for your first conditional formatting rule. Enter "Large Open Order Values" as the name.

11. Select the OPEN ORDER VALUE key figure for the BASED ON option.

12. The FORMAT option lets you select one of the following six options (see Figure 4.61):

Advanced Analysis Office — Microsoft Excel | **4.1**

- The BACKGROUND option lets you format the background color for the selected value.
- The VALUE option lets you format the color of the value itself.
- The STATUS SYMBOL option lets you assign a status symbol as part of the rules.
- The TREND ASCENDING option provides you with a list of color-coded arrows with the assumption that decreasing values are good. In this category, the green arrow symbols point down.
- The TREND DESCENDING option provides you with a list of color-coded arrows with the opposite assumption of TREND ASCENDING.
- The TREND GREY option provides you with a list of arrow symbols in grey.

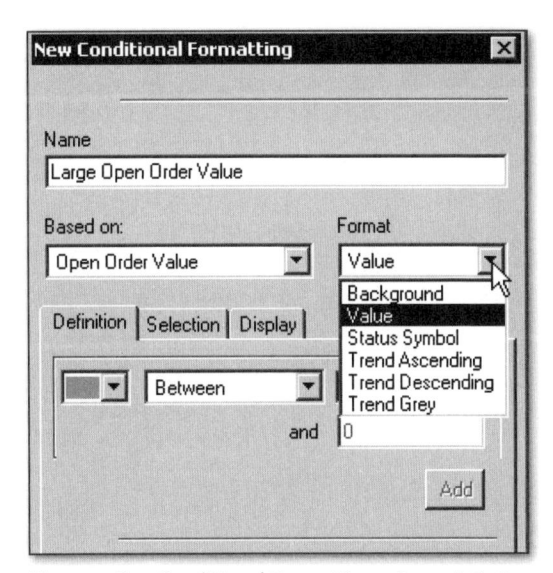

Figure 4.61 Conditional Formatting – Format Options

13. Select the VALUE option.
14. Define a set of three rules and click on the ADD button to make sure each rule is being added to the list (see Figure 4.62).

145

4 | Advanced Analysis Office — Basic Functions

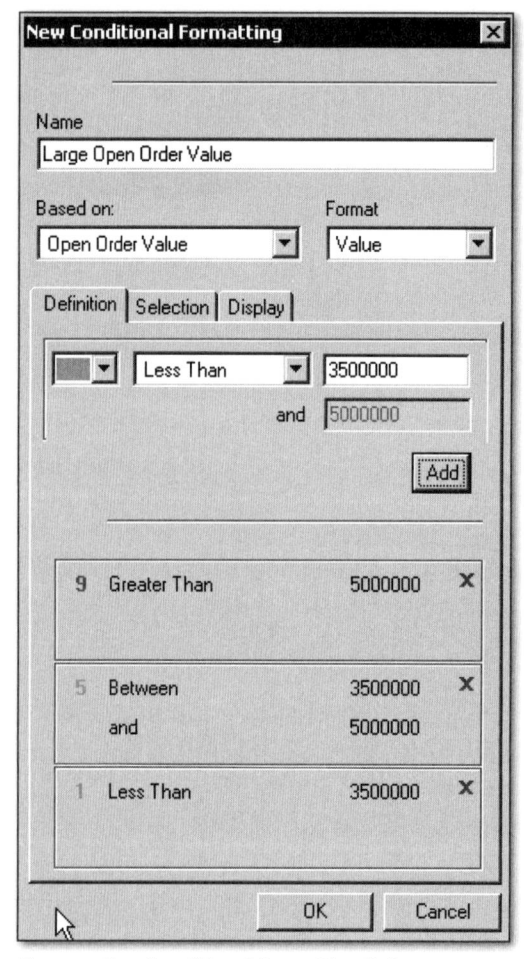

Figure 4.62 Conditional Formatting Rules

- Values less than 3.500.000 are shown in green.
- Values between 3.500.000 and 5.000.000 are shown in orange.
- Values higher than 5.000.000 are shown in red.

15. Navigate to the SELECTION tab (see Figure 4.63).

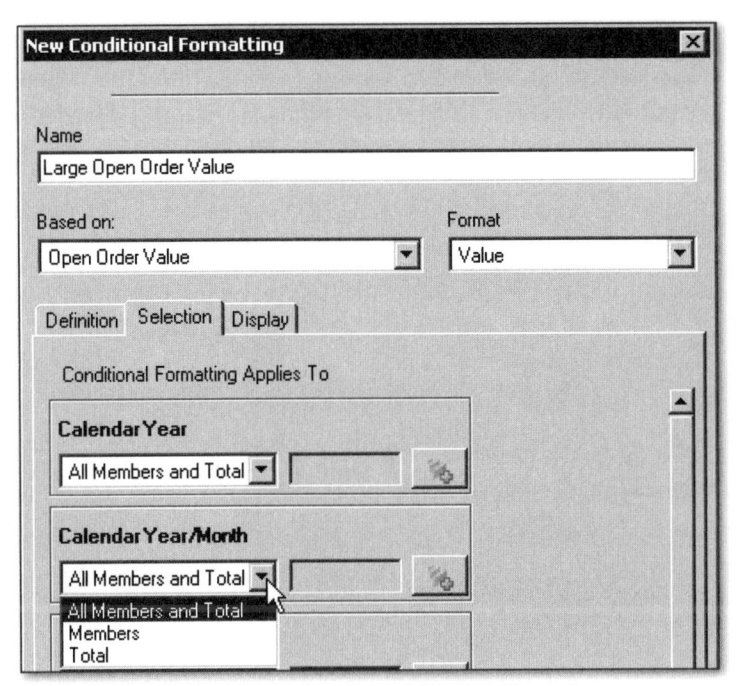

Figure 4.63 Conditional Formatting — Selections

On the SELECTION tab, you can define how the rules for conditional formatting get applied. You have the option of applying the formatting to ALL MEMBERS AND TOTAL or to MEMBERS or TOTAL separately. The MEMBERS option is very compelling, because it lets you select a dedicated list of members for your conditional formatting. This is helpful in situations where you want to apply different rules for members of the same characteristic, for example, a large list of Products for which you would like to define different rules for based on the Product members.

16. Navigate to the DISPLAY tab (see Figure 4.64).

4 | Advanced Analysis Office — Basic Functions

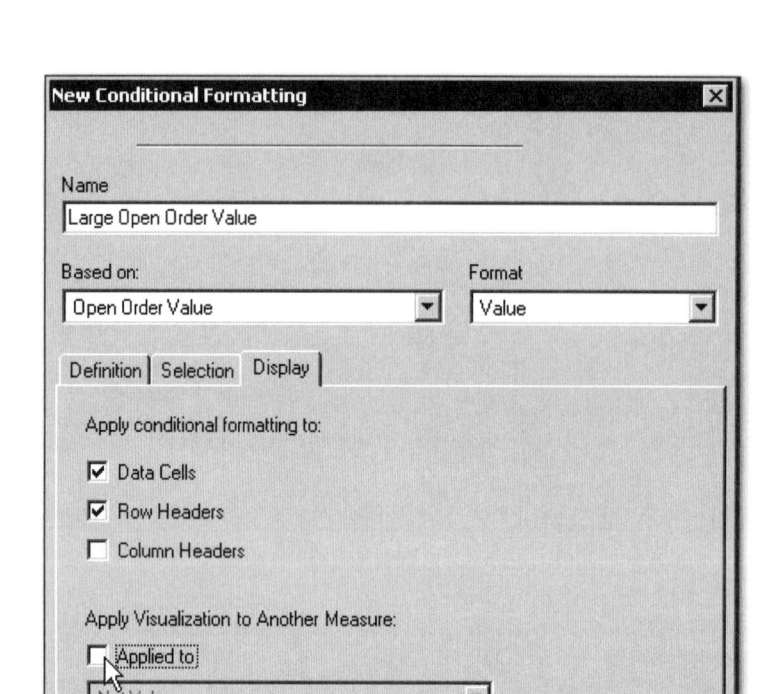

Figure 4.64 Conditional Formatting - Display

Here, you can configure which cells in the crosstab will be highlighted. By default, the DATA CELLS option is activated. The ROW HEADERS and COLUMN HEADERS options let you show an aggregated status of the rule in the rows or columns; the row header or column header will show the worst of all values in the rows or columns.

The APPLY VISUALIZATION TO ANOTHER MEASURE option lets you highlight, for example, the cells of the key figure NET VALUE based on the rules you defined for the key figure OPEN ORDER VALUE. You basically define rules on key figure A and apply the formatting to key figure B.

17. Activate the ROW HEADERS option so that, in our example, the CALENDAR YEAR/ MONTH value is highlighted.

18. Click OK. You should now see the actual key figure and values for CALENDAR YEAR/MONTH highlighted according to the rules we defined.

19. Next, exchange CALENDAR YEAR/MONTH with PRODUCT. Note that the conditional formatting is now applied to PRODUCT because we defined the rules based on the key figure and not on the characteristic.

20. Navigate to the CONDITIONAL FORMATTING menu (see Figure 4.65).

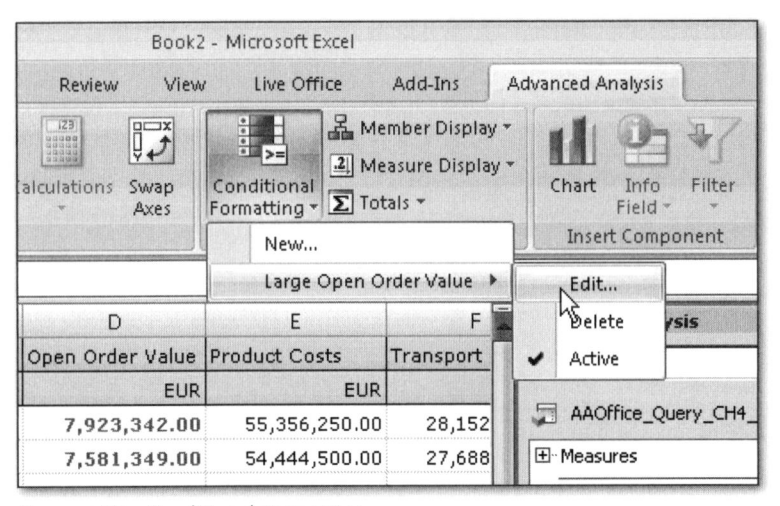

Figure 4.65 Conditional Formatting

21. Each of the defined rules is shown as a separate entry and you can select them based on the name we defined.

22. Follow the CONDITIONAL FORMATTING • NEW menu path to create an additional conditional formatting setup.

23. Define a new rule based on the NET VALUE key figure using the TREND DESCENDING format.

24. Define all values greater than 50.000.000 as Trend value 1 (green) and all values less than 40.000.000 as Trend value 9 (red) (see Figure 4.66).

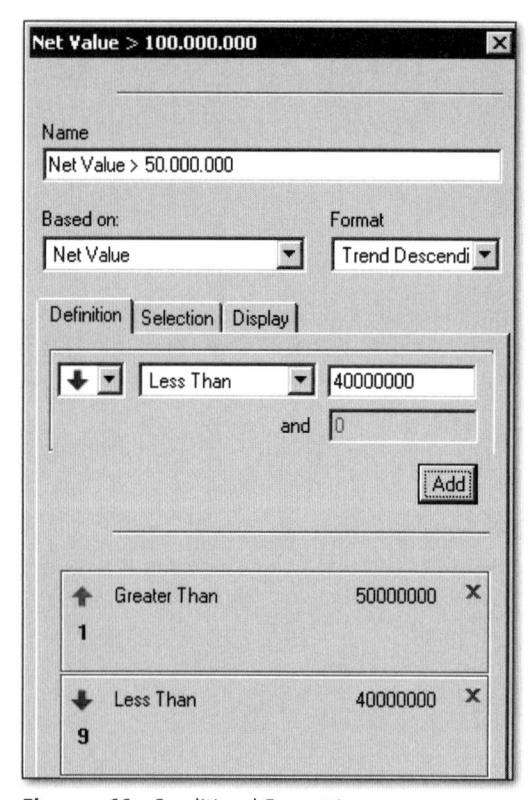

Figure 4.66 Conditional Formatting

25. Navigate to the SELECTION tab.
26. Set the option to MEMBERS for the COUNTRY characteristic (see Figure 4.67).
27. Click the icon and select GERMANY and the U.S.
28. Navigate to the DISPLAY tab and select DATA CELLS and ROW HEADERS.
29. Click OK.
30. Add COUNTRY to your crosstab so that COUNTRY is shown as the outer characteristic (see Figure 4.68).

Advanced Analysis Office — Microsoft Excel | **4.1**

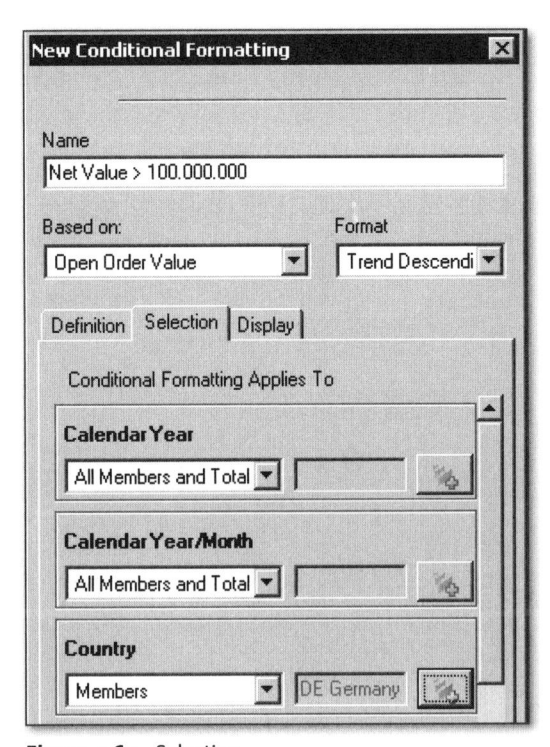

Figure 4.67 Selection

Figure 4.68 Advanced Analysis Crosstab

151

We created a conditional formatting based on the key figure NET VALUE, but restricted it to Germany and the U.S.; therefore, the rules are not applied to France.

31. To change an existing conditional formatting, or to simply disable the rules, you can use the CONDITIONAL FORMATTING menu to select the name of your configured rules and use the EDIT options or switch the ACTIVE option off (see Figure 4.69).

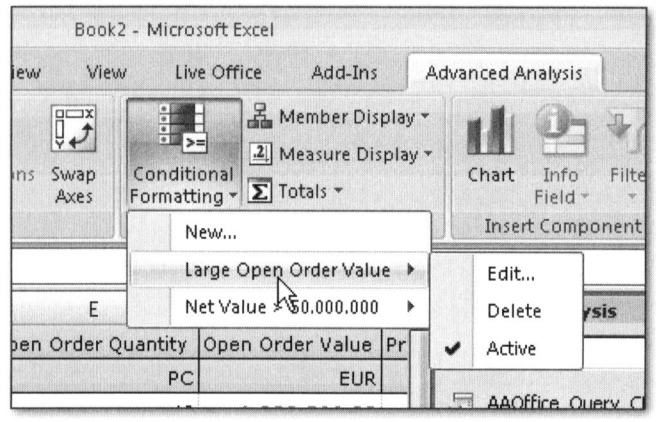

Figure 4.69 Conditional Formatting

> **Conditional Formatting and Exceptions**
>
> Exceptions, which have been defined as part of the BEx Query definition, are leveraged as part of Advanced Analysis Office in a read-only mode. All of the defined formatting is applied, but you need to make any necessary changes directly in the BEx Query.

In this section, we learned how to leverage rules to define conditional formatting as part of your crosstab. In the next section, we will take a look how you can extend this even further and define ranking and filtering based on key figures.

4.1.9 Ranking, Conditions, and Filter by Measures

You may know the term *condition* from the BEx Query Designer and BEx Analyzer. In Advanced Analysis Office you can create a condition, such as a top 10 filtering, with FILTER BY MEASURE.

1. Start Advanced Analysis Office with Microsoft Excel via the menu path START • PROGRAMS • SAP BUSINESSOBJECTS • ADVANCED ANALYSIS FOR MICROSOFT EXCEL. If you already started Advanced Analysis for Microsoft Excel, create a new empty spreadsheet.

2. Select the INSERT • SELECT DATA SOURCE option from the Advanced Analysis ribbon.

3. Select the connection to our previously created BW Query. The connection should be listed as part of the SELECT DATA SOURCE menu.

Based on the definition of the BW Query, you are presented with the PRODUCT GROUP and PRODUCT characteristics in the rows and the key figures in the columns.

4. Remove PRODUCT from your crosstab.

5. Exchange SOLD-TO PARTY with PRODUCT GROUP.

6. Right-click on a value of NET VALUE and follow the menu path FILTER BY MEASURE • ALL DIMENSIONS INDEPENDENTLY • EDIT (see Figure 4.70).

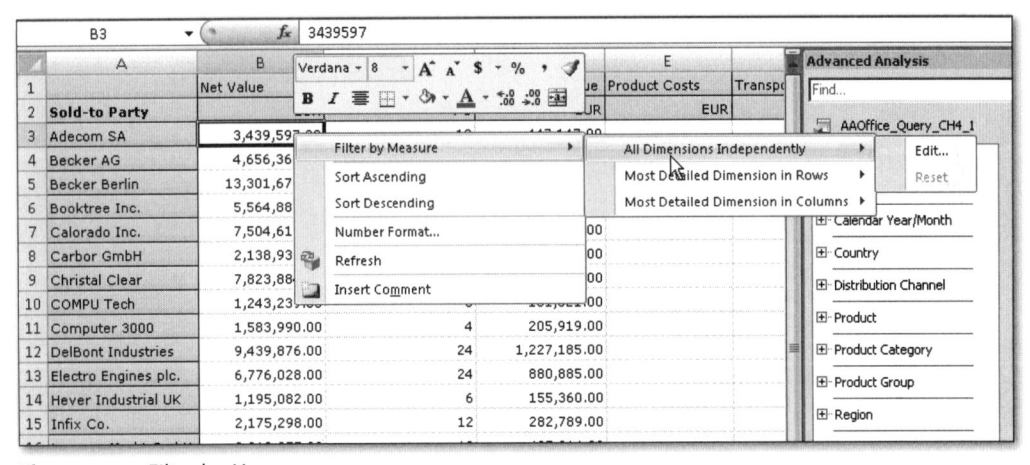

Figure 4.70 Filter by Measure

▶ The ALL DIMENSIONS INDEPENDENTLY option lets you define a filter based on a key figure, which will get applied to all used characteristics.

4 | Advanced Analysis Office — Basic Functions

▶ The MOST DETAILED DIMENSION IN ROWS option means that the filter gets applied to the most detailed characteristic in the rows and likewise the MOST DETAILED DIMENSION IN COLUMNS option.

7. Because we started by selecting a value from NET VALUE, the key figure is preselected and we can now define the filter (see Figure 4.71).

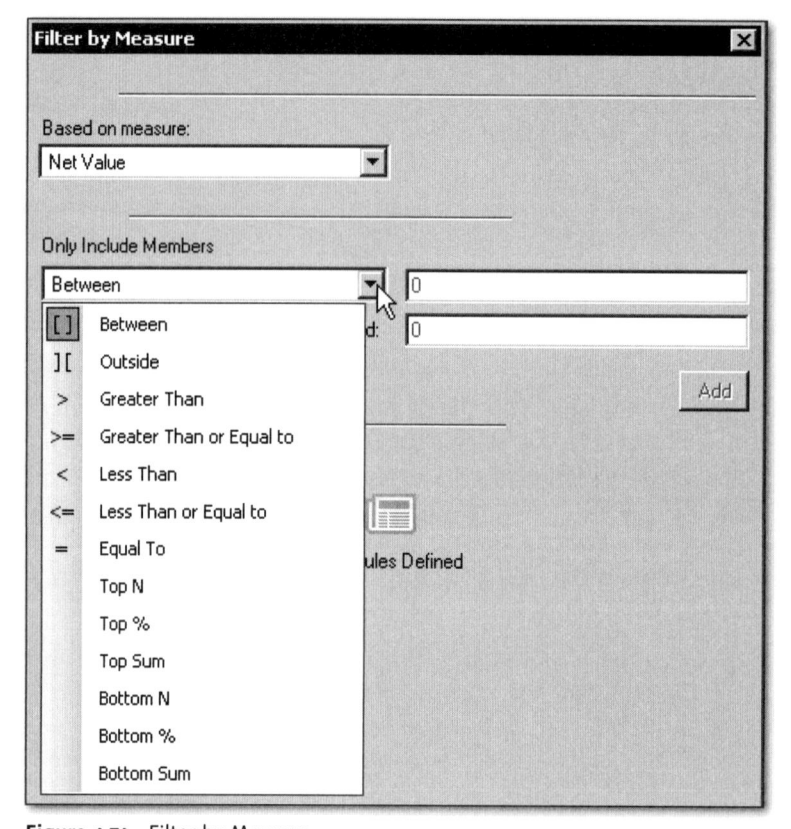

Figure 4.71 Filter by Measure

8. Select the TOP N option for ONLY INCLUDE MEMBERS and enter the value 3.
9. Click ADD to make sure your rule is added to the list (see Figure 4.72).

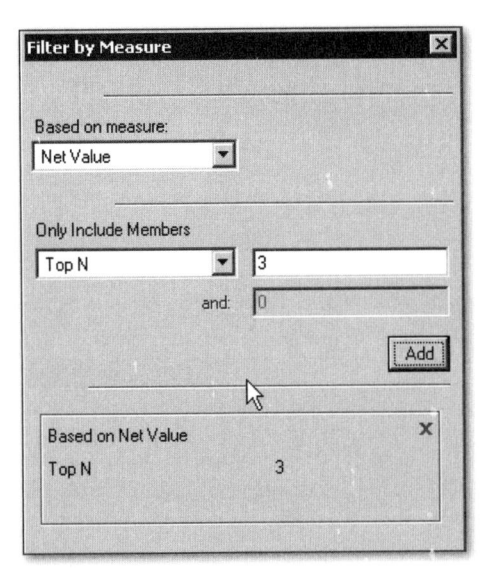

Figure 4.72 Filter by Measure

Editing Defined Rules

Just as with conditional formatting, you can't edit a defined rule in the FILTER BY MEASURE definition screen. The only option is to delete the rule and add a new one.

10. Click OK. Your list of customers is reduced to the top three (see Figure 4.73).

	A	B	C
1		Net Value	Open Order Quantity
2	**Sold-to Party**	EUR	PC
3	Becker Berlin	13,301,670.00	36
4	Toro Motor Company	16,322,887.00	48
5	Not assigned	219,000,000.00	0
6	**Overall Result**	323,648,056.00	324

Figure 4.73 Advanced Analysis Crosstab

> **Filter by Measure and Totals**
>
> It is important to note (see Figure 4.73) that the totals and subtotals are based on all of the information in your crosstab, not just on the entries based on the FILTER BY MEASURE configuration.

11. Next, add PRODUCT as an inner characteristic to your crosstab (see Figure 4.74).

	A	B	C	D
1			Net Value	Open Order Quan
2	Sold-to Party	Product	EUR	
3	Becker Berlin	CN00S2	4,661,758.00	
4		CN0F17	4,748,919.00	
5		CN0F21	3,890,993.00	
6		Result	13,301,670.00	
7	Toro Motor Company	CN00S1	4,480,293.00	
8		CN00S2	4,391,628.00	
9		CN0400	7,450,966.00	
10		Result	16,322,887.00	
11	Not assigned	CN00S1	21,200,000.00	
12		HT1000	37,800,000.00	
13		HT1001	33,600,000.00	
14		Result	219,000,000.00	
15	Overall Result		323,648,056.00	

Figure 4.74 Advanced Analysis Crosstab

Because we used the ALL DIMENSIONS INDEPENDENTLY option when we started the definition of our Filter by Measure, we now have a crosstab that shows the top three customers with the top three products for each customer. Our FILTER BY MEASURE is applied to any characteristic that is part of the crosstab.

12. Select a value for NET VALUE and follow the menu path FILTER • FILTER BY MEASURE • ALL DIMENSIONS INDEPENDENTLY • RESET.

13. Exchange PRODUCT with CALENDAR YEAR/MONTH. Your crosstab should now show all of the members of SOLD-TO PARTY in the first three months of 2010. The filter for the first three months is based on the filtering defined in the BW Query.

14. Select one member of CALENDAR YEAR/MONTH and follow the FILTER • FILTER BY MEMBER menu path and select all 12 months for 2010.

15. Next, select a value for NET VALUE and follow the menu path FILTER • FILTER BY MEASURE • MOST DETAILED DIMENSION IN ROWS • EDIT.

16. Define an identical rule just as we did to filter the NET VALUE key figure for the top three values.

17. Your crosstab should now show the top- three CALENDAR YEAR/MONTH members for all members of SOLD-TO PARTY (see Figure 4.75).

	A	B	C	D
1			Net Value	Open Order Quantity
2	Sold-to Party	Calendar Year/Month	EUR	PC
3	Adecom SA	02.2010	2,011,970.00	4
4		09.2010	1,498,754.00	2
5		12.2010	1,495,565.00	2
6		Result	11,099,330.00	28
7	Becker AG	02.2010	2,498,940.00	4
8		04.2010	2,739,980.00	4
9		07.2010	2,184,669.00	4
10		Result	15,913,176.00	48
11	Becker Berlin	02.2010	5,912,360.00	12
12		07.2010	6,267,522.00	12
13		11.2010	5,393,654.00	12
14		Result	48,398,976.00	144

Figure 4.75 Advanced Analysis Office – Filter by Measure

18. Now use the navigation panel to swap CALENDAR YEAR/MONTH with SOLD-TO PARTY and your crosstab shows the top three members of SOLD-TO PARTY for all 12 months of 2010 (see Figure 4.76).

4 | Advanced Analysis Office — Basic Functions

	A	B	C
1			Net Value
2	Calendar Year/Month	Sold-to Party	EUR
3	01.2010	Becker Berlin	4,460,941.00
4		DelBont Industries	3,797,773.00
5		Not assigned	75,200,000.00
6		Result	103,094,479.00
7	02.2010	Becker Berlin	5,912,360.00
8		Toro Motor Company	5,040,175.00
9		Not assigned	73,200,000.00
10		Result	111,543,037.00
11	03.2010	Christal Clear	3,571,130.00
12		Toro Motor Company	8,132,875.00
13		Not assigned	70,600,000.00
14		Result	109,010,540.00

Figure 4.76 Advanced Analysis Office – Filter by Measure

19. Now select a value of the keyfigure NET VALUE and use the menu FILTER • FILTER BY MEASURE • MOST DETAILED DIMENSION IN ROWS • RESET.

20. Now select a value of the keyfigure NET VALUE and use the menu FILTER • FILTER BY MEASURE • MOST DETAILED DIMENSION IN COLUMNS • EDIT.

21. Define an identical rule just as we did to filter the NET VALUE for the top three values.

22. Now use the navigation panel and move SOLD-TO PARTY into the columns (see Figure 4.77).

Now we are looking at our top three members of SOLD-TO PARTY based on NET VALUE and broken down by all 12 months of 2010.

So far, we started with key figure selection and then created a filter. Now let's select a characteristic and then apply the FILTER BY MEASURE functionality.

23. Select a value for NET VALUE and follow the menu path FILTER • FILTER BY MEASURE • MOST DETAILED DIMENSION IN COLUMNS • RESET.

24. Select a value for CALENDAR YEAR/MONTH and follow the menu path FILTER • FILTER BY MEASURE • EDIT (see Figure 4.78).

	A	B	C	D	E
1		Net Value			
2	Sold-to Party	Becker Berlin	Toro Motor Company	Not assigned	Overall Result
3	Calendar Year/Month	EUR	EUR	EUR	EUR
4	01.2010	4,460,941.00	3,149,837.00	75,200,000.00	103,094,479.00
5	02.2010	5,912,360.00	5,040,175.00	73,200,000.00	111,543,037.00
6	03.2010	2,928,369.00	8,132,875.00	70,600,000.00	109,010,540.00
7	04.2010	1,991,892.00	6,089,119.00	67,200,000.00	107,279,485.00
8	05.2010	4,314,146.00	3,346,542.00	69,400,000.00	101,779,708.00
9	06.2010	4,365,006.00	5,553,257.00	73,200,000.00	107,921,026.00
10	07.2010	6,267,522.00	4,943,446.00	72,000,000.00	106,524,422.00
11	08.2010	4,315,495.00	4,099,394.00	72,800,000.00	107,499,898.00
12	09.2010	1,609,929.00	5,073,529.00	74,200,000.00	107,614,639.00
13	10.2010	3,954,960.00	7,430,363.00	75,200,000.00	114,888,253.00
14	11.2010	5,393,654.00	4,798,653.00	74,400,000.00	111,502,360.00
15	12.2010	2,884,702.00	4,540,563.00	76,200,000.00	108,804,894.00
16	Overall Result	48,398,976.00	62,197,753.00	873,600,000.00	1,297,462,741.00

Figure 4.77 Advanced Analysis – Filter by Measure

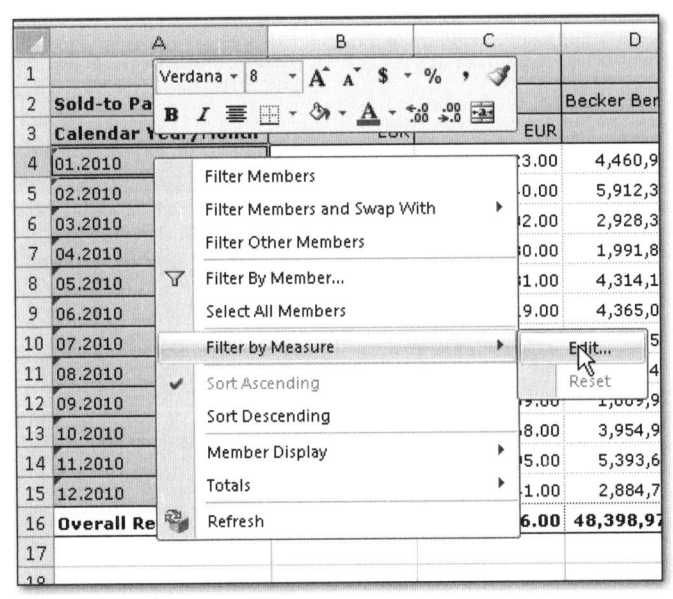

Figure 4.78 Filter by Measure

25. Define a top three rule based on NET VALUE and click ADD.

26. Click OK.

27. Your crosstab should show the top three members of 2010 based on NET VALUE.

28. Now use the navigation panel to move SOLD-TO PARTY back to the rows as an inner group (see Figure 4.79).

	A	B	C	D
1			Net Value	Open Order Quantity
2	Calendar Year/Month	Sold-to Party	EUR	PC
3	01.2010	Adecom SA	726,029.00	4
4		Becker AG	503,523.00	4
5		Becker Berlin	4,460,941.00	12
6		Booktree Inc.	825,510.00	8
7		Calorado Inc.	2,873,234.00	8
8		Carbor GmbH	686,351.00	4
9		Christal Clear	2,582,720.00	8
10		COMPU Tech	315,987.00	2
11		DelBont Industries	3,797,773.00	8
12		Electro Engines plc.	1,738,250.00	8
13		Hever Industrial UK	338,445.00	2
14		Infix Co.	971,414.00	4
15		Lampen-Markt GmbH	343,600.00	4
16		Minerva Industries	1,747,373.00	6
17		Nobil North Limited	220,143.00	2
18		Royal British Rail	985,015.00	2
19		Superplus	1,628,334.00	6
20		Toro Motor Company	3,149,837.00	16
21		Not assigned	75,200,000.00	0
22		Result	103,094,479.00	108
23	05.2010	Adecom SA	256,874.00	2
24		Becker AG	1,377,381.00	4
25		Becker Berlin	4,314,146.00	12

Figure 4.79 Filter by Measure

The crosstab still shows the top three months but now it's with all of the members of SOLD-TO PARTY for each of the top three months. Compared to the other options defined for the key figure, defining a filter by measure on the characteristic is just basically moving and staying with the characteristic itself and is not depending on which characteristic is the most detailed one in the rows or columns.

> **Filter by Measure Visibility**
>
> Unlike the Filter by Member option in the Advanced Analysis Office navigation panel, which has a ▽ icon next to the elements impacted by Filter by Member rules, the Filter by Measure rules are not visible in the Analysis tab of the navigation panel. Applied Filter by Measure rules are only visible in the Information tab of the navigation panel.

> **Conditions and Filter by Measure**
>
> Conditions defined as part of the BEx Query are leveraged by Advanced Analysis Office. The definitions of those conditions are not visible in Advanced Analysis and if changes are needed they need to be performed directly in the BEx Query. Please note that you can also define a Filter by Measure.

In this section, we reviewed the new capability for defining filter conditions based on measures. In the next section, we will look at the formatting options for the totals and subtotals in our crosstab.

4.1.10 Totals and Subtotals

In this section, we will look at the options for placing and formatting the subtotals and totals of our crosstab.

1. Start Advanced Analysis Office with Microsoft Excel via the menu path START • PROGRAMS • SAP BUSINESSOBJECTS • ADVANCED ANALYSIS FOR MICROSOFT EXCEL. If you already started Advanced Analysis for Microsoft Excel, create a new empty spreadsheet.

2. Select the INSERT • SELECT DATA SOURCE option from the Advanced Analysis ribbon.

3. Select the connection to our previously created BW Query. The connection should be listed as part of the SELECT DATA SOURCE menu.

4 | Advanced Analysis Office — Basic Functions

Based on the definition of the BW Query, you are presented with the PRODUCT GROUP and PRODUCT characteristics in the rows and the key figures in the columns.

4. Select the line for the subtotals for PRODUCT. To do so, select the cell with the word RESULT in the crosstab.

5. Navigate to the TOTALS menu (see Figure 4.80).

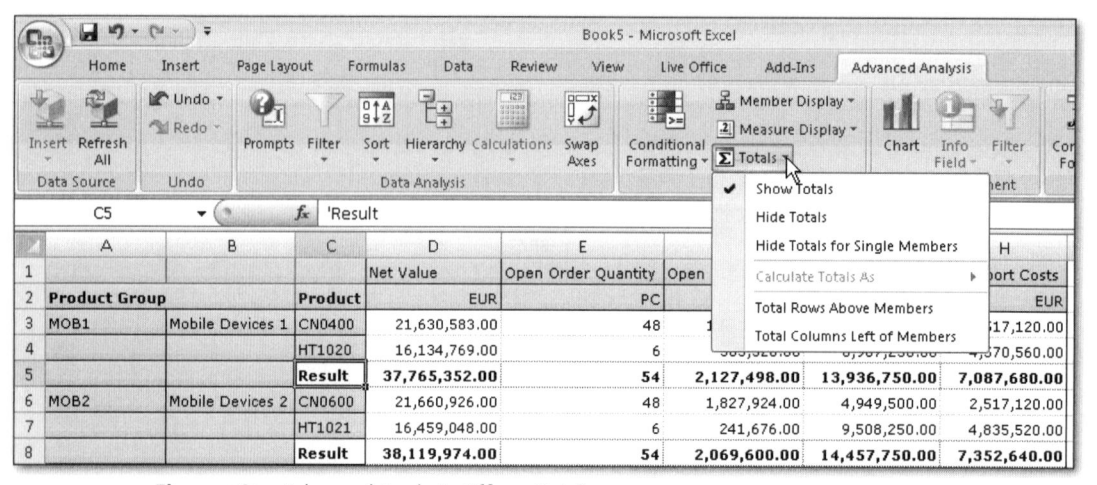

Figure 4.80 Advanced Analysis Office - Totals

The TOTALS menu gives you several options:

- HIDE TOTALS lets you hide the totals for the selected characteristic. In our example, the menu option would hide all subtotals for PRODUCT.

- HIDE TOTALS FOR SINGLE MEMBERS provides you with the option to hide the subtotal for cases where there is only a single member, which means the single member and the subtotal would be identical.

- The TOTAL ROWS ABOVE MEMBERS and TOTAL COLUMNS LEFT OF MEMBERS options let you define the position of the row and column totals.

Please note that all of the menu options in the TOTALS menu are enabled or disabled and have a checkmark in front of the option to show which ones have been activated. In addition, those menu options are also available in the context menu of each characteristic shown in the crosstab (see Figure 4.81).

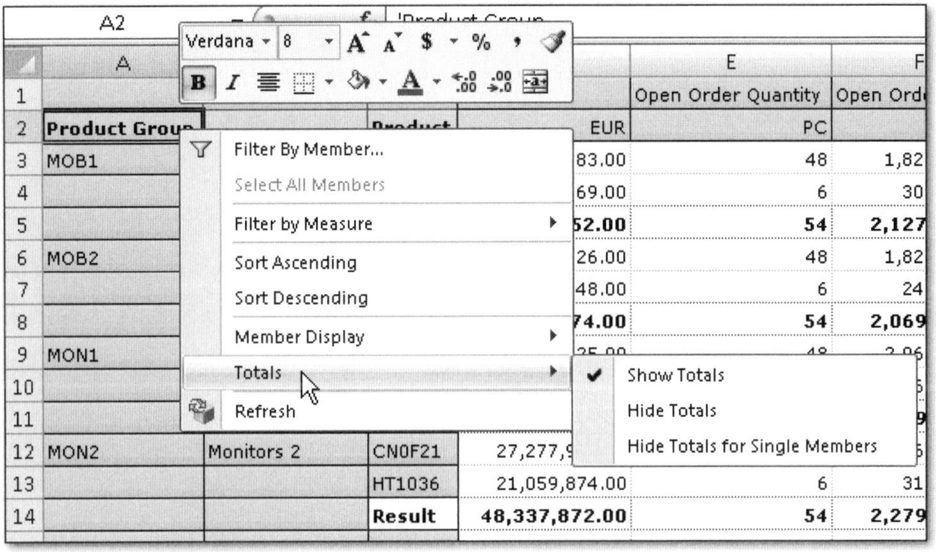

Figure 4.81 Context Menu

6. Now select the column header for NET VALUE.

7. Follow the TOTALS • CALCULATE TOTAL AS menu path or use the context menu (see Figure 4.82).

CALCULATE TOTAL AS allows you to define how the subtotals and totals are calculated. The DEFAULT entry refers to the type of aggregation defined in SAP NetWeaver BW.

4 | Advanced Analysis Office — Basic Functions

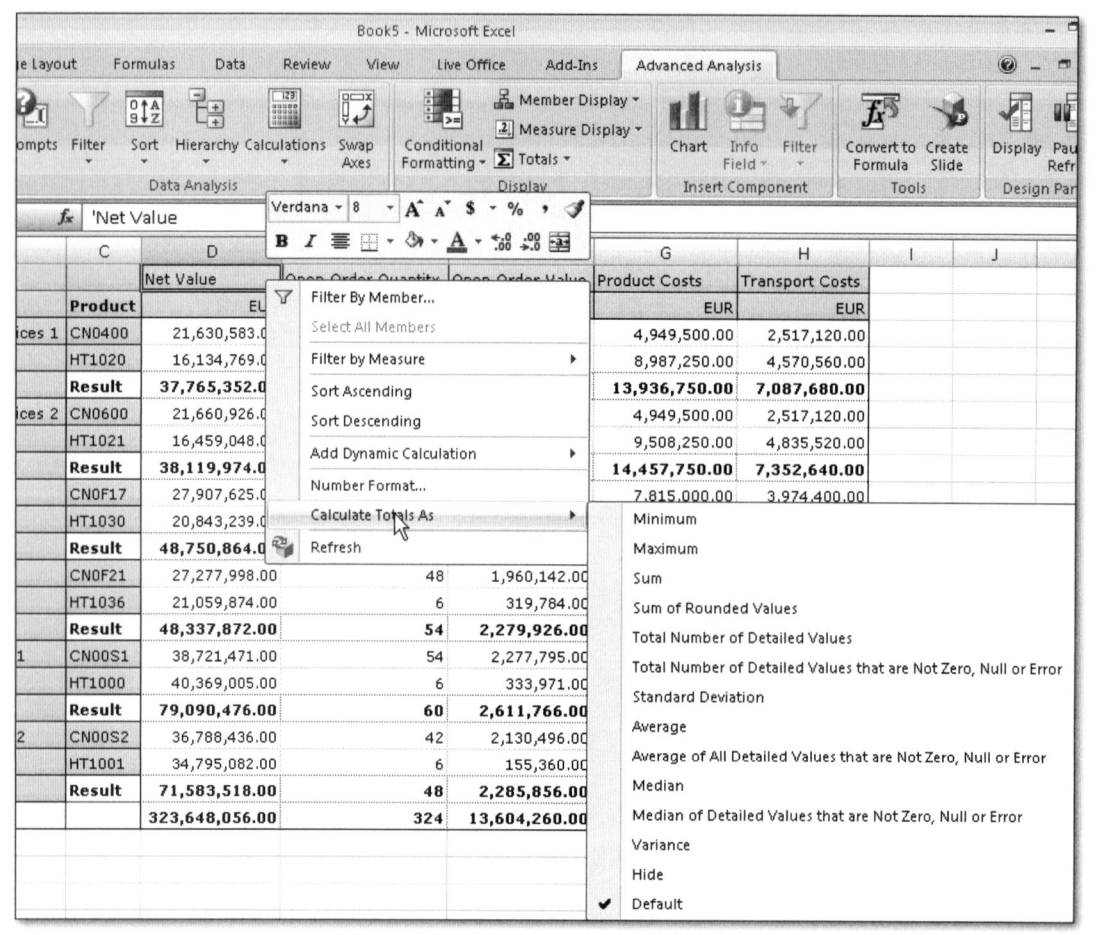

Figure 4.82 Calculate Total As

In this section, we reviewed the options for placing our subtotals and totals. In the next section, we will review the prompting user interface (UI) and functionality of Advanced Analysis Office.

4.1.11 Prompting and Variables

The initial release of Advanced Analysis Office only supports SAP NetWeaver BW as a data source and therefore all prompts represent variables from BW queries. Advanced Analysis Office will turn any variable that has been configured with the Ready for Input option into a prompt. Please note that if your underlying BW Query doesn't contain mandatory variables, then Advanced Analysis Office will not display a prompting screen when you insert the initial crosstab, because all of the variables are optional in such a case. In this situation you can access the PROMPT dialog in the ribbon.

1. Start Advanced Analysis Office with Microsoft Excel via the menu path START • PROGRAMS • SAP BUSINESSOBJECTS • ADVANCED ANALYSIS FOR MICROSOFT EXCEL. If you already started Advanced Analysis for Microsoft Excel, create a new empty spreadsheet.

2. Select the INSERT • SELECT DATA SOURCE option from the Advanced Analysis ribbon.

3. Select the connection to our previously created BW Query. The connection should be listed as part of the SELECT DATA SOURCE menu.

4. Because our underlying BW Query contains variables, you will be presented with the prompting dialog (see Figure 4.83).

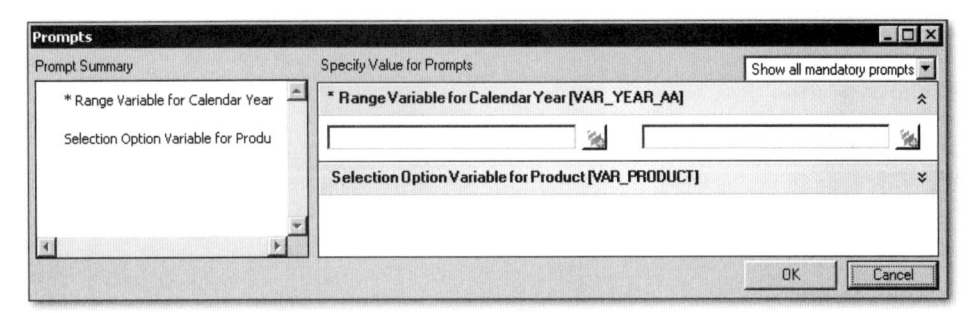

Figure 4.83 Advanced Analysis Prompting

You will notice a set of standard behaviors:

▶ All mandatory variables are shown in a collapsed view and have an * symbol in front of the variable description.

▶ All optional variables are listed, but not shown in an expanded view.

▶ You can use the list box in the top right corner (see Figure 4.84) to switch between different views of the list of variables.

4 | Advanced Analysis Office — Basic Functions

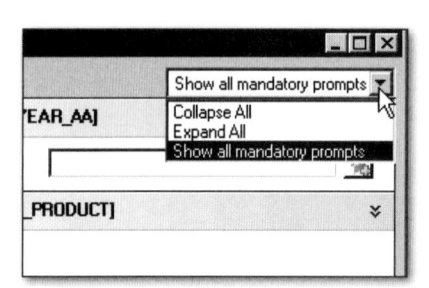

Figure 4.84 Advanced Analysis Prompting

You can always enter the values for the prompts manually or you can click on the icon and open the Member Selector, which provides you the same functionality as we discussed in Section 4.1.6, Sorting and Filtering.

The options for selecting a single or multiple values in the Member Selector always depend on the type of variable that you created in the underlying BW Query.

Advanced Analysis Office supports all of the variable options, which the BW Query gives you (including Text Variables). If you are using a SELECTION OPTION VARIABLE, Advanced Analysis Office will provide you the UI shown in Figure 4.85.

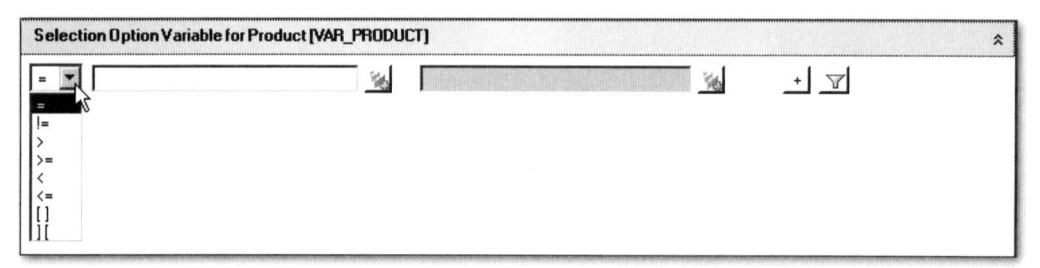

Figure 4.85 Selection Option Variable

Here, you can use the list of operators on the left side to define the type of member selection you would like to define. Depending on the operator, you have the option of either entering a single or multiple single values or entering ranges and you will either have one open box for entering values or two. On the right-hand side you can click the [+] icon to add an additional rule and you can click the icon to open the member selector. The icon gives you access to the Member

Selector and you can select several members in a single step and the selected values will be treated as values to be included into the selection (see Figure 4.86).

Figure 4.86 Selection Option Variable

After you enter the initial set of values for your variables, you can always use PROMPTS in the Advanced Analysis Office ribbon to bring up the prompting dialog for your variables (see Figure 4.87).

Figure 4.87 Advanced Analysis Office Ribbon

In this section, we reviewed the capabilities of Advanced Analysis Office with regard to leveraging prompting based on the variables in your BW Query. In the next section, we will demonstrate how to show additional information about the data shown in your crosstab.

4.1.12 Displaying Information about the Data

In addition to showing the actual data to the user, Advanced Analysis Office also provides you with the option to show metadata information for your data. Most people know these elements as BEx text elements from the BEx Analyzer.

4 | Advanced Analysis Office — Basic Functions

1. Start Advanced Analysis Office with Microsoft Excel via the menu path START • PROGRAMS • SAP BUSINESSOBJECTS • ADVANCED ANALYSIS FOR MICROSOFT EXCEL. If you already started Advanced Analysis for Microsoft Excel, create a new empty spreadsheet.

2. Select the INSERT • SELECT DATA SOURCE option from the Advanced Analysis ribbon.

3. Select the connection to our previously created BW query. The connection should be listed as part of the SELECT DATA SOURCE menu.

4. Provide the values for the variables we created as part of our BW Query.

5. Now insert a set of six rows on top of the actual crosstab.

6. Select the first empty cell above the crosstab and navigate to the INSERT FIELD menu (see Figure 4.88).

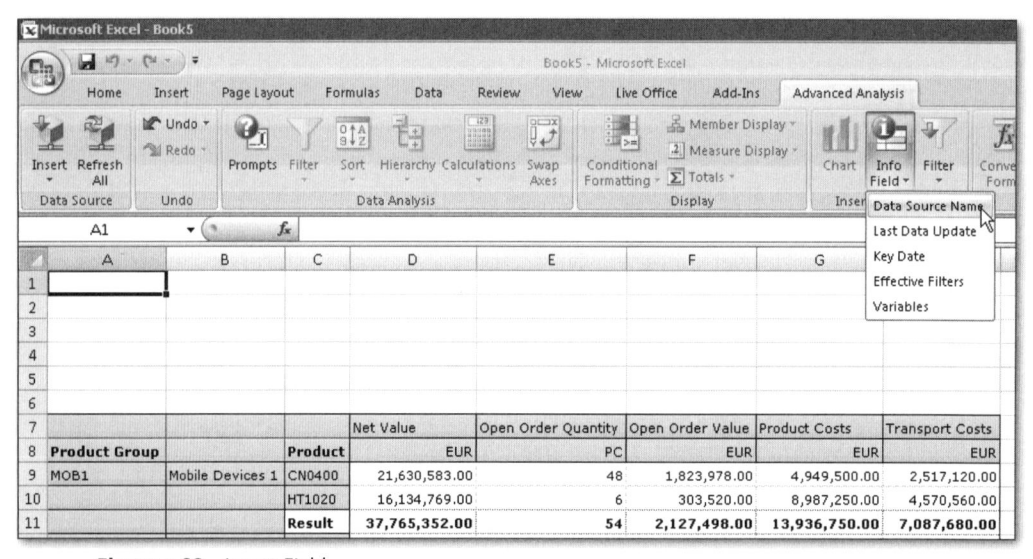

Figure 4.88 Insert Field

7. Now select five fields to provide further details on from our workbook:

    ▶ DATA SOURCE NAME
    ▶ LAST DATA UPDATE

- KEY DATE
- EFFECTIVE FILTERS
- VARIABLES

8. Insert all five text elements into your spreadsheet. Keep in mind that EFFECTIVE FILTERS and VARIABLES may need more than a single row in your spreadsheet (see Figure 4.89).

	A	B	C	D
1	Data Source Name	AAOffice_Query_CH4_1		
2	Last Data Update	Tuesday, March 09, 2010 9:05:50 AM		
3	Key Date	Monday, June 07, 2010		
4				
5	**Effective Filter**			
6	Calendar Year/Month	01.2010; 02.2010; 03.2010		
7	Calendar Year	2006 - 2011		
8				
9	**Variables**			
10	Range Variable for Calendar Year	2006 - 2011		
11				
12				
13				
14				Net Value
15	**Product Group**		**Product**	EUR
16	MOB1	Mobile Devices 1	CN0400	21,630,583.00
17			HT1020	16,134,769.00
18			**Result**	**37,765,352.00**
19	MOB2	Mobile Devices 2	CN0600	21,660,926.00

Figure 4.89 Text Elements

- DATA SOURCE NAME provides you with the technical name of the BW Query.
- LAST DATA UPDATE provides you with the date of the last update to the underlying InfoProvider. The date refers to the last update of the data, not data modeling.
- KEY DATE shows the date that is used as the key date for the BW Query, which is relevant to time-dependent elements such as a time-dependent hierarchy structure.

- EFFECTIVE FILTERS shows all of the filters configured for any of the characteristics in your workbook.
- VARIABLES shows all of the variables with their description and values.

All of the information in these fields is language dependent based on the language of the Microsoft Office installation and independent of the log-on language of the backend system. These fields are refreshed each time the workbook is opened or refreshed. If you edit the information manually, the changes will be overwritten with the updated information on the next refresh.

> **Multilingual Environments**
>
> Because the Info Fields are shown based on the language used for Microsoft Office and not based on the backend log-on language, this could lead to a situation where a user with German as the language for Microsoft Excel creates a workbook, and then the Info Fields are shown in German to a user with Microsoft Excel set in English. On the next refresh of the workbook set in English, the Info Fields will be shown in English.

In this section, we reviewed how to display further details about your workbook. In the next section, we will review the basic functionality for Advanced Analysis Office for Microsoft PowerPoint.

4.2 Advanced Analysis Office — Microsoft PowerPoint

In the previous sections, we reviewed the basic functionality of Advanced Analysis Office in a Microsoft Excel environment. Advanced Analysis Office in a Microsoft PowerPoint environment focuses on presenting information and not so much on actually analyzing the information. Advanced Analysis Office for Microsoft PowerPoint is designed to provide the functionality to create compelling presentations with the necessary information and data provided by Advanced Analysis Office and therefore there are some differences in the functionality compared to Advanced Analysis Office for Microsoft Excel. In this section, we will highlight those differences in functionality for the basic features of Advanced Analysis Office.

1. Start Advanced Analysis Office with Microsoft PowerPoint via the menu path START • PROGRAMS • SAP BUSINESSOBJECTS • ADVANCED ANALYSIS FOR MICROSOFT POWERPOINT.

Advanced Analysis Office — Microsoft PowerPoint | **4.2**

2. Select the INSERT • SELECT DATA SOURCE option from the Advanced Analysis ribbon.

3. Select the connection to our previously created BW Query. The list of connections is identical to the one we used in Advanced Analysis Office for Microsoft Excel.

4. Provide the values for the prompting part based on the variables from our BW Query.

5. Click OK.

6. Next, you will be asked how many rows of data you want to show in the table in Microsoft PowerPoint (see Figure 4.90).

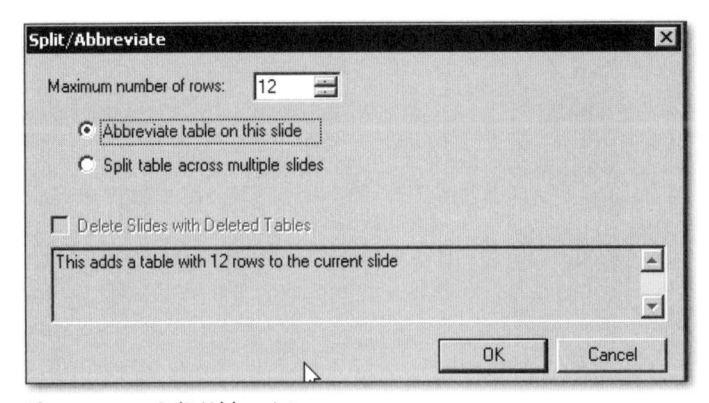

Figure 4.90 Split/Abbreviate

Because you are creating a presentation and you can only have a limited number of rows per slide in your presentation, Advanced Analysis Office is asking you how you want to split the information. You can define the number of rows (with 21 being the maximum) and decide if you want to abbreviate the table or split the table into multiple slides as part of your presentation.

7. We will use the ABBREVIATE TABLE ON THIS SLIDE option for now and look into this option in more detail in Chapter 5, Advanced Analysis Office — Advanced Functions.

8. Set the MAXIMUM NUMBER OF ROWS to 12.

9. Click OK.

171

4 | Advanced Analysis Office — Basic Functions

Next, you'll see a table as part of your slide (see Figure 4.91) and because we chose to abbreviate the table the last row in our crosstab shows "…" in each of the cells to highlight that the table does not show the complete set of data.

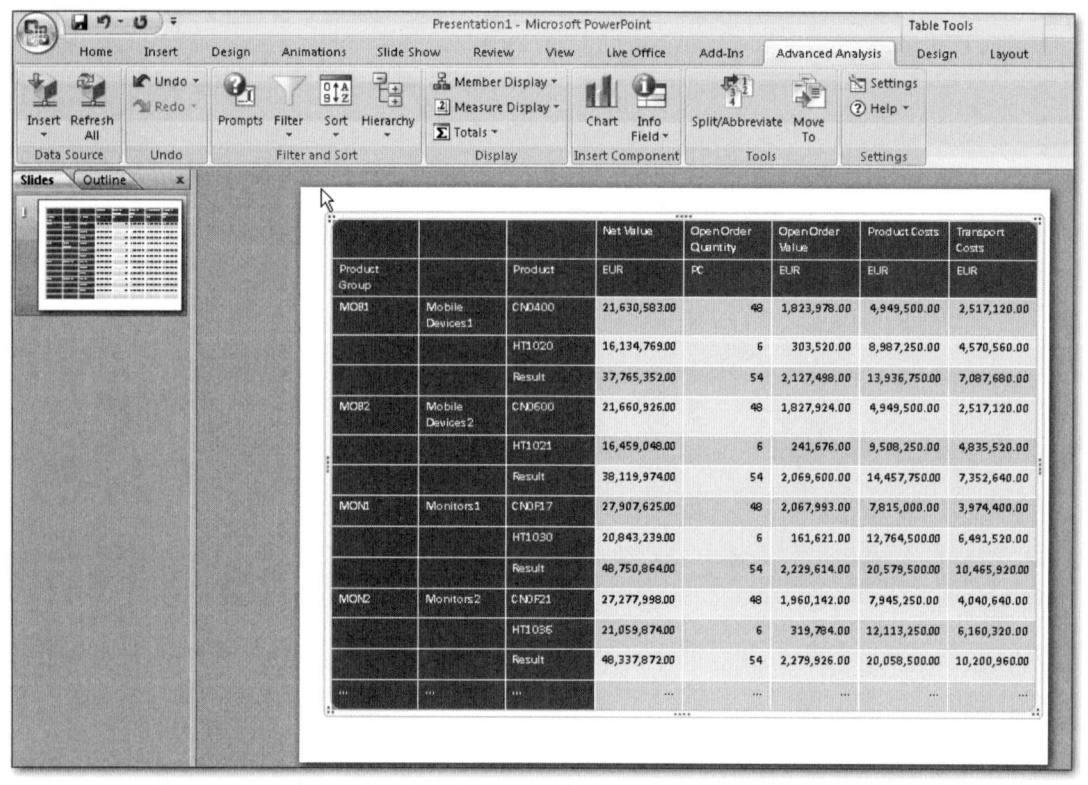

Figure 4.91 Advanced Analysis for Microsoft PowerPoint

Just as with Advanced Analysis Office for Microsoft Excel, the tools leverage the native Microsoft PowerPoint functionality as much as possible. When inserting a crosstab into your slide, you are able to use the standard TABLE TOOLS menus in Microsoft PowerPoint to format the table (see Figure 4.92).

Advanced Analysis Office — Microsoft PowerPoint | **4.2**

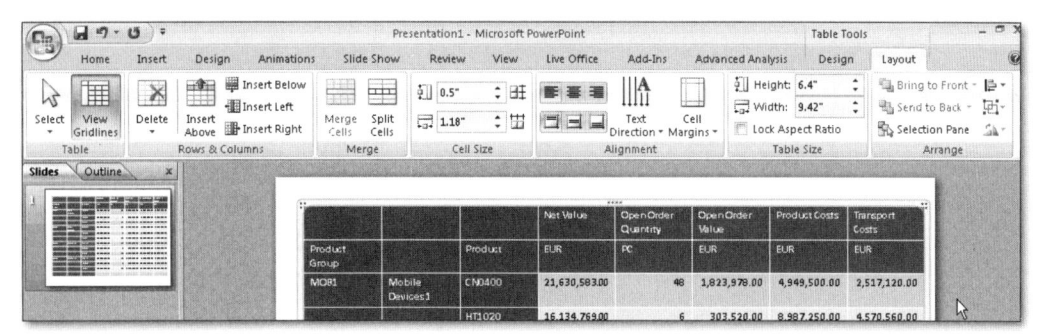

Figure 4.92 Table Tools

4.2.1 Advanced Analysis Office — Microsoft Excel versus Microsoft PowerPoint

You have now created your first Advanced Analysis Office crosstab as part of your presentation in Microsoft PowerPoint. The following are the elements that are different in functionality when compared to Advanced Analysis Office in Microsoft Excel:

- The first major difference is that in Microsoft PowerPoint you don't see the Advanced Analysis Office navigation panel and you can't pause the refresh when designing your slide.

- Advanced Analysis Office for Microsoft PowerPoint does not let you swap the axis of your table.

- Advanced Analysis Office for Microsoft PowerPoint does not let you create calculations.

- Advanced Analysis Office for Microsoft PowerPoint does not let you suppress empty rows or columns.

- Advanced Analysis Office for Microsoft PowerPoint does not let you filter and swap a characteristic at the same time like you can by using the context menu in Advanced Analysis Office for Microsoft Excel.

- Advanced Analysis Office for Microsoft PowerPoint does not let you create a conditional formatting.

In this short section, we reviewed the major differences between Advanced Analysis Office for Microsoft PowerPoint and for Microsoft Excel. In the next section, we will go through a basic workflow with Advanced Analysis Office integrated into Microsoft PowerPoint and take a closer look at the basic functionality.

4.2.2 Advanced Analysis Office for Microsoft PowerPoint — Basic Steps

Let's review the basic functionality in more detail, but not as close as we did for Advanced Analysis Office for Microsoft Excel, because most of the functionality is identical. Instead, let's look at the parts of the integration that differ between Microsoft PowerPoint and Microsoft Excel.

1. Start Advanced Analysis Office with Microsoft PowerPoint via the menu path START • PROGRAMS • SAP BUSINESSOBJECTS • ADVANCED ANALYSIS FOR MICROSOFT POWERPOINT.

2. Select the INSERT • SELECT DATA SOURCE option from the Advanced Analysis ribbon.

3. Select the connection to our previously created BW Query and provide your SAP credentials to log on to the SAP NetWeaver BW system.

4. Provide the values for the prompting part based on the variables from our BW Query.

5. Click OK.

6. In the FIT TABLE screen, set the MAXIMUM NUMBER OF ROWS to the value of 12 and use the ABBREVIATE TABLE ON THIS SLIDE option (see Figure 4.93).

7. Click OK.

8. Use the standard features and functions, such as resizing the table or decreasing the font size, to make sure the table fits onto your slide (see Figure 4.94).

Advanced Analysis Office — Microsoft PowerPoint | **4.2**

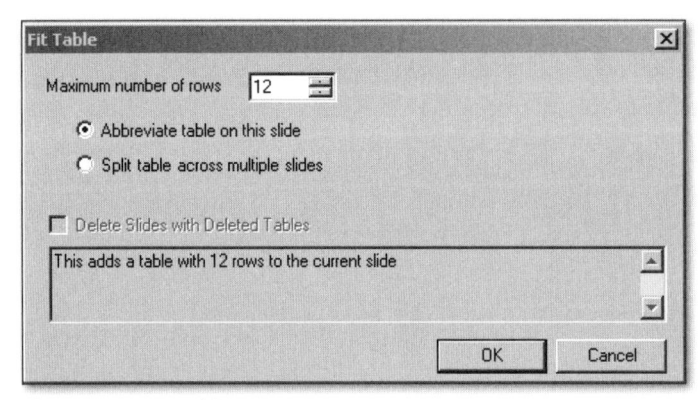

Figure 4.93 Fit Table

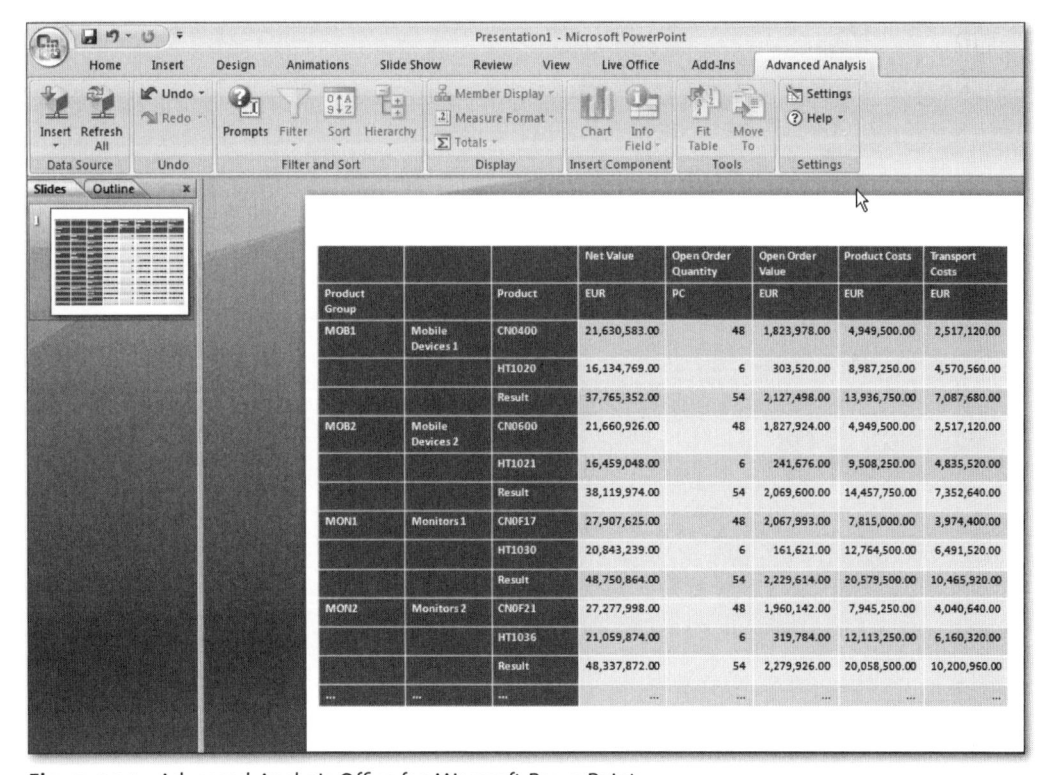

Figure 4.94 Advanced Analysis Office for Microsoft PowerPoint

175

Please note that Advanced Analysis Office for Microsoft PowerPoint does not provide you any capability to change the navigation status of your BEx Query. Advanced Analysis Office for Microsoft PowerPoint creates a table based on the definition of the BEx Query or the BEx Query View. Because of this inability to change the navigation status of your query, Advanced Analysis Office for Microsoft Excel gives you the option of creating a slide based on the workbook in Microsoft Excel, which is a functionality we will learn in the next chapter.

> **Advanced Analysis Office and Table Layout**
>
> After you insert your table into the Microsoft PowerPoint slide, you can use all of the standard menu options for Microsoft PowerPoint to change the layout and size of rows, columns, or the table overall.

9. Select the table column for PRODUCT GROUP.
10. Navigate to the SORT menu in the Advanced Analysis Office ribbon.
11. Select the MORE SORT OPTIONS... option (see Figure 4.95).

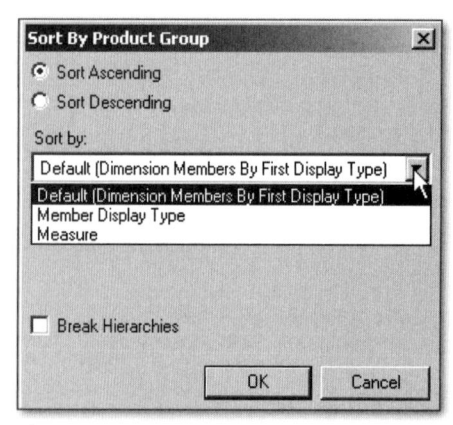

Figure 4.95 Sort Options

The Sort options are identical to those offered in Advanced Analysis Office for Microsoft Excel.

12. Select the option to sort PRODUCT GROUP based on the key value by setting the SORT BY option to MEMBER DISPLAY TYPE and the DISPLAY option to KEY.
13. Click OK.

Advanced Analysis Office — Microsoft PowerPoint | **4.2**

14. Now select PRODUCT GROUP and use the MEMBER DISPLAY menu in the ribbon (see Figure 4.96).

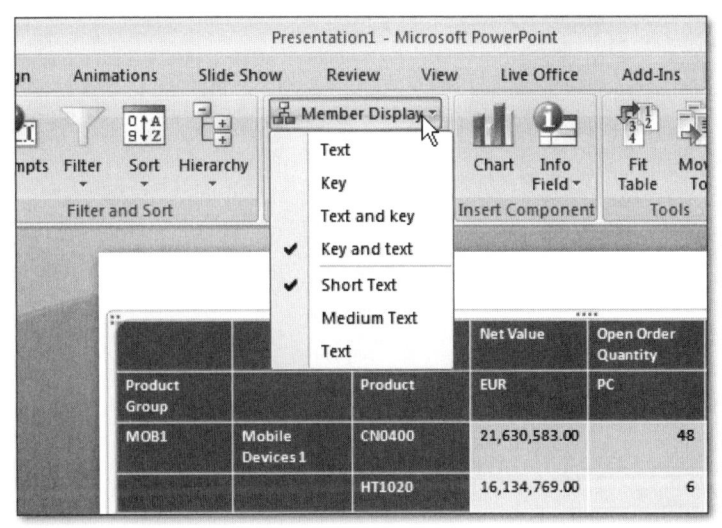

Figure 4.96 Member Display

15. Select the options to show the characteristic with KEY AND TEXT.
16. Now select the NET VALUE key figure in the crosstab and open the MEASURE FORMAT menu (see Figure 4.97).

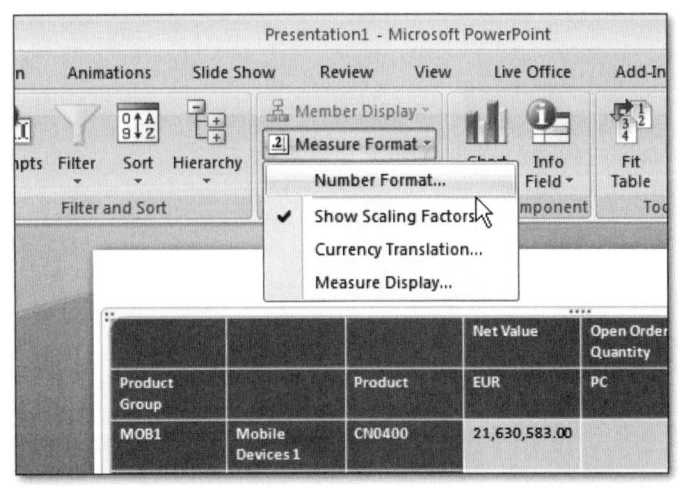

Figure 4.97 Measure Display

4 | Advanced Analysis Office — Basic Functions

17. Select the NUMBER FORMAT menu (see Figure 4.98).

Figure 4.98 Scaling Factor and Decimal Places

18. Set the SCALING FACTOR to THOUSANDS and set the DECIMAL PLACES to 0.

19. Make sure the DISPLAY SCALING FACTOR AND UNITS IN THE HEADER FOR ALL MEASURE option is activated.

20. Select the first row that represents a subtotal row in your crosstab. Navigate to the TOTALS menu in the ribbon (see Figure 4.99).

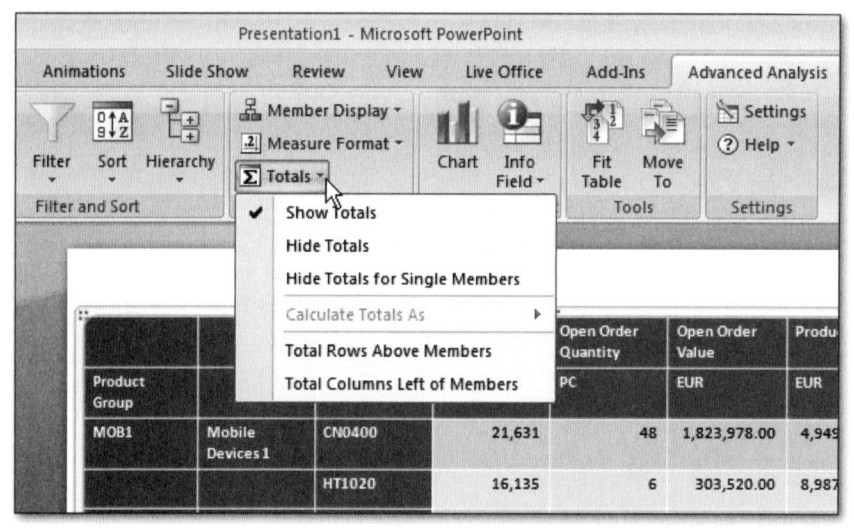

Figure 4.99 Menu Totals

The functionality for showing or hiding the grand totals or subtotals and the functionality to show the rows above the members or to the left of the members is identical to the workflow in Microsoft Excel shown in Section 4.1.10, Totals and Subtotals.

21. Select the HIDE TOTALS option.
22. Select the column header for NET VALUE.
23. Navigate to the FILTER menu.

    Please note that Advanced Analysis Office for Microsoft PowerPoint does not provide the same scope with regard to the FILTER BY MEASURE capability. As shown in Figure 4.100, you can only use the FILTER BY MEASURE feature for ALL DIMENSIONS INDEPENDENTLY and not for the most detailed rows or columns.

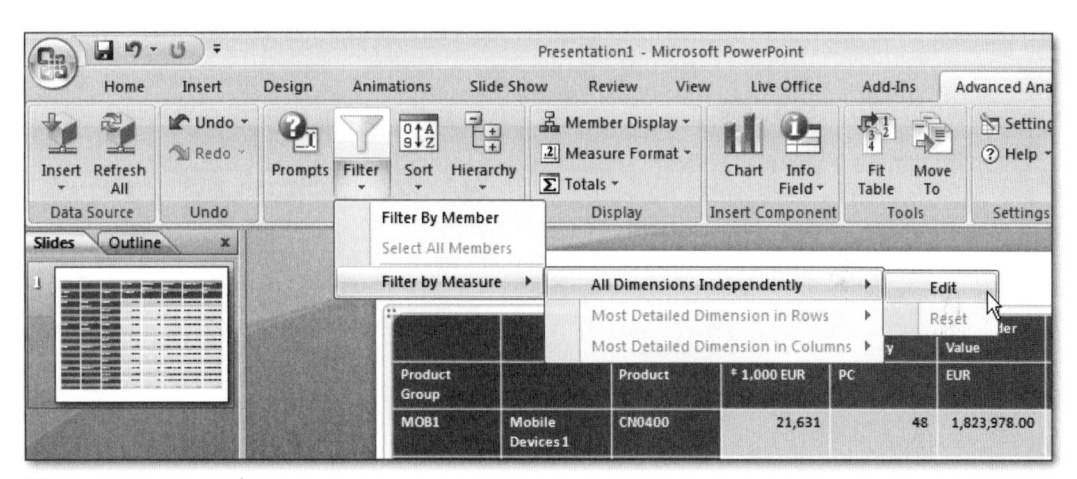

Figure 4.100 Menu Filter

24. Follow the menu path FILTER • FILTER BY MEASURE • ALL DIMENSIONS INDEPENDENTLY • EDIT.
25. Define a top three filter (see Figure 4.101).

4 | Advanced Analysis Office — Basic Functions

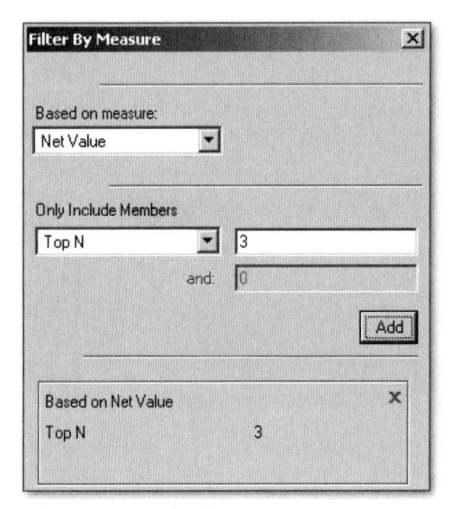

Figure 4.101 Filter by Measure

26. Click ADD.
27. Click OK (see Figure 4.102).

Product Group		Product	Net Value * 1,000 EUR	Open Order Quantity PC	Open Order Value * 1,000 EUR	Product Costs * 1,000 EUR	Transport Costs * 1,000 EUR
MON1	Monitors 1	CN0F17	27,908	48	2,068	7,815	3,974
		HT1030	20,843	6	162	12,765	6,492
NB1	Notebooks 1	CN00S1	38,721	54	2,278	13,807	7,021
		HT1000	40,369	6	334	24,617	12,519
NB2	Notebooks 2	CN00S2	36,788	42	2,130	13,286	6,756
		HT1001	34,795	6	155	21,882	11,128
Overall Result			323,648	324	13,604	142,624	72,533

Figure 4.102 Advanced Analysis Office for Microsoft PowerPoint

Filter by Member and Filter by Measure for Characteristics

The functionality of Filter by Member and Filter by Measure as part of the crosstab in Microsoft PowerPoint is identical to the functionality shown in Microsoft Excel. Therefore, we will not repeat those steps as part of this section.

28. Next, use the standard Microsoft PowerPoint menu options to reduce the overall size of the table by reducing the size of the rows and columns and place the table into the upper part of your slide (see Figure 4.103).

Product Group		Product	Net Value *1,000 EUR	Open Order Quantity PC	Open Order Value *1,000 EUR	Product Costs *1,000 EUR	Transport Costs *1,000 EUR
MON1	Monitors 1	CN0F17	27,908	48	2,068	7,815	3,974
		HT1030	20,843	6	162	12,765	6,492
NB1	Notebooks 1	CN00S1	38,721	54	2,278	13,807	7,021
		HT1000	40,369	6	334	24,617	12,519
NB2	Notebooks 2	CN00S2	36,788	42	2,130	13,286	6,756
		HT1001	34,795	6	155	21,882	11,128
Overall Result			323,648	324	13,604	142,624	72,533

Figure 4.103 Advanced Analysis Office for Microsoft PowerPoint

29. Select the crosstab you inserted into your slide.
30. Follow the INFO FIELD • DATA SOURCE NAME menu path from the Advanced Analysis Office ribbon.
31. Place the newly added textbox below your crosstab (see Figure 4.104).

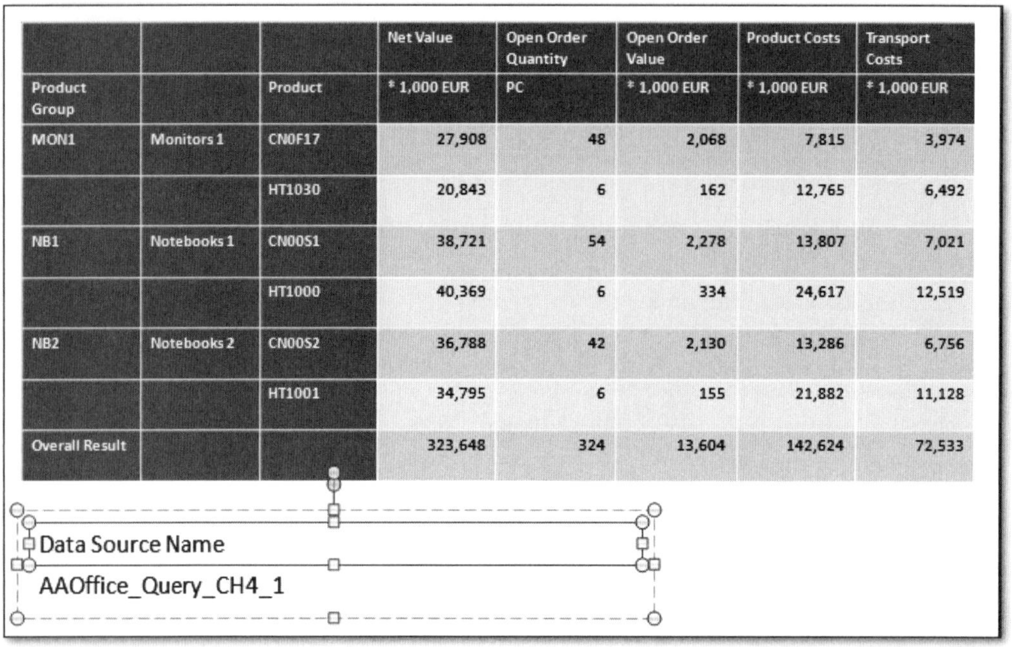

4 | Advanced Analysis Office — Basic Functions

Product Group		Product	Net Value * 1,000 EUR	Open Order Quantity PC	Open Order Value * 1,000 EUR	Product Costs * 1,000 EUR	Transport Costs * 1,000 EUR
MON1	Monitors 1	CN0F17	27,908	48	2,068	7,815	3,974
		HT1030	20,843	6	162	12,765	6,492
NB1	Notebooks 1	CN00S1	38,721	54	2,278	13,807	7,021
		HT1000	40,369	6	334	24,617	12,519
NB2	Notebooks 2	CN00S2	36,788	42	2,130	13,286	6,756
		HT1001	34,795	6	155	21,882	11,128
Overall Result			323,648	324	13,604	142,624	72,533

Data Source Name
AAOffice_Query_CH4_1

Figure 4.104 Info Fields

Advanced Analysis Office in Microsoft PowerPoint creates the Info Fields as a grouping of text boxes. The grouping is done using standard Microsoft PowerPoint menus. You can also ungroup the objects and place them as you wish.

32. Repeat the previous step and insert all of the available Info Fields, ungroup them, and then arrange them next to each other (see Figure 4.105).

33. Select your crosstab on the slide.

34. Select the CHART menu from the Advanced Analysis Office ribbon (see Figure 4.106).

The newly created chart is placed on top of your crosstab.

Advanced Analysis Office — Microsoft PowerPoint | **4.2**

Product Group		Product	Net Value * 1,000 EUR	Open Order Quantity PC	Open Order Value * 1,000 EUR	Product Costs * 1,000 EUR	Transport Costs * 1,000 EUR
MON1	Monitors 1	CN0F17	27,908	48	2,068	7,815	3,974
		HT1030	20,843	6	162	12,765	6,492
NB1	Notebooks 1	CN0051	38,721	54	2,278	13,807	7,021
		HT1000	40,369	6	334	24,617	12,519
NB2	Notebooks 2	CN0052	36,788	42	2,130	13,286	6,756
		HT1001	34,795	6	155	21,882	11,128
Overall Result			323,648	324	13,604	142,624	72,533

Data Source Name   AAOffice_Query_CH4_1
Last Data Update   3/9/2010 9:05:50 AM
Key Date   6/11/2010 5:00:00 AM
Effective Filters
Calendar Year/Month   01.2010; 02.2010; 03.2010
Calendar Year   2006 - 2011
Variables
Range Variable for Calendar Year   2006 - 2011

Figure 4.105   Info Fields

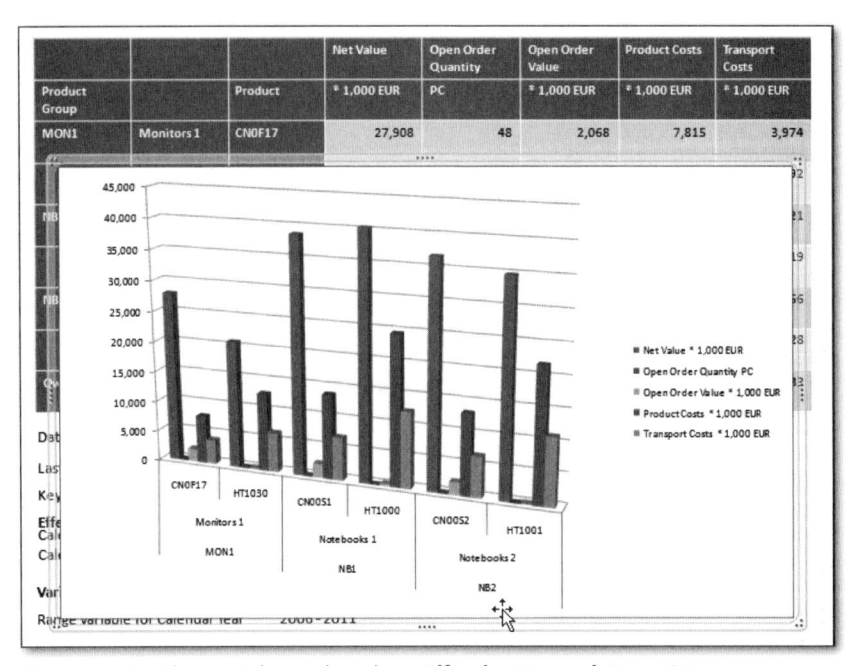

Figure 4.106   Chart in Advanced Analysis Office for Microsoft PowerPoint

183

35. Use the standard Microsoft PowerPoint NEW SLIDE menu on the HOME tab of the Microsoft PowerPoint ribbon.
36. Navigate back to the slide with your crosstab and chart.
37. Select the chart and use the MOVE TO menu from the Advanced Analysis Office ribbon.

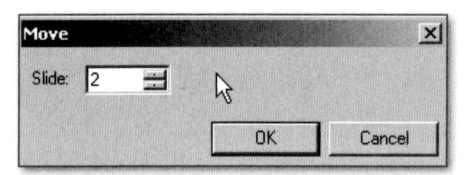

Figure 4.107 Menu Move To

38. Set the value for the SLIDE to 2.
39. Click OK.

    The chart you created with Advanced Analysis Office is moved to slide 2, but will still be connected to your crosstab; any changes performed on the crosstab that influence the actual data that is being displayed will also impact the chart.

40. Select the chart component.
41. Right-click the chart and navigate to the CHART OBJECT menu.

    You have the option of editing the chart inside Microsoft PowerPoint, and you can open the chart, which will open a separate window inside of Microsoft Excel.

42. Now click the OFFICE button in Microsoft PowerPoint (see Figure 4.108).
43. Select the SAVE PRESENTATION menu (see Figure 4.109).

Figure 4.108 Microsoft PowerPoint Office Button

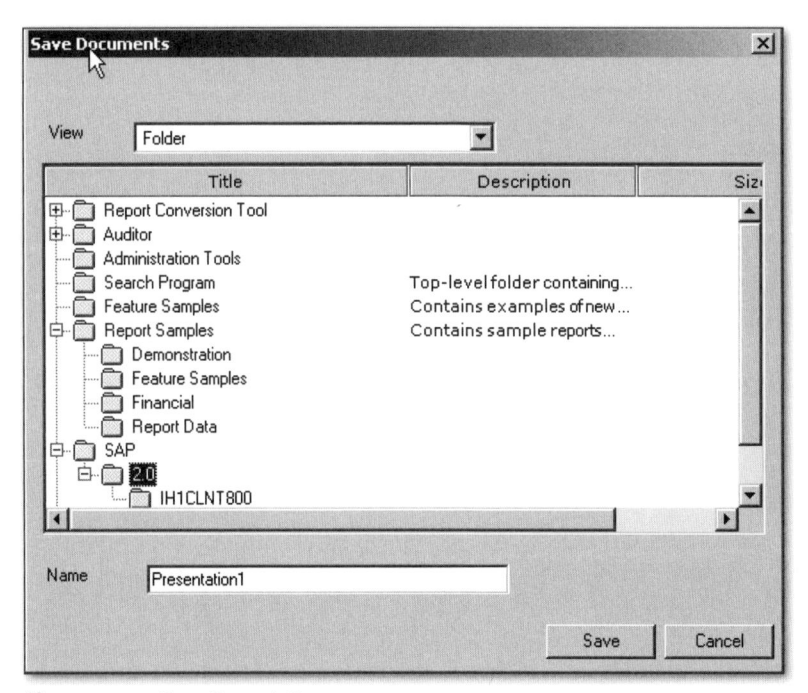

Figure 4.109 Save Presentation

Now you can enter a name for your presentation and save the presentation to your SAP BusinessObjects Enterprise system and share your design with other users.

44. Enter a name for the presentation and click SAVE.

> **Open and Saving Presentations**
>
> The menu options Open Presentation and Save Presentation work under the assumption that a connection to your SAP BusinessObjects Enterprise system already exists. If you work with a local connection for your SAP NetWeaver BW system, you need to follow the INSERT • SELECT DATA SOURCE menu path and log on to the SAP BusinessObjects Enterprise so Open Presentation and Save Presentation can leverage the connection to your SAP BusinessObjects Enterprise system.

In this section, you learned the basic steps in Advanced Analysis Office for Microsoft PowerPoint. In the next chapter, we will move to the more advanced capabilities of Advanced Analysis Office for Microsoft Excel and PowerPoint.

4.3 Summary

In this chapter, we reviewed the basic functionality of Advanced Analysis Office in Microsoft Excel and PowerPoint. In addition, we learned the differences between Advanced Analysis Office in Microsoft Excel and PowerPoint. In the next chapter, we will take a look at the more advanced capabilities of Advanced Analysis Office, such as working with hierarchies.

Now that we've gone over the basic functionality of Advanced Analysis Office, let's move on to more advanced topics such as hierarchies and custom calculations.

5 Advanced Analysis Office — Advanced Functions

So far, we've reviewed the basic features and functions of Advanced Analysis Office. In the next couple of sections, we will look at advanced topics, such as handling hierarchies and calculations, in Microsoft Excel and PowerPoint.

5.1 Advanced Functionality in Advanced Analysis Office for Microsoft Excel

In this section, we will look at some advanced functions of Advanced Analysis Office. All of the examples are based on the SAP NetWeaver Demo model and each SAP Business Explorer (BEx) Query is shown and explained.

5.1.1 Using Hierarchies

In this section, we will leverage Advanced Analysis Office in Microsoft Excel and leverage hierarchies we defined as part of our BEx Query. To do so, let's create a BEx Query that makes use of hierarchies.

Figure 5.1 shows the BEx Query we are going to use, which is based on the demo cube `SAP Demo Sales and Distribution`: Overview (technical name: 0D_SD_C03). The BEx Query contains the following characteristics:

- SOLD-TO PARTY
- SALES GROUP

- Material
- Sales organization
- Distribution channel

The BEx Query contains the following key figures:

- Net val. in statCur
- Costs stats currency
- Open orders
- Open orders qty

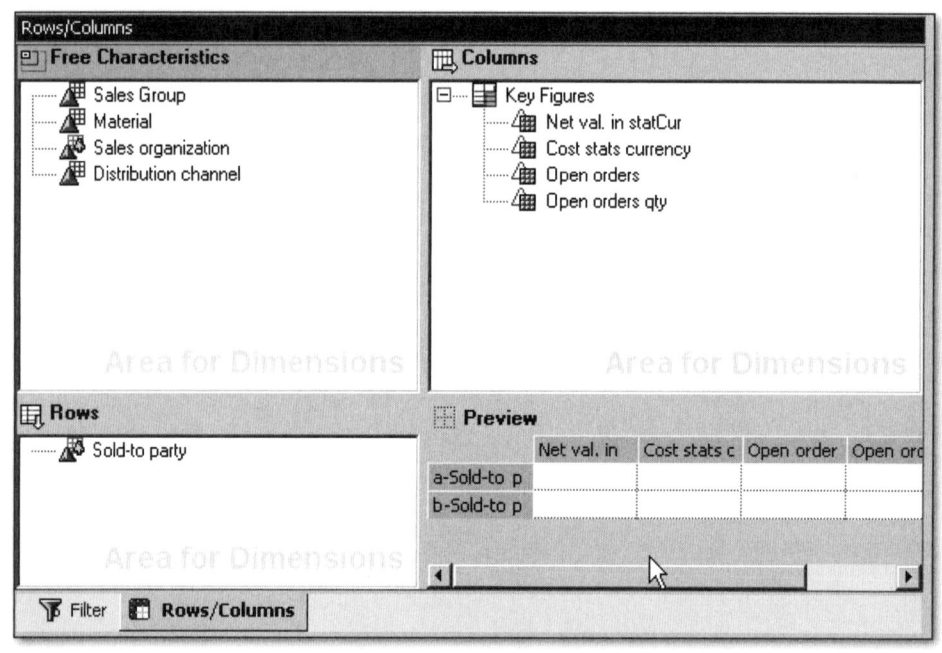

Figure 5.1 BEx Query

In addition, the BEx Query contains hierarchies for two of the characteristics.

Figure 5.2 shows the details of the hierarchy configuration. The Sold-to party characteristic is configured with a time-dependent hierarchy structure.

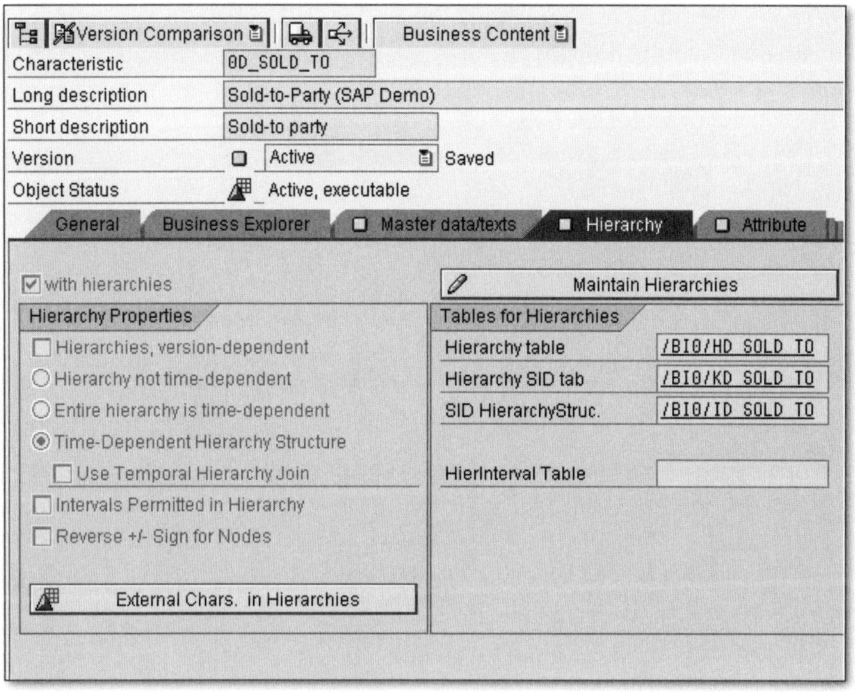

Advanced Functionality in Advanced Analysis Office for Microsoft Excel | 5.1

Figure 5.2 Characteristic Sold-to-Party

Figure 5.3 shows the hierarchy we will use in our SOLD-TO PARTY example. In the SOLD-TO PARTY hierarchy, all members are available at any time.

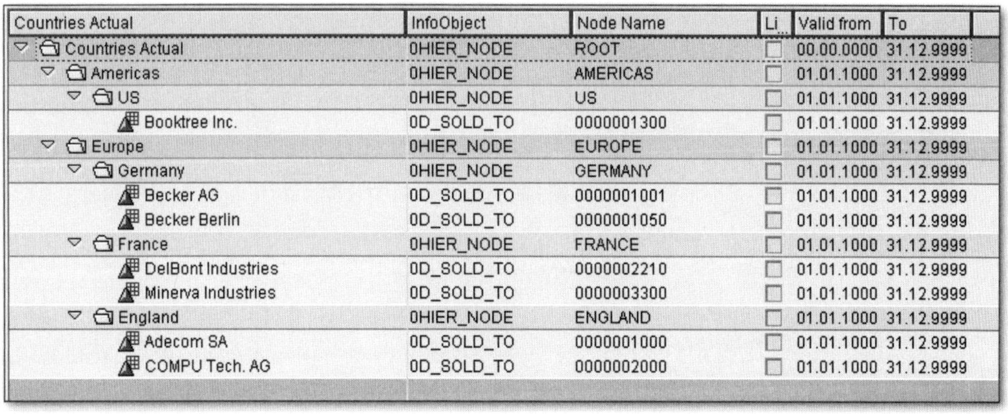

Figure 5.3 Hierarchy Countries Actual

Figure 5.4 shows the configuration details for the SALES ORGANIZATION hierarchy. The characteristic is configured with a time-dependent hierarchy structure.

```
Version Comparison              Business Content
Characteristic         0D_SALE_ORG
Long description       Sales Organization (SAP Demo)
Short description      Sales organization
Version                ☐ Active           ≣ Saved
Object Status             Active, executable
    General    Business Explorer   ☐ Master data/texts   ■ Hierarchy    ☐ Attribute

☑ with hierarchies                          ✎       Maintain Hierarchies
Hierarchy Properties                        Tables for Hierarchies
☐ Hierarchies, version-dependent            Hierarchy table        /BI0/HD_SALE_ORG
○ Hierarchy not time-dependent              Hierarchy SID tab      /BI0/KD_SALE_ORG
○ Entire hierarchy is time-dependent        SID HierarchyStruc.    /BI0/ID_SALE_ORG
◉ Time-Dependent Hierarchy Structure
    ☐ Use Temporal Hierarchy Join           HierInterval Table
☐ Intervals Permitted in Hierarchy
☐ Reverse +/- Sign for Nodes

       External Chars. in Hierarchies
```

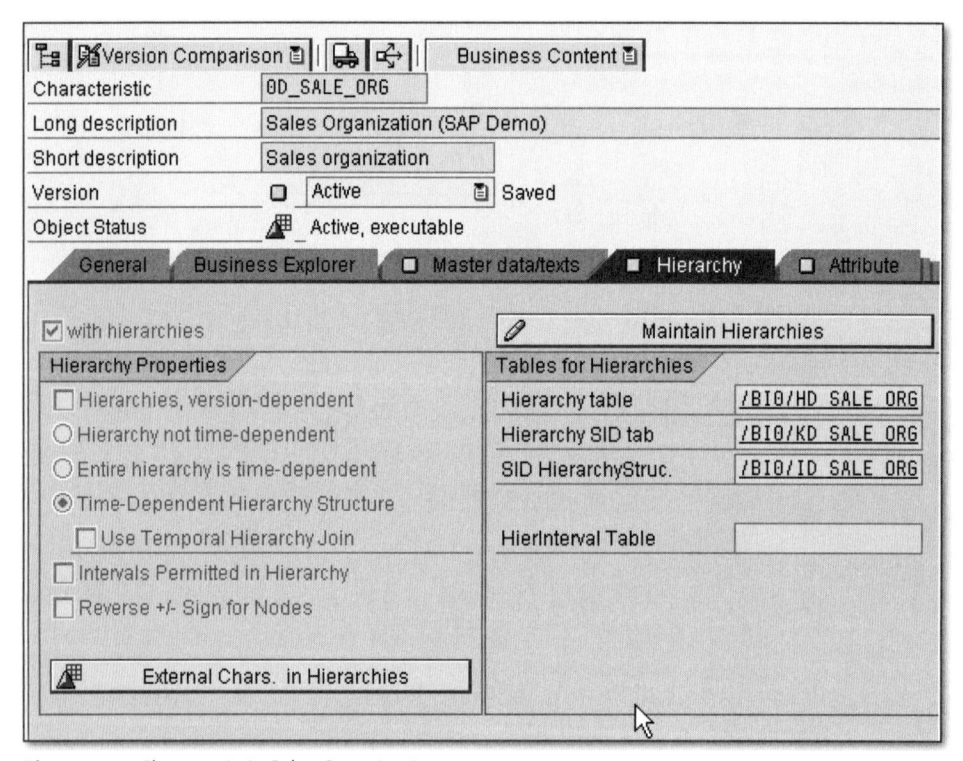

Figure 5.4 Characteristic Sales Organization

Figure 5.5 shows the configured hierarchy for SALES ORGANIZATION with a time-dependent hierarchy structure. Note that the offices in MARSEILLE and BIRMINGHAM were opened in January 2010.

In addition, the BEx Query contains a global key date variable and both hierarchies are configured to leverage it to resolve any time dependency.

PM Sales Organization	InfoObject	Node name	Li	Valid from	To
▽ 🗀 PM Sales Organization	0HIER_NODE	ROOT	☐	01.01.2002	31.12.9999
▽ 🗀 Europe	0HIER_NODE	EUROPE	☐	01.01.1000	31.12.9999
▽ 🗀 Germany	0HIER_NODE	GERMANY	☐	01.01.1000	31.12.9999
Frankfurt	0D_SALE_ORG	1512	☐	01.01.1000	31.12.9999
Berlin	0D_SALE_ORG	1514	☐	01.01.1000	31.12.9999
Munich	0D_SALE_ORG	1516	☐	01.01.1000	31.12.9999
Hamburg	0D_SALE_ORG	1518	☐	01.01.1000	31.12.9999
▽ 🗀 France	0HIER_NODE	FRANCE	☐	01.01.1000	31.12.9999
Paris	0D_SALE_ORG	1592	☐	01.01.1000	31.12.9999
Marseille	0D_SALE_ORG	1594	☐	01.01.2010	31.12.9999
▽ 🗀 GB	0HIER_NODE	GB	☐	01.01.1000	31.12.9999
London	0D_SALE_ORG	1552	☐	01.01.1000	31.12.9999
Birmingham	0D_SALE_ORG	1554	☐	01.01.2010	31.12.9999
▽ 🗀 Switzerland	0HIER_NODE	SWITZERLAND	☐	01.01.1000	31.12.9999
Grenoble	0D_SALE_ORG	1596	☐	01.01.1000	31.12.2009
▽ 🗀 Americas	0HIER_NODE	AMERICAS	☐	01.01.1000	31.12.9999
▽ 🗀 USA	0HIER_NODE	USA	☐	01.01.1000	31.12.9999
New York	0D_SALE_ORG	1612	☐	01.01.1000	31.12.9999
San Francisco	0D_SALE_ORG	1614	☐	01.01.1000	31.12.9999
Illinois	0D_SALE_ORG	1616	☐	01.01.1000	31.12.9999
Colorado	0D_SALE_ORG	1618	☐	01.01.1000	31.12.9999
Alaska	0D_SALE_ORG	1620	☐	01.01.1000	31.12.9999
▽ 🗀 Canada	0HIER_NODE	CANADA	☐	01.01.1000	31.12.9999
Toronto	0D_SALE_ORG	1662	☐	01.01.1000	31.12.9999
Vancouver	0D_SALE_ORG	1664	☐	01.01.1000	31.12.2009

Figure 5.5 Hierarchy for Sales Organization

Let's use the BEx Query to leverage the hierarchies in Advanced Analysis Office for Microsoft Excel:

1. Start Advanced Analysis Office with Microsoft Excel via the menu path START • PROGRAMS • SAP BUSINESSOBJECTS • ADVANCED ANALYSIS FOR MICROSOFT EXCEL.

2. Select the INSERT • SELECT DATA SOURCE option from the Advanced Analysis ribbon.

3. You should see the log-on screen for SAP BusinessObjects Enterprise.

4. If you do not want to share the workbook with your colleagues, or do not want to use a shared connection, you can click on the Skip button. In our example, we use the Skip option.

5. Click Skip.

6. Now you are presented with the list of available SAP systems based on entries in your SAP Logon pad.

7. Select the entry for your SAP system.

8. Click Next.

9. Enter your SAP credentials in the log-on screen and click Next.

10. Select the BEx Query that we created based on the definition shown above.

11. You need to provide an input value for the key date variable. In our example, we will use January 01, 2010, as the value for now (see Figure 5.6).

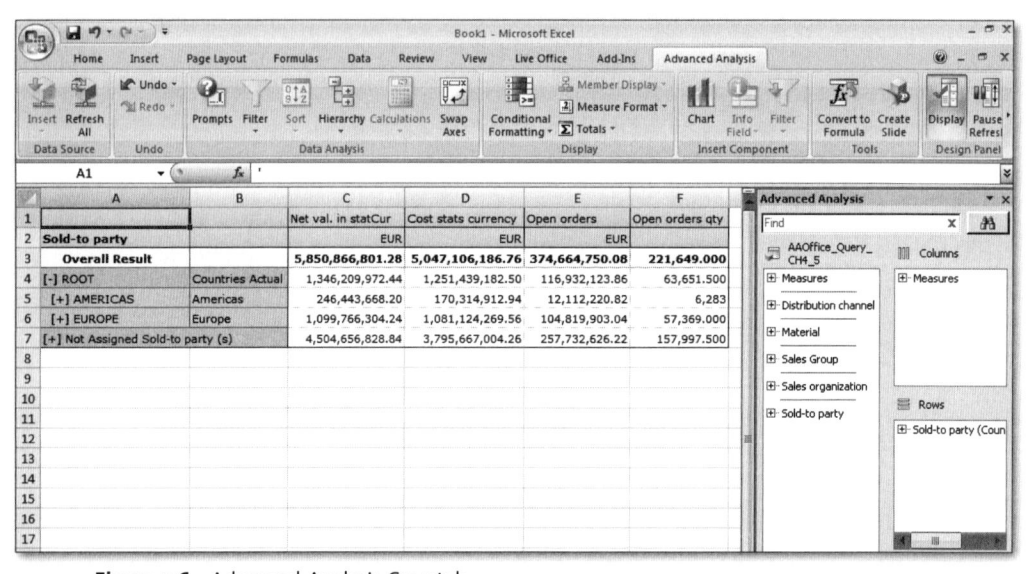

Figure 5.6 Advanced Analysis Crosstab

You are presented with the crosstab (see Figure 5.6) based on the BEx Query definition. Now you can leverage the hierarchies of both characteristics.

12. Navigate to the panel on the right-hand side and open both SOLD-TO PARTY and SALES ORGANIZATION (see Figure 5.7).

   Even though we activated specific hierarchies, Advanced Analysis Office still lets us leverage the nonhierarchical display (FLAT PRESENTATION) or any other available hierarchy. Those hierarchies configured as part of the underlying BEx Query are shown in bold. You can use any available hierarchy and add them to your crosstab via drag-and-drop navigation or by leveraging the context menu.

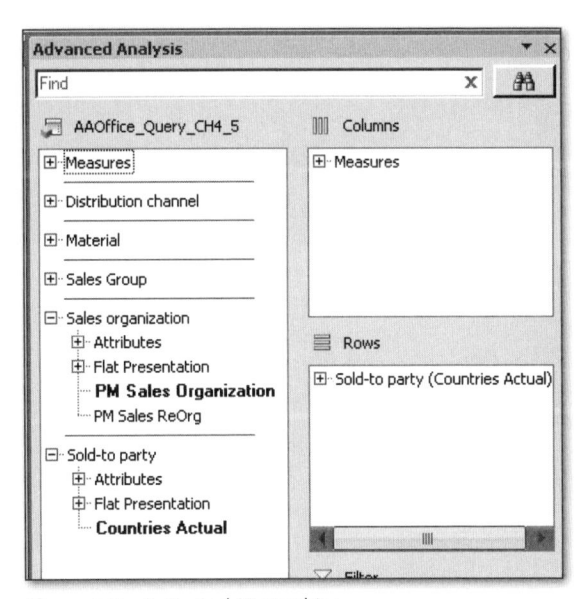

Figure 5.7 Activated Hierarchies

13. To collapse the hierarchical display, use the + and - symbols in front of each member of the hierarchy individually (see Figure 5.8).

5 | Advanced Analysis Office — Advanced Functions

	A	B	C
1			Net val. in statCur
2	**Sold-to party**		EUR
3	**Overall Result**		**5,850,866,801.28**
4	[-] ROOT	Countries Actual	1,346,209,972.44
5	[-] AMERICAS	Americas	246,443,668.20
6	[-] US	US	246,443,668.20
7	1300	Booktree Inc.	246,443,668.20
8	[-] EUROPE	Europe	1,099,766,304.24
9	[+] GERMANY	Germany	186,487,011.64
10	[+] FRANCE	France	666,842,998.70
11	[+] ENGLAND	England	246,436,293.90
12	[+] Not Assigned Sold-to party (s)		4,504,656,828.84
13			

Figure 5.8 Expanded Hierarchy

14. Select the hierarchy node element GERMANY.

15. Right-click to open the context menu and select the EXPAND option (see Figure 5.9).

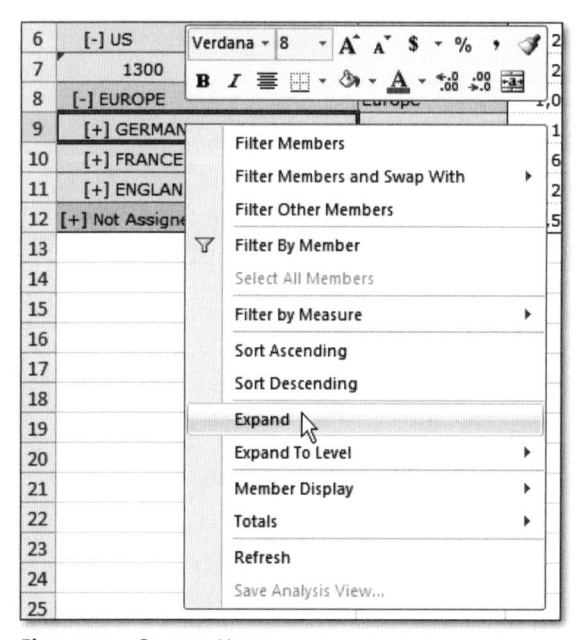

Figure 5.9 Context Menu

194

Advanced Functionality in Advanced Analysis Office for Microsoft Excel | **5.1**

The EXPAND option is also available in the HIERARCHY menu of the Advanced Analysis Office ribbon (see Figure 5.10).

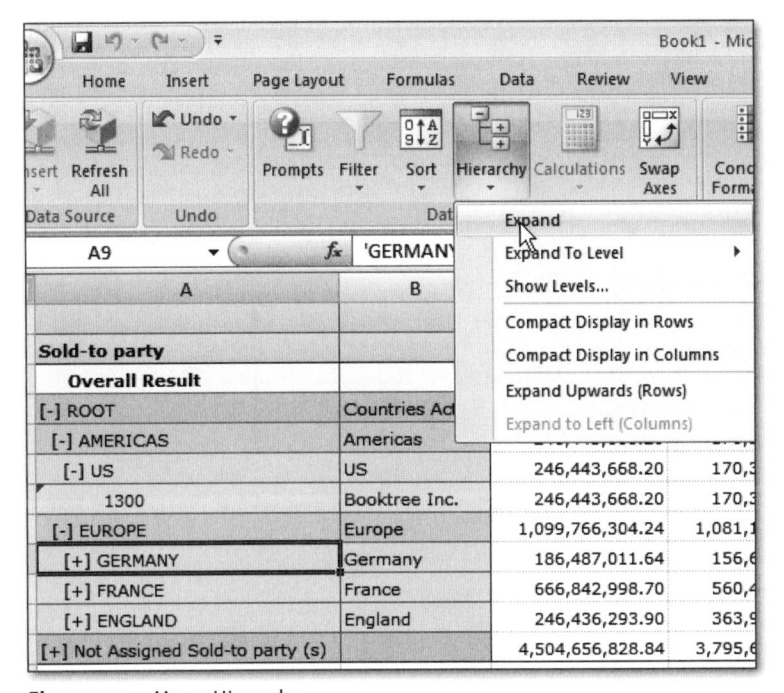

Figure 5.10 Menu Hierarchy

16. Select the hierarchy node element EUROPE.

17. Right-click to open the context menu and select EXPAND TO LEVEL (see Figure 5.11).

    The EXPAND TO LEVEL option lets you expand several hierarchy nodes below the selected member to the level of depth you select. The number of levels shown depends on the depth of the hierarchical structure and the member you selected.

18. Select the LEVEL 04 option (see Figure 5.12).

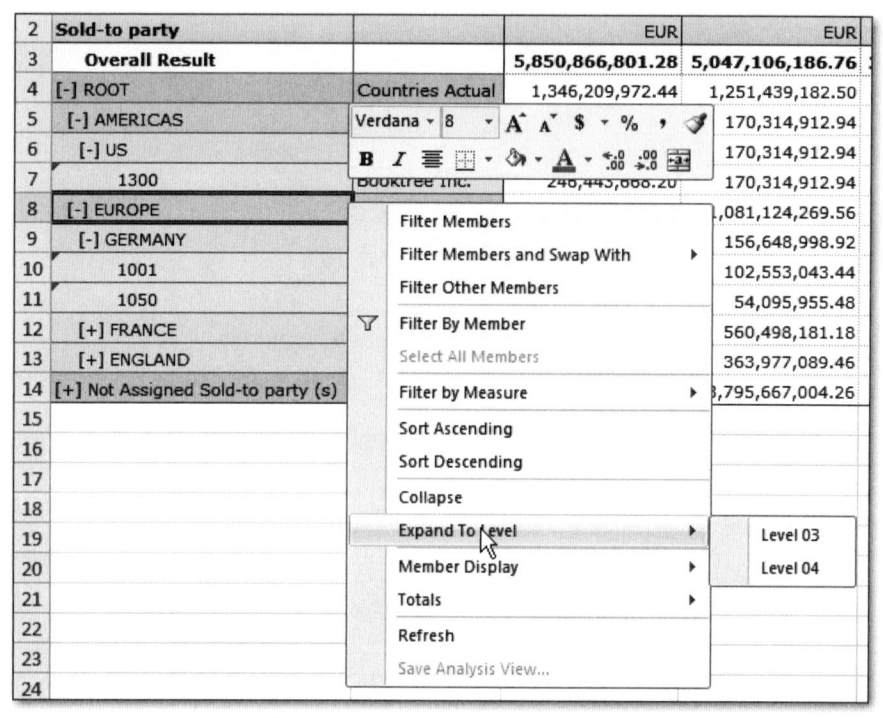

5 | Advanced Analysis Office — Advanced Functions

Figure 5.11 Expand to Level

Figure 5.12 Expanded Hierarchical Structure

196

Now EUROPE has been expanded down to level 04 for all elements below the hierarchy node EUROPE. Hierarchy nodes on the same level as EUROPE — in our example the NOT ASSIGNED SOLD-TO PARTY node — are not impacted by this command because only elements below EUROPE are expanded.

Please note that EXPAND TO LEVEL is also available in the HIERARCHY menu in the Advanced Analysis Office ribbon.

19. Navigate to the top level of your hierarchy.
20. Follow the HIERARCHY • SHOW LEVELS menu path from the Advanced Analysis Office ribbon (see Figure 5.13).

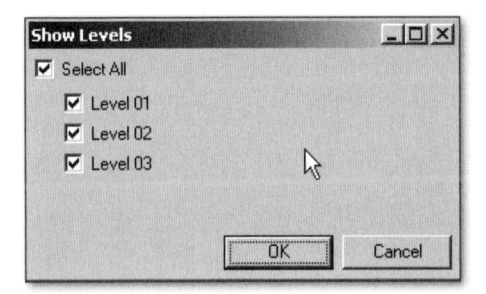

Figure 5.13 Show Levels

Now you can select hierarchy levels as you need them in your workbook. The list you see does not include the lowest level of members — the levels shown are the actual hierarchical levels. You can also skip levels.

21. Select LEVEL 01 and LEVEL 03.
22. Click OK.

Based on our selections, the workbook (see Figure 5.14) now shows countries from Europe on the same level as the hierarchy node US, because we removed LEVEL 02 from our hierarchical display.

23. Select the top-level member ROOT from your hierarchy.
24. Select EXPAND UPWARDS (ROWS) (see Figure 5.15).

5 | Advanced Analysis Office — Advanced Functions

	A	B	C
1			Net val. in statCur
2	**Sold-to party**		EUR
3	**Overall Result**		5,850,866,801.28
4	[-] ROOT	Countries Actual	1,346,209,972.44
5	[-] US	US	246,443,668.20
6	1300	Booktree Inc.	246,443,668.20
7	[-] GERMANY	Germany	186,487,011.64
8	1001	Becker AG	122,086,994.64
9	1050	Becker Berlin	64,400,017.00
10	[-] FRANCE	France	666,842,998.70
11	2210	DelBont Industries	266,880,688.80
12	3300	Minerva Industries	399,962,309.90
13	[-] ENGLAND	England	246,436,293.90
14	1000	Adecom SA	138,148,847.80
15	2000	COMPU Tech. AG	108,287,446.10
16	[+] Not Assigned Sold-to party (s)		4,504,656,828.84
17			
18			

Figure 5.14 Shown Hierarchy Levels

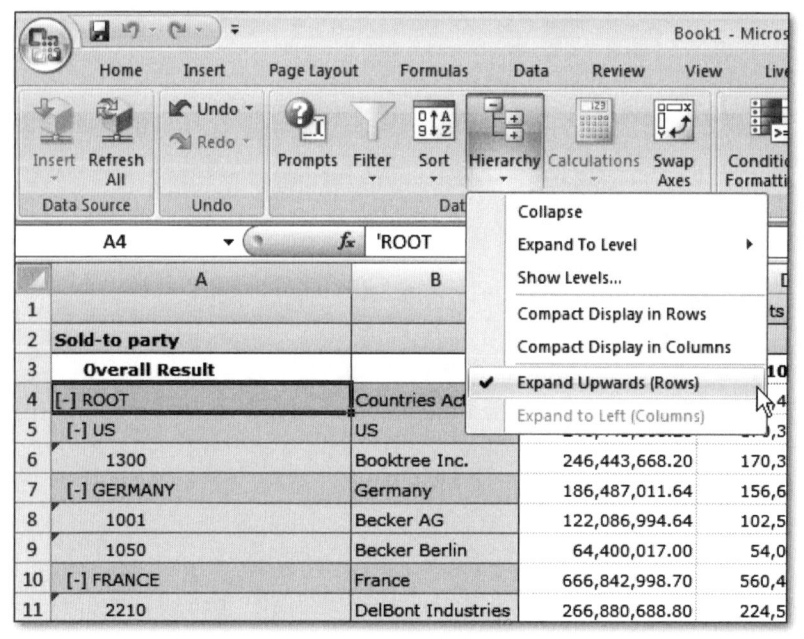

Figure 5.15 Menu Hierarchy

Please note that EXPAND UPWARDS (ROWS) is a simple menu option that can be activated or deactivated.

Based on our selection, the totals and subtotals for the hierarchy nodes are now displayed below the leaves in our hierarchy (see Figure 5.16).

	A	B	C
1			Net val. in statCur
2	**Sold-to party**		EUR
3	1300	Booktree Inc.	246,443,668.20
4	[-] US	US	246,443,668.20
5	1001	Becker AG	122,086,994.64
6	1050	Becker Berlin	64,400,017.00
7	[-] GERMANY	Germany	186,487,011.64
8	2210	DelBont Industries	266,880,688.80
9	3300	Minerva Industries	399,962,309.90
10	[-] FRANCE	France	666,842,998.70
11	1000	Adecom SA	138,148,847.80
12	2000	COMPU Tech. AG	108,287,446.10
13	[-] ENGLAND	England	246,436,293.90
14	[-] ROOT	Countries Actual	1,346,209,972.44
15	[+] Not Assigned Sold-to party (s)		4,504,656,828.84
16	**Overall Result**		**5,850,866,801.28**

Figure 5.16 Hierarchical Crosstab

25. Select the top-level node ROOT from your hierarchy.
26. Follow the SORT • MORE SORT OPTIONS menu from the Advanced Analysis Office ribbon (see Figure 5.17).

The options provided in the sort dialog when using a hierarchy are identical to those options provided when using a standard characteristic. In addition to those standard options, you can also leverage HIERARCHY DEFINITION for the SORT BY options to leverage the defined hierarchy structure for the sorting.

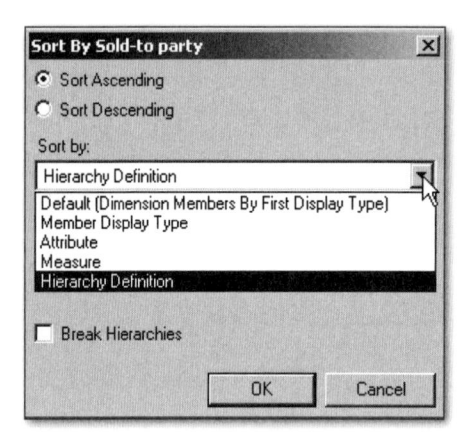

5 | Advanced Analysis Office — Advanced Functions

Figure 5.17 More Sort Options

27. Set the SORT BY option to MEASURE (see Figure 5.18).

Figure 5.18 Break Hierarchies

28. Set MEASURE to the NET VALUE key figure.
29. Activate the BREAK HIERARCHIES options.

   As shown in Figure 5.19, all members of the hierarchy — including hierarchy nodes — are now sorted in an ascending manner based on the value of NET VALUE. The BREAK HIERARCHIES option provides you with the ability to arrange

200

for a sort independent of the hierarchical order while still keeping all hierarchy nodes as part of the crosstab. This way, you can quickly recognize, for example, that FRANCE has the highest value for Net Sales out of all of the countries.

	A	B	C
1			Net val. in statCur	Cos
2	Sold-to party		EUR
3	1050	Becker Berlin	64,400,017.00
4	2000	COMPU Tech. AG	108,287,446.10
5	1001	Becker AG	122,086,994.64
6	1000	Adecom SA	138,148,847.80
7	GERMANY	Germany	186,487,011.64
8	ENGLAND	England	246,436,293.90
9	1300	Booktree Inc.	246,443,668.20
10	US	US	246,443,668.20
11	2210	DelBont Industries	266,880,688.80
12	3300	Minerva Industries	399,962,309.90
13	FRANCE	France	666,842,998.70
14	ROOT	Countries Actual	1,346,209,972.44
15	Not Assigned Sold-to party (s)		4,504,656,828.84
16	Overall Result		5,850,866,801.28

Figure 5.19 Sort with Break Hierarchies

30. Select a member of your hierarchy.

31. Right-click to open the context menu and select FILTER BY MEMBER (see Figure 5.20).

The Member Selector is shown in a hierarchical display and lets you select complete hierarchy nodes with all children below (for example, ENGLAND) or explicitly select elements of a hierarchy node (for example, FRANCE) or exclude complete hierarchy nodes (for example, GERMANY), and depending on your selection the symbols will change. In addition, the Member Selector also lets you change the type of display (see Figure 5.21).

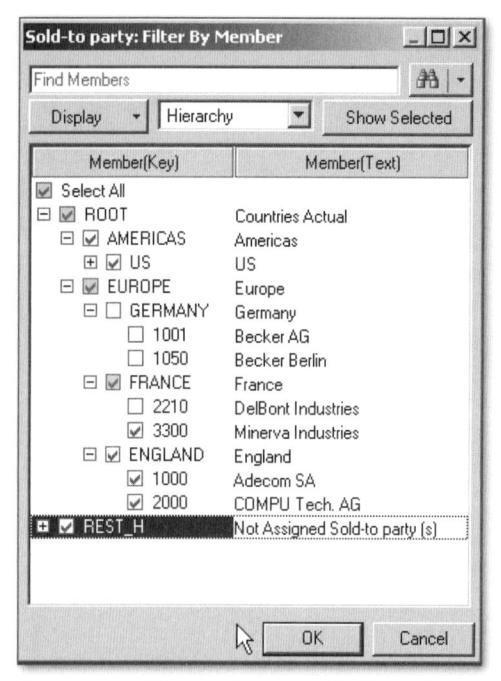

Figure 5.20 Filter by Member with Hierarchy

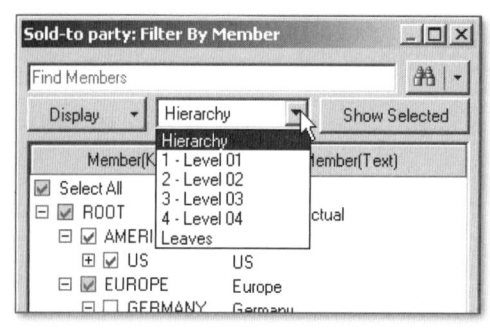

Figure 5.21 Member Selector

The Member Selector lets you select a specific level, the complete hierarchy, or just the leaves.

32. Limit your crosstab to EUROPE and AMERICAS and exclude NOT ASSIGNED SOLD-TO-PARTY(S).

33. Click OK.

In this section, we reviewed the specific elements of Advanced Analysis Office for Microsoft Excel when you use hierarchies as part of your crosstab. In the next section, we'll use the functionality to display standard characteristics in a hierarchical manner.

5.1.2 Displaying Characteristics as Hierarchy

In this section, we'll learn how to display standard characteristics in a hierarchical way. This functionality is also known as the DISPLAY AS HIERARCHY option in the BEx Query Designer.

1. Start Advanced Analysis Office with Microsoft Excel via the menu path START • PROGRAMS • SAP BUSINESSOBJECTS • ADVANCED ANALYSIS FOR MICROSOFT EXCEL.
2. Select the INSERT • SELECT DATA SOURCE option from the Advanced Analysis ribbon.
3. You will see the log-on screen for SAP BusinessObjects Enterprise.

    If you do not want to share the workbook with your colleagues or use a shared connection, you can click the SKIP button. In our example, we use the SKIP option.
4. Click SKIP.
5. You are presented with the list of available SAP systems based on the entries of your SAP Logon pad.
6. Select the entry for your SAP system.
7. Click NEXT.
8. Enter your SAP credentials in the log-on screen and click NEXT.
9. Select the BEx Query that we created in Chapter 4, Advanced Analysis Office — Basic Functions, which shows Product Group and Product in the rows.
10. Next is the prompting screen. Enter the values for the variables and click OK (see Figure 5.22).

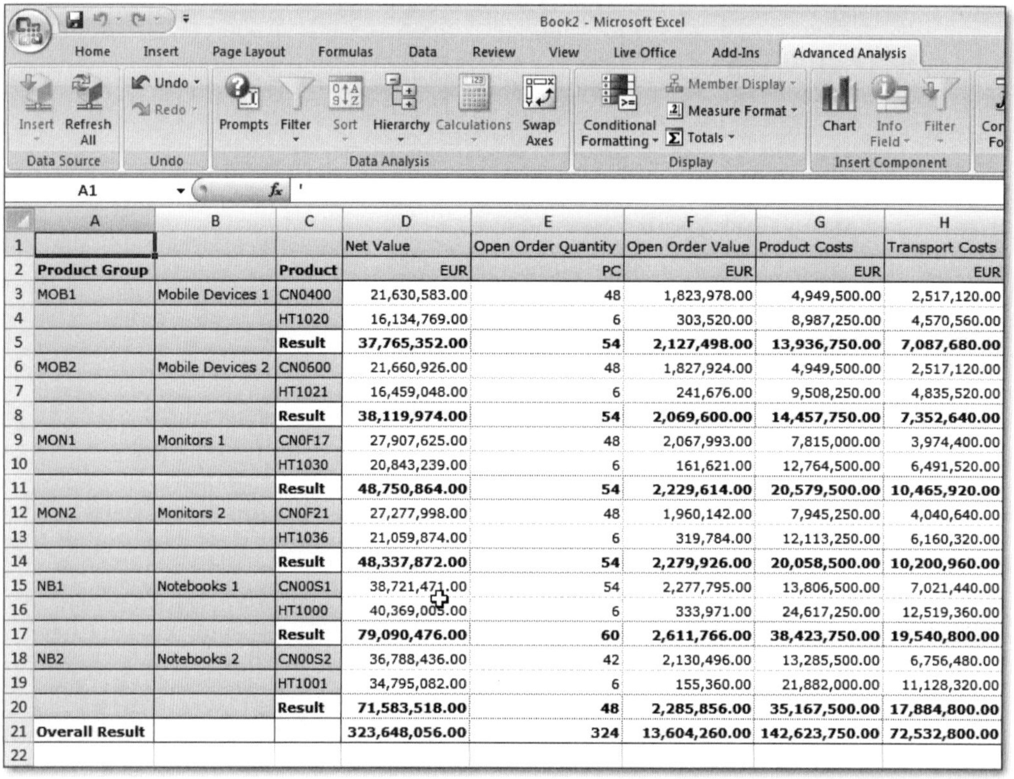

	A	B	C	D	E	F	G	H
1				Net Value	Open Order Quantity	Open Order Value	Product Costs	Transport Costs
2	**Product Group**		**Product**	EUR	PC	EUR	EUR	EUR
3	MOB1	Mobile Devices 1	CN0400	21,630,583.00	48	1,823,978.00	4,949,500.00	2,517,120.00
4			HT1020	16,134,769.00	6	303,520.00	8,987,250.00	4,570,560.00
5			**Result**	**37,765,352.00**	**54**	**2,127,498.00**	**13,936,750.00**	**7,087,680.00**
6	MOB2	Mobile Devices 2	CN0600	21,660,926.00	48	1,827,924.00	4,949,500.00	2,517,120.00
7			HT1021	16,459,048.00	6	241,676.00	9,508,250.00	4,835,520.00
8			**Result**	**38,119,974.00**	**54**	**2,069,600.00**	**14,457,750.00**	**7,352,640.00**
9	MON1	Monitors 1	CNOF17	27,907,625.00	48	2,067,993.00	7,815,000.00	3,974,400.00
10			HT1030	20,843,239.00	6	161,621.00	12,764,500.00	6,491,520.00
11			**Result**	**48,750,864.00**	**54**	**2,229,614.00**	**20,579,500.00**	**10,465,920.00**
12	MON2	Monitors 2	CNOF21	27,277,998.00	48	1,960,142.00	7,945,250.00	4,040,640.00
13			HT1036	21,059,874.00	6	319,784.00	12,113,250.00	6,160,320.00
14			**Result**	**48,337,872.00**	**54**	**2,279,926.00**	**20,058,500.00**	**10,200,960.00**
15	NB1	Notebooks 1	CN00S1	38,721,471.00	54	2,277,795.00	13,806,500.00	7,021,440.00
16			HT1000	40,369,005.00	6	333,971.00	24,617,250.00	12,519,360.00
17			**Result**	**79,090,476.00**	**60**	**2,611,766.00**	**38,423,750.00**	**19,540,800.00**
18	NB2	Notebooks 2	CN00S2	36,788,436.00	42	2,130,496.00	13,285,500.00	6,756,480.00
19			HT1001	34,795,082.00	6	155,360.00	21,882,000.00	11,128,320.00
20			**Result**	**71,583,518.00**	**48**	**2,285,856.00**	**35,167,500.00**	**17,884,800.00**
21	**Overall Result**			**323,648,056.00**	**324**	**13,604,260.00**	**142,623,750.00**	**72,532,800.00**
22								

Figure 5.22 Advanced Analysis Crosstab

11. Select a member of the PRODUCT GROUP.
12. Follow the HIERARCHY • COMPACT DISPLAY IN ROWS menu path from the Advanced Analysis Office ribbon (see Figure 5.23).

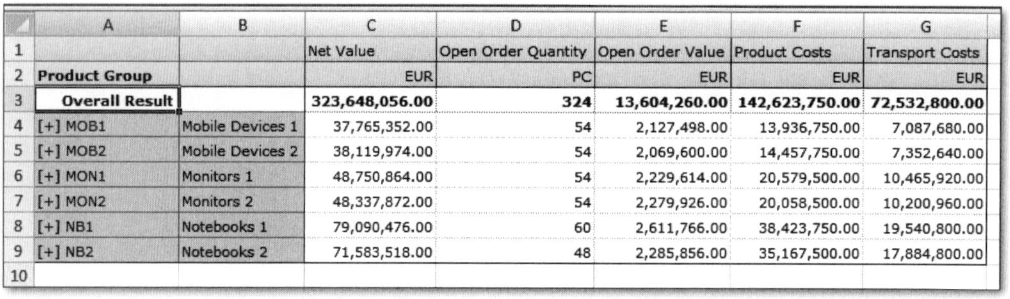

	A	B	C	D	E	F	G
1			Net Value	Open Order Quantity	Open Order Value	Product Costs	Transport Costs
2	**Product Group**		EUR	PC	EUR	EUR	EUR
3	**Overall Result**		**323,648,056.00**	**324**	**13,604,260.00**	**142,623,750.00**	**72,532,800.00**
4	[+] MOB1	Mobile Devices 1	37,765,352.00	54	2,127,498.00	13,936,750.00	7,087,680.00
5	[+] MOB2	Mobile Devices 2	38,119,974.00	54	2,069,600.00	14,457,750.00	7,352,640.00
6	[+] MON1	Monitors 1	48,750,864.00	54	2,229,614.00	20,579,500.00	10,465,920.00
7	[+] MON2	Monitors 2	48,337,872.00	54	2,279,926.00	20,058,500.00	10,200,960.00
8	[+] NB1	Notebooks 1	79,090,476.00	60	2,611,766.00	38,423,750.00	19,540,800.00
9	[+] NB2	Notebooks 2	71,583,518.00	48	2,285,856.00	35,167,500.00	17,884,800.00
10							

Figure 5.23 Compact Display in Rows

Now PRODUCT GROUP and PRODUCT are shown in a hierarchical manner and you can navigate by using the + and - symbols to open and close specific elements. The SHOW LEVELS and EXPAND TO LEVEL options from the HIERARCHY menu are not available for this feature. Instead of EXPAND TO LEVEL you have the EXPAND DIMENSION PRODUCT option in the HIERARCHY menu. In our example, we used PRODUCT GROUP and PRODUCT; therefore, the menu shows EXPAND DIMENSION PRODUCT (see Figure 5.24).

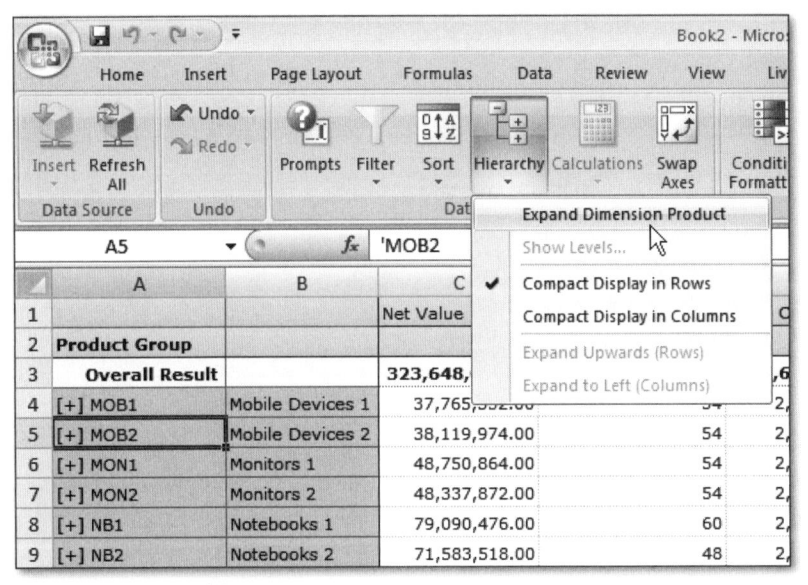

Figure 5.24 Expand Dimension

Using the COMPACT DISPLAY IN ROWS option results in the HIERARCHY menu always showing the next level as an expendable option. The HIERARCHY menu does not have an option to expand all levels.

Please note that the COMPACT DISPLAY option in the HIERARCHY menu can be used in the rows and columns.

In this section, we learned how to display a set of characteristics as a hierarchy. In the next section, we will create our own custom calculations as part of our crosstab.

5 | Advanced Analysis Office — Advanced Functions

5.1.3 Creating Calculations

In this section, we'll take a look how we can add our own calculations outside the BEx Query as part of our crosstab in Microsoft Excel. Let's use the BEx Query we created in Chapter 4 for this exercise.

1. Start Advanced Analysis Office with Microsoft Excel via the menu path START • PROGRAMS • SAP BUSINESSOBJECTS • ADVANCED ANALYSIS FOR MICROSOFT EXCEL.

2. Select the INSERT • SELECT DATA SOURCE option from the Advanced Analysis ribbon.

3. You will see the log-on screen for SAP BusinessObjects Enterprise.

4. Click SKIP.

5. You are then presented with a list of available SAP systems based on the entries of your SAP Logon pad.

6. Select the entry for your SAP system.

7. Click NEXT.

8. Enter your SAP credentials in the log-on screen and click NEXT.

9. Select the BEx Query that we created in Chapter 4 that shows Product Group and Product in the rows.

10. Enter the values for the variables when you are prompted.

> **Insert Data Source**
>
> The connection for the BEx queries is shown in the list of available connections and you can click on it without going through all of the separate steps. The number of connections shown in the list depends on your configuration, which you can change in the SETTINGS menu.

11. Select the OPEN ORDER VALUE column and OPEN ORDER QUANTITY column (see Figure 5.25). Just select the actual column header and not the complete column.

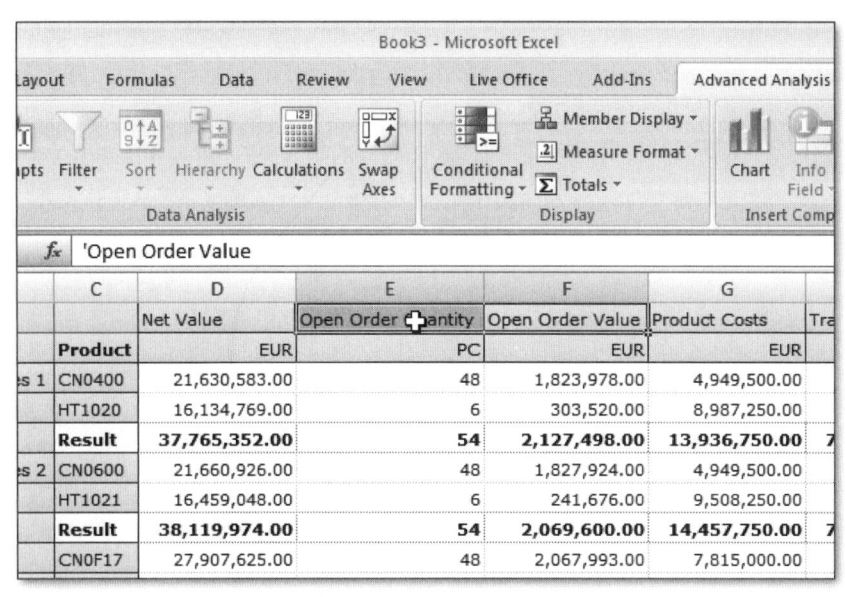

5.1 Advanced Functionality in Advanced Analysis Office for Microsoft Excel

Figure 5.25 Column Header Selection

12. Open the CALCULATIONS menu in the Advanced Analysis Office ribbon (see Figure 5.26).

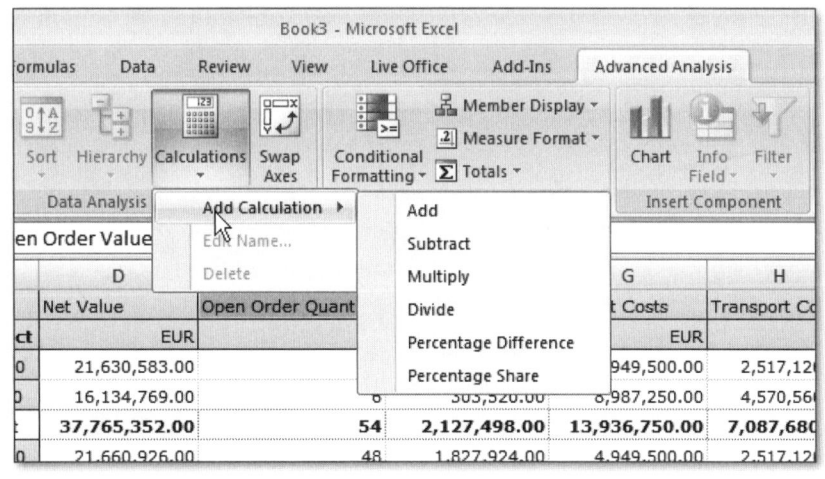

Figure 5.26 Calculations

207

5 | Advanced Analysis Office — Advanced Functions

The available options in the CALCULATIONS menu depend on your selection. In our first example, we selected two columns and a list of basic mathematical functions is shown to us.

13. We would like to know the price per piece, so we need to divide the OPEN ORDER VALUE by OPEN ORDER QUANTITY; therefore, we follow the menu path CALCULATIONS • ADD CALCULATION • DIVIDE (see Figure 5.27).

	B	C	D	E	F	G	H	I
1			Net Value	Open Order Quantity	Open Order Value	Product Costs	Transport Costs	Open Order Value/Open Order Quantity
2	Group	Product	EUR	PC	EUR	EUR	EUR	EUR / PC
3	Mobile Devices 1	CN0400	21,630,583.00	48	1,823,978.00	4,949,500.00	2,517,120.00	37,999.54
4		HT1020	16,134,769.00	6	303,520.00	8,987,250.00	4,570,560.00	50,586.67
5		Result	37,765,352.00	54	2,127,498.00	13,936,750.00	7,087,680.00	39,398.11
6	Mobile Devices 2	CN0600	21,660,926.00	48	1,827,924.00	4,949,500.00	2,517,120.00	38,081.75
7		HT1021	16,459,048.00	6	241,676.00	9,508,250.00	4,835,520.00	40,279.33
8		Result	38,119,974.00	54	2,069,600.00	14,457,750.00	7,352,640.00	38,325.93
9	Monitors 1	CN0F17	27,907,625.00	48	2,067,993.00	7,815,000.00	3,974,400.00	43,083.19
10		HT1030	20,843,239.00	6	161,621.00	12,764,500.00	6,491,520.00	26,936.83
11		Result	48,750,864.00	54	2,229,614.00	20,579,500.00	10,465,920.00	41,289.15
12	Monitors 2	CN0F21	27,277,998.00	48	1,960,142.00	7,945,250.00	4,040,640.00	40,836.29
13		HT1036	21,059,874.00	6	319,784.00	12,113,250.00	6,160,320.00	53,297.33
14		Result	48,337,872.00	54	2,279,926.00	20,058,500.00	10,200,960.00	42,220.85
15	Notebooks 1	CN00S1	38,721,471.00	54	2,277,795.00	13,806,500.00	7,021,440.00	42,181.39
16		HT1000	40,369,005.00	6	333,971.00	24,617,250.00	12,519,360.00	55,661.83
17		Result	79,090,476.00	60	2,611,766.00	38,423,750.00	19,540,800.00	43,529.43
18	Notebooks 2	CN00S2	36,788,436.00	42	2,130,496.00	13,285,500.00	6,756,480.00	50,726.10
19		HT1001	34,795,082.00	6	155,360.00	21,882,000.00	11,128,320.00	25,893.33
20		Result	71,583,518.00	48	2,285,856.00	35,167,500.00	17,884,800.00	47,622.00
21	Result		323,648,056.00	324	13,604,260.00	142,623,750.00	72,532,800.00	41,988.46

Figure 5.27 New Calculation

The CALCULATION is added on the right-hand side of the crosstab. The reason for selecting OPEN ORDER VALUE first and OPEN ORDER QUANTITY second should be clear —we were not asked to create an actual formula. Advanced Analysis Office uses the first column as the left operand and the second column as the right operand.

14. Use the DISPLAY menu in the ribbon to be sure that the navigation panel is shown (see Figure 5.28).

The newly added calculation becomes part of the navigation panel and can be used just as any other key figure.

15. Select the column header of the newly created calculation in the crosstab.

16. Right-click to open the context menu.

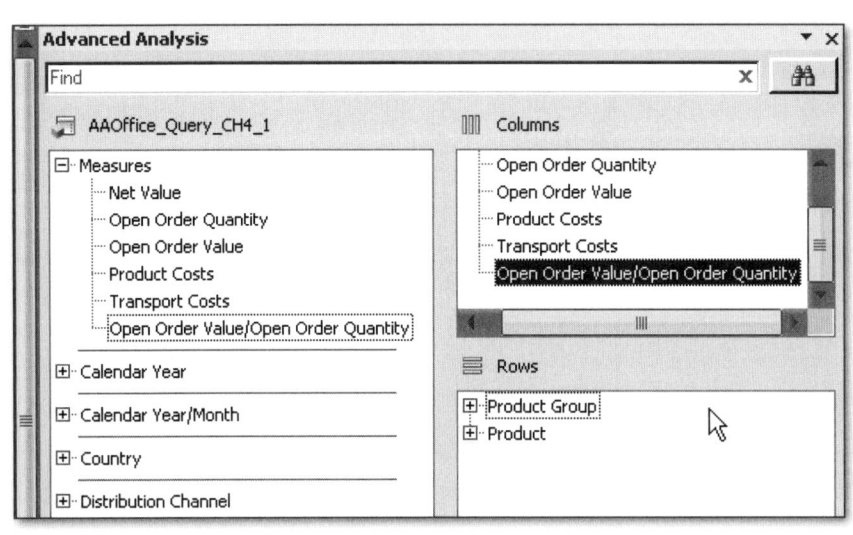

Advanced Functionality in Advanced Analysis Office for Microsoft Excel | **5.1**

Figure 5.28 Navigation Panel

17. Use EDIT NAME to rename the calculation. The EDIT NAME option is also available in the CALCULATIONS menu (see Figure 5.29).

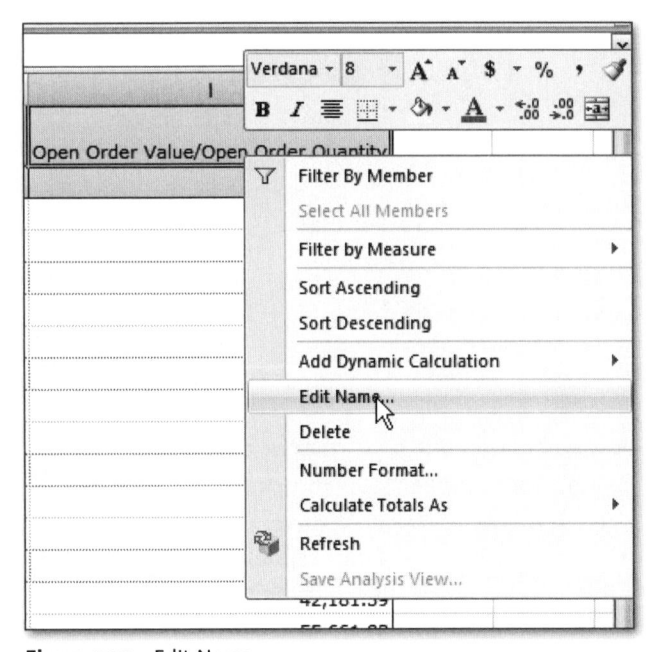

Figure 5.29 Edit Name

209

5 | Advanced Analysis Office — Advanced Functions

18. Now select the NET VALUE column header.

19. Open the CALCULATIONS menu (see Figure 5.30).

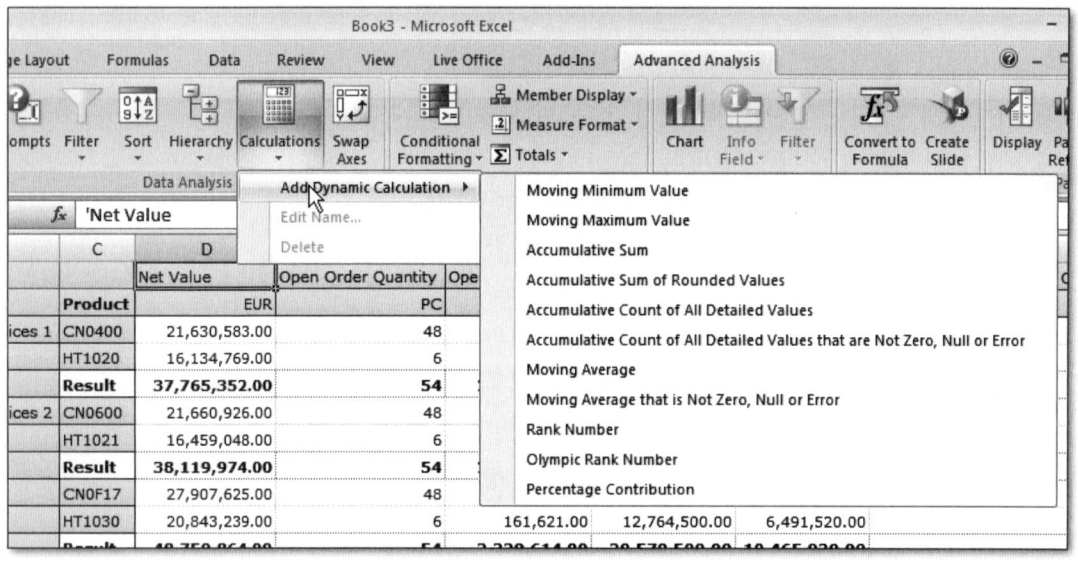

Figure 5.30 Menu Calculations

In this example we only selected a single key figure; therefore, we are offered a different list of calculation options.

20. Follow the menu path CALCULATIONS • ADD DYNAMIC CALCULATION • PERCENTAGE CONTRIBUTION (see Figure 5.31).

As opposed to the previous calculation, this time the calculation is added next to the key figure you selected. Now the crosstab includes the percentage value based on the contribution to the NET VALUE for each PRODUCT and PRODUCT GROUP.

In this section, you learned how to create your own custom calculations as part of your crosstab. In the next section, we'll look at how to turn your crosstab into standard Microsoft Excel formulas and how you can use those as part of Advanced Analysis Office for Microsoft Excel.

Advanced Functionality in Advanced Analysis Office for Microsoft Excel | **5.1**

	A	B	C	D	E
1				Net Value	Percentage Contribution: Net Value
2	**Product Group**		**Product**	EUR	%
3	MOB1	Mobile Devices 1	CN0400	21,630,583.00	57.276
4			HT1020	16,134,769.00	42.724
5			Result	37,765,352.00	11.669
6	MOB2	Mobile Devices 2	CN0600	21,660,926.00	56.823
7			HT1021	16,459,048.00	43.177
8			Result	38,119,974.00	11.778
9	MON1	Monitors 1	CN0F17	27,907,625.00	57.245
10			HT1030	20,843,239.00	42.755
11			Result	48,750,864.00	15.063
12	MON2	Monitors 2	CN0F21	27,277,998.00	56.432
13			HT1036	21,059,874.00	43.568
14			Result	48,337,872.00	14.935
15	NB1	Notebooks 1	CN00S1	38,721,471.00	48.958
16			HT1000	40,369,005.00	51.042
17			Result	79,090,476.00	24.437
18	NB2	Notebooks 2	CN00S2	36,788,436.00	51.392
19			HT1001	34,795,082.00	48.608
20			Result	71,583,518.00	22.118
21	**Overall Result**			323,648,056.00	100.000
22					

Figure 5.31 Percentage Contribution

5.1.4 Using Data as a "Formula"

In this section, we'll look at how to use standard Microsoft Excel functions provided by Advanced Analysis Office to create custom layouts for our crosstab.

1. Start Advanced Analysis Office with Microsoft Excel via the menu path START • PROGRAMS • SAP BUSINESSOBJECTS • ADVANCED ANALYSIS FOR MICROSOFT EXCEL.

2. Select the INSERT • SELECT DATA SOURCE option from the Advanced Analysis ribbon.

3. You will see the log-on screen for SAP BusinessObjects Enterprise system.

4. Click SKIP.

5. You are now presented with a list of available SAP systems based on the entries in your SAP Logon pad.

6. Select the entry for your SAP system.

7. Click NEXT.

8. Enter your SAP credentials in the log-on screen and click NEXT.

9. Select the BEx Query that we created in Chapter 4 that shows Product Group and Product in the rows.

10. Enter 2009 and 2010 for the Calendar Year when prompted.

11. Click OK.

12. Now exchange PRODUCT with CALENDAR YEAR.

13. Open the CALENDAR YEAR/MONTH context menu and choose SELECT ALL MEMBERS (see Figure 5.32). Your overall crosstab should now look similar to Figure 5.33.

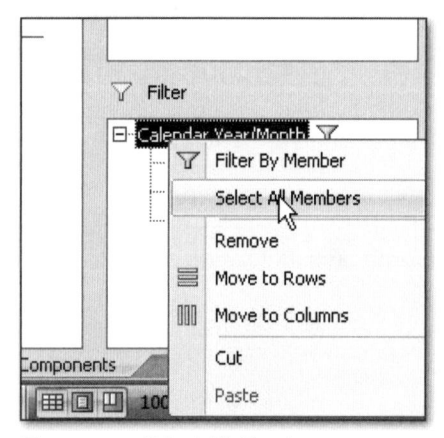

Figure 5.32 Select All Members

	A	B	C	D	E	F	G
1				Net Value	Open Order Quantity	Open Order Value	Product Costs
2	**Product Group**		Calendar Year	EUR	PC	EUR	EUR
3	MOB1	Mobile Devices 1	2009	161,526,975.00	216	9,688,506.00	56,658,750.00
4			2010	158,897,844.00	216	9,346,730.00	56,658,750.00
5			Result	320,424,819.00	432	19,035,236.00	113,317,500.00
6	MOB2	Mobile Devices 2	2009	153,036,188.00	216	9,156,711.00	53,793,250.00
7			2010	151,160,072.00	216	8,912,819.00	53,793,250.00
8			Result	304,196,260.00	432	18,069,530.00	107,586,500.00
9	MON1	Monitors 1	2009	208,897,159.00	216	9,866,637.00	86,616,250.00
10			2010	201,104,561.00	216	8,853,604.00	86,616,250.00
11			Result	410,001,720.00	432	18,720,241.00	173,232,500.00
12	MON2	Monitors 2	2009	204,359,070.00	216	9,406,682.00	85,965,000.00
13			2010	207,002,836.00	216	9,750,372.00	85,965,000.00
14			Result	411,361,906.00	432	19,157,054.00	171,930,000.00
15	NB1	Notebooks 1	2009	300,765,016.00	222	10,083,452.00	145,359,000.00
16			2010	295,127,024.00	222	9,350,523.00	145,359,000.00
17			Result	595,892,040.00	444	19,433,975.00	290,718,000.00
18	NB2	Notebooks 2	2009	283,671,490.00	210	8,823,297.00	140,539,750.00
19			2010	284,170,404.00	210	8,888,156.00	140,539,750.00
20			Result	567,841,894.00	420	17,711,453.00	281,079,500.00
21	**Overall Result**			2,609,718,639.00	2,592	112,127,489.00	1,137,864,000.00

Figure 5.33 Advanced Analysis Crosstab

14. Select any cell from your crosstab.

15. Navigate to the CONVERT TO FORMULA menu in the Advanced Analysis Office ribbon.

Now every element in your crosstab has been turned into a standard Microsoft Excel function provided by Advanced Analysis Office (see Figure 5.34).

The functionality for converting your crosstab into a set of formulas or leveraging a set of functions provides you with a great amount of flexibility for when the standard options are not enough. In the next couple of steps, we will create a custom layout for our BEx Query in Advanced Analysis Office. The goal is to create a crosstab that results in a layout similar to the one shown in Figure 5.34. You can create this layout using the BEx Query Designer, which Advanced Analysis Office would inherit, but the following steps are designed to show you the functions in Microsoft Excel. Therefore, we will start with a simple example (see Figure 5.35).

5 Advanced Analysis Office — Advanced Functions

	A	B	C	D	E	F	G	H
1			Measures	Net Value	Open Order Quantity	Open Order Value	Product Costs	Transport Costs
2	Product Group	Product Group	Calendar Year	EUR	PC	EUR	EUR	EUR
3	MOB1	Mobile Devices 1	2009	161,526,975.00	216	9,688,506.00	56,658,750.00	28,814,400.00
4	MOB1	Mobile Devices 1	2010	158,897,844.00	216	9,346,730.00	56,658,750.00	28,814,400.00
5	MOB1	Mobile Devices 1	Result	320,424,819.00	432	19,035,236.00	113,317,500.00	57,628,800.00
6	MOB2	Mobile Devices 2	2009	153,036,188.00	216	9,156,711.00	53,793,250.00	27,357,120.00
7	MOB2	Mobile Devices 2	2010	151,160,072.00	216	8,912,819.00	53,793,250.00	27,357,120.00
8	MOB2	Mobile Devices 2	Result	304,196,260.00	432	18,069,530.00	107,586,500.00	54,714,240.00
9	MON1	Monitors 1	2009	208,897,159.00	216	9,866,637.00	86,616,250.00	44,049,600.00
10	MON1	Monitors 1	2010	201,104,561.00	216	8,853,604.00	86,616,250.00	44,049,600.00
11	MON1	Monitors 1	Result	410,001,720.00	432	18,720,241.00	173,232,500.00	88,099,200.00
12	MON2	Monitors 2	2009	204,359,070.00	216	9,406,682.00	85,965,000.00	43,718,400.00
13	MON2	Monitors 2	2010	207,002,836.00	216	9,750,372.00	85,965,000.00	43,718,400.00
14	MON2	Monitors 2	Result	411,361,906.00	432	19,157,054.00	171,930,000.00	87,436,800.00
15	NB1	Notebooks 1	2009	300,765,016.00	222	10,083,452.00	145,359,000.00	73,923,840.00
16	NB1	Notebooks 1	2010	295,127,024.00	222	9,350,523.00	145,359,000.00	73,923,840.00
17	NB1	Notebooks 1	Result	595,892,040.00	444	19,433,975.00	290,718,000.00	147,847,680.00
18	NB2	Notebooks 2	2009	283,671,490.00	210	8,823,297.00	140,539,750.00	71,472,960.00
19	NB2	Notebooks 2	2010	284,170,404.00	210	8,888,156.00	140,539,750.00	71,472,960.00
20	NB2	Notebooks 2	Result	567,841,894.00	420	17,711,453.00	281,079,500.00	142,945,920.00
21	Overall Result	Overall Result	Result	2,609,718,639.00	2,592	112,127,489.00	1,137,864,000.00	578,672,640.00

Figure 5.34 Convert to Formula

	A	B	C	D	E	F	G	H
1								
2					Net Value		Product Costs	
3	Product Group			2009	2010 Variance		2009	2010 Variance
4	Key	Description						
5								
6								
7								
8								
9								

Figure 5.35 Layout Structure

1. Create a new empty sheet in Advanced Analysis for Microsoft Excel.
2. Use the DISPLAY menu to make sure the navigation panel is being displayed.
3. Select the COMPONENTS tab in the navigation panel.
4. Right-click on BOOK2, which represents the workbook, and use the USE DATA SOURCE menu (see Figure 5.36).

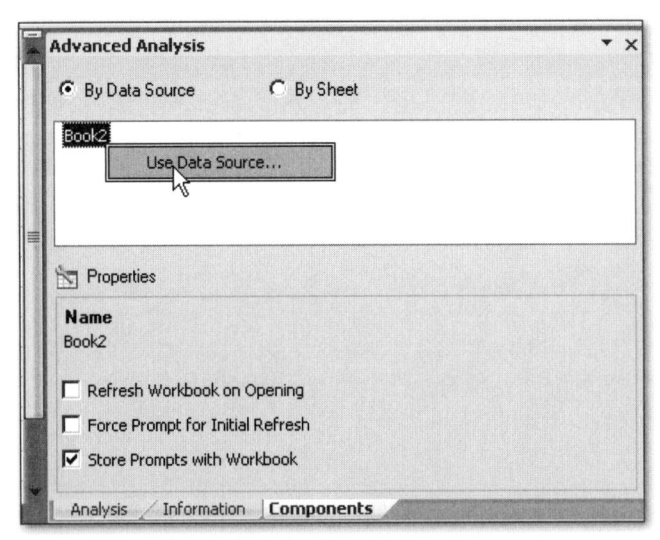

Figure 5.36 Advanced Analysis Components

Instead of using the SELECT DATA SOURCE menu, which would automatically insert a crosstab into our spreadsheet, let's start with an empty spreadsheet and attach a data source to it by using the USE DATA SOURCE menu from the COMPONENTS tab.

5. You are now presented with the standard dialogs to select your Business Information Warehouse (BW) Query.

6. Click SKIP.

7. You should now see the list of available SAP systems based on the entries in your SAP Logon pad.

8. Select the entry in your SAP system.

9. Click NEXT.

10. Enter your SAP credentials to the log on screen and click NEXT.

11. Select the BEx Query we created in Chapter 4 that shows Product Group and Product in the rows.

12. Enter 2009 and 2010 for the Calendar Year when prompted.

5 | Advanced Analysis Office — Advanced Functions

13. Click OK.

14. Navigate to the ANALYSIS tab.

15. Open the CALENDAR YEAR/MONTH context menu and choose SELECT ALL MEMBERS.

16. Move Calendar Year into the ROWS.

> **Functions and Available Characteristics or Key Figures**
>
> In the initial release of Advanced Analysis Office, you can only leverage characteristics or key figures that are shown in the Rows or Columns of your crosstab or navigation panel. Elements that are not part of the result set are not available to formulas in the initial release.

17. Navigate back to the COMPONENTS tab.

18. Select the entry for your BW Query in the COMPONENTS screen (see Figure 5.37).

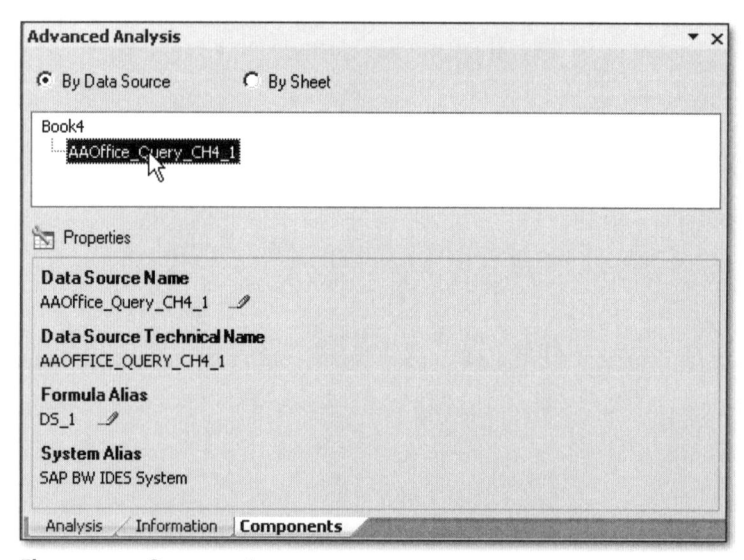

Figure 5.37 Components

Below the BEx Query is PROPERTIES, and you can change some of them. You can change the actual BEx Query to a different one and you can change the

216

Advanced Functionality in Advanced Analysis Office for Microsoft Excel | 5.1

FORMULA ALIAS. The FORMULA ALIAS is very important, because we need the names of all of our formulas to reference the correct BEx Query.

19. Click the ✎ icon next to FORMULA ALIAS and enter "DATA_SOURCE_1" as the new FORMULA ALIAS (see Figure 5.38).

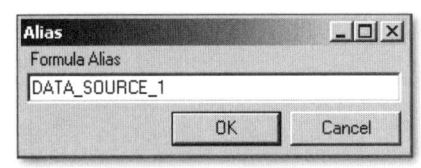

Figure 5.38 Alias

20. Click OK.
21. Create a structure in your empty spreadsheet identical to Figure 5.35.
22. Click on the first cell below the header for PRODUCT GROUP.
23. Use the standard Microsoft Excel HOME • MORE FUNCTIONS menu path to open the list of available functions.
24. Select ADVANCED ANALYSIS (see Figure 5.39).

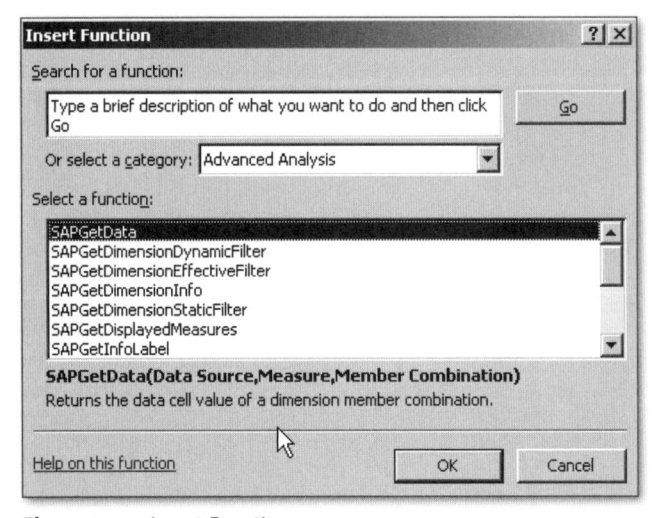

Figure 5.39 Insert Function

25. In the first column, we need the key value of PRODUCT GROUP, which is possible with the SAPGETMEMBER function.

26. Select SAPGETMEMBER (see Figure 5.40)

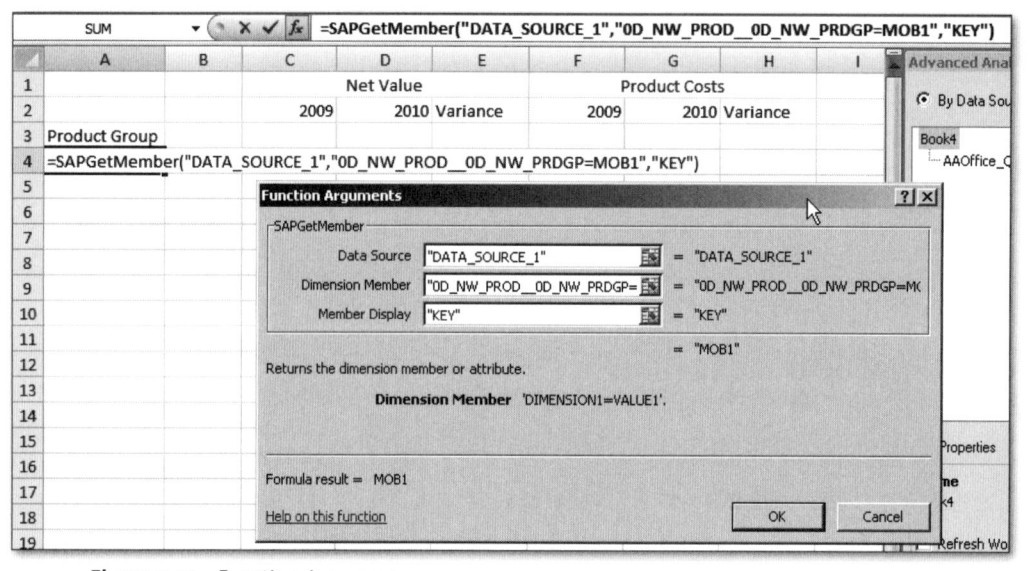

Figure 5.40 Function Arguments

- DATA SOURCE: Here, we need to enter the name of our Data Source in quotes. In our example: "DATA_SOURCE_1".

- DIMENSION MEMBER: Here, we need to enter the technical name of the characteristic and the value we want to show. In our example: "0D_NW_PROD__0D_NW_PRDGP=MOB1" where 0D_NW_PROD__0D_NW_PRDGP represents the technical name of the characteristic and MOB1 represents the key value of the member we would like to show. The formula needs to be written in quotes.

- MEMBER DISPLAY as the option TEXT or KEY and needs to be written in quotes as well. In our example, it is "KEY" for the first part.

Please note that the technical name of the characteristic might be different in your BEx Query if you didn't use the standard SAP NetWeaver Demo model.

You can easily check the correct technical name in the BEx Query Designer or in the spreadsheet we converted to a set of formulas in the previous steps.

27. Enter the values into the dialog as described above. In our example: "SAPGetMember("DATA_SOURCE_1", "0D_NW_PROD__0D_NW_PRDGP=MOB1", "Key")".

> **Referencing Key Figures or Characteristics**
>
> When you use functions from Advanced Analysis Office in Microsoft Excel you have the option of referencing a value by either typing the value in quotes, referencing another cell in your spreadsheet, or by using a formula.

28. Repeat the previous steps for the first value in the second column that represents the Text for PRODUCT GROUP, but this time use the value "TEXT" for the MEMBER DISPLAY option.

29. You should now see the key and text for the first entry of the PRODUCT GROUP.

30. Now click on the first cell below the NET SALES column in 2009.

31. Use the standard Microsoft Excel HOME • MORE FUNCTIONS menu to open the list of available functions.

32. SELECT ADVANCED ANALYSIS.

33. Select SAPGETDATA (see Figure 5.41).

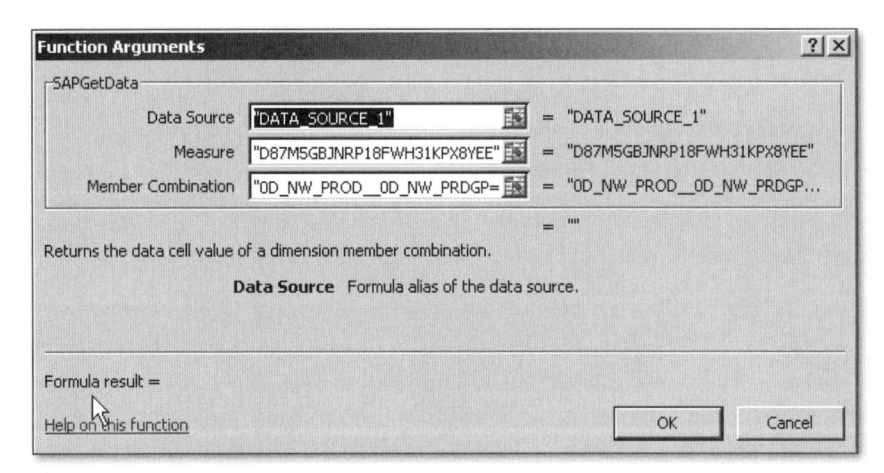

Figure 5.41 Function Arguments

SAPGetData requires the DATA SOURCE, MEASURE, and a MEMBER COMBINATION as valid arguments. The DATA SOURCE is identical to the previous step, in our example, DATA_SOURCE_1. In the case of the MEASURE argument, you can either use the name of the measure or you can use the key, which is the actual globally unique identifier (GUID) of the measure that you can retrieve from the BEx Query Designer. For MEMBER COMBINATION, you need to enter the technical names and the value of the characteristics you want to combine, for example, `0D_NW_PROD__0D_NW_PRDGP=MOB1;0CALYEAR=2009` for PRODUCT GROUP with the value MOB1 and CALENDAR YEAR with the value 2009; each value pair needs to be separated with a semicolon.

In our example, the formula looks like:

`=SAPGetData("DATA_SOURCE_1","Net Value","0D_NW_PROD__0D_NW_PRDGP=MOB1;0CALYEAR=2009")` when using the name of the measure or `=SAPGetData("DATA_SOURCE_1","D87M5GBJNRP18FWH31KPX8YEE","0D_NW_PROD__0D_NW_PRDGP=MOB1;0CALYEAR=2009")` when using the technical name for the measure.

34. Enter the formula into the cell of the first product for 2009 as described above.

35. Repeat the above step and enter the formula for 2010 by simply changing the value for Calendar Year to 2010.

36. Now copy and paste those two formulas and exchange the Net Value with Product Costs.

    By now you have a spreadsheet that shows one member of your PRODUCT GROUP and the NET SALES and PRODUCT COSTS for two years. You can easily use the standard Microsoft Excel formulas to add the VARIANCE between the years to your spreadsheet (see Figure 5.42).

37. Add an additional member of Product Group following the same steps, but with the key MOB2.

38. After you add the additional line you can have two Product Groups shown in your spreadsheet. Now we would like to use the same function to display the subtotals.

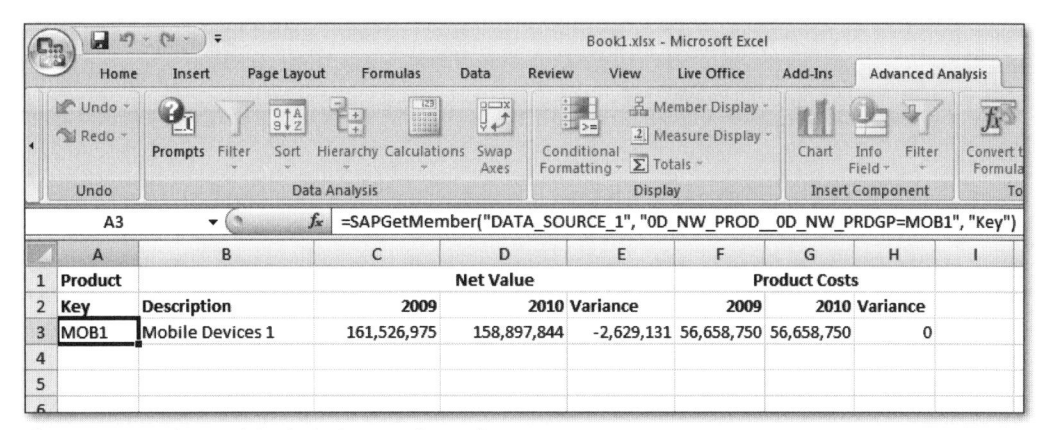

Advanced Functionality in Advanced Analysis Office for Microsoft Excel | **5.1**

	A	B	C	D	E	F	G	H	I
1	Product			Net Value			Product Costs		
2	Key	Description	2009	2010	Variance	2009	2010	Variance	
3	MOB1	Mobile Devices 1	161,526,975	158,897,844	-2,629,131	56,658,750	56,658,750	0	

Figure 5.42 Advanced Analysis Custom Crosstab

39. Navigate to the cell below the description of Product Group. Enter the following syntax:

    =SAPGetMember("DATA_SOURCE_1","0D_NW_PROD__0D_NW_PRDGP=SUMME", "Text")

    The SAPGetMember function lets you use the word "Summe" (German word for subtotal) with the Display Type Text as well so that you can put descriptions for the subtotals into the spreadsheet. Please note that the characteristic shown in this example, 0D_NW_PROD__0D_NW_PRDGP, might be different for your example.

40. Navigate to the subtotal cell for both Product Groups for the Net Sales value for 2009.

41. Enter the following formula:

    =SAPGetData("DATA_SOURCE_1","Net Value","0D_NW_PROD__0D_NW_PRDGP=SUMME;0CALYEAR=2009")

    This formula lets you receive the subtotal for the Product Group for 2009. Please note that the subtotal is based on the overall navigation, not on the elements that we previously created in our custom table. If you are interested in only summarizing the custom elements, you could use the standard Microsoft Excel summary functions or you could change the formula to the one shown below, so that only a specific list of members for characteristic Product Group is being used.

42. Use the syntax described below to create subtotals for 2009 and 2010 for Net Value and Product Costs:

- =SAPGetData("DATA_SOURCE_1", "Net Value", "0D_NW_PROD__0D_NW_PRDGP=SUMME;0CALYEAR=2009")
- =SAPGetData("DATA_SOURCE_1", "Net Value", "0D_NW_PROD__0D_NW_PRDGP=SUMME;0CALYEAR=2010")
- =SAPGetData("DATA_SOURCE_1", "Product Costs", "0D_NW_PROD__0D_NW_PRDGP=SUMME;0CALYEAR=2009")
- =SAPGetData("DATA_SOURCE_1", "Product Costs", "0D_NW_PROD__0D_NW_PRDGP=SUMME;0CALYEAR=2010")

In the last few steps, we used the Advanced Analysis functions in Microsoft Excel to show how you can leverage the functions to create a custom design. Table 5.1 shows a list of the available Advanced Analysis functions and a brief description of the returned value(s).

Advanced Analysis Function	Description
SAPGetDimensionDynamicFilter	Returns a description of the dynamic filter of a dimension.
SAPGetDimensionEffectiveFilter	Returns a description of the effective filter of a dimension.
SAPGetDimensionInfo	Returns the name of a dimension or an active hierarchy.
SAPGetDimensionStaticFilter	Returns the description of the static filter defined in the underlying source for a dimension.
SAPGetDisplayedMeasures	Returns the descriptions of the displayed measure(s).
SAPGetInfoLabel	Returns the label for an Info Field.
SAPGetMeasureFilter	Returns the measure filter.
SAPGetMember	Returns the text or key of a member of a dimension.

Table 5.1 Advanced Analysis Functions

Advanced Analysis Function	Description
SAPGetSourceInfo	Returns the value of a selected property underlying source.
SAPGetVariable	Returns the value or the description of a variable.
SAPGetWorkbookInfo	Returns a property of the workbook.
SAPListOfEffectiveFilters	Returns a list of all effective filters.
SAPListOfVariables	Returns a list of all variables.
SAPSetFilterComponent	Creates a filter component in the workbook.

Table 5.1 Advanced Analysis Functions (Cont.)

In the next couple of steps, we will add some additional functions to our workbook to see their returned values.

43. Navigate to a cell below the actual data in your spreadsheet.
44. Use the Microsoft Excel HOME • MORE FUNCTIONS menu path to open the list of available functions (see Figure 5.43).

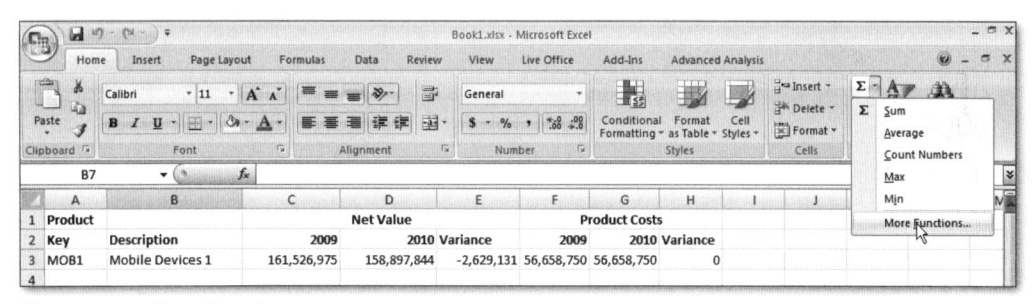

Figure 5.43 More Functions

45. Select ADVANCED ANALYSIS.
46. Select SAPGETDIMENSIONEFFECTIVEFILTER.
47. Click OK (see Figure 5.44).

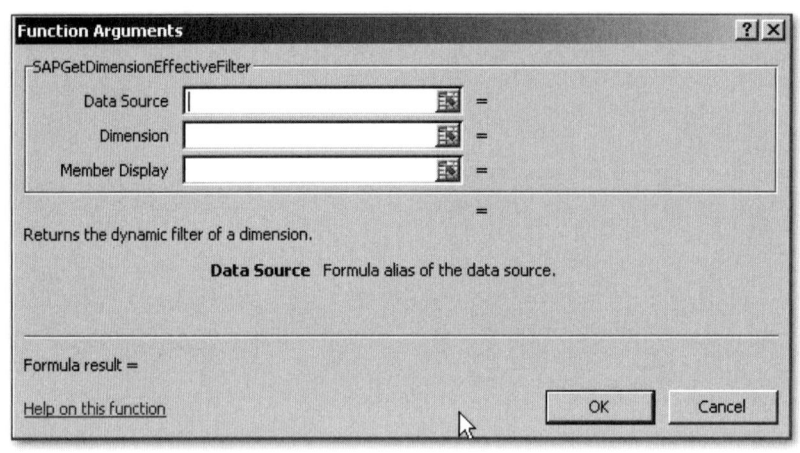

5 | Advanced Analysis Office — Advanced Functions

Figure 5.44 Function Arguments

The SAPGetDimensionEffectiveFilter function returns a description of the effective filters of a specific characteristic and Data Source.

48. Enter "DATA_SOURCE_1" (including the quotes) as the DATA SOURCE.
49. Enter "0CALYEAR" (with quotes) as the DIMENSION.
50. Enter "KEY" as the Member Display.

You'll receive the effective filters for 0CALYEAR, which in our example is filtered based on the variable settings (see Figure 5.45).

Figure 5.45 Advanced Analysis Custom Crosstab

51. Now navigate to one cell further down your spreadsheet to add another function.
52. Follow the Microsoft Excel HOME • MORE FUNCTIONS menu path to open the list of available functions.
53. Select ADVANCED ANALYSIS.
54. Select SAPGETDISPLAYEDMEASURES.
55. Click OK.
56. The SAPGETDISPLAYEDMEASURE function only expects the value for the Data Source, in our example "DATA_SOURCE_1" (with quotes).

    As a result of the function, you get the descriptions of the displayed key figures (see Figure 5.46).

	A	B	C
1	Product		Net Vaue
2	Key	Description	2,009
3	MOB1	Mobile Devices 1	161,526,975
4	MOB2	Mobile Devices 2	153,036,188
5			
6			
7		Overall Result	1,312,255,898
8			
9			
10			
11	SAPGetDimensionEffectiveFilter	2009 - 2010	
12	SAPGetDisplayedMeasures	Net Value; Product Costs	
13			
14			
15			
16			
17			
18			

Figure 5.46 Advanced Analysis Custom Crosstab

57. Now navigate to one cell further down in your spreadsheet to add another function.

58. Use the Microsoft Excel HOME • MORE FUNCTIONS menu path to open the list of available functions.
59. Select ADVANCED ANALYSIS.
60. Select SAPGETINFOLABEL.
61. Click OK.
62. The SAPGETINFOLABEL function expects the property name of an Info Field and will return the actual label for the property (not the value).

Table 5.2 shows the valid values.

Property Name	Description
QueryTechName	Technical name of the BEx Query.
InfoProviderTechName	Technical name of the InfoProvider.
InfoProviderName	Description value for the InfoProvider.
QueryCreatedBy	User account for creating the BEx Query.
QueryLastChangedBy	User account for the last change of the BEx Query.
QueryLastChangedAt	Date value for the last change to the BEx Query.
System	System alias for the backend system.
LastDataUpdate	Date for the last data update for the InfoProvider.
KeyDate	Date value for the key date.
DataSourceName	Description value for BEx Query.

Table 5.2 Info Field Values

Info Fields

In addition to using the INFO FIELDS menu in the Advanced Analysis Office ribbon, you can also drag and drop the INFO FIELDS from the navigation panel in the INFORMATION tab directly onto the spreadsheet.

Advanced Functionality in Advanced Analysis Office for Microsoft Excel | 5.1

63. Use LASTDATAUPDATE as the value of the function.
64. Click OK.
65. Now navigate to the cell next to the one we used for the label.
66. Follow the Microsoft Excel HOME • MORE FUNCTIONS menu path to open the list of available functions.
67. Select ADVANCED ANALYSIS.
68. Select SAPGETSOURCEINFO.
69. Click OK.
70. The SAPGETSOURCEINFO function expects the value for the Data Source (in our example "DATA_SOURCE_1") and the property name of an Info Field. The list of available properties is identical to Table 5.2.
71. Enter "DATA_SOURCE_1" as the value for the Data Source.
72. Enter "LASTDATAUPDATE" as the value for the property.
73. Your spreadsheet should look similar to Figure 5.47.

	A	B	C
1	Product		Net Vaue
2	Key	Description	2,009
3	MOB1	Mobile Devices 1	161,526,975
4	MOB2	Mobile Devices 2	153,036,188
5			
6			
7		Overall Result	1,312,255,898
8			
9			
10			
11	SAPGetDimensionEffectiveFilter	2009 - 2010	
12	SAPGetDisplayedMeasures	Net Value; Product Costs	
13	Last Data Update	Tuesday, March 09, 2010 9:05:50 AM	
14			
15			

Figure 5.47 Advanced Analysis Custom Crosstab

> **Technical Name versus Description**
>
> In general, you can reference a key figure or a characteristic in the functions using the description value or the technical name. For key figures the technical name would be the GUID, which can be retrieved from the BEx Query Designer. It is highly recommended to use the technical names as they are unique, and in a multilingual scenario the technical names ensure that users will see the correct results.

In this section, we reviewed the option for leveraging standard Advanced Analysis Office functions in Microsoft Excel to display data from your underlying source system. In the next section, we will add a filter panel for easier navigation to our workbook.

5.1.5 Adding a Filter Panel

In this section, we will add more flexibility and usability to our workbook by adding a filter panel to it.

1. Start Advanced Analysis Office with Microsoft Excel via the menu path START • PROGRAMS • SAP BUSINESSOBJECTS • ADVANCED ANALYSIS FOR MICROSOFT EXCEL.

2. Select the INSERT • SELECT DATA SOURCE option from the Advanced Analysis ribbon.

3. You will see the log-on screen for SAP BusinessObjects Enterprise.

4. Click SKIP.

5. You are now presented with the list of available SAP systems based on the entries in your SAP Logon pad.

6. Select the entry for your SAP system.

7. Click NEXT.

8. Enter your SAP credentials in the log-on screen and click NEXT.

9. Select the BEx Query that we created in Chapter 4 that shows Product Group and Product in the rows.

5.1 Advanced Functionality in Advanced Analysis Office for Microsoft Excel

10. Enter 2009 and 2010 for the variable for Calendar Year when prompted.
11. Click OK.
12. Now add five empty rows above your crosstab.
13. Select the cell A1 in your spreadsheet.
14. Select the FILTER menu from the INSERT COMPONENT area in the Advanced Analysis Office ribbon (see Figure 5.48).

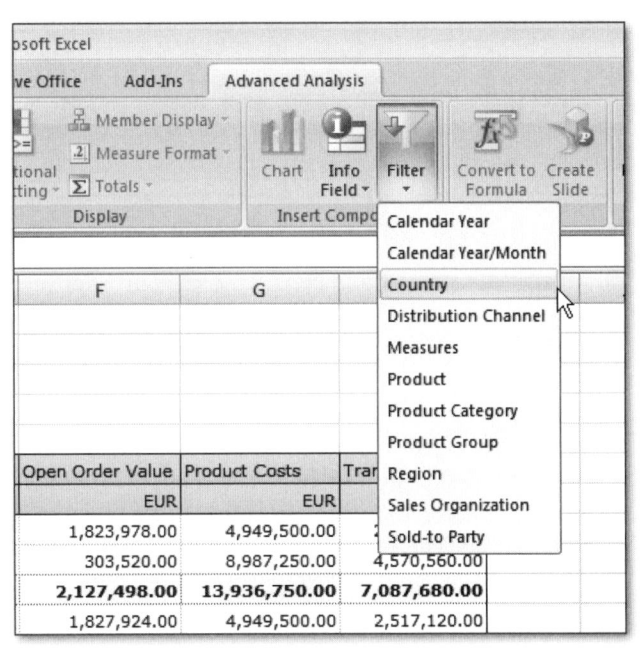

Figure 5.48 Insert Filter Component

15. Select COUNTRY.
16. Select cell B1 and repeat the steps and this time select the CALENDAR YEAR/ MONTH.
17. Select cell C1 and repeat the steps and select the PRODUCT GROUP.
18. Select cell D1 and repeat the steps and select MEASURES (see Figure 5.49).

5 | Advanced Analysis Office — Advanced Functions

	A	B	C	D	E	F	G
		B4		fx	=SAPSetFilterComponent("DS_1", "D87M5GBJNRNHV78YFYPHSE5UU","ALL")		
1	Country						
2	Calendar Year/Month	01.2010; 02.2010; 03.2010					
3	Product Group						
4	Measures						
5							
6				Net Value	Open Order Quantity	Open Order Value	Product Costs
7	**Product Group**		**Product**	EUR	PC	EUR	E
8	MOB1	Mobile Devices 1	CN0400	21,630,583.00	48	1,823,978.00	4,949,500
9			HT1020	16,134,769.00	6	303,520.00	8,987,250
10			Result	37,765,352.00	54	2,127,498.00	13,936,750
11	MOB2	Mobile Devices 2	CN0600	21,660,926.00	48	1,827,924.00	4,949,500
12			HT1021	16,459,048.00	6	241,676.00	9,508,250
13			Result	38,119,974.00	54	2,069,600.00	14,457,750
14	MON1	Monitors 1	CN0F17	27,907,625.00	48	2,067,993.00	7,815,000
15			HT1030	20,843,239.00	6	161,621.00	12,764,500
16			Result	48,750,864.00	54	2,229,614.00	20,579,500

Figure 5.49 Filter Components

You can add a FILTER COMPONENT for each characteristic and key figure from the underlying BEx Query. You can click on the filter icon to get the Member Selector to define the filter criteria.

Please note that the filter icon is only visible when the user is clicking on the actual cell. Therefore, it might not be obvious right away that the user has to click the cell and then click the filter icon to select the members for the characteristic. One way to make it more user-friendly could be to highlight those cells with a background color.

In this section, we created a separate filter panel as part of our workbook to provide our end users a more user-friendly way to define the filter criteria. In the next section, we'll look at how we can generate a Microsoft PowerPoint slide from Advanced Analysis Office for Microsoft Excel.

5.1.6 Creating a Microsoft PowerPoint Slide

In this section, we will leverage Advanced Analysis Office for Microsoft Excel to generate a slide based on navigation status so that information is automatically transferred to Advanced Analysis Office for Microsoft PowerPoint.

1. Start Advanced Analysis Office with Microsoft Excel via the menu path START •
   PROGRAMS • SAP BUSINESSOBJECTS • ADVANCED ANALYSIS FOR MICROSOFT
   EXCEL.
2. Select the INSERT • SELECT DATA SOURCE option from the Advanced Analysis ribbon.
3. You will see the log-on screen for SAP BusinessObjects Enterprise.
4. Click SKIP.
5. You are now presented with the list of available SAP systems based on the entries in your SAP Logon pad.
6. Select the entry for your SAP system.
7. Click NEXT.
8. Enter your SAP credentials in the log-on screen and click NEXT.
9. Select the BEx Query that we created in Chapter 4 that shows Product Group and Product in the rows.
10. Enter 2009 and 2010 for the variable for Calendar Year when prompted.
11. Click OK.
12. Use the DISPLAY menu in the ribbon to see the navigation panel.
13. Replace PRODUCT GROUP with CALENDAR YEAR.
14. Replace PRODUCT with CALENDAR YEAR/MONTH.
15. Open the context menu for CALENDAR YEAR/MONTH in the Rows in the navigation panel and choose SELECT ALL MEMBERS.
16. Open the context menu for MEASURES in the navigation panel and select FILTER BY MEMBER.
17. In the Member Selector, select NET VALUE and OPEN ORDERS VALUE (see Figure 5.50).

5 | Advanced Analysis Office — Advanced Functions

	A	B	C	D
			Net Value	Open Order Value
	Calendar Year	Calendar Year/Month	EUR	EUR
	2009	01.2009	111,679,314.00	4,742,310.00
		02.2009	117,127,173.00	5,710,534.00
		03.2009	107,472,855.00	4,793,471.00
		04.2009	103,324,258.00	4,696,155.00
		05.2009	105,661,264.00	4,713,968.00
		06.2009	100,020,912.00	3,486,723.00
		07.2009	107,587,959.00	4,626,439.00
		08.2009	107,849,039.00	4,556,374.00
		09.2009	111,936,646.00	4,905,766.00
		10.2009	115,875,801.00	5,287,853.00
		11.2009	113,144,471.00	5,036,785.00
		12.2009	110,576,206.00	4,468,907.00
		Result	1,312,255,898.00	57,025,285.00
	2010	01.2010	103,094,479.00	3,626,286.00
		02.2010	111,543,037.00	4,984,600.00
		03.2010	109,010,540.00	4,993,374.00
		04.2010	107,279,485.00	5,210,338.00
		05.2010	101,779,708.00	4,209,363.00
		06.2010	107,921,026.00	4,513,737.00

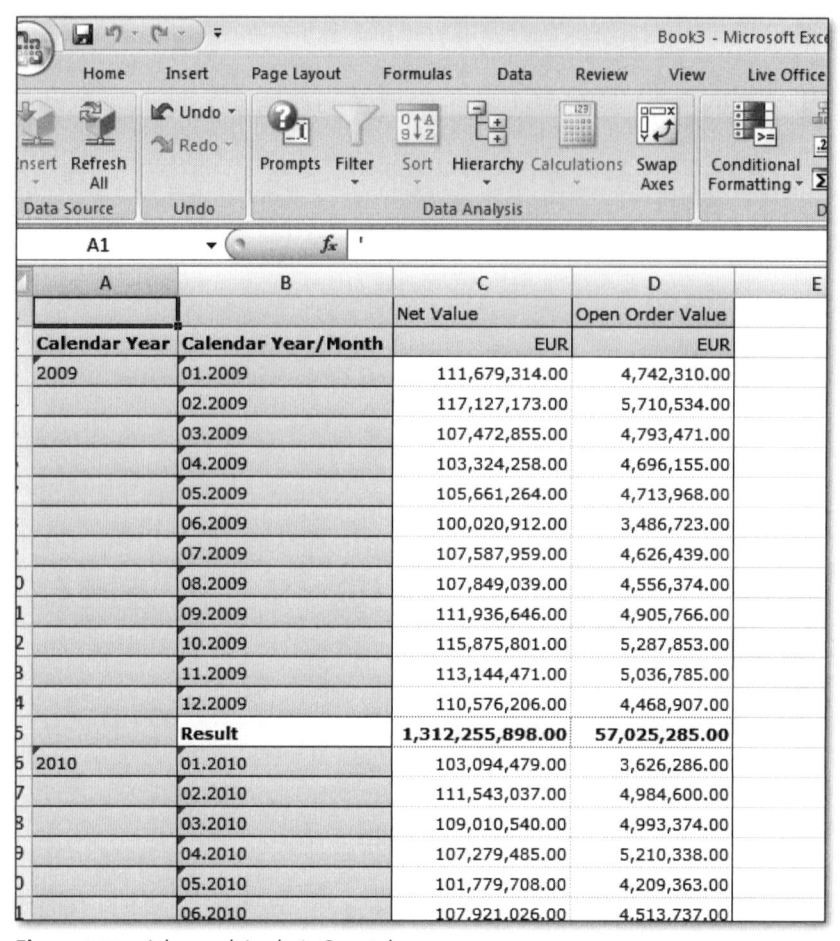

Figure 5.50 Advanced Analysis Crosstab

18. Select the CREATE SLIDE menu in the Advanced Analysis Office ribbon.

19. Advanced Analysis for Microsoft PowerPoint is started and you should see a log-on screen.

20. After you authenticate against the SAP BW system you will be asked how you want to split the material into several slides (see Figure 5.51).

    This step is identical to the question for creating a new slide with Advanced Analysis Office for Microsoft PowerPoint.

Advanced Functionality in Advanced Analysis Office for Microsoft Excel | **5.1**

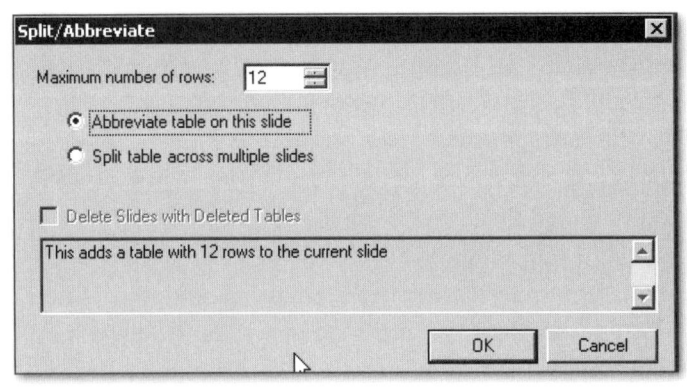

Figure 5.51 Split/Abbreviate

21. Set the MAXIMUM NUMBER OF ROWS to 12 and click OK.

    The information from your workbook is transferred to the slide deck in Advanced Analysis Office for Microsoft Excel (see Figure 5.52).

Calendar Year	Calendar Year/Month	Net Value EUR	Open Order Value EUR
2009	01.2009	111,679,314.00	4,742,310.00
	02.2009	117,127,173.00	5,710,534.00
	03.2009	107,472,855.00	4,793,471.00
	04.2009	103,324,258.00	4,696,155.00
	05.2009	105,661,264.00	4,713,968.00
	06.2009	100,020,912.00	3,486,723.00
	07.2009	107,587,959.00	4,626,439.00
	08.2009	107,849,039.00	4,556,374.00
	09.2009	111,936,646.00	4,905,766.00
	10.2009	115,875,801.00	5,287,853.00
	11.2009	113,144,471.00	5,036,785.00
	12.2009	110,576,206.00	4,468,907.00

Figure 5.52 Advanced Analysis for Microsoft PowerPoint

233

This time, you used the CREATE SLIDE menu from Advanced Analysis Office for Microsoft Excel, and the crosstab on the slide leverages the layout, which we defined previously in Microsoft Excel. When you create a new crosstab directly within Advanced Analysis Office for Microsoft PowerPoint, Advanced Analysis Office leverages the settings from the BEx Query and the layout of the crosstab with regard to rows and columns are based on the BEx Query definition. Now with the additional option of using the Create Slide menu in Advanced Analysis Office for Microsoft Excel, you can access the functionality to create a crosstab based on the navigation you did in Microsoft Excel as part of your Microsoft PowerPoint slide deck. Remember, in Advanced Analysis Office for Microsoft PowerPoint you cannot navigate the actual crosstab, it is created based on the definition of the BEx Query; therefore, the CREATE SLIDE menu can save you several changes and steps by letting you reuse the navigation status from Microsoft Excel for your Microsoft PowerPoint slide.

In this section, we learned how we can improve the process for creating slides for Microsoft PowerPoint by using the CREATE SLIDE option in Advanced Analysis Office for Microsoft Excel. In the next section, we will leverage additional metadata information as part of our workbook.

5.1.7 Using Additional Information and Settings

In addition to the information available in Info Fields, you can also use the Information Panel shown in Advanced Analysis Office for Microsoft Excel and simply drag and drop the fields onto your workbook.

1. Leverage the workbook from our previous activity.

2. Open the INFORMATION tab in the navigation panel (see Figure 5.53).

3. You can simply drag and drop any of the fields to your workbook and you will see the label and actual value in two separate cells.

Advanced Functionality in Advanced Analysis Office for Microsoft Excel | **5.1**

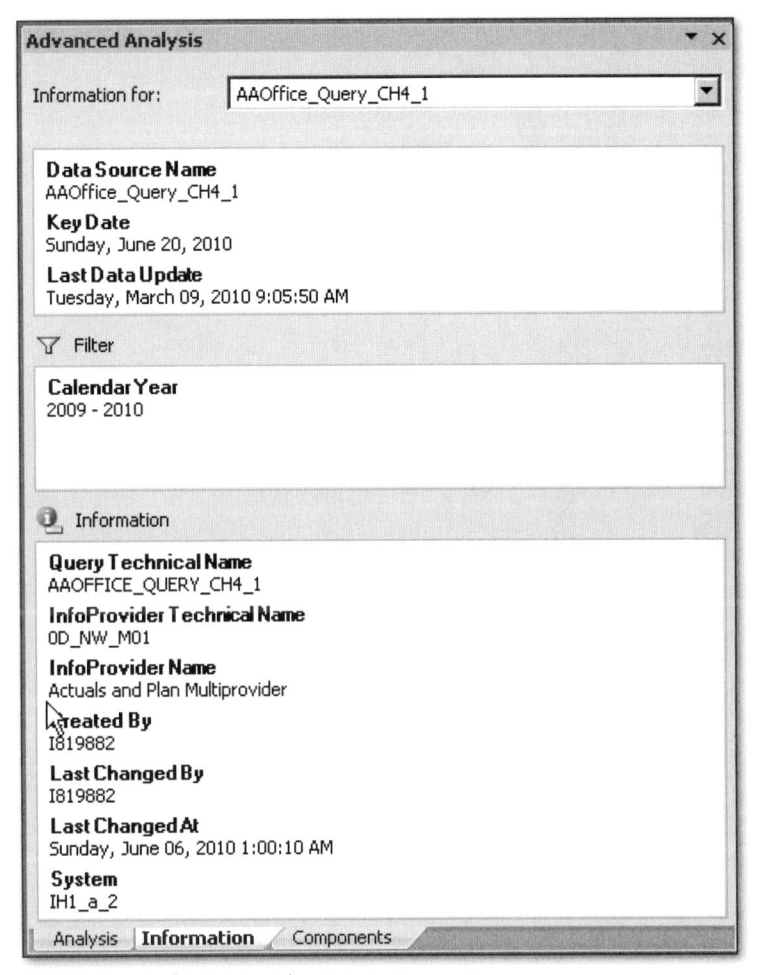

Figure 5.53 Information Tab

4. Drag and drop the LAST DATA UPDATE information to your workbook.

5. Select the workbook information on the INFORMATION tab by selecting the workbook in the top list box (see Figure 5.54).

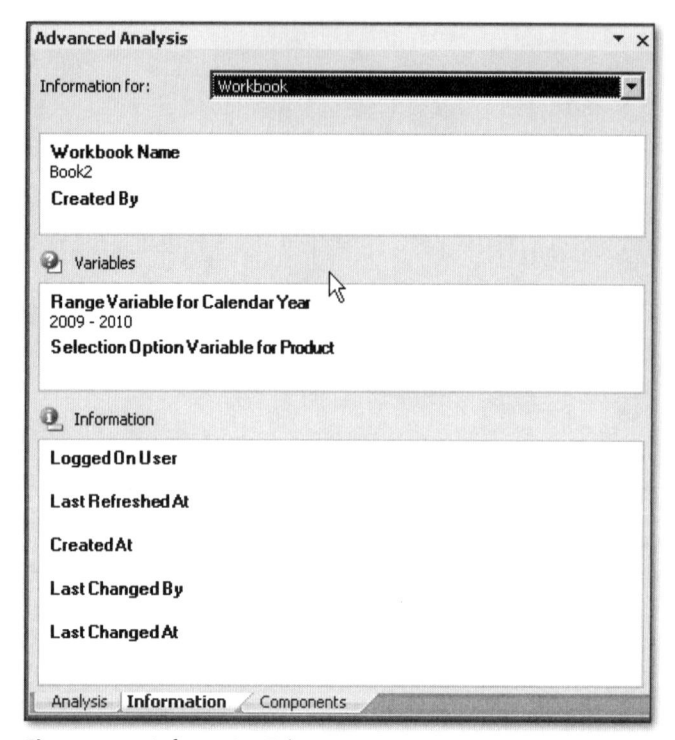

5 | Advanced Analysis Office — Advanced Functions

Figure 5.54 Information Tab

You have a set of information available for the workbook and a set of information available per underlying source.

All of the values and labels shown on the INFORMATION tab are also available in the INFO FIELDS menu in the ribbon and via the functions provided by Advanced Analysis Office.

6. Navigate to an empty sheet as part of your workbook.

7. Select the INSERT • SELECT DATA SOURCE from the Advanced Analysis ribbon.

8. You will see the log-on screen for SAP BusinessObjects Enterprise.

9. Click SKIP.

10. Because we are already logged on to the SAP NetWeaver BW system we are presented with the list of available source.

Advanced Functionality in Advanced Analysis Office for Microsoft Excel | 5.1

11. Select the BEx Query we used previously.
12. We now have a workbook with two BEx queries in two sheets.
13. Navigate to the COMPONENTS tab in the navigation panel (see Figure 5.55).

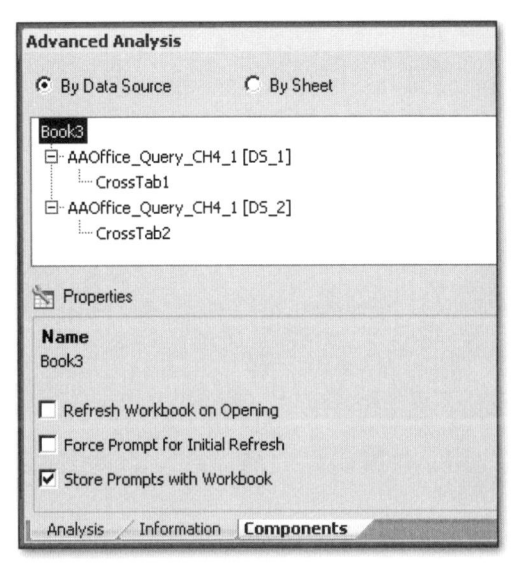

Figure 5.55 Components

14. You have the option to view the COMPONENTS by DATA SOURCE (see Figure 5.55) or by SHEET (see Figure 5.56).

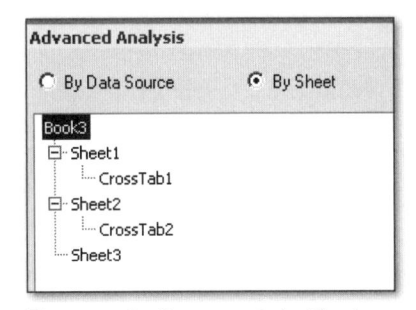

Figure 5.56 Components by Sheet

237

15. Select the BY DATA SOURCE option and choose the first Data Source on the list (see Figure 5.57).

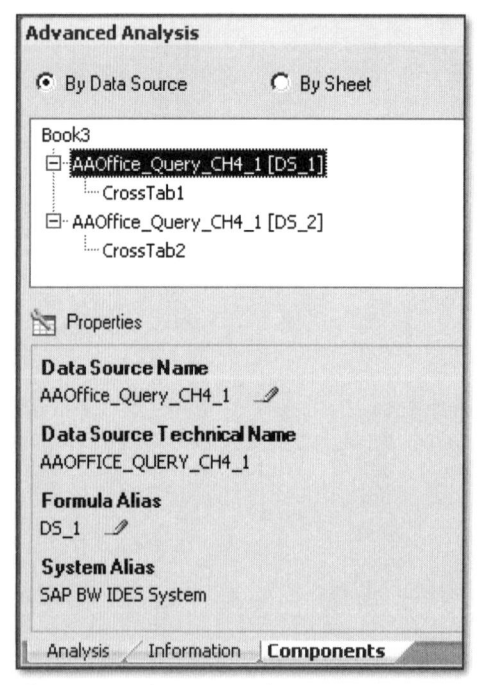

Figure 5.57 Components by Data Source

Each DATA SOURCE and COMPONENT has a set of PROPERTIES that is shown on the COMPONENTS tab. Each property with the ✎ icon next to it can be changed by clicking on the ✎ icon and choosing a new name or source. FORMULA ALIAS is used for situations where you want to leverage the formula functions of Advanced Analysis Office.

16. Now select the crosstab component below the first Data Source (see Figure 5.58).

Each COMPONENT also has a set of PROPERTIES that can be configured on the COMPONENTS tab.

▶ FORMULA ALIAS is relevant for situations where you are using the formula functions in Advanced Analysis Office and lets you choose an Alias.

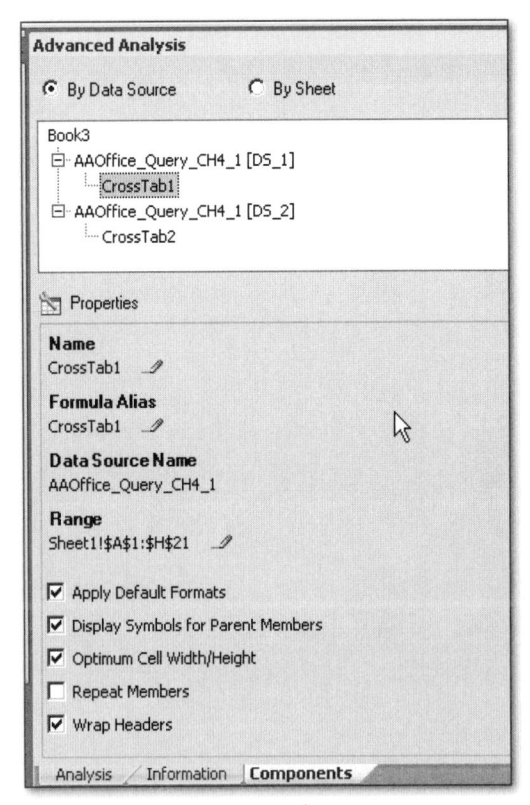

Figure 5.58 Components and Properties

- The RANGE option lets you move the component to another area or sheet in your workbook.

- The DISPLAY SYMBOLS FOR PARENT MEMBERS property lets you enable or disable the [+] and [-] symbols of a hierarchical structure for the parent members.

- The OPTIMUM CELL WIDTH/HEIGHT property lets you configure the component automatically with the optimum width and height for the cells.

- The REPEAT MEMBERS option provides you with the functionality to either repeat the members of each dimension/characteristic for each line or to only show the member once and not repeat it each line.

- The WRAP HEADERS option lets you enable or disable the option to wrap the header texts.

17. Next, select the top-level workbook entry on the COMPONENTS tab (see Figure 5.59).

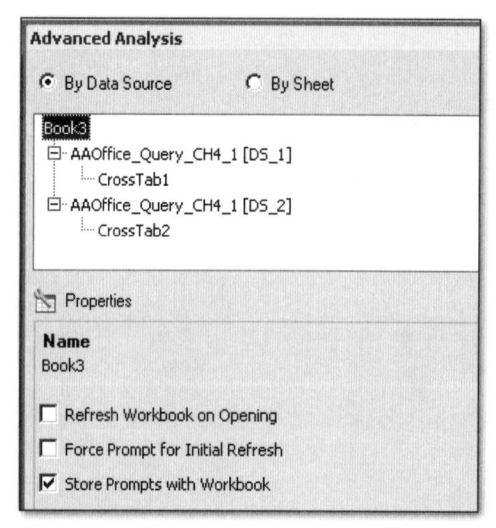

Figure 5.59 Components

On the workbook level, you can enable three properties:

▶ REFRESH WORKBOOK ON OPENING lets you configure the complete workbook, including any data source in the workbook that needs to be refreshed each time the workbook is opened.

▶ FORCE PROMPTS ON INITIAL REFRESH results in the prompt dialog being shown to the user on the initial refresh when the user opens the workbook — even when the workbook only contains optional prompts.

▶ STORE PROMPTS WITH WORKBOOK results in the used values for the prompts being stored as part of the workbook. If the FORCE PROMPT FOR INITIAL REFRESH option is disabled the stored values for the prompts are used for the initial refresh.

In the previous steps we used the menu INSERT • SELECT DATA SOURCE to insert a new BEx query into our workbook but you can also use the COMPONENTS tab in the navigation panel to achieve them same goal.

Advanced Functionality in Advanced Analysis Office for Microsoft Excel | **5.1**

18. Navigate to the COMPONENTS tab in your Advanced Analysis Office workbook.

19. Select the option BY SHEET and right-click on one of the existing crosstabs in your workbook (see Figure 5.60).

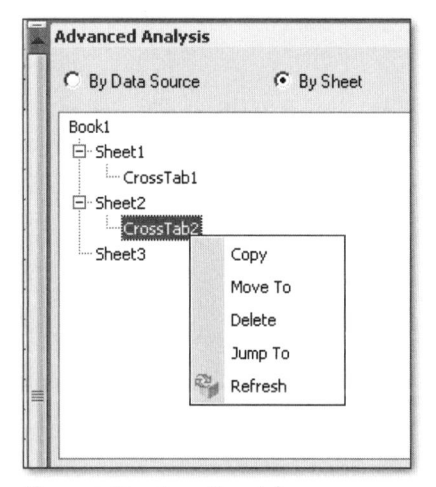

Figure 5.60 Copy Crosstab

20. After using the menu COPY of the context menu you will be asked where you would like to place the crosstab (see Figure 5.61) and you can also select one of the empty sheets in your crosstab.

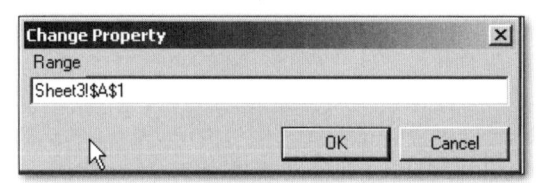

Figure 5.61 Copy Crosstab

21. Now use the option BY DATA SOURCE in the COMPONENTS tab and open the context menu for one of the existing data sources (see Figure 5.62).

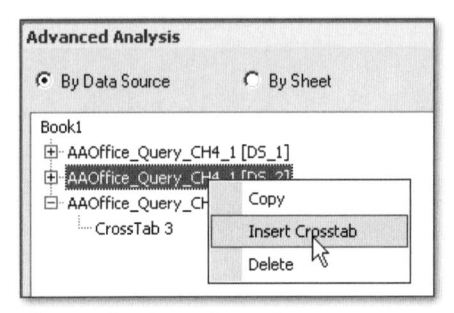

Figure 5.62 Insert Crosstab

22. Use the menu INSERT CROSSTAB and you will be asked where you would like to insert a new crosstab based on the selected data source.

These are additional options to create additional crosstabs in your existing workbook.

In this section, we reviewed the additional metadata information available in Advanced Analysis Office. In the next section, we will learn how we can define our own styles and how to leverage them.

5.1.8 Working with Styles

In this section, we will leverage the styles in Microsoft Excel to provide all of our workbooks a common look and feel. Styles is a standard functionality of Microsoft Excel and Advanced Analysis Office can leverage it for the crosstabs as well by providing you with a set of prebuilt styles and a set of preconfigured types of cells that you can use to define the formatting details.

1. Start Advanced Analysis Office with Microsoft Excel via the menu path START • PROGRAMS • SAP BUSINESSOBJECTS • ADVANCED ANALYSIS FOR MICROSOFT EXCEL.

2. Select the INSERT • SELECT DATA SOURCE option from the Advanced Analysis ribbon.

3. You will see the log-on screen for SAP BusinessObjects Enterprise.

4. Click SKIP.

Advanced Functionality in Advanced Analysis Office for Microsoft Excel | **5.1**

5. You are now presented with the list of available SAP systems based on the entries in your SAP Logon pad.
6. Select the entry for your SAP system.
7. Click NEXT.
8. Enter your SAP credentials in the log-on screen and click NEXT.
9. Select the BEx Query that we created in Chapter 4 that shows Product Group and Product in the rows.
10. Enter 2009 and 2010 for the variable for Calendar Year when being prompted.
11. Click OK.
12. Navigate to the STYLES menu in the Advanced Analysis Office ribbon (see Figure 5.63).

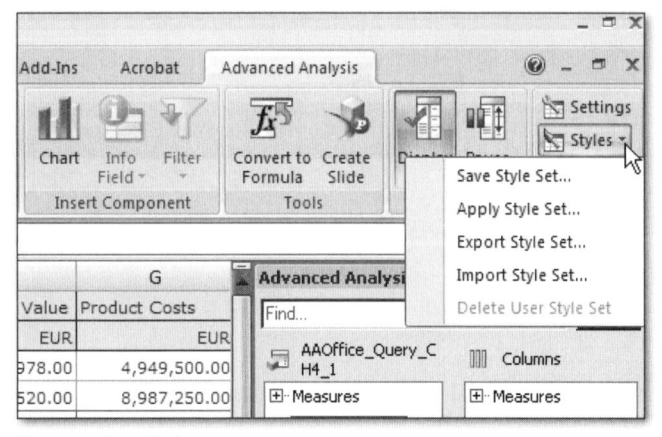

Figure 5.63 Styles

13. Follow the menu path STYLES • APPLY STYLE SET (see Figure 5.64).

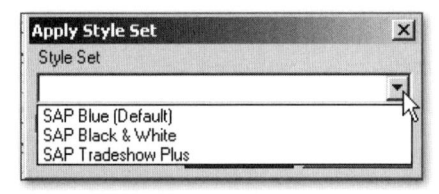

Figure 5.64 Apply Style Set

243

5 | Advanced Analysis Office — Advanced Functions

14. Now you can select any of the available style sets and apply it to your crosstab. The three style sets shown in Figure 5.64 are part of the Advanced Analysis Office installation.

15. Select each style — one after the other — and click OK to see the impact of the styles to your crosstab.

16. Next, navigate to the Microsoft Excel CELL STYLES menu on the HOME tab (see Figure 5.65).

Figure 5.65 Cell Styles

Advanced Functionality in Advanced Analysis Office for Microsoft Excel | **5.1**

17. Select SAPDimensionCell (first row and fourth item from the left).
18. Right-click on the elements and use the context menu Modify (see Figure 5.66).

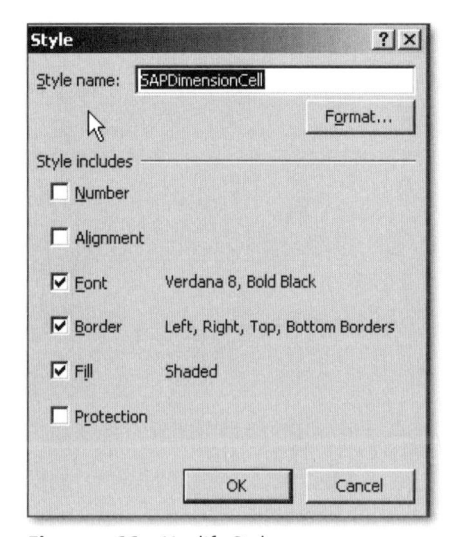

Figure 5.66 Modify Style

19. Click Format.
20. Now the detailed settings for fonts, background, alignments, and so on are shown and you can make changes.
21. Make the changes to the settings.
22. Click OK to confirm the changes.
23. Click OK to confirm the changes to the style.
24. Repeat the steps for the SAPMemberCell Cell Style.

    You now have a style with two customized format options and the changes should already be shown in your crosstab.

25. Follow the Styles • Save Style Set menu path in the Advanced Analysis Office ribbon (see Figure 5.67).

245

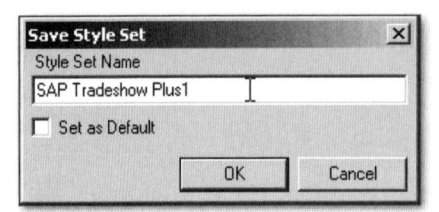

5 | Advanced Analysis Office — Advanced Functions

Figure 5.67 Save Style Set

26. Enter a STYLE SET NAME.

27. Click OK.

28. Follow the STYLES • APPLY STYLE SET menu path in the Advanced Analysis Office ribbon.

29. Select your newly saved style and click OK. Your style is applied with the name we entered when saving the style.

In the previous steps, you used an existing style from Advanced Analysis Office and modified it to your needs. We then saved the modified style with a new name. In a scenario where you would like to share the style with other users, so that all users have the same look and feel for the workbooks, you can use the EXPORT STYLE SET menu and IMPORT STYLE SET from the STYLE menu in the Advanced Analysis Office ribbon to create a common, shared definition for a style.

Export and Import Style Sets
With the Export Style Set menu and Import Style Set you can export your style set definition as an XML file and share the definition with other users who can use the Import Style Set menu to leverage your definitions.

Table 5.3 lists the available Cell Styles for Advanced Analysis Office.

Cell Style Name	Description
SAPBorder	Formatting for the borders of the cells as part of the crosstab.
SAPDataCell	Formatting for the detailed cells displaying the actual data.

Table 5.3 Available Cell Styles

Cell Style Name	Description
SAPDataTotalCell	Formatting for the Totals and Subtotals line items.
SAPDimensionCell	Formatting for dimension/characteristic header cells.
SAPEmphasized	Formatting for highlighted cells displaying the actual data. The highlighting is based on the BEx Query definition.
SAPExceptionLevel1 to SAPExceptionLevel9	Formatting settings for rules leveraged in Exceptions defined in the BEx query or via conditional formatting of Advanced Analysis Office.
SAPHierarchyCell	Formatting for members of the hierarchy for even levels (0, 2, 4,...).
SAPHierarchyCell0 to SAPHierarchyCell4	Formatting for members of the specific hierarchy level. This setting will override SAPHierarchyCell and SAPHierarchyOddCell.
SAPHierarchyOddCell	Formatting for members of the hierarchy for odd levels (1, 3, 5,...).
SAPMemberCell	Formatting for members of the dimension/ characteristic.
SAPMemberTotalCell	Formatting for the Total and Subtotal lines for the dimensions/characteristics.

Table 5.3 Available Cell Styles (Cont.)

In this section, we learned how to use a style set to provide all of our users via a common look and feel. In the next section, we will take a look at the advanced funtionalities of Advanced Analysis Office in Microsoft PowerPoint.

5.2 Advanced Functionality in Advanced Analysis Office for Microsoft PowerPoint

In this section, we will take a look at some of the more advanced functionality of Advanced Analysis for Microsoft PowerPoint, in particular, the Fit Table functionality and its behavior.

5 | Advanced Analysis Office — Advanced Functions

1. Start Advanced Analysis Office with Microsoft PowerPoint via the menu path START • PROGRAMS • SAP BUSINESSOBJECTS • ADVANCED ANALYSIS FOR MICROSOFT POWERPOINT.
2. Select the NEW menu and create a new blank presentation.
3. Select the INSERT • SELECT DATA SOURCE option from the Advanced Analysis ribbon.
4. You will see the log-on screen for SAP BusinessObjects Enterprise.
5. Click SKIP.
6. You are now presented with the list of available SAP systems based on the entries in your SAP Logon pad.
7. Select the entry for your SAP system.
8. Click NEXT.
9. Enter your SAP credentials in the log-on screen and click NEXT.
10. Select the BEx query that we created in Chapter 4 that shows Product Group and Product in the rows.
11. Enter 2009 and 2010 for the variable for Calendar Year when prompted.
12. Click OK.
13. You will be asked if you would like to SPLIT or ABBREVIATE the table for the slides (see Figure 5.68).

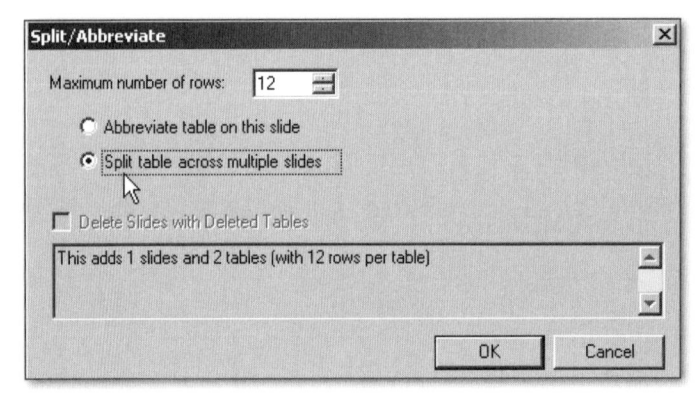

Figure 5.68 Split /Abbreviate

14. Select the SPLIT TABLE ACROSS MULTIPLE SLIDES option and set the value for MAXIMUM NUMBER OF ROWS to 12 (see Figure 5.69).

15. Click OK.

Product Group		Product	Net Value EUR	Open Order Quantity PC	Open Order Value EUR	Product Costs EUR	Transport Costs EUR
MOB1	Mobile Devices 1	CN0400	21,630,583.00	48	1,823,978.00	4,949,500.00	2,517,120.00
		HT1020	16,134,769.00	6	303,520.00	8,987,250.00	4,570,560.00
		Result	37,765,352.00	54	2,127,498.00	13,936,750.00	7,087,680.00
MOB2	Mobile Devices 2	CN0600	21,660,926.00	48	1,827,924.00	4,949,500.00	2,517,120.00
		HT1021	16,459,048.00	6	241,676.00	9,508,250.00	4,835,520.00
		Result	38,119,974.00	54	2,069,600.00	14,457,750.00	7,352,640.00
MON1	Monitors 1	CN0F17	27,907,625.00	48	2,067,993.00	7,815,000.00	3,974,400.00
		HT1030	20,843,239.00	6	161,621.00	12,764,500.00	6,491,520.00
		Result	48,750,864.00	54	2,229,614.00	20,579,500.00	10,465,920.00
MON2	Monitors 2	CN0F21	27,277,998.00	48	1,960,142.00	7,945,250.00	4,040,640.00
		HT1036	21,059,874.00	6	319,784.00	12,113,250.00	6,160,320.00
		Result	48,337,872.00	54	2,279,926.00	20,058,500.00	10,200,960.00

Figure 5.69 Split Table

When using the SPLIT THE TABLE ACROSS MULTIPLE SLIDES option the table is split based on the configured number. For example, a table with 40 rows with a maximum number of rows set to 12 would be split into 4 slides with three slides having 12 rows each and one slide with 4 rows. After each refresh the number of slides is recalculated and the number of slides can grow based on the actual data volume.

16. Select the table on the first slide and navigate to the SPLIT/ABBREVIATE menu in the Advanced Analysis Office ribbon (see Figure 5.70).

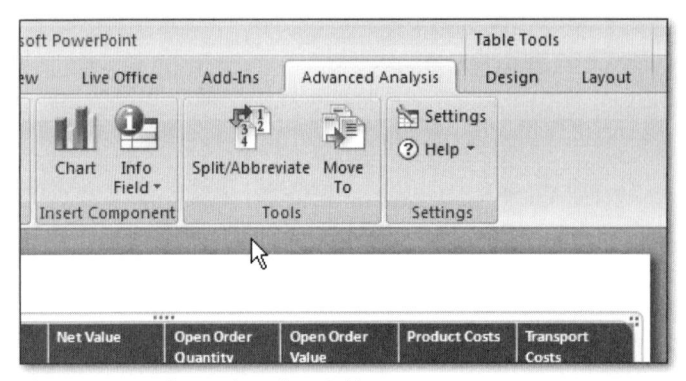

5 | Advanced Analysis Office — Advanced Functions

Figure 5.70 Advanced Analysis Ribbon

17. Select the SPLIT/ABBREVIATE menu.

    Next, abbreviate the table and the dialog shows that this will result in the table on our second slide being deleted. In addition, we have the option of also deleting the slides that will become empty because of the deleted tables (see Figure 5.71).

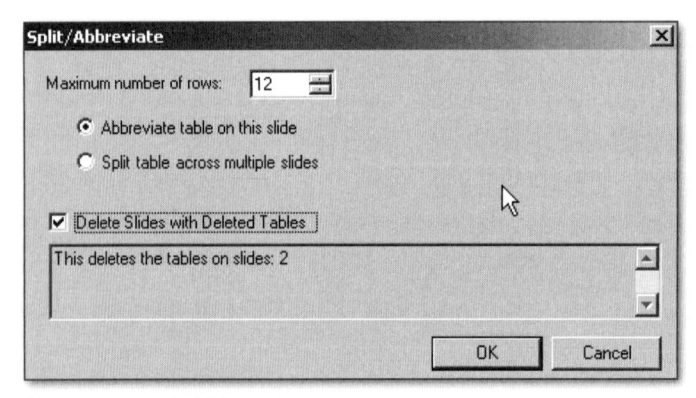

Figure 5.71 Split/Abbreviate

18. Select the ABBREVIATE TABLE ON THIS SLIDE option and configure the value for MAXIMUM NUMBER OF ROWS to 12.

19. Activate the DELETE SLIDES WITH DELETED TABLES option.

20. Click OK (see Figure 5.72).

250

Advanced Functionality in Advanced Analysis Office for Microsoft PowerPoint | 5.2

Product Group		Product	Net Value EUR	Open Order Quantity PC	Open Order Value EUR	Product Costs EUR	Transport Costs EUR
MOB1	Mobile Devices 1	CN0400	21,630,583.00	48	1,823,978.00	4,949,500.00	2,517,120.00
		HT1020	16,134,769.00	6	303,520.00	8,987,250.00	4,570,560.00
		Result	37,765,352.00	54	2,127,498.00	13,936,750.00	7,087,680.00
MOB2	Mobile Devices 2	CN0600	21,660,926.00	48	1,827,924.00	4,949,500.00	2,517,120.00
		HT1021	16,459,048.00	6	241,676.00	9,508,250.00	4,835,520.00
		Result	38,119,974.00	54	2,069,600.00	14,457,750.00	7,352,640.00
MON1	Monitors 1	CN0F17	27,907,625.00	48	2,067,993.00	7,815,000.00	3,974,400.00
		HT1030	20,843,239.00	6	161,621.00	12,764,500.00	6,491,520.00
		Result	48,750,864.00	54	2,229,614.00	20,579,500.00	10,465,920.00
MON2	Monitors 2	CN0F21	27,277,998.00	48	1,960,142.00	7,945,250.00	4,040,640.00
		HT1036	21,059,874.00	6	319,784.00	12,113,250.00	6,160,320.00
		Result	48,337,872.00	54	2,279,926.00	20,058,500.00	10,200,960.00
...	...	...	...	...	...	...	...

Figure 5.72 Abbreviated Table

Because we chose to abbreviate the table in the last row of the table, you should see "..." symbols to indicate that there are more rows of data in the underlying source. Please note that the actual rows that are shown are not fixed because, for example, a simple sort can change which 12 rows are shown on the first slide.

21. Select the table on the first slide and navigate to the SPLIT/ABBREVIATE menu.
22. Select the SPLIT TABLE ACROSS MULTIPLE SLIDES option. The dialog will indicate that a slide will be added to the presentation (see Figure 5.73).
23. Click OK.
24. Now manually delete the second slide of the presentation.

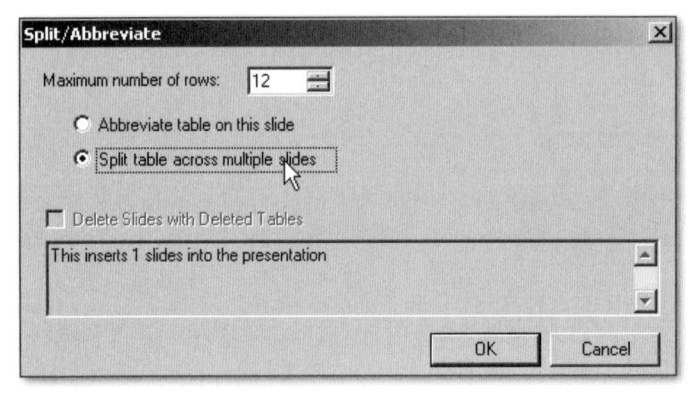

5 Advanced Analysis Office — Advanced Functions

Figure 5.73 Split/Abbreviate

25. Select the REFRESH ALL menu in the Advanced Analysis Office ribbon.

    Because we configured our presentation to split the table, the manually deleted slide is added back to the overall presentation.

26. Now change the order of the slides inside the overall presentation.

27. Select the REFRESH ALL menu in the Advanced Analysis Office ribbon (see Figure 5.74).

Figure 5.74 Advanced Analysis Office Presentation

Here, you will notice that the manually changed order stays as manually rearranged and is not overwritten by a refresh.

252

In this section, we reviewed the behavior of splitting and abbreviating the table from Advanced Analysis Office in Microsoft PowerPoint. In the next chapter, we will compare Advanced Analysis Office with BEx Analyzer.

5.3 Summary

In this chapter, you learned the more advanced features and functions of Advanced Analysis Office for Microsoft Excel and PowerPoint. We learned how to leverage hierarchies, create calculations, use a Filter Panel, use Formulas, how to work with styles, and how to fit our information into a Microsoft PowerPoint slide deck. In the next chapter, we will compare Advanced Analysis Office with BEx Analyzer.

Advanced Analysis Office is quickly becoming the new Business Explorer (BEx) Analyzer. In this chapter, we'll see how the first version of Advanced Analysis Office compares to BEx Analyzer.

6 Advanced Analysis Office and BEx Analyzer — a Comparison

In this chapter, we will compare the features and functions of the initial release of Advanced Analysis Office to BEx Analyzer to give you a good idea of what to expect from the product itself. We grouped the comparison into two main categories: Supported and Missing Functionality.

6.1 Supported Functionality

In this section, we will highlight the features and functions of BEx Analyzer that are fully supported by Advanced Analysis Office.

Table 6.1 contains a list of features and functions supported by Advanced Analysis Office.

Category	Feature/Functionality
General Functionality	
	Support for Currency/Quantity translation defined in BEx Query
	Support for Currency/Quantity translation by end users
	Exception aggregation
	Simple calculations by end users
	Support for conditions defined in the BEx Query
	Support for conditions defined by end users

Table 6.1 Supported Features and Functions

6 | Advanced Analysis Office and BEx Analyzer — a Comparison

Category	Feature/Functionality
	Support for exceptions defined in the BEx Query
	Support for exceptions defined by end users
	Zero/Null suppression
	Multiple data sources in a single workbook
Metadata Support	
	Characteristics
	Key Figures
	Restricted Key Figures
	Calculated Key Figures
	Navigational Attributes
	Display Attributes
	Hierarchies
	Structures
	Filter
	Exceptions
	Conditions
	Cell Editor changes
	Compounded Characteristics
	Constant Selection
Variable Support	
	Characteristic Variables
	Formula Variables
	Text Variables
	Hierarchy Variables
	Hierarchy Node Variables

Table 6.1 Supported Features and Functions (Cont.)

Category	Feature/Functionality
	Variables based on Authorization
	Variables based on EXIT
	Variables based on Replacement Paths
	Optional Variables
	Mandatory Variables
	Default Values for Variables
	Variables used in the Default area of BEx Query
Hierarchy Support	
	Expanding to a specified Hierarchy Level
	Expanding to the Hierarchy Level specified in BEx Query
	Position Parent Nodes above or below their children
	Temporal Hierarchy Join
	Hierarchical display of characteristics configured in BEx Query
	Hierarchical display of Key Figures
	Exchange of Hierarchies at runtime by end users

Table 6.1 Supported Features and Functions (Cont.)

As you can see in Table 6.1, and based on the overview of the basic and advanced functionality in the previous chapters, Advanced Analysis Office offers a broad range of functionality that is offered by BEx Analyzer.

In the next section, we will look at the gaps in functionality between Advanced Analysis Office and BEx Analyzer.

6.2 Missing Functionality

In this section, we will highlight the features and functions that are not available with Advanced Analysis Office. Please note, this book is based on the initial release of Advanced Analysis Office and most of these gaps will be closed in future releases.

Table 6.2 lists the features and functions that are available with BEx Analyzer but not yet supported by Advanced Analysis Office.

Category	Feature/Functionality
General Functionality	
	Support for Report Report Interface (RRI)
	Support for precalculating workbooks
	Support for scheduling workbooks
	Integration with SAP NetWeaver Business Information Warehouse (BW) documents
	Integration with the Planning functionality
	Support for SAP NetWeaver BW 3.x
Variables	
	Support for Variants
	Support for Variable Personalization

Table 6.2 Missing Features and Functions

In addition to the items listed in Table 6.2, there are two important facts to consider. Advanced Analysis Office, in its initial release, does not offer an actual migration of your BEx Analyzer workbooks. However, because both products are based on the BEx Query as a data source you should have no problem creating new workbooks using Advanced Analysis Office for workbooks that don't use VBA coding or a lot of custom designs. The other fact is that there is only support for SAP NetWeaver BW 7.x or higher; Advanced Analysis Office will not support SAP NetWeaver BW 3.x.

In terms of the timeframe for closing some of the previously mentioned gaps, we will discuss the future roadmap in Chapter 9, Advanced Analysis — Product Outlook.

6.3 Summary and Conclusion

The two tables in this chapter should provide you with a good indication of how close Advanced Analysis Office is, in its initial release, to the full functionality of BEx Analyzer. In addition, Advanced Analysis Office will be bringing new features and a totally redesigned usability to your end users, such as:

- A navigation panel that can be used for filtering and slice-and-dice navigation via drag and drop.
- The capability to select specific hierarchy levels for display, which includes skipping hierarchy levels.
- The option for creating calculations without having to write formulas, but instead by simply selecting the needed elements and type of calculation.
- Integration into the full charting capabilities of Microsoft Office, which also provides functions such as Trend Analysis.
- A complete integration into Microsoft PowerPoint, allowing you to create presentations with live and updated data.
- Interoperability with other SAP BusinessObjects Business Intelligence (BI) client tools like Crystal Reports and Web Intelligence within the BusinessObjects XI 4.0 timeframe.

Overall, Advanced Analysis Office is the right choice for those looking to replace their BEx Analyzer workbooks with a more modern and user-friendly product that provides end users with a BI client, which allows for more in-depth analysis compared to the other BI client tools.

With the option of having Advanced Analysis Office deployed in combination with SAP BusinessObjects XI 3.1, customers have the opportunity to leverage an existing investment into the XI 3.1 platform and add a long-awaited component to their portfolio. Based on their needs, requirements, and project timeframe they can then decide when to move to SAP BusinessObjects XI 4.x.

For those that are worried about an automatic migration of their BEx Analyzer workbooks, they may want to group their workbooks into workbooks that just basically show the data from the underlying BEx Query and the workbooks that make use of VBA coding or custom designs. These workbooks, which are basic workbooks not making use of VBA coding or custom design, should be very easy to create with Advanced Analysis Office and customers should consider consolidating all of their BI requirements and tools on top of SAP BusinessObjects XI. For workbooks that do leverage VBA coding or custom designs, or do require the missing functionality listed in the previous section, it is recommended to wait for an updated version of Advanced Analysis Office with migration functionality for the BEx Analyzer workbooks.

Advanced Analysis Office is one of several Business Intelligence (BI) client tools that integrate with SAP BusinessObjects Enterprise. In this chapter, we'll learn how Advanced Analysis Office benefits from this integration.

7 Advanced Analysis Office Integrated with SAP BusinessObjects Enterprise

This chapter contains an overview of how Advanced Analysis Office is integrated with SAP BusinessObjects Enterprise. The focus is on XI 3.1, because XI 4.0 has not been released as of this book's writing (June 2010). Chapter 9, Advanced Analysis – Product Outlook, contains an outlook into the XI 4.0 integration.

In general, the SAP BusinessObjects integration can be grouped into five areas:

- Lifecycle Management
- Object Level and Data Level Security
- Sharing of common objects (for example, connections or workbooks)
- Single Sign On (SSO) and User Authentication
- Integration into InfoView

We will now look at each of these areas in more detail.

7.1 Lifecycle Management

In this section, we will review the Lifecycle Management options that you will have after integrating Advanced Analysis Office with SAP BusinessObjects Enterprise. Lifecycle Management, in this context, means the capability to move an Advanced Analysis Office workbook or presentation and its connections from your development environment to the test or production environment.

The Lifecycle Manager for SAP BusinessObjects Enterprise can be downloaded for free from the SAP Service Marketplace at *http://service.sap.com/swdc*. It lets you move objects from SAP BusinessObjects Enterprise system to either an external archive file or to another SAP BusinessObjects system.

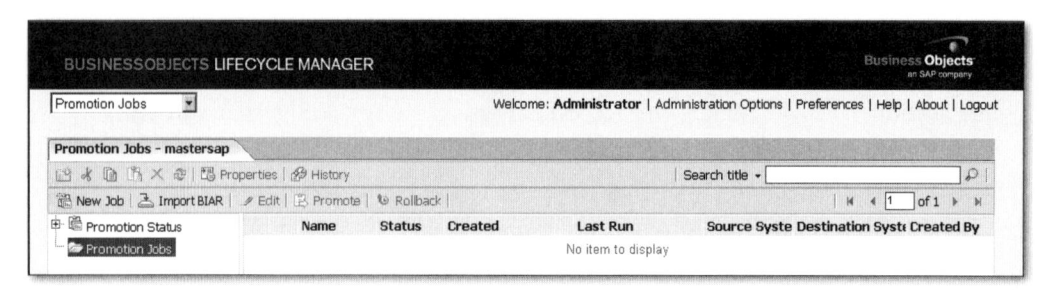

SAP BusinessObjects Lifecycle Manager

For more details on the SAP BusinessObjects Lifecycle Manager, you can find the complete documentation at *http://help.sap.com* in the area for SAP BusinessObjects. You can also use the following links for the Installation Guide and User Guide:

Installation Guide (Windows):

http://service.sap.com/~sapidb/011000358700000565232010E/xi31_sp3_lcm_inst_win_en.pdf

User Guide:

http://help.sap.com/businessobject/product_guides/boexir31SP3/en/xi31_sp3_lcm_user_en.pdf

---

For the following steps, it is assumed that you have installed SAP BusinessObjects Lifecycle Manager on your SAP BusinessObjects Enterprise system, that you have at least one defined server-side connection for Advanced Analysis Office, and that you have one workbook stored in SAP BusinessObjects Enterprise.

1. Start the Lifecycle Manager via the menu path: START • PROGRAMS • BUSINESSOBJECTS XI 3.1 • BUSINESSOBJECTS ENTERPRISE • BUSINESSOBJECTS ENTERPRISE LIFECYCLE MANAGER.

2. Log on to your system with an administrative account. The start screen from the Lifecycle Manager will appear (see Figure 7.1).

Figure 7.1 BusinessObjects Lifecycle Manager

3. Select ADMINISTRATION OPTIONS in the top menu bar (see Figure 7.2).

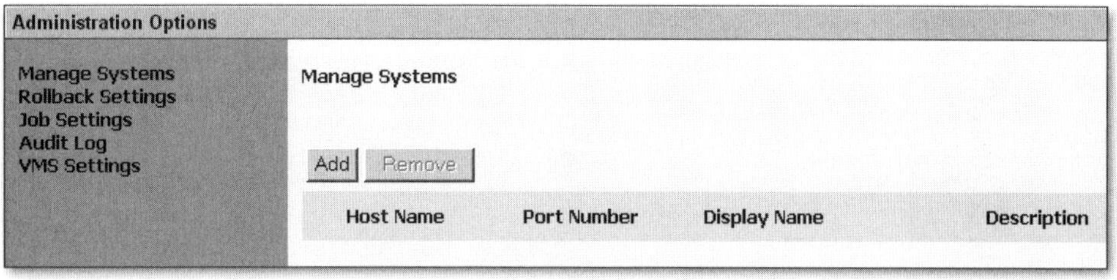

Figure 7.2 Administration Options

4. Next, we need to define our SAP BusinessObjects Enterprise system as the source system for the Lifecycle Manager.
5. Click ADD.
6. Enter the details of your SAP BusinessObjects Enterprise system (see Figure 7.3).

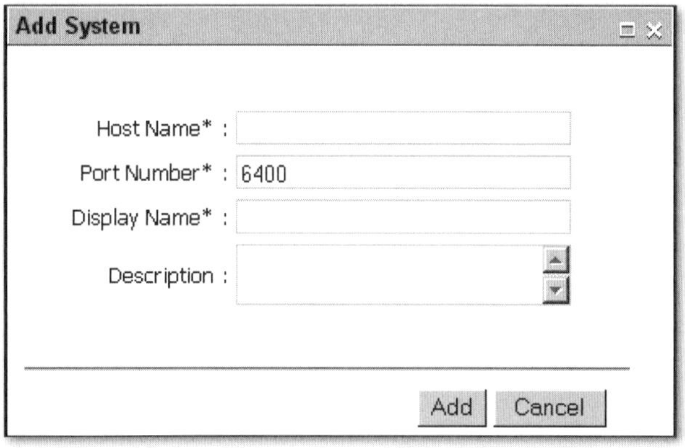

Figure 7.3 Add System

7. Click ADD.
8. Click CLOSE.
9. Use the menu item NEW JOB to create a new PROMOTION JOB for your objects (see Figure 7.4).

7 | Advanced Analysis Office Integrated with SAP BusinessObjects Enterprise

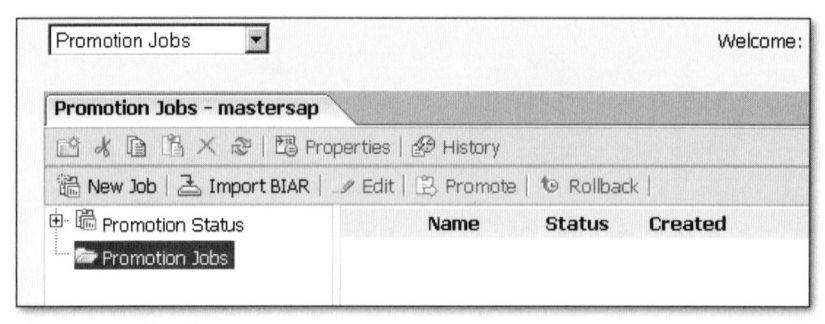

Figure 7.4 Lifecycle Manager

10. Enter a name for the new job (see Figure 7.5).

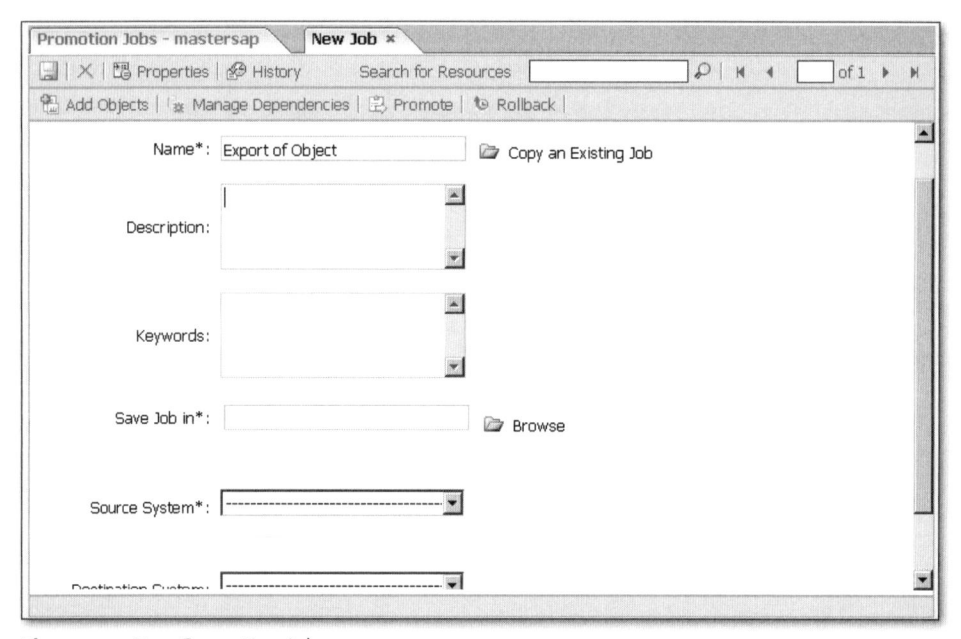

Figure 7.5 New Promotion Job

11. Select a folder to save the job to by clicking the Browse button.
12. Select the LOGIN TO A NEW CMS option for the SOURCE SYSTEM option.
13. Then select the system and provide credentials for authentication (see Figure 7.6).

Lifecycle Management | **7.1**

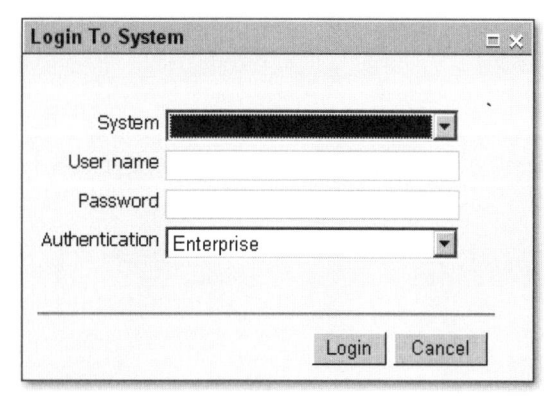

Figure 7.6 Login to System

14. Select the system you defined previously from the list.
15. Enter the administrator account and password.
16. Click LOGIN.
17. Select OUTPUT TO BIAR FILE for the DESTINATION SYSTEM.
18. Click CREATE.
19. You can now use the different object types on the left side to select the objects (see Figure 7.7).

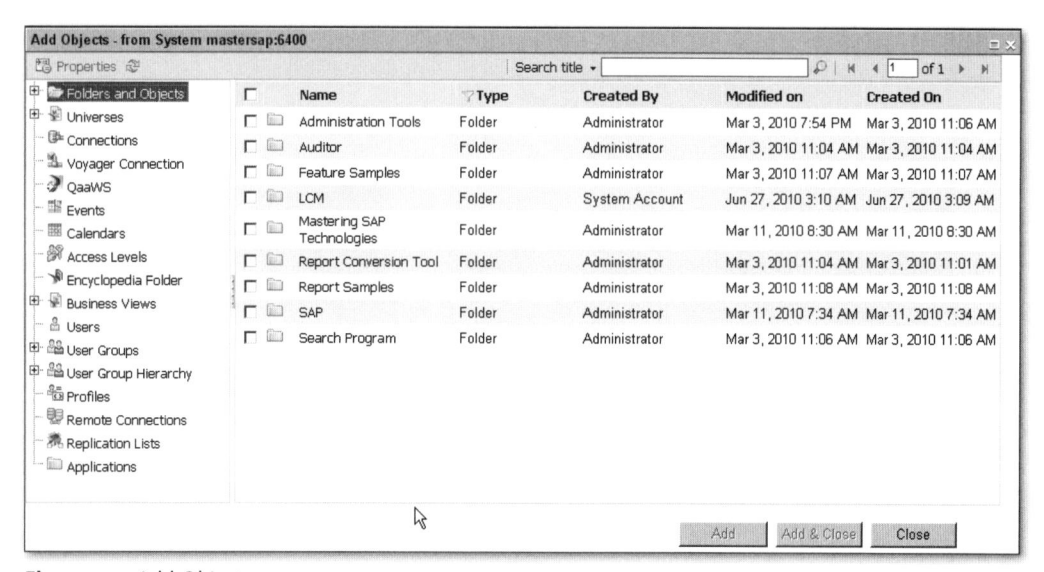

Figure 7.7 Add Objects

265

7 | Advanced Analysis Office Integrated with SAP BusinessObjects Enterprise

20. Select FOLDERS AND OBJECTS and navigate to the folder for the Advanced Analysis Office workbook (see Figure 7.8).

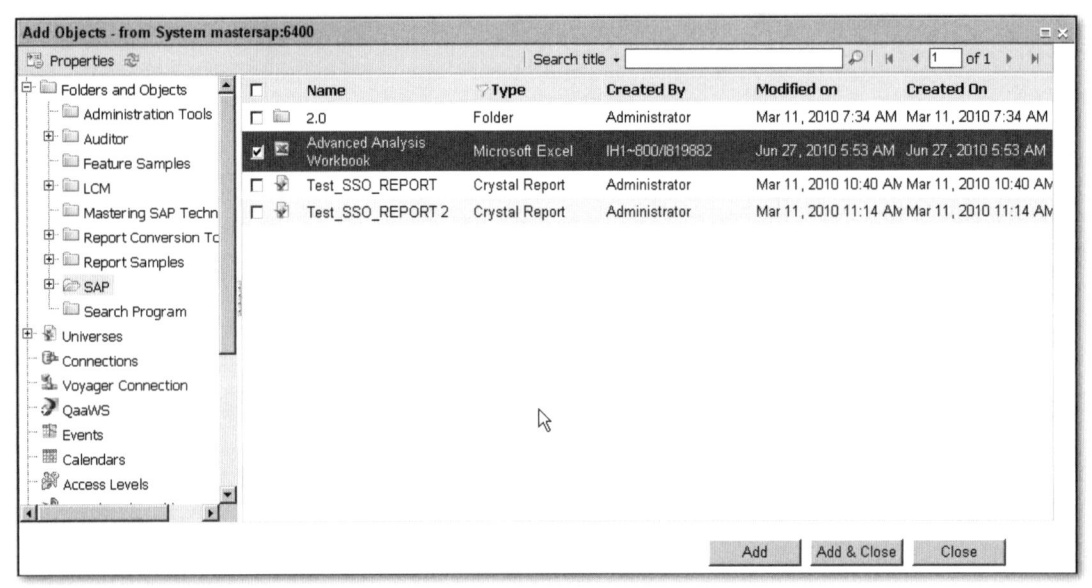

Figure 7.8 Add Objects

21. Select the Advanced Analysis workbook.
22. Click ADD.
23. Select VOYAGER CONNECTIONS.
24. Select the defined connection (see Figure 7.9).
25. Click ADD & CLOSE.

> **Advanced Analysis Office and Lifecycle Manager**
>
> Please note that the Advanced Analysis Office workbooks and presentations are treated as Microsoft Excel and PowerPoint object types in SAP BusinessObjects Enterprise XI 3.1. In terms of connections, Advanced Analysis Office shares the Voyager connections.

Lifecycle Management | **7.1**

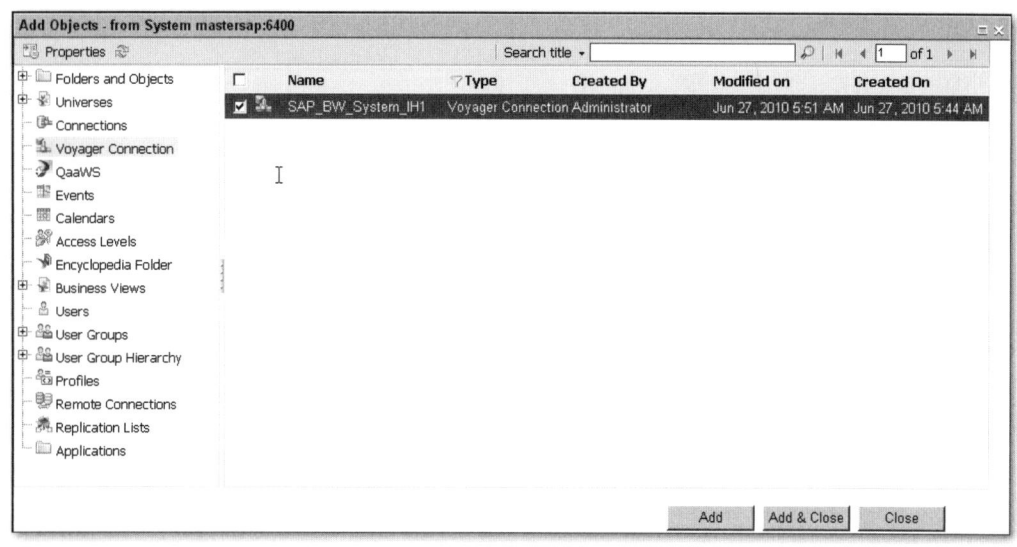

Figure 7.9 Voyager Connections

All of the selected objects are now shown (see Figure 7.10) and now you can create a BI archive package, manage dependencies, or transport the objects directly to another SAP BusinessObjects Enterprise system.

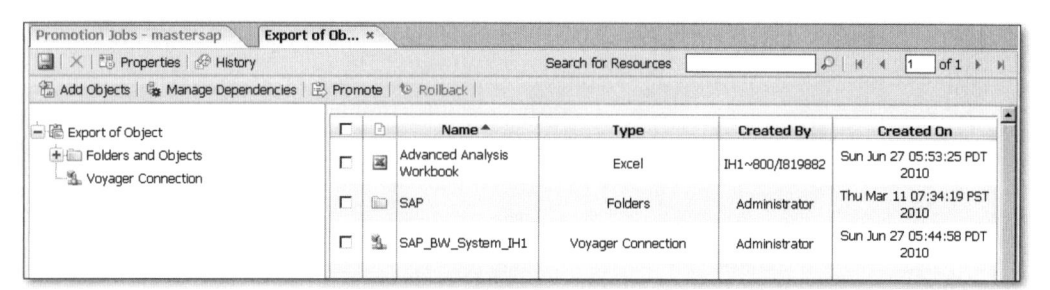

Figure 7.10 Promotion

26. Click MANAGE DEPENDENCIES (see Figure 7.11).

267

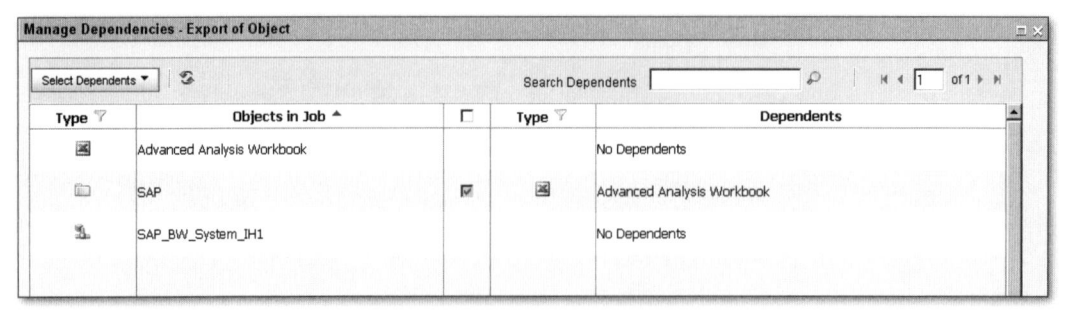

Figure 7.11 Manage Dependencies

It is important to note that the workbook states that there are no dependents. This is the most important limitation of integrating Advanced Analysis Office with SAP BusinessObjects Lifecycle Manager XI 3.1 — the inability to show dependencies to the underlying Voyager connections.

Based on this limitation, you have to select workbooks and presentations from Advanced Analysis Office and Voyager connections manually.

27. Click CLOSE.
28. Click PROMOTE.

Now you can review the summary (see Figure 7.12) of your configured job promotion.

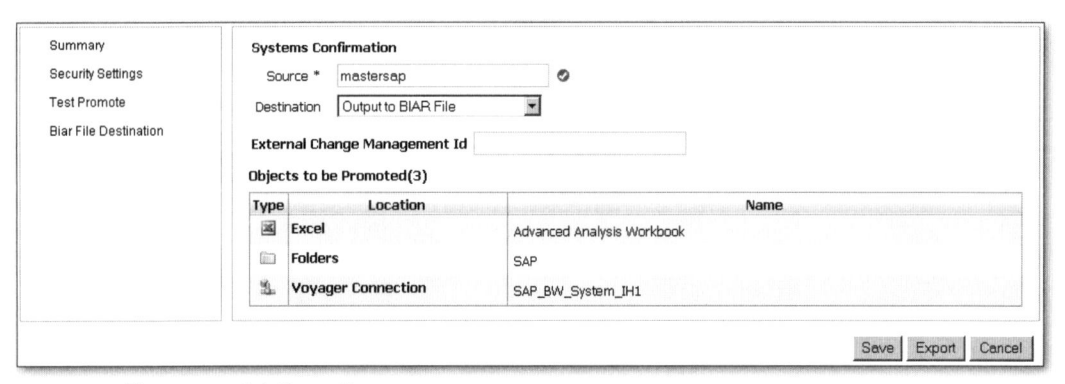

Figure 7.12 Job Promotion

29. Click EXPORT.

30. Based on our example, and the configuration to output the object to a BI Archive file, you will be prompted to save the file to the local disk.

The preceding steps outline a basic workflow of exporting a set of objects from Advanced Analysis Office to a locally stored BI Archive file. These steps also show the limitations of combining Lifecycle Manager with Advanced Analysis Office.

When importing a configured BI Archive file to another SAP BusinessObjects Enterprise system, you will notice that you can't change the settings of the Voyager connection before the object is imported into the target system.

> **Lifecycle Manager Limitations with Advanced Analysis Office**
>
> When using the Lifecycle Manager for Advanced Analysis Office–related objects, you need to take the following limitations into consideration:
>
> - Advanced Analysis Office workbooks and presentations do not show dependent connections.
> - Voyager connections cannot be mapped or edited when being moved from one system to another, unlike Universal connections.

The preceding limitations should be addressed with the release of XI 4.0, which is planned to provide integration between SAP BusinessObjects Lifecycle Manager and the transport system on the SAP NetWeaver side.

In this section, we reviewed the option to use the Lifecycle Manager from your SAP BusinessObjects Enterprise system for transporting Advanced Analysis Office objects from a development environment to a test or production environment. In the next section, we will take a closer look at data-level and object-level security.

7.2 Object-Level and Data-Level Security

In this section, we will review the options for object-level and data-level security. Object-level security refers to the option of securing the actual workbooks and limiting access to those workbooks to a specified list of users. Data-level security refers to defining security for the actual data, often referred to as row-level or column-level security.

7.2.1 Data-Level Security

With regard to data-level security, the integration with SAP BusinessObjects Enterprise doesn't impact any of your existing practices, because data-level, or column-level security for SAP NetWeaver Business Information Warehouse (BW) is defined as part of the BI authorizations. It is important to remember that the recommended approach is to leverage the BEx Query as the data source so that you can leverage authorization variables as part of the BEx Query definition. BI authorizations defined in SAP NetWeaver BW do not automatically work as a filter; therefore, it is highly recommended to leverage the BEx query with authorization variables as the source for Advanced Analysis Office (and any other SAP BusinessObjects BI client tool). Integrating with SAP BusinessObjects Enterprise does not change the rule as there is no option for defining row-level or column-level security outside of SAP NetWeaver BW that is leveraged by Advanced Analysis Office.

7.2.2 Object-Level Security

When referring to object-level security we mean the functionality to secure the Advanced Analysis Office workbook or the underlying connection. Overall, there are three levels of object security:

- You can secure the connection to SAP NetWeaver BW.
- You can secure access to the folder containing the Advanced Analysis Office workbook or presentation.
- You can define security on the individual workbook or presentation.

All of these steps can be performed using the SAP BusinessObjects Enterprise Central Management Console (CMC). Section 2.2.10 Setting Up User Authorizations and Rights contains details on how to define these object security levels. It is recommended to leverage security from the folder level to the object level to avoid having to define object-level security down to the actual workbook or presentation.

> **SAP BusinessObjects Enterprise Administrator Guide**
>
> You can find more details on the administration of SAP BusinessObjects Enterprise and the definition of security as part of your BI platform in the SAP BusinessObjects Enterprise Administrator Guide, which is available at *http://help.sap.com*. You can also use this direct link to the guide: *http://help.sap.com/businessobject/product_guides/boex-ir31SP3/en/xi31_sp3_bip_admin_en.pdf*.

In this section, we reviewed the options for defining data-level security and object-level security when integrating Advanced Analysis Office with SAP BusinessObjects Enterprise. In the next section, we will look at the capability to share objects like workbooks and connections.

7.3 Sharing of Common Objects

In this section we will review the functionality to share objects like a workbook or presentation and sharing the connection to the SAP NetWeaver BW system with multiple users by using SAP BusinessObjects Enterprise as central BI platform.

7.3.1 Sharing Connections

When using Advanced Analysis Office in conjunction with SAP BusinessObjects Enterprise, you can define the connections for Advanced Analysis Office as part of the central repository of your SAP BusinessObjects Enterprise system.

The following steps outline how to create a connection in the CMC of your SAP BusinessObjects Enterprise system:

1. Start the CMC via the menu path: START • PROGRAMS • BUSINESSOBJECTS XI 3.1 • BUSINESSOBJECTS ENTERPRISE • BUSINESSOBJECTS ENTERPRISE CENTRAL MANAGEMENT CONSOLE.

2. Log on to your SAP BusinessObjects Enterprise CMC with an administrative account.

3. Select the Voyager Connections option. Advanced Analysis Office combined with SAP BusinessObjects XI 3.1 is sharing connection definitions with Voyager.

4. Click on the [symbol] symbol to start the new connection process.

5. Enter the necessary details for your SAP NetWeaver BW system (see Figure 7.13). You can see more details in Table 2.2 in Chapter 2, Installation, Deployment, and Configuration of Advanced Analysis Office.

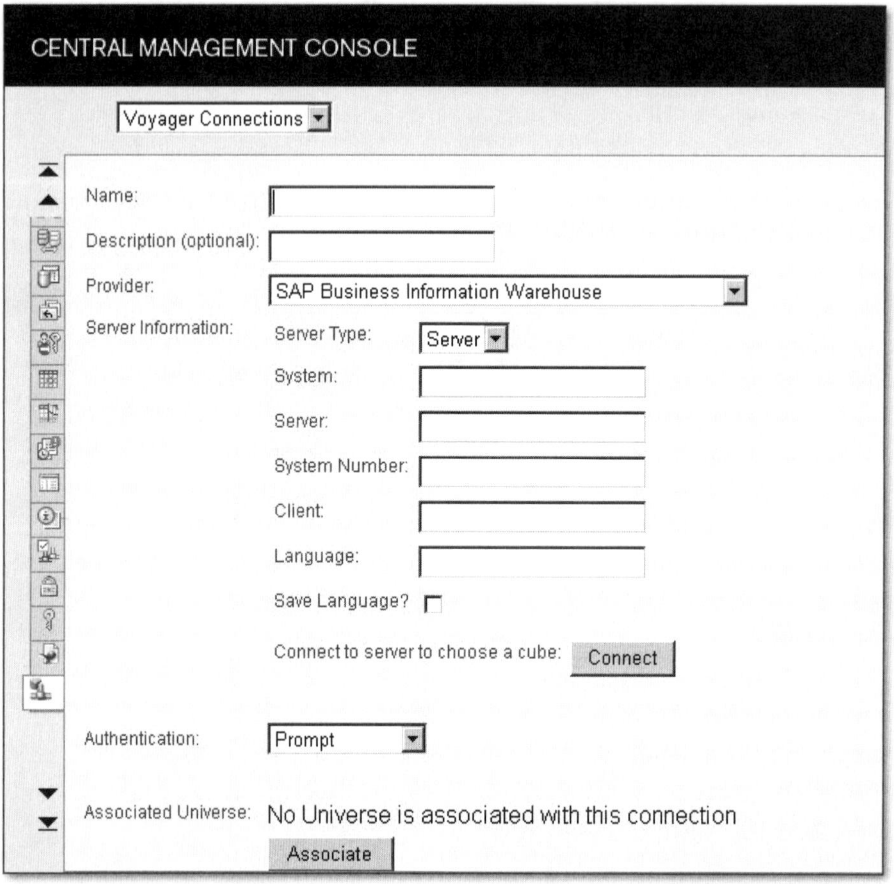

Figure 7.13 Voyager Connection

6. After you enter the details of your SAP NetWeaver BW system, click on the CONNECT button.

7. Enter the USER and PASSWORD to connect to the SAP NetWeaver BW system.

8. Click OK.

9. You will be presented with the CUBE BROWSER, which lets you select an InfoProvider or a BW Query based on the CAPTION or the NAME.

10. Select any BW Query from your SAP NetWeaver BW system and click SELECT.

11. Click SAVE to save your connection.

Now that we've created the connection as part of SAP BusinessObjects Enterprise, let's create a new Advanced Analysis Office workbook based on the connection.

1. Start Advanced Analysis Office with Microsoft Excel via the menu path: START • PROGRAMS • SAP BUSINESSOBJECTS • ADVANCED ANALYSIS FOR MICROSOFT EXCEL.

2. Select INSERT • SELECT DATA SOURCE from the Advanced Analysis Ribbon.

3. In the dialog to log on to your SAP BusinessObjects Enterprise system, click OPTIONS and set SAP as the AUTHENTICATION (see Figure 7.14).

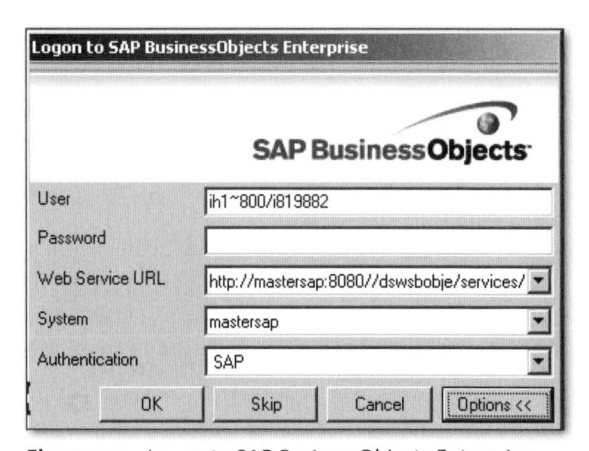

Figure 7.14 Logon to SAP BusinessObjects Enterprise

4. Enter your SAP credentials and password.

   Please note that using SAP as the AUTHENTICATION requires that your SAP BusinessObjects Enterprise system be configured with SAP authentication. In addition, you cannot enter the SAP System ID or SAP Client number as separate fields, you need to enter them as part of the User in the syntax:

   `<SAP System ID>~<SAP Client number>/<SAP User>`, for example, `IH1~800/i819882`

5. Click OK.

6. Select the QUERY/QUERY VIEW option in the listbox for the type of connection (see Figure 7.15).

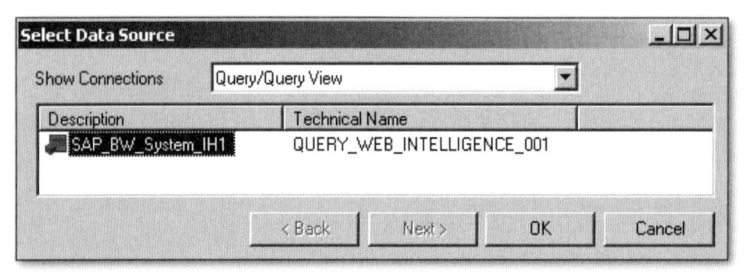

Figure 7.15 Select Data Source

The connection we defined previously should now be shown in the list of available connections.

7. Select the connection and click OK.

   Even though we authenticated with our SAP credentials for our SAP BusinessObjects Enterprise system, we have to authenticate again for the SAP NetWeaver BW system (see Figure 7.16). The reason for this is that the integration with SAP BusinessObjects Enterprise XI 3.1 does not provide a server-based SSO. SSO, in conjunction with SAP BusinessObjects Enterprise XI 3.1, is limited to a client-side SSO. This will be addressed with the release of XI 4.0.

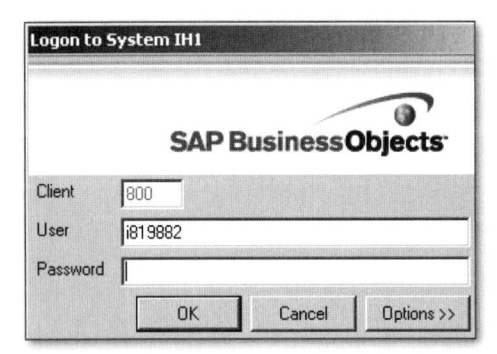

Figure 7.16 SAP Logon

8. After this step you should see the default crosstab in Advanced Analysis Office (see Figure 7.17).

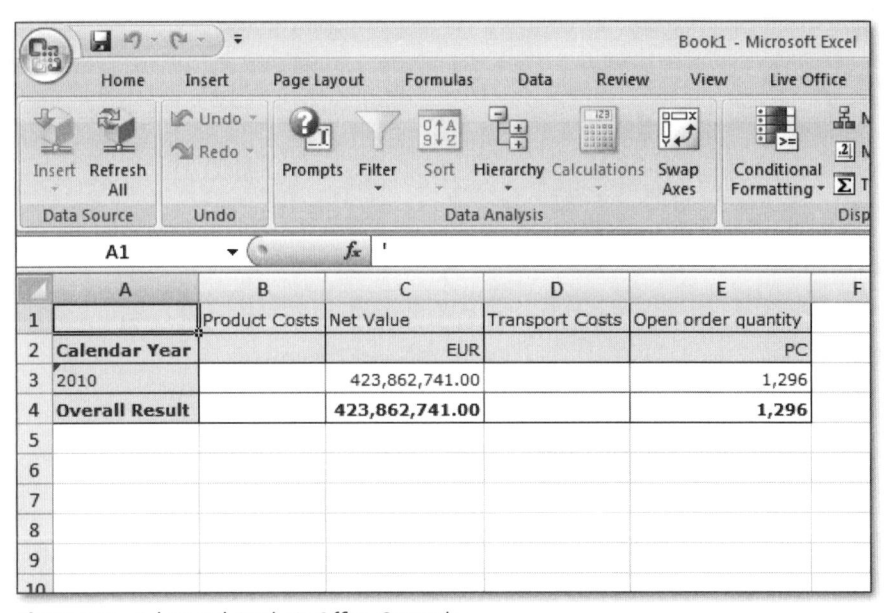

Figure 7.17 Advanced Analysis Office Crosstab

You can find more details on how to secure connections as part of your SAP BusinessObjects Enterprise system in Section 2.2.10 Setting Up User Authorizations and Rights.

In this section, we reviewed the workflow for creating and sharing a connection as part of your SAP BusinessObjects Enterprise system, so that it can be used with Advanced Analysis Office. In the next section, we will look at how to share workbooks and presentations by using SAP BusinessObjects Enterprise as a BI platform.

7.3.2 Sharing Workbooks and Presentations

When using SAP BusinessObjects Enterprise as a BI platform, you can also share workbooks and presentations by using SAP BusinessObjects Enterprise as a repository.

1. Continue with the Advanced Analysis workbook from the previous section.
2. Click the MICROSOFT OFFICE button and select the SAVE WORKBOOK menu (see Figure 7.18).

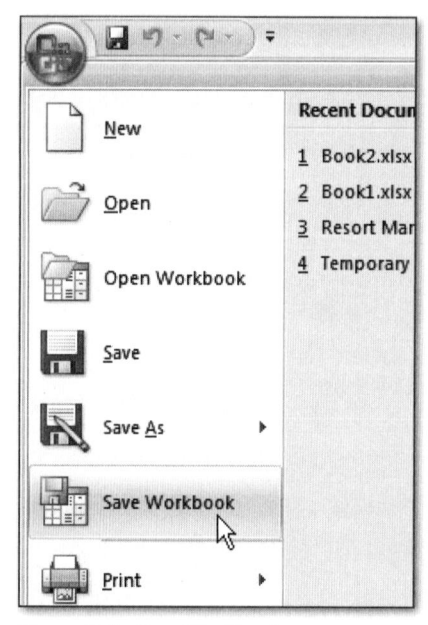

Figure 7.18 Save Workbook

3. Because we already authenticated against the SAP BusinessObjects Enterprise system, we are presented with the folder structure (see Figure 7.19).

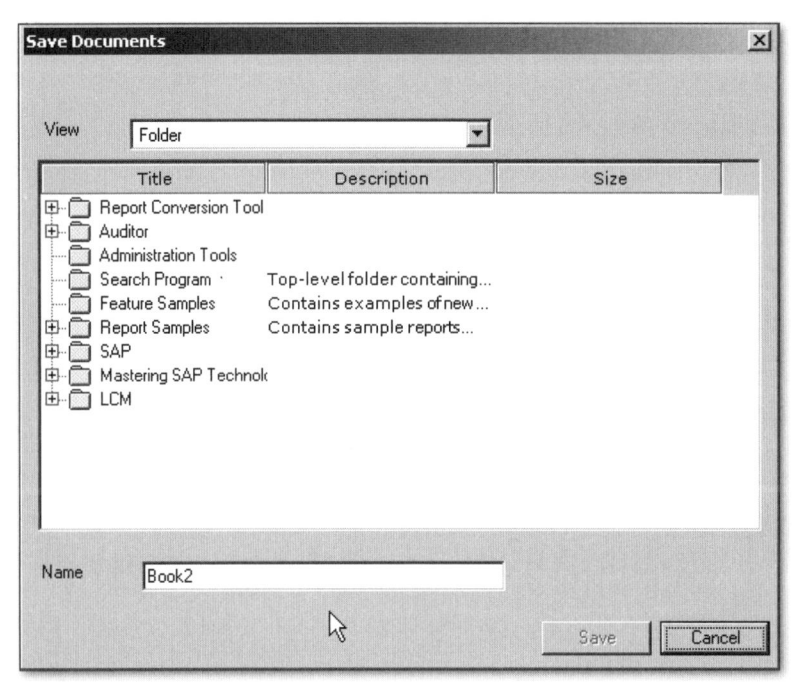

Figure 7.19 Save Documents

4. We can now select a folder and enter a NAME for our workbook.

5. Click SAVE.

The option for opening a workbook from SAP BusinessObjects Enterprise is the same as saving a workbook to SAP BusinessObjects Enterprise. For more details on how to configure the connection to your SAP BusinessObjects Enterprise system for Advanced Analysis Office, see Section 2.2.7 Configuring Connections to SAP BusinessObjects Enterprise.

In this section, we reviewed how you can share workbooks and presentations from Advanced Analysis Office via SAP BusinessObjects Enterprise. In the next section, we will look into the details of user management and user authentication when using Advanced Analysis Office with SAP BusinessObjects Enterprise XI 3.1.

7.4 User Authentication and SSO

In this section, we will provide more details on the integration of Advanced Analysis Office with SAP BusinessObjects Enterprise XI 3.1 with regard to user management and user authentication.

Advanced Analysis Office integrated with SAP BusinessObjects Enterprise XI 3.1 only provides you with a client side–based SSO — not with a server-side SSO. Even when leveraging connections defined as Voyager connections in SAP BusinessObjects Enterprise and leveraging the SAP authentication, users can only achieve real SSO when using a client-side configuration using Secure Network Communication (SNC).

Such a configuration involves the following steps:

- Configuring the necessary profile parameters of SNC for SAP NetWeaver BW, including an SNC name for the SAP NetWeaver BW System.
- Configuring server-side trust between SAP BusinessObjects Enterprise and SAP NetWeaver BW, including an SNC name for the SAP BusinessObjects Enterprise system.
- Configuring the SAP authentication for SAP BusinessObjects Enterprise. The configuration needs to include the SNC options for SAP NetWeaver BW as part of the SAP authentication configuration.
- Configuring the SNC name for the SAP credentials in Transaction SU01.
- Configuring an SNC name for your SAP BusinessObjects Enterprise system in Transaction SNC0.
- The client computer needs to be configured with the necessary SNC software as well.

> **Further Information**
>
> For configuring server-side trust and the SAP Authentication, you can find the complete details in the Installation Guide for the SAP BusinessObjects Integration for SAP Solutions at *http://help.sap.com*:
>
> *http://service.sap.com/~sapidb/011000358700000559912010E/xi31_sp3_bip_sap_inst_en.pdf*.

The workflow to achieve SSO with a connection defined as part of your SAP BusinessObjects Enterprise system is as follows (see Figure 7.20):

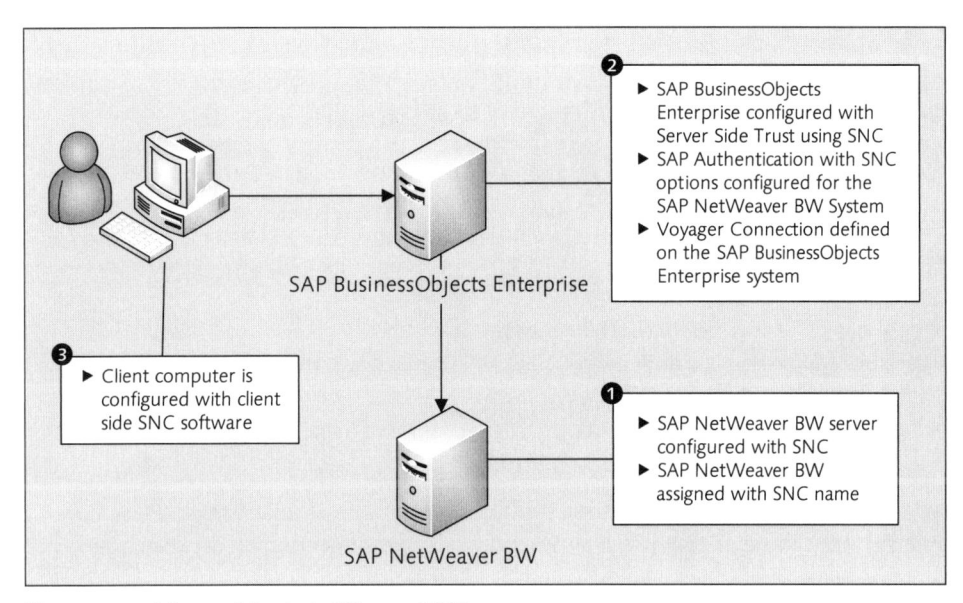

Figure 7.20 Advanced Analysis Office and SSO

❶ You configure SAP NetWeaver BW with SNC.

❷ You configure SAP BusinessObjects Enterprise with server-side trust.

You configure the SNC options for SAP authentication of SAP BusinessObjects Enterprise for SAP NetWeaver BW.

You configure the Voyager connection on SAP BusinessObjects Enterprise.

❸ You configure your client computer with the client-side SNC software.

Now the workflow of opening or creating an Advanced Analysis Office workbook with Single Sign On is as follows:

- You start Advanced Analysis Office for Microsoft Excel.
- You log on to SAP BusinessObjects Enterprise.
- You select the connection stored in SAP BusinessObjects Enterprise.

- Advanced Analysis Office retrieves the connection details from SAP BusinessObjects Enterprise, including the SNC name for the SAP NetWeaver BW system and the System ID.
- The System ID is retrieved from the Voyager Connection and the SNC name is being retrieved from the SNC options for the SAP authentication. The correct SNC options are retrieved by using the System ID as the identifier.
- Advanced Analysis Office leverages the client-side SNC configuration on the local computer with the SAP NetWeaver BW system to achieve SSO.

> **Important: System Details**
>
> Please note that it is very important that the entries on the client computer, the Voyager connection entries, and the SAP authentication for the System ID of your SAP NetWeaver BW system are identical, otherwise Advanced Analysis Office will not be able to identify the system.

If you are using Advanced Analysis Office without an SAP BusinessObjects Enterprise system, you can also use a client-side SNC configuration to achieve SSO.

In this section, we reviewed the options for providing users with a client- or server-based SSO user experience. In the next section, we will take a look at how Advanced Analysis Office integrates with InfoView.

7.5 Integration with InfoView

In this section, we will learn how Advanced Analysis Office is integrated with InfoView from SAP BusinessObjects Enterprise and what steps are necessary to make the integration seamless.

When you save an Advanced Analysis Office workbook or presentation to SAP BusinessObjects Enterprise, the objects are treated as a normal Microsoft Excel or PowerPoint object. You can use the option for opening or saving the workbook and presentation as described in Section 7.3.2, Sharing Workbooks and Presentations, but you can also open Microsoft Excel and PowerPoint objects directly from InfoView.

Before we open a workbook directly from InfoView, we need to make sure that the Advanced Analysis Office add-in is loaded when Microsoft Excel or PowerPoint are used.

You can configure the load behavior of the Advanced Analysis Office add-in by configuring the `LoadBehavior` registry setting in the branch `HKEY_LOCAL_MACHINE\SOFTWARE\Microsoft\Office\Excel\AddIns\SBOP.AdvancedAnalysis.Addin.1` to the value 3 for enabling and to the value 2 for disabling the add-in.

After we configured the load behavior we can open the Advanced Analysis Office documents directly from InfoView.

1. Start InfoView via the menu path: START • PROGRAMS • BUSINESSOBJECTS XI 3.1 • BUSINESSOBJECTS ENTERPRISE • BUSINESSOBJECTS ENTERPRISE JAVA INFOVIEW.
2. Log on to InfoView with your credentials.
3. Click DOCUMENT LIST.
4. Navigate to the Advanced Analysis Office document folder (see Figure 7.21).

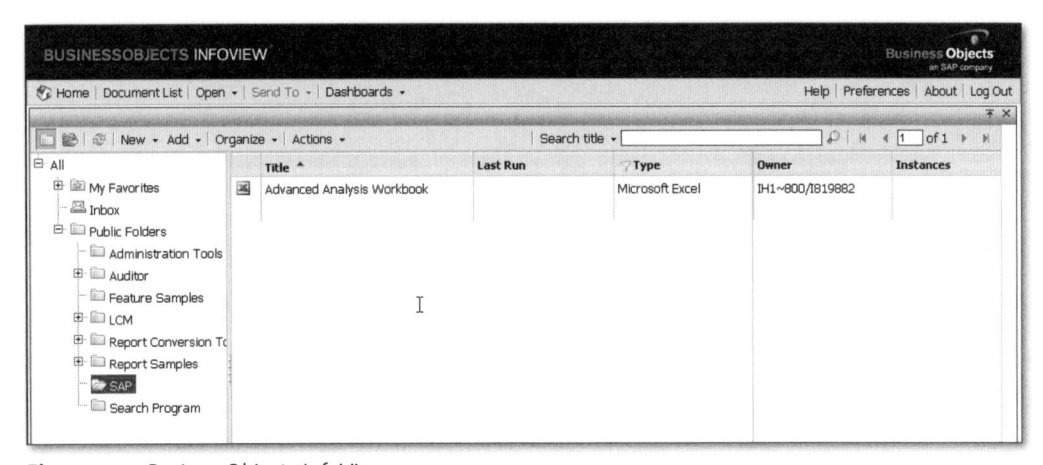

Figure 7.21 BusinessObjects InfoView

5. Right-click the Advanced Analysis Office workbook (see Figure 7.22).

7 | Advanced Analysis Office Integrated with SAP BusinessObjects Enterprise

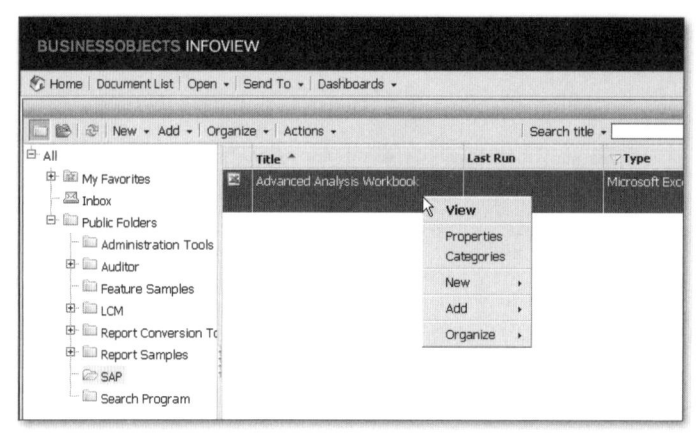

Figure 7.22 SAP BusinessObjects InfoView

6. Select the VIEW menu option (see Figure 7.23).

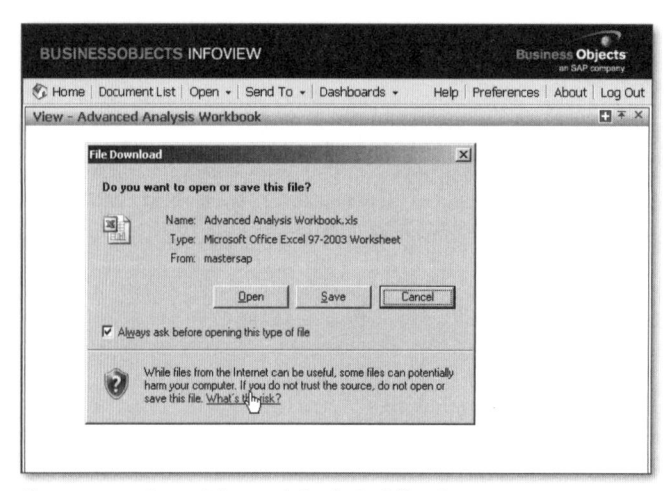

Figure 7.23 Open Advanced Analysis Office Document

7. Click OPEN.

The Advanced Analysis Office workbook is opened in Microsoft Excel and the Advanced Analysis Office add-in is automatically enabled because we configured the load behavior in the registry (see Figure 7.24).

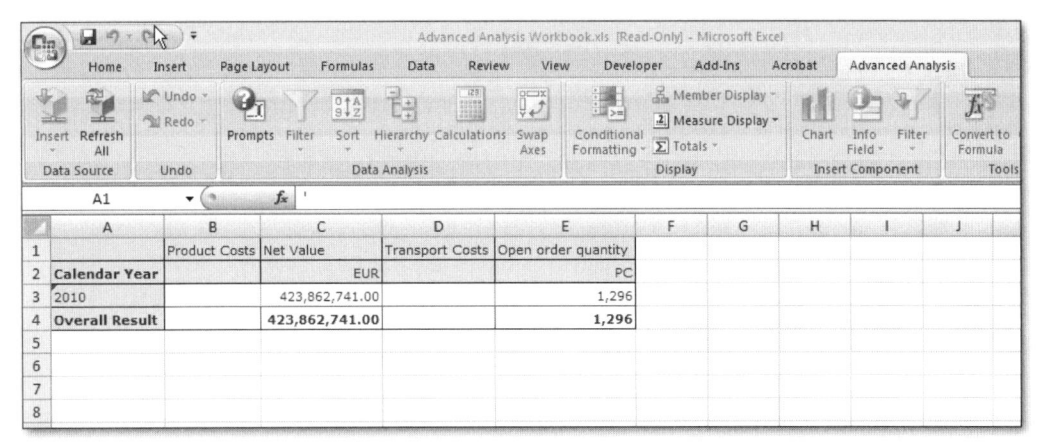

Figure 7.24 Advanced Analysis Office

In this section, we looked at how to configure the load behavior of Advanced Analysis Office and open an Advanced Analysis Office workbook directly from InfoView.

7.6 Summary

In this chapter, we reviewed the different areas of integration, such as Lifecycle Management, between Advanced Analysis Office and SAP BusinessObjects Enterprise. In the next chapter, we will look at a set of business scenarios to see how you can leverage Advanced Analysis Office as part of your day-to-day work.

This chapter uses practical examples to show you how to use the features and functions of Advanced Analysis Office to provide end users greater usability and the correct information.

8 Advanced Analysis Office — Usage Scenarios

In this chapter, we will use practical examples to show you how to leverage Advanced Analysis Office as part of your overall Business Intelligence (BI) portfolio and provide end users with a tool for more detailed analysis.

8.1 Advanced Analysis Office and Customer Support

In this section, we'll assume the role of a Customer Service Center manager. Our main responsibilities are to make sure that customers' problems and issues are resolved quickly, that our resources are leveraged in the best possible way, and that more experienced employees are not spending time on cases that can be solved by others.

In this example, we'll use a BEx Query based on the InfoProvider ACRM_SRV1, which is part of the SAP NetWeaver Business Information Warehouse (BW) Internet Demonstration and Evaluation System (IDES) installation (see Figure 8.1).

The BEx Query includes the following characteristics:

- PRODUCT CATEGORY
- COUNTRY
- PRODUCT

8 | Advanced Analysis Office — Usage Scenarios

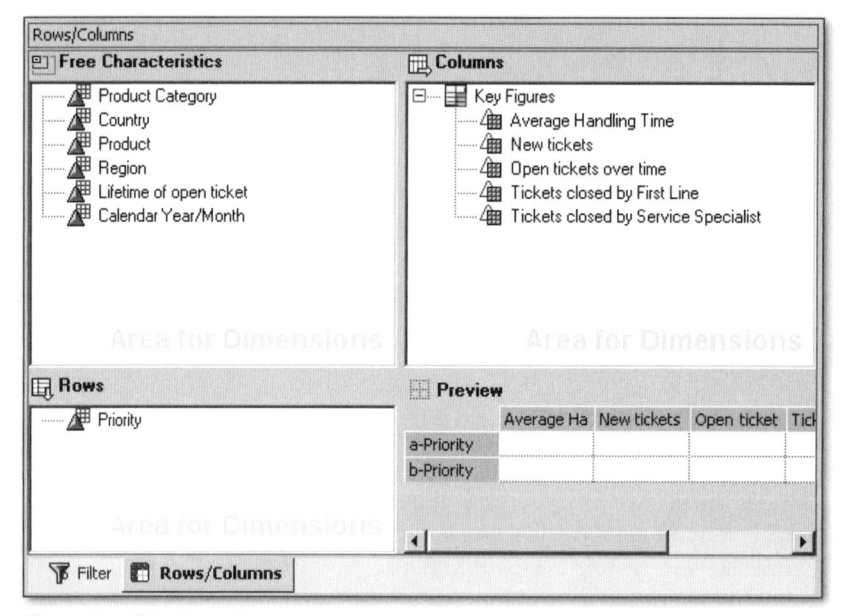

Figure 8.1 BEx Query Design

- REGION
- LIFETIME OF OPEN TICKET
- CALENDAR YEAR/MONTH
- PRIORITY

and the following key figures:

- AVERAGE HANDLING TIME
- NEW TICKETS
- OPEN TICKETS OVER TIME
- TICKETS CLOSED BY FIRST LINE
- TICKETS CLOSED BY SERVICE SPECIALIST

Let's start our analysis with an overview of our customer cases from the last 12 months (see Figure 8.2).

Advanced Analysis Office and Customer Support | **8.1**

	A	B	C	D	E	F
1	Priority	Average Handling Time	New tickets	Open tickets over time	Tickets closed by First Line	Tickets closed by Service Specialist
2	High	579.917	6,360.000	998.000	4,326.000	1,409.000
3	Low	472.167	5,415.000	852.000	4,226.000	730.000
4	Medium	805.583	12,155.000	1,316.000	8,915.000	2,330.000
5	Very High	447.455	3,413.000	784.000	2,453.000	529.000

Figure 8.2 Customer Cases Overview

At first, everything looks fine. The distribution of cases based on priority, and those closed by the first line and by a service specialist are in the range of what we would expect. To verify our assumption, we are adding a dynamic calculation for two key figures — Tickets closed by First Line and Tickets closed by Service Specialist — using the Calculations option in the Advanced Analysis Office ribbon. Then, add the Percentage Contribution to the crosstab (see Figure 8.3).

	A	B	C	D	E	F	G	H
1		Average Handling Time	New tickets	Open tickets over time	Tickets closed by First Line	Percentage Contribution: Tickets closed by First Line	Tickets closed by Service Specialist	Percentage Contribution: Tickets closed by Service Specialist
2	Priority					%		%
3	High	579.917	6,360.000	998.000	4,326.000	21.717	1,409.000	28.191
4	Low	472.167	5,415.000	852.000	4,226.000	21.215	730.000	14.606
5	Medium	805.583	12,155.000	1,316.000	8,915.000	44.754	2,330.000	46.619
6	Very High	447.455	3,413.000	784.000	2,453.000	12.314	529.000	10.584

Figure 8.3 Percentage Contribution

Now we can see that only 28% of the Priority High and 10% of the Very High cases are being closed by a Service Specialist. However, 46% of the Medium cases are also closed by Service Specialists. This raises a red flag because the Service Specialists should spend their time on the more important cases and not on ones with Medium or Low priority.

8   Advanced Analysis Office — Usage Scenarios

Now let's focus on the TICKETS CLOSED BY FIRST LINE and TICKETS CLOSED BY SERVICE SPECIALIST key figures, including the PERCENTAGE CONTRIBUTION. In addition, let's add the LIFETIME OF OPEN TICKET characteristic to our analysis, so that we can see the duration of the ticket based on defined time ranges (see Figure 8.4).

	A	B	C	D	E	F
1			Tickets closed by First Line	Percentage Contribution: Tickets closed by First Line	Tickets closed by Service Specialist	Percentage Contribution: Tickets closed by Service Specialist
2	Priority	Lifetime of open ticket		%		%
3	High	> 48 hours	12.000	0.060	23.000	0.460
4		0 - 12 hours	2,621.000	13.158	901.000	18.027
5		13 - 24 hours	881.000	4.423	338.000	6.763
6		25 - 48 hours	812.000	4.076	147.000	2.941
7	Low	> 48 hours	305.000	1.531	49.000	0.980
8		0 - 12 hours	2,540.000	12.751	365.000	7.303
9		13 - 24 hours	1,134.000	5.693	234.000	4.682
10		25 - 48 hours	247.000	1.240	82.000	1.641
11	Medium	> 48 hours	121.000	0.607	45.000	0.900
12		0 - 12 hours	6,298.000	31.616	1,715.000	34.314
13		13 - 24 hours	167.000	0.838	22.000	0.440
14		25 - 48 hours	2,329.000	11.692	548.000	10.964
15	Very High	0 - 12 hours	1,434.000	7.199	232.000	4.642
16		13 - 24 hours	938.000	4.709	271.000	5.422
17		25 - 48 hours	81.000	0.407	26.000	0.520
18						

Figure 8.4   Lifetime of Open Ticket

Next, so we can easily identify the areas we should focus on, add some conditional formatting to the two key figures representing the percentage contribution to show a symbol for those cases where the percentage contribution is greater than 25% (see Figure 8.5).

8.1 Advanced Analysis Office and Customer Support

	A	B	C	D	E	F
1			Tickets closed by First	Percentage Contribution	Tickets closed by Service Specialist	Percentage Contribution: Tickets closed by Service Specialist
2	Priority	Lifetime of open ticket		%		%
3	High	> 48 hours	12.000	0.060	23.000	0.460
4		0 - 12 hours	2,621.000	13.158	901.000	18.027
5		13 - 24 hours	881.000	4.423	338.000	6.763
6		25 - 48 hours	812.000	4.076	147.000	2.941
7	Low	> 48 hours	305.000	1.531	49.000	0.980
8		0 - 12 hours	2,540.000	12.751	365.000	7.303
9		13 - 24 hours	1,134.000	5.693	234.000	4.682
10		25 - 48 hours	247.000	1.240	82.000	1.641
11	Medium	> 48 hours	121.000	0.607	45.000	0.900
12		0 - 12 hours	6,298.000 ■	31.616	1,715.000 ■	34.314
13		13 - 24 hours	167.000	0.838	22.000	0.440
14		25 - 48 hours	2,329.000	11.692	548.000	10.964
15	Very High	0 - 12 hours	1,434.000	7.199	232.000	4.642
16		13 - 24 hours	938.000	4.709	271.000	5.422
17		25 - 48 hours	81.000	0.407	26.000	0.520
18						
19						

Figure 8.5 Conditional Formatting

With the help of the conditional formatting we can see that our first-line support and our Service Specialists focus more than 30% of their time on cases with MEDIUM priority. These customer cases fall into the lifetime category of 0 - 12 HOURS. Next, compare the effort spent on these cases to all of the other categories by adding the AVERAGE HANDLING TIME key figure back onto the crosstab (see Figure 8.6).

In addition to AVERAGE HANDLING TIME, we also created a Dynamic Calculation to determine the rank in our crosstab. Now we can see that the AVERAGE HANDLING TIME for the cases we're focusing on is in the top 3 in the analysis.

8 | Advanced Analysis Office — Usage Scenarios

	A	B	C	D	E	F	G	H
1			Average Handling Time	Rank Number: Average Handling Time	Tickets closed by First Line	Percentage Contribution: Tickets closed by First Line	Tickets closed by Service Specialist	Percentage Contribution: Tickets closed by Service Specialist
2	Priority	Lifetime of open ticket				%		%
3	High	> 48 hours	0.000	15	12.000	0.060	23.000	0.460
4		0 - 12 hours	319.300		2,621.000	13.158	901.000	18.027
5		13 - 24 hours	318.833	6	881.000	4.423	338.000	6.763
6		25 - 48 hours	264.714	7	812.000	4.076	147.000	2.941
7	Low	> 48 hours	109.667	14	305.000	1.531	49.000	0.980
8		0 - 12 hours	199.727	12	2,540.000	12.751	365.000	7.303
9		13 - 24 hours	323.429	4	1,134.000	5.693	234.000	4.682
10		25 - 48 hours	219.000	10	247.000	1.240	82.000	1.641
11	Medium	> 48 hours	259.500	8	121.000	0.607	45.000	0.900
12		0 - 12 hours	367.750	3	6,298.000	31.616	1,715.000	34.314
13		13 - 24 hours	589.500	1	167.000	0.838	22.000	0.440
14		25 - 48 hours	237.700	9	2,329.000	11.692	548.000	10.964
15	Very High	0 - 12 hours	200.667	11	1,434.000	7.199	232.000	4.642
16		13 - 24 hours	490.000	2	938.000	4.709	271.000	5.422
17		25 - 48 hours	155.600	13	81.000	0.407	26.000	0.520

Figure 8.6 Ranking

Let's continue our analysis and drill down into some further details. First, filter the PRIORITY characteristic to only show cases with MEDIUM priority and then use this option to filter and swap the LIFETIME characteristic in a single step (see Figure 8.7).

	A	B	C	D	E	F	G	H
1								Percentage Contribution: Tickets closed by
					Tickets closed by Fir	Percentage Contrib	Tickets closed by S	Service Specialist
2	Priority	Lifetime of open ticke				%		%
3	Medium	> 48 hours			121.000	1.357	45.000	1.931
4		0 - 12 hours	367.750		6,298.000	70.645	1,715.000	73.605
5		13 - 24 hours		Insert Comment	167.000	1.873	22.000	0.944
6		25 - 48 hours		Filter Members	2,329.000	26.125	548.000	23.519
7				Filter Members and Swap With ▸	Product Category			
8				Filter Other Members	Country			
9				Filter By Member...	Product			
10				Select All Members	Region			
11					Calendar Year/Month			
12				Filter by Measure ▸				
13				Sort Ascending				
14				Sort Descending				
15				Member Display ▸				
16				Totals ▸				
17				Refresh				

Figure 8.7 Filter Members and Swap

Swap LIFETIME with the COUNTRY characteristic so that we can see where the most cases with MEDIUM priority are that our Support Specialists worked on (see Figure 8.8).

	A	B	C	D	E	F	G	H	I	J
1				Average Handling Time	Rank Number: Average Handling Time	Tickets closed by First Line	Percentage Contribution: Tickets closed by First Line	Tickets closed by Service Specialist	Percentage Contribution: Tickets closed by Service Specialist	
2	Priority	Country					%		%	
3	Medium	CH	Switzerland	149.000	3	1,262.000	20.038	327.000	19.067	
4		DE	Germany	190.600	1	2,304.000	36.583	856.000	49.913	
5		US	United States	162.667	2	2,732.000	43.379	532.000	31.020	
6										
7										
8										

Figure 8.8 Customer Cases by Country

We can see that the U.S. and Germany are ranked as first and second with regard to AVERAGE HANDLING TIME and that our Service Specialists solve a large portion of these cases. Continue the analysis by filtering the data for Germany and the U.S. and focusing on the REGIONS (see Figure 8.9).

	A	B	C	D	E	F	G	H	I
1				Average Handling Time	Rank Number: Average Handling Time	Tickets closed by First Line	Percentage Contribution: Tickets closed by First Line	Tickets closed by Service Specialist	Percentage Contribution: Tickets closed by Service Specialist
2	Priority	Region					%		%
3	Medium	DE/N	North	153.250	3	464.000	9.214	89.000	6.412
4		DE/O	East	64.333	6	317.000	6.295	210.000	15.130
5		DE/S	South	219.333	1	671.000	13.324	170.000	12.248
6		DE/W	West	88.400	4	852.000	16.918	387.000	27.882
7		US/CA	California	73.667	5	741.000	14.714	170.000	12.248
8		US/IL	Illinois	0.000	7	289.000	5.739	94.000	6.772
9		US/NY	New York	177.571	2	1,702.000	33.797	268.000	19.308
10									
11									

Figure 8.9 Customer Cases by Regions

8 | Advanced Analysis Office — Usage Scenarios

Based on the customer cases by REGION, we can see — highlighted by the conditional formatting — that the second and fourth ranked regions consume 33% of our first-line support and 27% of our Service Specialists. In addition, according to the percentage contribution for the Service Specialists, they are involved in about 15% of the second-ranked region's cases. Based on this information, let's ignore the regional aspect for now and exchange REGION with the PRODUCT characteristic (see Figure 8.10).

	A	B	C	D	E	F	G	H
1			Average Handling Time	Rank Number: Average Handling Time	Tickets closed by First Line	Percentage Contribution: Tickets closed by First Line	Tickets closed by Service Specialist	Percentage Contribution: Tickets closed by Service Specialist
2	Priority	Product				%		%
3	Medium	Billing Question	329.000	1	0.000	0.000	0.000	0.000
4		Desktop PC	163.000	4	1,163.000	23.094	248.000	17.867
5		ERP	78.400	7	795.000	15.786	277.000	19.957
6		Human Resources	164.500	3	1,210.000	24.027	190.000	13.689
7		Info	0.000	8	0.000	0.000	0.000	0.000
8		Laptop PC	96.500	6	424.000	8.419	159.000	11.455
9		Microsoft Office	0.000	8	182.000	3.614	145.000	10.447
10		PC Peripherals	0.000	8	0.000	0.000	0.000	0.000
11		Platform	126.286	5	1,262.000 ■	25.060	369.000 ■	26.585
12		Service & Quality	262.000	2	0.000	0.000	0.000	0.000

Figure 8.10 Customer Cases by Product

Now that we are on a different level compared to when we started, we need to change the conditional formatting to highlight percentage volumes above 15%. Remember, when we started we configured the conditional formatting to highlight values of 25% or higher on a global level, but now that we are on a more detailed level, it makes sense to reconfigure the highlighting to a lower level (see Figure 8.11).

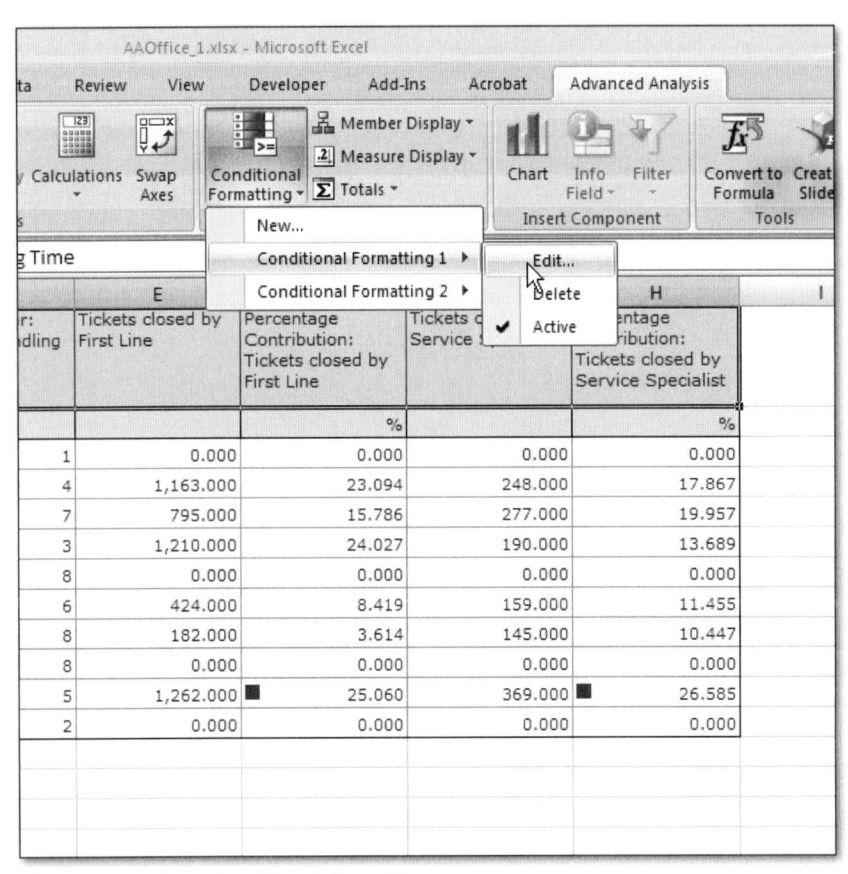

Figure 8.11 Editing Conditional Formatting

After we change the CONDITIONAL FORMATTING to lower percentage values, we can see that we have three main areas that combined are responsible for close to 75% of customer cases (see Figure 8.12).

8 | Advanced Analysis Office — Usage Scenarios

	A	B	C	D	E	F	G	H
1			Average Handling Time	Rank Number: Average Handling Time	Tickets closed by First Line	Percentage Contribution: Tickets closed by First Line	Tickets closed by Service Specialist	Percentage Contribution: Tickets closed by Service Specialist
2	Priority	Product				%		%
3	Medium	Billing Question	329.000	1	0.000	0.000	0.000	0.000
4		Desktop PC	163.000	4	1,163.000 ■	23.094	248.000 ◆	17.867
5		ERP	78.400	7	795.000	15.786	277.000 ◆	19.957
6		Human Resources	164.500	3	1,210.000 ■	24.027	190.000	13.689
7		Info	0.000	8	0.000	0.000	0.000	0.000
8		Laptop PC	96.500	6	424.000	8.419	159.000	11.455
9		Microsoft Office	0.000	8	182.000	3.614	145.000	10.447
10		PC Peripherals	0.000	8	0.000	0.000	0.000	0.000
11		Platform	126.286	5	1,262.000 ■	25.060	369.000 ■	26.585
12		Service & Quality	262.000	2	0.000	0.000	0.000	0.000

Figure 8.12 Percentage Contribution

We are now using three products — DESKTOP PC, HUMAN RESOURCES, and PLATFORM — to filter our data. In addition, let's add CALENDAR YEAR/MONTH as part of our analysis (see Figure 8.13).

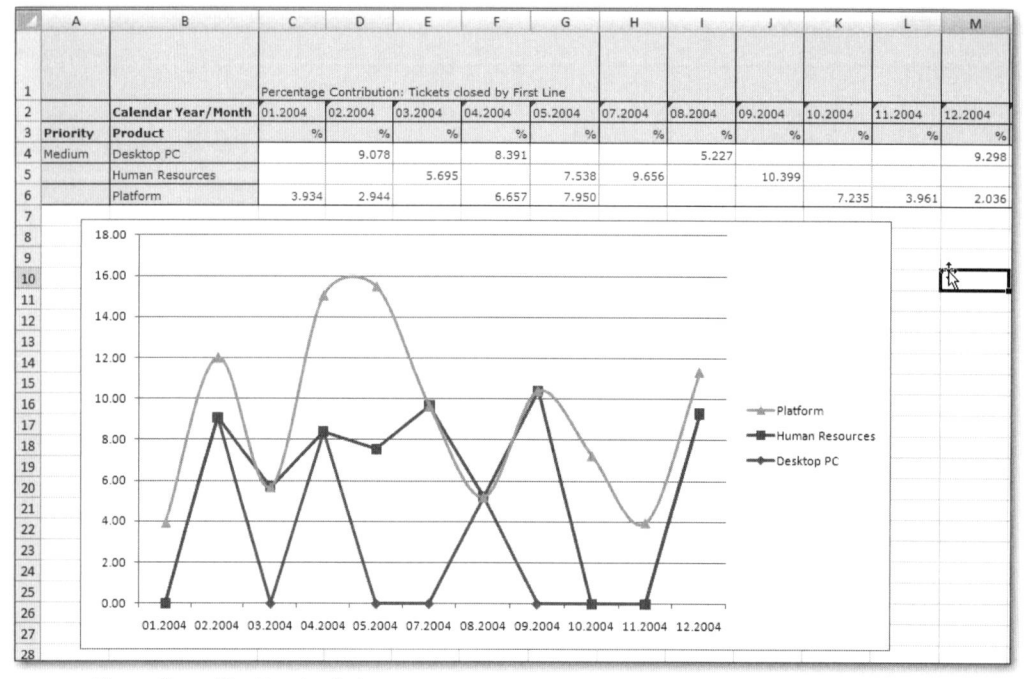

Figure 8.13 Charting Analysis

Let's also add a chart to our workbook showing the three previously mentioned products and the trend in the percentage distribution of cases over 12 months. The trend we see is that in the beginning of each quarter there is a large uptake in the number of cases and a slow down toward the end of the quarter. So, not only did we identify a set of products in Germany and the U.S. that are taking up far too much of our Support Specialists' time, we also identified a trend in the twelve months of our support cases showing an interesting trend in the customer cases.

Before we are going to share the workbook with our Customer Service managers in the regions we are adding the necessary InfoFields, such as the effective filters, to the workbook so that everyone can recognize the displayed information and the overall context (see Figure 8.14).

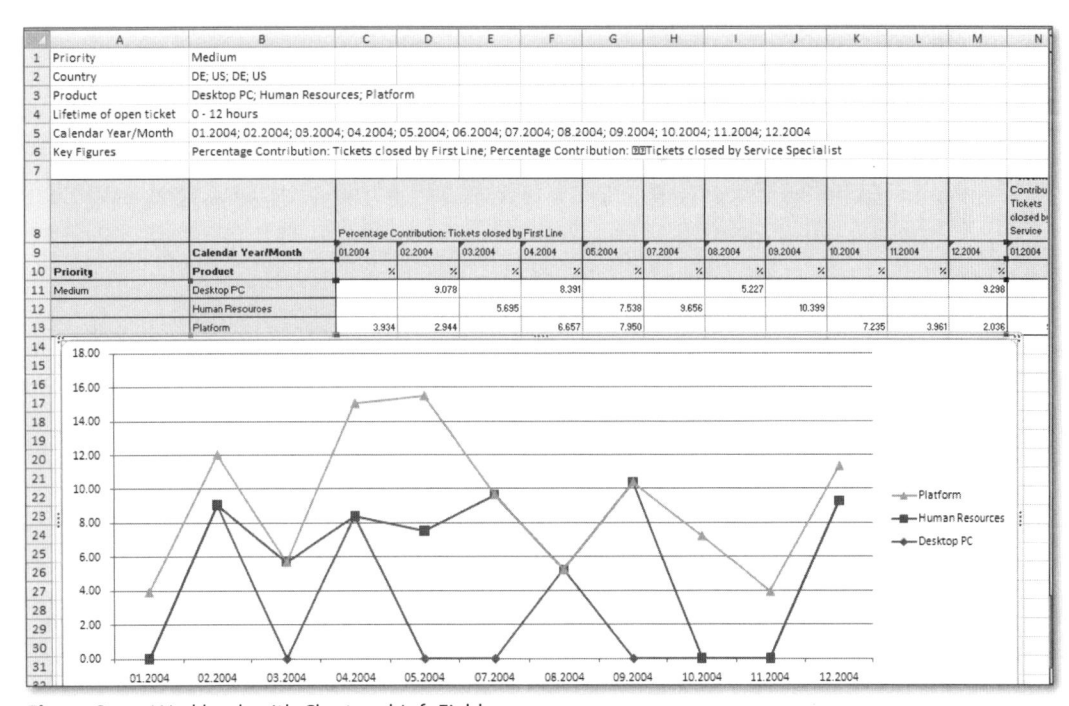

Figure 8.14 Workbook with Chart and InfoFields

8 | Advanced Analysis Office — Usage Scenarios

In this example, we used Advanced Analysis Office to identify the areas in our customer service support organization that we might want to refocus to a different product segment or a different area of priority to increase our overall customer satisfaction. In addition, we recognized a trend in the volume of our customer messages, which can provide us further insight into the products our customers use and lead to actions on our side.

In the next section, we will take a look at a product profitability example and how we can use Advanced Analysis Office as an analysis tool in this area.

8.2 Advanced Analysis Office and Product Profitability

In this section, we'll look at our product and customer profitability. Let's assume the role of a general manager where our responsibilities include achieving our overall revenue goals and maintaining our profitability level.

For this example, let's use a BEx Query based on the InfoProvider CO-PA Sales Data (technical name: IDESSLS1), which is part of the SAP NetWeaver BW IDES installation (see Figure 8.15).

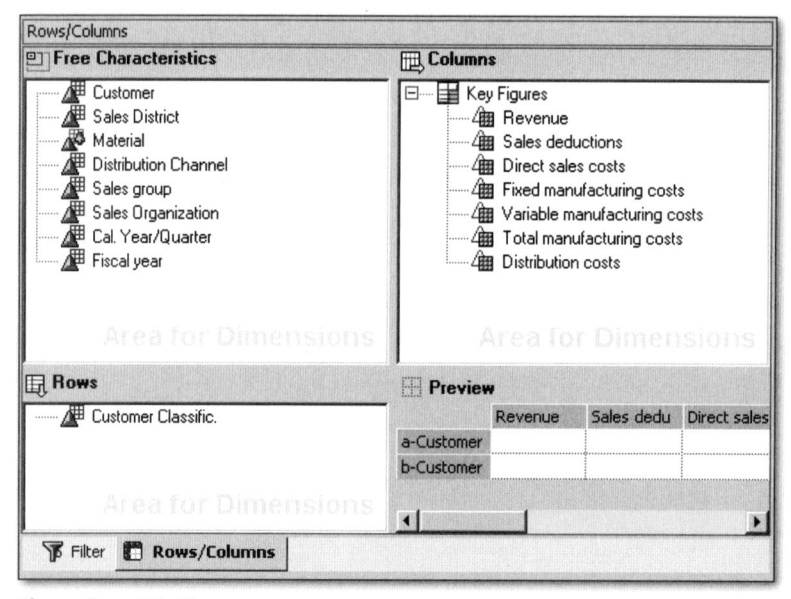

Figure 8.15 BEx Query

The BEx query contains the following characteristics:

- CUSTOMER
- SALES DISTRICT
- MATERIAL
- DISTRIBUTION CHANNEL
- SALES GROUP
- SALES ORGANIZATION
- CAL. YEAR/QUARTER
- FISCAL YEAR
- CUSTOMER CLASSIFIC.

and the following key figures:

- REVENUE
- SALES DEDUCTIONS
- DIRECT SALES COSTS
- FIXED MANUFACTURING COSTS
- VARIABLE MANUFACTURING COSTS
- TOTAL MANUFACTURING COSTS
- DISTRIBUTION COSTS

Let's start off our analysis by looking at the key figures broken down by CUSTOMER CLASSIFICATION (see Figure 8.16).

Next, we'll add a calculation to create the MARGIN by subtracting all of the detailed cost elements from our revenue. In addition, we'll add a calculation showing us the percentage share of the margin in relationship to the revenue (see Figure 8.17).

8 | Advanced Analysis Office — Usage Scenarios

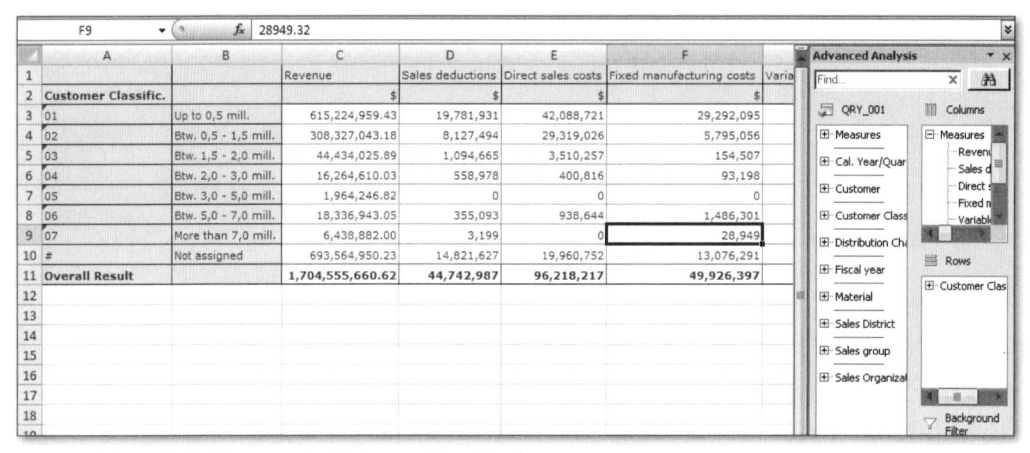

Figure 8.16 Revenue by Customer Classification

Figure 8.17 Margin and Margin in %

Note that we have two CUSTOMER CLASSIFICATION groups with a negative MARGIN, which is clearly something we need to investigate further.

Select those two customer classifications and use the FILTER BY MEMBER option to reduce the amount of data to those selected members so that we can focus on finding the root cause of the negative margins. In addition, swap the axis of our crosstab so that we have an easier comparison (see Figure 8.18). We can quickly see that the VARIABLE MANUFACTURING COSTS are the cause of the negative margins, so we reduce the list of key figures to those that are relevant to our analysis: REVENUE, MARGIN, MARGIN IN %, FIXED, VARIABLE, and TOTAL MANUFACTURING COSTS.

	A	B	C	D	E
1		Customer Classific.	05	07	Overall Result
2			Btw. 3,0 - 5,0 mill.	More than 7,0 mill.	
3	Revenue	$	1,964,246.82	6,438,882.00	8,403,128.82
4	Margin	$	-2,264,059.18	-10,561,160.73	-12,825,219.91
5	Margin in %	%	-115.26348	-164.02165	-152.62434
6	Sales deductions	$	0	3,199	3,199
7	Fixed manufacturing costs	$	0	28,949	28,949
8	Variable manufacturing costs	$	4,228,306	16,967,895	21,196,201
9	Total manufacturing costs	$	4,228,306	16,996,844	21,225,150
10	Distribution costs	$	0.00	0.00	0.00
11	Direct sales costs	$	0	0	0

Figure 8.18 Swapped Axis

Because we have a huge amount of VARIABLE MANUFACTURING COSTS, move the CUSTOMER CLASSIFICATION characteristic to the BACKGROUND FILTER and move MATERIAL to the rows of the workbook. In the hierarchical display of the MATERIAL characteristic, only show the lowest level of the hierarchy nodes to compare the lowest level of the MATERIAL hierarchy (see Figure 8.19).

	A	B	C	D	E	F	G	H
1			Revenue	Margin	Margin in %	Fixed manufacturing costs	Variable manufacturing costs	Total manufacturing costs
2	Material		$	$	%	$	$	$
3	[+] 001250010000000100	PC ensemble	146,095.50	6,932.73	4.74534	28,949	107,015	135,964
4	[+] 001250010000000110	Monitor	791,100.64	596,850.66	75.44560	0	194,250	194,250
5	[+] 001250010000000120	Processor	975,349.57	-1,176,690.46	-120.64295	0	2,152,040	2,152,040
6	[+] 001250010000000125	Memory	640,399.57	-1,984,680.48	-309.91284	0	2,625,080	2,625,080
7	[+] 001250010000000130	Drive	3,934,941.03	-9,012,192.95	-229.02994	0	12,947,134	12,947,134
8	[+] 001250010000000135	Input device	1,915,242.51	-1,255,439.41	-65.54989	0	3,170,682	3,170,682

Figure 8.19 Lowest Level Hierarchy

Next, select the four hierarchy nodes PROCESSOR, MEMORY, DRIVE, and INPUT DEVICE and use the Filter by Member option to select those hierarchy nodes as additional filters for our crosstab. These hierarchy nodes are the only nodes with a negative margin.

Now we can sort all hierarchy elements based on the MARGIN IN % and leverage the option to sort across the hierarchy (see Figure 8.20).

	A	B	C	D	E	
1			Revenue	Margin	Margin in %	Fixed
2	Material		$	$	%	
3	Overall Result		7,465,932.69	-13,429,003.30	-179.87040	
4	DPC1014	SIM-Modul M8M x 32, 128MB DDR-RAM	183,487.98	-1,241,472.05	-676.59583	
5	DPC1002	Harddisk 10.80 GB / SCSI-2-Fast	878,740.22	-3,477,169.79	-395.69940	
6	001250010000000125	Memory	640,399.57	-1,984,680.48	-309.91284	
7	DPC1003	Harddisk 180 GB / SCSI-2-Fast	1,004,498.41	-2,911,221.57	-289.81843	
8	001250010000000130	Drive	3,934,941.03	-9,012,192.95	-229.02994	
9	DPC1016	SIM-Module 8M x 36, 70 ns	103,738.81	-212,789.21	-205.12015	
10	DPC1020	3Processor 500 MHz	606,479.99	-1,057,920.04	-174.43610	
11	DPC1015	SIM-Modul 256 MB 16M x 32, 70 ns	253,876.79	-426,483.25	-167.98828	
12	DPC1004	Harddisk 42.94 GB / SCSI-2-Fast	578,212.82	-782,507.19	-135.33204	
13	DPC1005	Harddisk 21.13 GB / ATA-2	1,473,489.59	-1,841,294.41	-124.96148	
14	001250010000000120	Processor	975,349.57	-1,176,690.46	-120.64295	
15	DPC1017	SIM-Module 4M x 36, 70 ns	99,295.99	-103,935.98	-104.67288	
16	DPC1010	Standard Keyboard - EURO-Special Model	322,719.61	-308,876.38	-95.71045	
17	DPC1009	Standard Keyboard - EURO Model	437,754.90	-361,814.06	-82.65220	
18	DPC1011	Professional keyboard - PROFITEC Model	391,949.98	-268,335.00	-68.46154	
19	001250010000000135	Input device	1,915,242.51	-1,255,439.41	-65.54989	
20	DPC1012	Professional keyboard - MAXITEC Model	369,100.43	-227,893.56	-61.74297	
21	DPC1019	Processor 700 MHz	368,869.57	-118,770.42	-32.19849	
22	DPC1013	Professional keyboard - NATURAL Model	393,717.59	-88,520.41	-22.48322	
23						

Figure 8.20 Sort across Hierarchy

Now we can identify the least profitable products and use this information to improve profitability. Right now, these products cost twice as much as the revenue they generate, which is not a sustainable business practice.

In addition to the lowest performing products, we are also interested in our best performing products. Because we want to share our findings on the lowest performing products, we can create a second sheet in Advanced Analysis Office for Microsoft Excel and insert the BEx Query we used previously into this new worksheet. Instead of following the INSERT • INSERT DATA SOURCE menu path we can use the navigation panel and copy the existing crosstab to a new sheet (see Figure 8.21) — you can also see Chapter 5, Section 5.1.7, Using Additional Information and Settings, for further details.

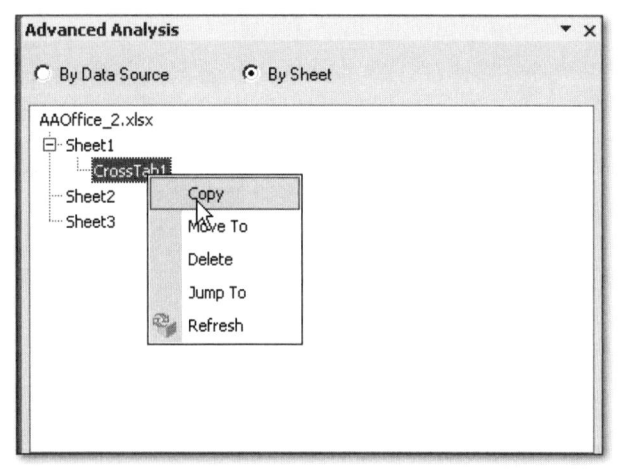

Figure 8.21 Copy Crosstab

Use the MATERIAL hierarchy in the rows and show the key figures REVENUE, MARGIN, and MARGIN IN %, which we created for our first crosstab (see Figure 8.22).

	A	B	C	D	E
1			Revenue	Margin	Margin in %
2	Material		$	$	%
3	Overall Result		1,704,555,660.62	1,066,673,197.41	62.57779
4	[-] ~ROOT	Product hierarchy	1,659,746,413.65	1,044,499,135.39	62.93125
5	[+] 000000000000000100	000000000000000100	325,972,030.62	263,169,859.24	80.73388
6	[+] 00105	Vehicles	238,431,039.24	129,183,748.21	54.18076
7	[+] 00110	Paints	139,785.47	-8,865,287.37	-6,342.06661
8	[+] 00115	Lighting	277,100,915.71	93,115,702.83	33.60353
9	[+] 00120	Elevators	44,052,166.09	44,053,350.51	100.00269
10	[+] 00125	Hardware	773,496,253.62	523,318,437.02	67.65623
11	[+] 00130	Software	2,921.80	2,887.39	98.82235
12	[+] 00135	Shipping units	34.18	32.81	95.98413
13	[+] 00140	Services	546,401.60	515,571.42	94.35760
14	[+] 00145	Foodstuffs	4,865.33	4,833.34	99.34241
15	[+] Not Assigned Material (s)		44,809,246.97	22,174,062.02	49.48546
16					
17					

Figure 8.22 Margin by Material Hierarchy

8 | Advanced Analysis Office — Usage Scenarios

Because we are mainly interested in the profitability of each product, use the option to only show the lowest hierarchy level (see Figure 8.23).

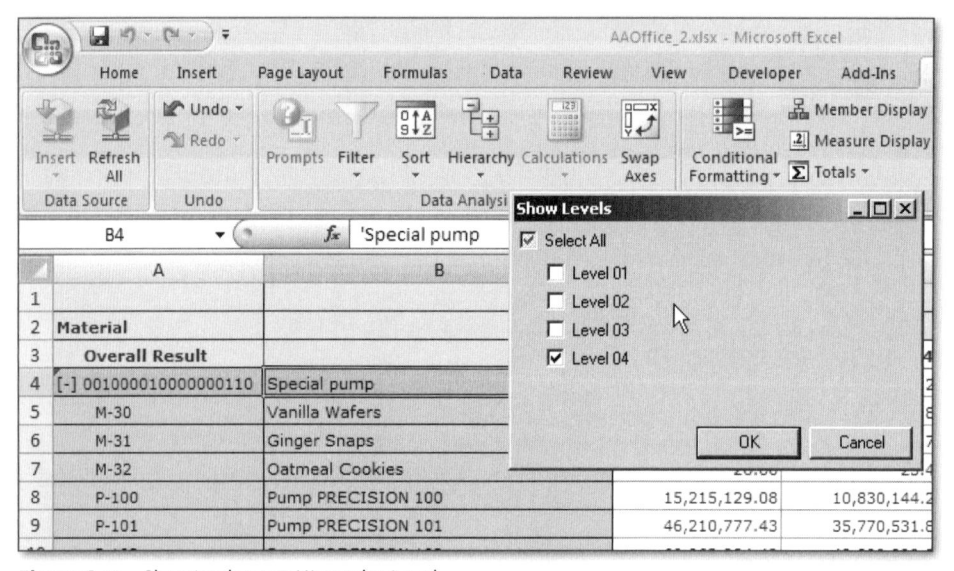

Figure 8.23 Showing lowest Hierarchy Level

To quickly identify the most profitable products, Advanced Analysis Office provides the option to sort the MATERIAL based on the measure and lets us sort across the hierarchy (see Figure 8.24).

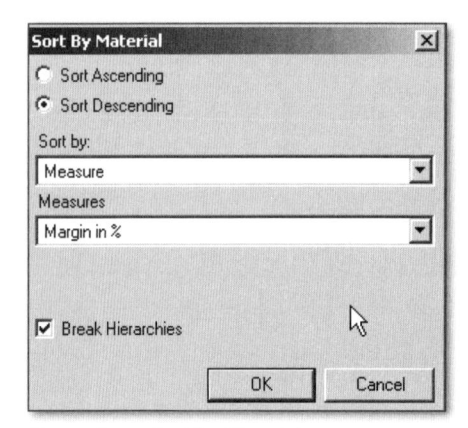

Figure 8.24 Sort by Material

302

Advanced Analysis Office and Product Profitability | **8.2**

As a result, we get a list of sorted products based on the margin percentage (see Figure 8.25) and we can now quickly identify our most profitable products.

1			Revenue	Margin	Margin in %
2	**Material**		$	$	%
3	**Overall Result**		1,704,555,660.62	1,066,673,197.41	62.57779
4	HT-1104	Smart Games	220.00	215.59	97.99861
5	HT-1106	Smart Firewall	68.00	66.20	97.35576
6	HT-1056	Multi Color	476.00	458.80	96.38652
7	PC_SERVICE_CONF	PC Service (Configurable)	339,167.89	326,871.18	96.37445
8	001250010000000100	PC ensemble	268,383,961.36	258,357,757.41	96.26423
9	001350010500000100	Pallet	9.74	9.37	96.17391
10	PK-102	Pallet 120 x 80 x 12,5 Type B	9.74	9.37	96.17391
11	HT-1040	Laser Professional Eco	36,519.97	35,111.92	96.14445
12	001350010000000100	Carton	24.44	23.44	95.90846
13	PK-100	Special carton high tech	24.44	23.44	95.90846
14	DPC3	Desktop PC3 / Assembly Planned Order	146,360.88	140,323.50	95.87500
15	HT-1042	Laser Allround	1,396.01	1,336.01	95.70242
16	M-32	Oatmeal Cookies	26.66	25.49	95.61348
17	HT-1080	Photo Scan	306.00	292.21	95.49389
18	HT-1052	Deskjet Super Highspeed	680.00	644.80	94.82373
19	001400010000000115	HiTech maintenance	546,401.60	515,571.42	94.35760

Figure 8.25 Material by Margin in %

Because we are responsible for the complete product portfolio, we are also interested in how many products make up a large portion of our margin. We want to know how many products we need to reach the 80% mark of our current total margin. To do such an analysis, use the Filter by Measure functionality in Advanced Analysis Office, but first deactivate the MATERIAL hierarchy, because the Filter by Measure option is not available with hierarchies activated in the crosstab.

Therefore, exchange MATERIAL with the activated hierarchy with the flat presentation by simply dragging the flat presentation from the navigation panel to the crosstab (see Figure 8.26).

303

8 | Advanced Analysis Office — Usage Scenarios

	A	B	C	D	E
1			Revenue	Margin	Margin in %
2	**Material**		$	$	%
3	HT-1117	ADSL progress T1	76.00	75.20	98.94972
4	HT-1102	Smart Network	276.01	272.82	98.84318
5	HT-1037	Flat X-large	14,300.00	14,130.00	98.81118
6	HT-1061	Speed Mouse	14.00	13.82	98.69129
7	HT-1100	Smart Office	1,797.99	1,773.98	98.66436
8	HT-1107	Smart Homebanking	59.80	58.80	98.32795
9	HT-1104	Smart Games	220.00	215.59	97.99861
10	AZ2-730	Navigation system	37,281.08	36,356.15	97.51904
11	AZ2-000	Viscous Fan Drive	86.64	84.48	97.49658
12	HT-1106	Smart Firewall	68.00	66.20	97.35576
13	AZ2-600	Air conditioning	233,639.11	226,629.97	97.00001
14	1400-510	MSI 350 Motorcycle	2,665.95	2,580.50	96.79476
15	C-100	CMR Component 100	51.99	50.18	96.51239
16	ISA-1002	CITTA	458.00	442.00	96.50687
17	HT-1056	Multi Color	476.00	458.80	96.38652
18	PC_SERVICE_CONF	PC Service (Configurable)	339,167.89	326,871.18	96.37445
19	AI-1000	Fruit drink 0.1 l concentrate/liter	34.67	33.38	96.28543
20	PK-102	Pallet 120 x 80 x 12,5 Type B	9.74	9.37	96.17391
21	HT-1040	Laser Professional Eco	36,519.97	35,111.92	96.14445
22	PK-100	Special carton high tech	24.44	23.44	95.90846
23	DPC3	Desktop PC3 / Assembly Planned	146,360.88	140,323.50	95.87500
24	HT-1042	Laser Allround	1,396.01	1,336.01	95.70242

Figure 8.26 Material by Margin

Now use the Filter by Measure option in Advanced Analysis Office and limit the list of products based on the top 80% of our MARGIN (see Figure 8.27).

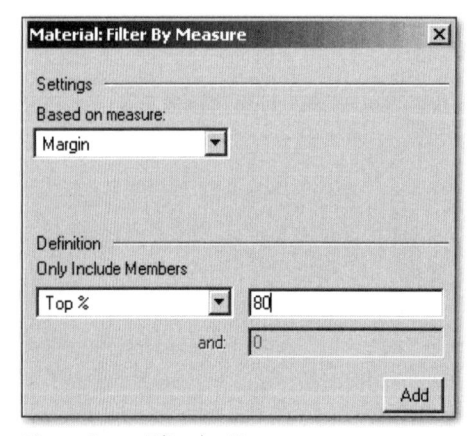

Figure 8.27 Filter by Measure

Now we can see that only a very small set of products — 21, in fact — are responsible for 80% of our total margin (see Figure 8.28).

	A	B	C	D	E
1			Revenue	Margin	Margin in %
2	**Material**		$	$	%
3	E-1521	Engine unit 20 KW 460V AC	41,223,255.04	41,223,847.25	100.00144
4	DPC4000	Desktop PC 4000	262,529,872.22	262,529,872.22	100.00000
5	P-103	Pump PRECISION 103	59,288,204.52	51,114,381.67	86.21341
6	P-109	Pump cast steel IDESNORM 170-230	21,182,480.99	17,858,450.05	84.30764
7	P-104	Pump PRECISION 104	78,488,316.01	65,272,520.23	83.16209
8	P-102	Pump PRECISION 102	60,062,884.42	49,890,899.83	83.06444
9	1400-400	Motorcycle Helmet - Standard	18,612,595.33	14,877,008.15	79.92979
10	P-101	Pump PRECISION 101	46,210,777.43	35,770,531.85	77.40734
11	M-01	Sunny Sunny 01	21,971,076.56	16,144,455.27	73.48049
12	M-02	Sunny Xa1	26,146,206.92	18,744,405.83	71.69073
13	P-402	Pump standard IDESNORM 100-402	45,523,619.65	32,435,583.01	71.25001
14	M-10	Flatscreen MS 1775P	35,072,250.67	24,957,394.38	71.15995
15	M-09	Flatscreen MS 1585	32,075,508.09	22,772,715.19	70.99721
16	M-04	Sunny Extreme	28,315,263.85	19,788,459.97	69.88619
17	M-03	Sunny Tetral3	26,357,761.33	18,259,633.85	69.27612
18	M-08	Flatscreen MS 1575P	29,691,227.97	20,448,271.09	68.86974
19	M-06	Flatscreen MS 1460 P	19,194,342.06	12,079,404.09	62.93211
20	1400-300	SunFun / 1200 cm3	142,007,521.21	88,827,252.37	62.55109
21	M-11	Flatscreen MS 1785P	23,552,320.92	11,588,501.96	49.20323
22	L-40C	Light Bulb 40 Watt clear 220/235V	58,343,416.63	18,511,958.25	31.72930
23	1400-310	CrossFun / 350 cm3	62,561,524.27	17,785,046.85	28.42809
24	**Overall Result**		1,704,555,660.62	1,066,673,197.41	62.57779

Figure 8.28 Material based on Top 80% Margin

Because we're not only interested in our most profitable products but also our most profitable customers, use the option in Advanced Analysis Office to define the FILTER BY MEASURE based on Margin (see Figure 8.29).

By changing the definition of our FILTER BY MEASURE from MATERIAL to MARGIN, we can define the top 80% ranking on all characteristics in a single step. By doing so, we are then in a position where we can simply exchange MATERIAL with CUSTOMER and the displayed customers will be automatically filtered, representing the top 80% MARGIN (see Figure 8.30).

8 | Advanced Analysis Office — Usage Scenarios

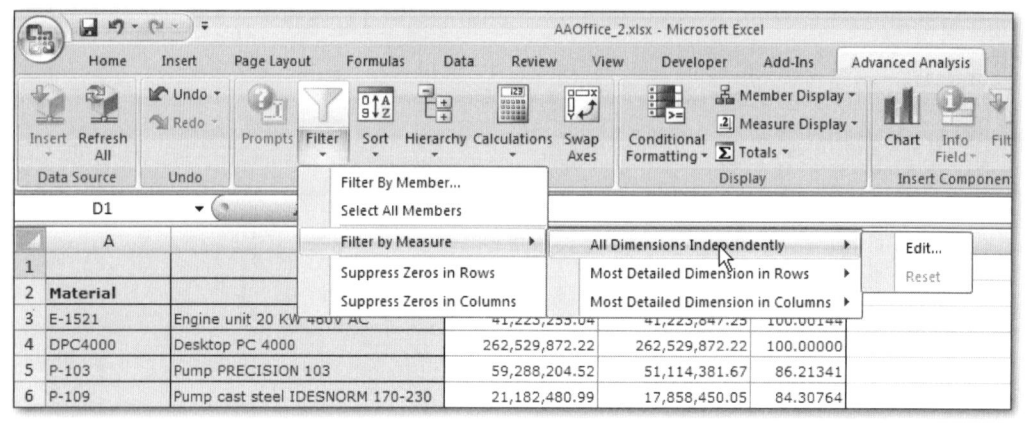

Figure 8.29 Filter by Measure

	A	B	C	D	E
1			Revenue	Margin	Margin in %
2	**Customer**		$	$	%
3	1000	Becker Berlin	25,161,642.50	21,128,555.83	83.97129
4	1001	Lampen-Markt GmbH	66,132,437.72	22,378,707.18	33.83923
5	1033	Karsson High Tech Markt	57,824,315.55	33,348,402.61	57.67194
6	1174	Motomarkt Stuttgart GmbH	56,306,877.17	27,836,933.54	49.43789
7	1175	Elektromarkt Bamby	86,580,996.85	30,591,058.00	35.33230
8	1300	Christal Clear	63,068,877.90	21,438,824.97	33.99272
9	1321	Becker Stuttgart	39,137,124.13	27,621,686.34	70.57669
10	1900	J & P	57,248,099.62	31,834,938.07	55.60872
11	1901	Motor Sports	48,142,662.61	28,122,695.62	58.41533
12	2000	Carbor GmbH	48,297,880.02	37,892,157.76	78.45512
13	2004	SudaTech GmbH	43,288,809.68	21,242,776.86	49.07221
14	2130	COMPU Tech. AG	42,615,664.62	25,834,394.43	60.62183
15	2140	N.I.C. High Tech	59,358,155.04	35,141,055.84	59.20173
16	2503	Norwegian Import & Export Group	23,940,630.96	22,650,280.98	94.61021
17	#	Not assigned	627,055,334.54	477,929,394.30	76.21806
18	**Overall Result**		1,704,555,660.62	1,066,673,197.41	62.57779

Figure 8.30 Customers for Top 80% Margin

In this section, we used Advanced Analysis Office in conjunction with ranking, filters, and hierarchies to see which products are the least and most profitable in our overall portfolio. We created several crosstabs that we can now use as part of

306

our continuous review of our overall profitability. In the next section, we will learn how to use Advanced Analysis Office in sales forecasting and planning.

8.3 Advanced Analysis Office and Sales Planning

In this section, we'll use Advanced Analysis Office as a tool for our Sales Planning and Forecasting process. Please note that we are not using an actual Planning workflow from SAP NetWeaver BI Integrated Planning. Instead, we'll use Advanced Analysis Office as an analysis tool for our sales numbers so that we can evaluate our next steps.

The BEx Query is based on the SAP Demo: DalSegno Company Reporting Cube (0D_DX_M01) InfoProvider from the SAP Demo content (see Figure 8.31).

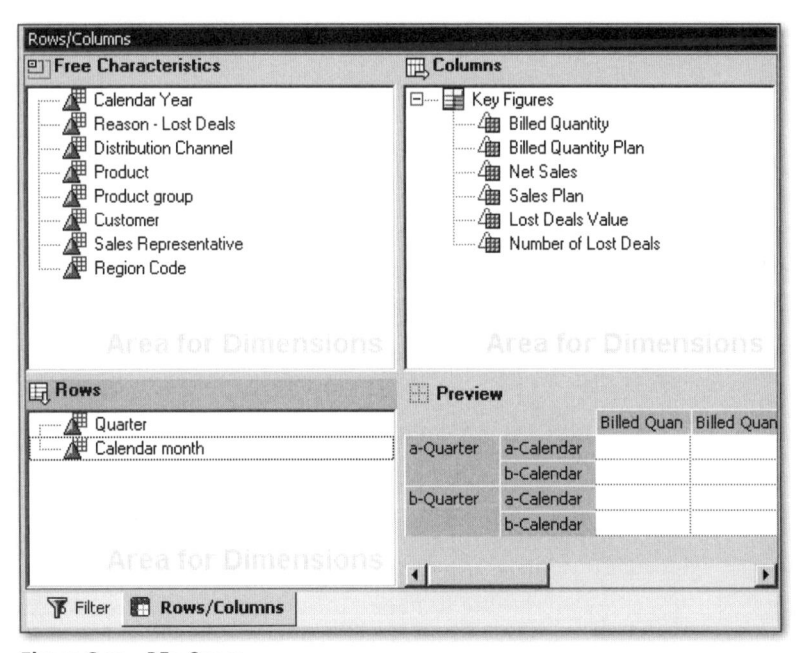

Figure 8.31 BEx Query

The BEx Query (see Figure 8.31) contains the following characteristics:

- CALENDAR YEAR
- REASON – LOST DEALS
- DISTRIBUTION CHANNEL
- PRODUCT
- PRODUCT GROUP
- CUSTOMER
- SALES REPRESENTATIVE
- REGION CODE
- QUARTER
- CALENDAR MONTH

and the following key figures:

- BILLED QUANTITY
- BILLED QUANTITY PLAN
- NET SALES
- SALES PLAN
- LOST DEALS VALUE
- NUMBER OF LOST DEALS

Let's start our analysis in Advanced Analysis Office for Microsoft Excel by looking at the actual and planned numbers broken down per quarter and month (see Figure 8.32).

Without adding any additional highlighting or calculations, it is very difficult to actually identify how our achievement rate has been in past quarters and how we are doing in the fourth quarter compared to our plans. Therefore, we need to add calculations to our crosstab to show the percentage share of our actual sold quantity and the resulting revenue compared to the plan numbers (see Figure 8.33).

8.3 Advanced Analysis Office and Sales Planning

Figure 8.32 Advanced Analysis Office Crosstab

Figure 8.33 Percentage Share

First, add conditional formatting to the crosstab to highlight the values that are below our expectations (see Figure 8.34).

8 | Advanced Analysis Office — Usage Scenarios

	A	B	C	D	E	F	G	H
1			Billed Quantity	Billed Quantity Plan	% Achievement Qty	Net Sales	Sales Plan	% Achievment Sales
2	Quarter	Calendar month	PC	* 1,000 PC	%	* 1,000 $	* 1,000 $	%
3	1	1	131,791,213	129,656	102	617,067.50	608,846	101
4		2	130,092,989	129,006	101	609,970.34	601,604	101
5		3	131,651,939	134,916	98	617,682.93	643,486	96
6		Result	393,536,141	393,578	100	1,844,720.78	1,853,936	100
7	2	4	131,368,632	129,091	102	615,928.03	603,693	102
8		5	129,118,460	128,380	101	606,096.12	604,287	100
9		6	131,383,972	133,644	98	617,618.83	634,771	97
10		Result	391,871,064	391,114	100	1,839,642.98	1,842,751	100
11	3	7	131,433,415	132,820	99	617,290.91	629,574	98
12		8	130,103,580	130,306	100	611,453.65	617,601	99
13		9	131,982,786	124,036	106	618,508.34	564,642	110
14		Result	393,519,781	387,162	102	1,847,252.90	1,811,818	102
15	4	10	130,205,175	127,243	102	612,018.93	591,797	103
16		11	116,381,635	115,524	101	621,909.72	615,187	101
17		12	118,946,119	119,723	99	636,012.15	642,840	99
18		Result	365,532,929	362,491	101	1,869,940.79	1,849,824	101
19	Overall Result		1,544,459,915	1,534,345	101	7,401,557.44	7,358,328	101

Figure 8.34 Conditional Formatting

Because we added conditional formatting to the percentage share calculation, we can now easily change the characteristics used in our crosstab and exchange CALENDAR MONTH with DISTRIBUTION CHANNEL and quickly identify which sales channels are above or below sales revenue expectations (see Figure 8.35).

	A	B	C	D	E	F	G	H
1			Billed Quantity	Billed Quantity Plan	% Achievement Qty	Net Sales	Sales Plan	% Achievment Sales
2	Quarter	Distribution Channel	PC	* 1,000 PC	%	* 1,000 $	* 1,000 $	%
3	1	EDI	79,037,748	77,413	102	368,195.83	358,938	103
4		Fax	127,226,562	128,354	99	601,229.93	611,504	98
5		Internet	67,905,131	68,386	99	313,713.65	317,489	99
6		Others	30,244,905	30,261	100	145,107.67	146,403	99
7		Phone	89,121,795	89,164	100	416,473.70	419,601	99
8		Result	393,536,141	393,578	100	1,844,720.78	1,853,936	100
9	2	EDI	78,873,855	78,654	100	369,204.23	369,164	100
10		Fax	122,630,000	124,915	98	578,689.78	600,596	96
11		Internet	72,720,459	70,267	103	338,166.34	323,352	105
12		Others	29,877,689	29,225	102	143,723.14	139,080	103
13		Phone	87,768,871	88,053	100	409,859.48	410,559	100
14		Result	391,871,064	391,114	100	1,839,642.98	1,842,751	100
15	3	EDI	78,866,227	78,731	100	368,454.92	368,950	100
16		Fax	123,157,622	121,766	101	582,015.32	574,819	101
17		Internet	72,445,936	69,537	104	336,959.91	317,227	106
18		Others	30,106,297	29,463	102	144,643.57	140,355	103
19		Phone	88,943,699	87,666	101	415,179.18	410,467	101
20		Result	393,519,781	387,162	102	1,847,252.90	1,811,818	102
21	4	EDI	72,588,843	73,611	99	370,639.83	379,734	98
22		Fax	114,222,042	113,189	101	589,461.23	582,485	101
23		Internet	67,969,503	65,838	103	341,631.77	326,062	105
24		Others	28,166,029	28,164	100	147,982.89	148,409	100
25		Phone	82,586,512	81,689	101	420,225.07	413,135	102

Figure 8.35 Revenue by Distribution Channel

Advanced Analysis Office and Sales Planning | **8.3**

Now we can see that in the first and second quarter all of our distribution channels missed the target revenue — just barely, but they missed the goals. Because this happened across all of our distribution channels we need to look at the Lost Deals Value key figure (see Figure 8.36) broken down by Distribution Channel and Quarter.

	A	B	C	D	E	F	G
1			Net Sales	Sales Plan	% Achievment Sales	Lost Deals Value	Number of Lost Deals
2	Distribution Channel	Quarter	* 1,000 $	* 1,000 $	%	* 1,000 $	* 1,000 PC
3	EDI	1	368,195.83	358,938	103	116,916	26,698
4		2	369,204.23	369,164	100	99,879	21,468
5		3	368,454.92	368,950	100	96,429	19,876
6		4	370,639.83	379,734	98	90,875	19,780
7		Result	1,476,494.81	1,476,785	100	404,099	87,822
8	Fax	1	601,229.93	611,504	98	150,436	31,529
9		2	578,689.78	600,596	96	148,280	32,369
10		3	582,015.32	574,819	101	121,855	26,463
11		4	589,461.23	582,485	101	122,294	26,602
12		Result	2,351,396.26	2,369,405	99	542,865	116,962
13	Internet	1	313,713.65	317,489	99	83,678	18,577
14		2	338,166.34	323,352	105	84,263	18,404
15		3	336,959.91	317,227	106	62,537	13,545
16		4	341,631.77	326,062	105	71,452	16,767
17		Result	1,330,471.67	1,284,129	104	301,930	67,294
18	Others	1	145,107.67	146,403	99	35,046	7,933
19		2	143,723.14	139,080	103	40,000	9,206
20		3	144,643.57	140,355	103	30,522	6,238
21		4	147,982.89	148,409	100	28,247	6,009
22		Result	581,457.27	574,248	101	133,815	29,386

Figure 8.36 Lost Deals by Distribution Channel

Now we can see the lost revenue number and the number of lost deals, but we can't easily identify any trends. Therefore, let's change the navigation to show the revenue from our lost deals by Distribution Channel and Calendar month in a chart (see Figure 8.37).

Now we can quickly see that our Distribution Channel Fax has the highest amount of lost revenue and that there is a pattern with a peak of lost revenue in each quarter.

With this in mind, we look at the lost revenue for the Distribution Channel Fax — which we moved to the Background Filter — by Customer. Add the Customer characteristic because these are lost deals and we are looking for more information on either a particular product or perhaps a particular sales organization–related pattern (see Figure 8.38).

8 | Advanced Analysis Office — Usage Scenarios

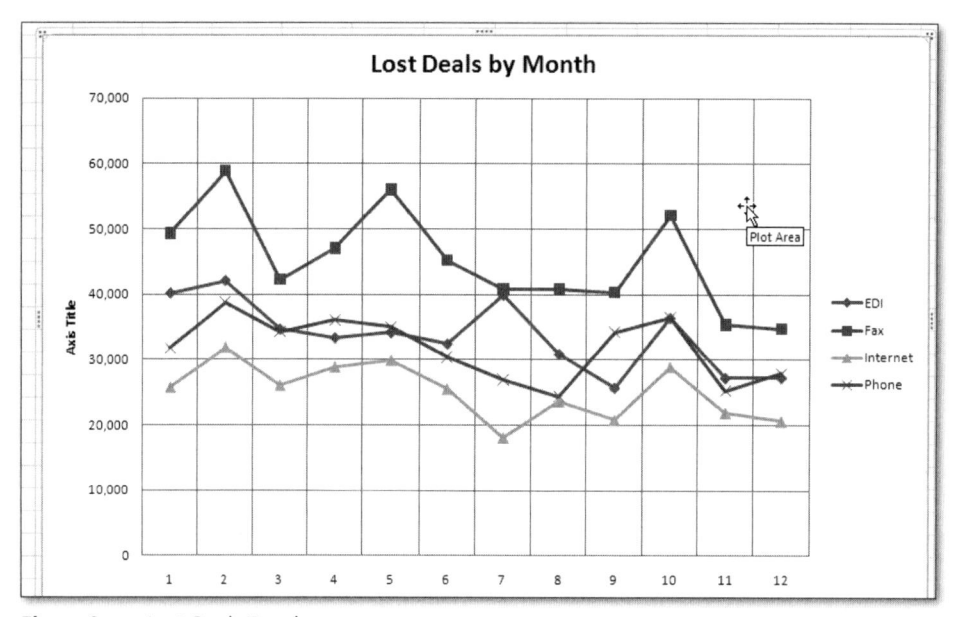

Figure 8.37 Lost Deals Trend

Figure 8.38 Top 25 Customers

Add a sort based on the lost revenue value and a Filter by Measure to filter the top 25 customers based on the LOST DEALS VALUE.

Next, we need to find out two things:

- Are there any specific products related to large portions of this lost revenue?
- Are there any particular sales representatives related to large portions of this list revenue?

First, select the top 25 customers and use the FILTER functionality to swap the characteristic with the PRODUCT characteristic (see Figure 8.39). The result is a list of the products responsible for the lost revenue of our top 25 customers. The LOST DEALS VALUE is empty on the PRODUCT level because the key figure is only maintained on the CUSTOMER level.

	A	B
1		Lost Deals Value
2	**Product**	* 1,000 $
3	Camera Connector	
4	Flatscreen Vision I	
5	Harddrive onTour	
6	iPhones PX2	
7	Notebook Speedy I	
8	Notebook Speedy II	
9	PC Thinkbox I	
10	PC Thinktank Is	
11	Stereo Kit	
12	USB Adaptor	
13	USB Mega Storage	
14	USB Storage	
15	#	47,837
16	**Overall Result**	**47,837**

Figure 8.39 Product with Lost Revenue

Keep the list of products for a more detailed analysis later. Because we filtered our crosstab based on the top 25 customers based on lost revenue, we can exchange PRODUCT with SALES REPRESENTATIVE to get the list of sales reps assigned to these top 25 customers (see Figure 8.40).

8 | Advanced Analysis Office — Usage Scenarios

	A	B
1		Lost Deals Value
2	**Sales Representative**	* 1,000 $
3	Thomas Byrnes	4,890
4	Nina Zeidler	3,409
5	Barbara Burningham	2,892
6	Krishnakumar Voss	2,733
7	Charles Subramani	2,563
8	Dean Callahan	2,508
9	Angela Housworth	2,451
10	Paul Herold	2,259
11	Charles Wible	2,044
12	Adam Riede	2,031
13	Michael Sawran	1,849
14	Jeffrey Battleson	1,840
15	JoAnna Edwards	1,821
16	Matthew Seymour	1,758
17	Erika Rainey	1,736
18	Antonio Barrett	1,636
19	Mills Sirkot	1,617
20	Denise Salmon	1,605
21	David DeVoue	1,559
22	Scott Stanley	1,557
23	Frank Becker	1,557
24	Gary Sandoval	1,523
25	**Overall Result**	**47,837**

Figure 8.40 Lost Revenue by Sales Representative

Before we use the new information and talk to our sales reps about the situation, let's quickly replace SALES REPRESENTATIVE with the actual reason for the lost deals (see Figure 8.41).

	A	B
1		Lost Deals Value
2	**Reason - Lost Deals**	* 1,000 $
3	Delivery Time	8,134
4	Prices	12,535
5	Service	27,168
6	Not assigned	
7	**Overall Result**	**47,837**

Figure 8.41 Reason – Lost Deals

Now we can see that the sales department has been underperforming for several quarters and we can identify the customers that we lost to our competition. In addition, we can see the reasons why we lost the revenue, which, according to our information, was because more than 50% of our customers were not satisfied with their service (see Figure 8.41). We can use this information in conjunction with the list of Sales Representatives to take steps to address this problem.

In this section, we leveraged Advanced Analysis Office in a sales planning- and sales review–related situation. In the next section, we will use Advanced Analysis Office combined with data from our procurement department.

8.4 Advanced Analysis Office and Procurement

In this section, we'll review how Advanced Analysis Office can help us find the right vendor for the right product. Let's assume we are part of the procurement department and that our responsibility is to make the correct delivery at the best possible price of the required products.

The BEx Query we'll use in this example is based on the SAP Demo cube Purchasing Data (0D_PU_C01) (see Figure 8.42).

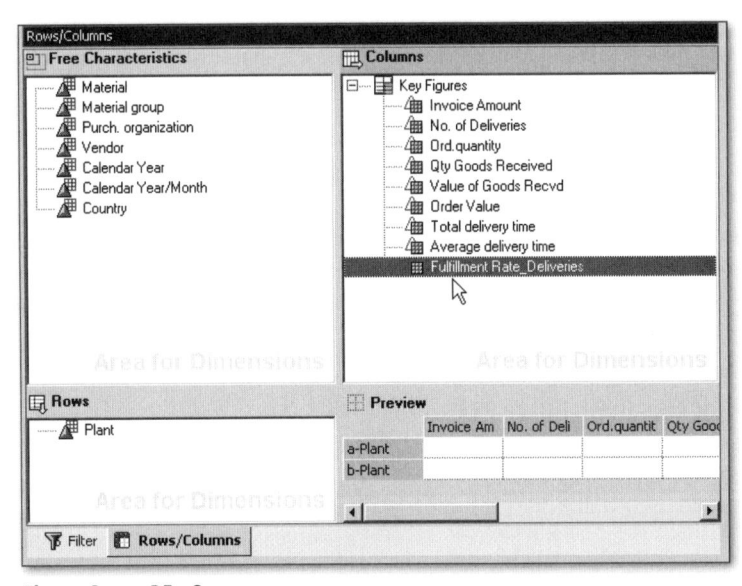

Figure 8.42 BEx Query

8 | Advanced Analysis Office — Usage Scenarios

The BEx Query contains the characteristics:

- Material
- Material group
- Purch. organization
- Vendor
- Calendar Year
- Calendar Year/Month
- Country
- Plan

And the following key figures:

- Invoice Amount
- No. of Deliveries
- Ord. quantity
- Qty Goods Received
- Values of Goods Recvd
- Order Value
- Total delivery time
- Average delivery time
- Fulfillment Rate_Deliveries

Let's start our analysis with an overview of our material and the No. of Deliveries, Invoice Amount, and Ord. quantity key figures (see Figure 8.43).

Based on the Invoice Amount and No. of Deliveries, the Casings and Motherboards product groups are the two most expensive product areas. Use them to start the analysis and search for better prices and faster delivery. Use the Material Group members Casings and Motherboards as filters and then look at the key figures by the actual Material (see Figure 8.44).

	A	B	C	D	E	F	G
1		Invoice Amount	No. of Deliveries	Ord.quantity	Qty Goods Received	Value of Goods Recvd	Order Value
2	Material group			***	***		
3	Casings	159,977,566.00	1,942	941,672.000	893,654.000	160,850,248.00	173,567,524.00
4	Motherboards	116,501,774.00	1,096	535,162.000	504,560.000	117,871,396.00	127,470,592.00
5	Monitors	58,071,467.00	724	406,510.000	389,094.000	58,103,246.00	60,803,455.00
6	Processors	89,539,417.00	1,134	535,162.000	504,560.000	88,325,838.00	96,871,369.00
7	Logics	45,754,131.00	762	406,510.000	389,094.000	45,992,311.00	48,224,559.00
8	Overall Result	469,844,355.00	5,658	2,825,016.000	2,680,962.000	471,143,039.00	506,937,499.00

Figure 8.43 Invoice Amount by Material Group

	A	B	C	D	E	F	G
1		Invoice Amount	No. of Deliveries	Ord.quantity	Qty Goods Received	Value of Goods Recvd	Order Value
2	Material			***	***		
3	Casing Notebook Speedy I CN	58,229,012.00	198	84,062.000	78,362.000	58,359,532.00	63,968,276.00
4	Motherboard Terminal P600 CN	43,390,140.00	408	225,878.000	215,166.000	43,699,237.00	45,517,526.00
5	Motherboard Terminal P400 CN	33,792,088.00	354	182,798.000	172,576.000	34,786,942.00	38,238,305.00
6	Motherboard Notebook Speedy I CN	29,146,832.00	200	84,062.000	78,362.000	29,172,832.00	31,977,131.00
7	Casing Terminal P600 CN	24,784,058.00	444	225,878.000	215,166.000	25,025,901.00	26,063,063.00
8	Casing Notebook Speedy II CN	21,845,006.00	130	42,424.000	38,456.000	21,845,006.00	25,105,327.00
9	Casing Terminal P400 CN	20,446,419.00	374	182,798.000	172,576.000	20,795,610.00	21,972,480.00
10	Casing Monitor flat 21 CN	18,719,756.00	286	165,560.000	160,880.000	18,780,207.00	19,156,978.00
11	Casing Monitor flat 17 CN	15,953,315.00	510	240,950.000	228,214.000	16,043,992.00	17,301,400.00
12	Motherboard Notebook Speedy II CN	10,172,714.00	134	42,424.000	38,456.000	10,212,385.00	11,737,630.00
13	Overall Result	276,479,340.00	3,038	1,476,834.000	1,398,214.000	278,721,644.00	301,038,116.00

Figure 8.44 Key Figures by Material

We are also interested in finding better prices for the products; therefore, reduce the list of key figures to INVOICE AMOUNT and ORD. QUANTITY and show the MATERIAL and VENDOR characteristics (see Figure 8.45). In addition, add a new calculation by dividing the INVOICE AMOUNT by the ORD. QUANTITY so that we can compare the per unit price from each Vendor.

Now we can compare the prices per Unit, but we have to go line item by line item through the list to find the most profitable price. In our example, we use the capability to add a dynamic calculation to our crosstab to add a Ranking based on the just-added calculation. After we add the Ranking, we only need to add a sort based on the Ranking to get an overview, which will provide us the most expensive MATERIAL with all possible VENDOR ranked on the per unit price (see Figure 8.46).

8 | Advanced Analysis Office — Usage Scenarios

	A	B	C	D	E
1			Invoice Amount	Ord.quantity	Invoice Amount/Ord.quantity
2	Material	Vendor		***	
3	Casing Notebook Speedy I CN	ABC Technology	7,017,600.00	11,910.000	589.22
4		Asia Technologies	461,020.00	1,182.000	390.03
5		Becker Components AG	10,802,711.00	19,650.000	549.76
6		CompuMax Corp	818,400.00	1,364.000	600.00
7		Générale Electronique	30,568,481.00	25,144.000	1,215.74
8		Hatushiba Co. Ltd	5,713,800.00	12,840.000	445.00
9		HiTech Corp	2,505,360.00	10,658.000	235.07
10		SAPSOTA Corp	341,640.00	1,314.000	260.00
11		Result	58,229,012.00	84,062.000	692.69
12	Motherboard Terminal P600 CN	CompSmart Inc.	9,062,760.00	46,236.000	196.01
13		Computer 3000 Inc.	4,043,400.00	27,028.000	149.60
14		Omnium	12,342,727.00	25,500.000	484.03
15		PAQ Germany GmbH	12,576,365.00	64,530.000	194.89
16		Sunny Electronics Inc.	5,364,888.00	62,584.000	85.72
17		Result	43,390,140.00	225,878.000	192.10
18	Motherboard Terminal P400 CN	Becker Components AG	5,230,288.00	30,240.000	172.96
19		C.E.B Paris	8,582,998.00	21,350.000	402.01
20		CompuMax Corp	8,442,000.00	43,560.000	193.80
21		Hatushiba Co. Ltd	6,150,000.00	42,340.000	145.25
22		Logo Systems	2,318,032.00	29,928.000	77.45
23		Technik und Systeme GmbH	3,068,770.00	15,380.000	199.53
24		Result	33,792,088.00	182,798.000	184.86

Figure 8.45 Per Unit Price

	A	B	C	D	E	F
1			Invoice Amount	Ord.quantity	Invoice Amount/Ord.quantity	Olympic Rank Number: Invoice Amount/Ord.quantity
2	Material	Vendor		***		
3	Casing Notebook Speedy I CN	HiTech Corp	2,505,360.00	10,658.000	235.07	8
4		SAPSOTA Corp	341,640.00	1,314.000	260.00	7
5		Asia Technologies	461,020.00	1,182.000	390.03	6
6		Hatushiba Co. Ltd	5,713,800.00	12,840.000	445.00	5
7		Becker Components AG	10,802,711.00	19,650.000	549.76	4
8		ABC Technology	7,017,600.00	11,910.000	589.22	3
9		CompuMax Corp	818,400.00	1,364.000	600.00	2
10		Générale Electronique	30,568,481.00	25,144.000	1,215.74	1
11		Result	58,229,012.00	84,062.000	692.69	1
12	Motherboard Terminal P600 CN	Sunny Electronics Inc.	5,364,888.00	62,584.000	85.72	5
13		Computer 3000 Inc.	4,043,400.00	27,028.000	149.60	4
14		PAQ Germany GmbH	12,576,365.00	64,530.000	194.89	3
15		CompSmart Inc.	9,062,760.00	46,236.000	196.01	2
16		Omnium	12,342,727.00	25,500.000	484.03	1
17		Result	43,390,140.00	225,878.000	192.10	5
18	Motherboard Terminal P400 CN	Logo Systems	2,318,032.00	29,928.000	77.45	6
19		Hatushiba Co. Ltd	6,150,000.00	42,340.000	145.25	5
20		Becker Components AG	5,230,288.00	30,240.000	172.96	4
21		CompuMax Corp	8,442,000.00	43,560.000	193.80	3
22		Technik und Systeme GmbH	3,068,770.00	15,380.000	199.53	2
23		C.E.B Paris	8,582,998.00	21,350.000	402.01	1

Figure 8.46 Ranking

Now we can add several other key figures, such as AVERAGE DELIVERY TIME and FULFILLMENT RATE, but not as simple key figures. In our example, we added dynamic calculations to represent the Ranking for these key figures in our crosstab (see Figure 8.47).

	B	C	D	E	F	G	H
1		Invoice Amount	Ord.quantity	Invoice Amount/Ord.quantity	Olympic Rank Number: Invoice Amount/Ord.quantity	Rank Number: Average delivery time	Rank Number: Fulfillment Rate_Deliveries
2	**Vendor**		***				
3	HiTech Corp	2,505,360.00	10,658.000	235.07	8	4	3
4	SAPSOTA Corp	341,640.00	1,314.000	260.00	7	8	1
5	Asia Technologies	461,020.00	1,182.000	390.03	6	1	6
6	Hatushiba Co. Ltd	5,713,800.00	12,840.000	445.00	5	7	1
7	Becker Components AG	10,802,711.00	19,650.000	549.76	4	5	4
8	ABC Technology	7,017,600.00	11,910.000	589.22	3	6	2
9	CompuMax Corp	818,400.00	1,364.000	600.00	2	2	1
10	Générale Electronique	30,568,481.00	25,144.000	1,215.74	1	3	5
11	**Result**	58,229,012.00	84,062.000	692.69	1	3	5

Figure 8.47 Ranking for Key Figures

In addition, we can enable a compact display in the rows to see all of the key figures without having to scroll (see Figure 8.48).

	Invoice Amount	Ord.quantity	Invoice Amount/Ord.quantity	Olympic Rank Number: Invoice Amount/Ord.quantity	Rank Number: Average delivery time	Rank Number: Fulfillment Rate_Deliveries
Material		***				
Overall Result	276,479,340.00	1,476,834.000	187.21	1	1	1
[-] Casing Notebook Speedy I CN	58,229,012.00	84,062.000	692.69	1	3	5
HiTech Corp	2,505,360.00	10,658.000	235.07	8	4	3
SAPSOTA Corp	341,640.00	1,314.000	260.00	7	8	1
Asia Technologies	461,020.00	1,182.000	390.03	6	1	6
Hatushiba Co. Ltd	5,713,800.00	12,840.000	445.00	5	7	1
Becker Components AG	10,802,711.00	19,650.000	549.76	4	5	4
ABC Technology	7,017,600.00	11,910.000	589.22	3	6	2
CompuMax Corp	818,400.00	1,364.000	600.00	2	2	1
Générale Electronique	30,568,481.00	25,144.000	1,215.74	1	3	5
[+] Motherboard Terminal P600 CN	43,390,140.00	225,878.000	192.10	5	5	2
[+] Motherboard Terminal P400 CN	33,792,088.00	182,798.000	184.86	6	7	4
[+] Motherboard Notebook Speedy I CN	29,146,832.00	84,062.000	346.73	3	4	5
[+] Casing Terminal P600 CN	24,784,058.00	225,878.000	109.72	9	8	2
[+] Casing Notebook Speedy II CN	21,845,006.00	42,424.000	514.92	2	1	6
[+] Casing Terminal P400 CN	20,446,419.00	182,798.000	111.85	8	9	4
[+] Casing Monitor flat 21 CN	18,719,756.00	165,560.000	113.07	7	6	1
[+] Casing Monitor flat 17 CN	15,953,315.00	240,950.000	66.21	10	10	3
[+] Motherboard Notebook Speedy II CN	10,172,714.00	42,424.000	239.79	4	2	6

Figure 8.48 Compact Display

8 | Advanced Analysis Office — Usage Scenarios

Now we can see all of our VENDORS per product and compare the PRICE PER UNIT, the AVERAGE DELIVERY TIME, and the FULFILLMENT RATE — all Ranked. That way, we can quickly identify the best combination of price and delivery. Please note that in our example the higher the Ranking value, the better the VENDOR. For example, SAPSOTA CORP is shown Ranked eighth for the price per unit, which is the lowest ranking value, but this also means it is the lowest price per unit for the product.

Before we start contacting our vendors to negotiate better terms, create a Microsoft PowerPoint presentation from the crosstab that we can share with our colleagues. Use the Create Slide option in Advanced Analysis Office for Microsoft Excel to create the presentation (see Figure 8.49).

	Invoice Amount	Ord. Quantity	Invoice Amount/Ord. Quantity	Olympic Rank Number: Invoice Amount/Ord. Quantity	Rank Number: Average Delivery Time	Rank Number: Fulfillment Rate_Deliveries
Material		***				
Overall Result	276,479,340.00 MIX	1,476,834.000	187.21 MIX / ***	1	1	1
[-] Casing Notebook Speedy I CN	58,229,012.00 MIX	84,062.000	692.69 MIX / ***	1	3	5
ABC Technology	7,017,600.00 CAD	11,910.000	589.22 CAD / ***	3	6	2
Asia Technologies	$ 461,020.00	1,182.000	$ 390.03 / ***	6	1	6
Becker Components AG	10,802,711.00 MIX	19,650.000	549.76 MIX / ***	4	5	4
CompuMax Corp	818,400.00 CAD	1,364.000	600.00 CAD / ***	2	2	1
Générale Electronique	30,568,481.00 MIX	25,144.000	1,215.74 MIX / ***	1	3	5
Hatushiba Co. Ltd	$ 5,713,800.00	12,840.000	$ 445.00 / ***	5	7	1
HiTech Corp	£ 2,505,360.00	10,658.000	£ 235.07 / ***	8	4	3
SAPSOTA Corp	£ 341,640.00	1,314.000	£ 260.00 / ***	7	8	1
[+] Motherboard Terminal P600 CN	43,390,140.00 MIX	225,878.000	192.10 MIX / ***	5	5	2
[+] Motherboard Terminal P400 CN	33,792,088.00 MIX	182,798.000	184.86 MIX / ***	6	7	4

Figure 8.49 Advanced Analysis Office Presentation

Now we have a shareable presentation and we negotiate with our vendors for better prices and delivery.

In this section, we reviewed the option for leveraging the capabilities of Advanced Analysis Office in procurement and we ranked values against each other to find the best possible vendor for our products.

8.5 Summary

In this chapter, we provided you with a set of scenarios to highlight the options of how you can use Advanced Analysis Office as part of your day-to-day business and leverage its capabilities as much as possible. In the next chapter, we'll provide you with an overview of the product roadmap for Advanced Analysis Office.

Advanced Analysis Office combines features from SAP BusinessObjects Voyager and functions from SAP Business Explorer (BEx) Analyzer. This chapter contains an outlook into the product roadmap for Advanced Analysis Office.

9 Advanced Analysis — Product Outlook

In this chapter, we will look at the roadmap for Advanced Analysis as the successor to BEx Analyzer and BEx Web Reporting. This roadmap will cover details on Advanced Analysis Office and details on the upcoming release of Advanced Analysis, Web Edition, and integration with the upcoming release of SAP BusinessObjects XI 4.0.

> **Product Roadmap Disclaimer**
>
> The preceding descriptions of future functionality are the author's interpretation of the publicly available product integration roadmap. These items are subject to change at any time without notice, and the author does not provide any warranty on these statements.

9.1 Advanced Analysis, Edition for Microsoft Office

In this section, we will review the product roadmap for Advanced Analysis Office and how it will evolve from its initial release on SAP BusinessObjects XI 3.1 to its integration with XI 4.0, fully replacing the BEx Analyzer.

As you can see in Figure 9.1, the focus of the initial release of Advanced Analysis Office is to provide a best-in-class integration with SAP NetWeaver Business Information Warehouse (BW) and a great user experience by providing a product that lets you conduct interactive multidimensional workflows. For the second release,

9 | Advanced Analysis — Product Outlook

which is planned for 2011 in conjunction with the SAP BusinessObjects XI 4.0 release, the focus is on letting customers migrate their BEx Analyzer workbooks to Advanced Analysis workbooks. In addition, there are two major enhancements for the 2011 release — a write-back capability with integration into SAP NetWeaver BW Integrated Planning (BW-IP), and support for additional data sources, including the semantic layer from SAP BusinessObjects. The support for the semantic layer will enable new types of workflows within Advanced Analysis Office, as you will be able to leverage Advanced Analysis Office against any data source that is supported by the semantic layer — even relational sources.

Preliminary Roadmap – SAP BusinessObjects Advanced Analysis, Edition for Microsoft Office

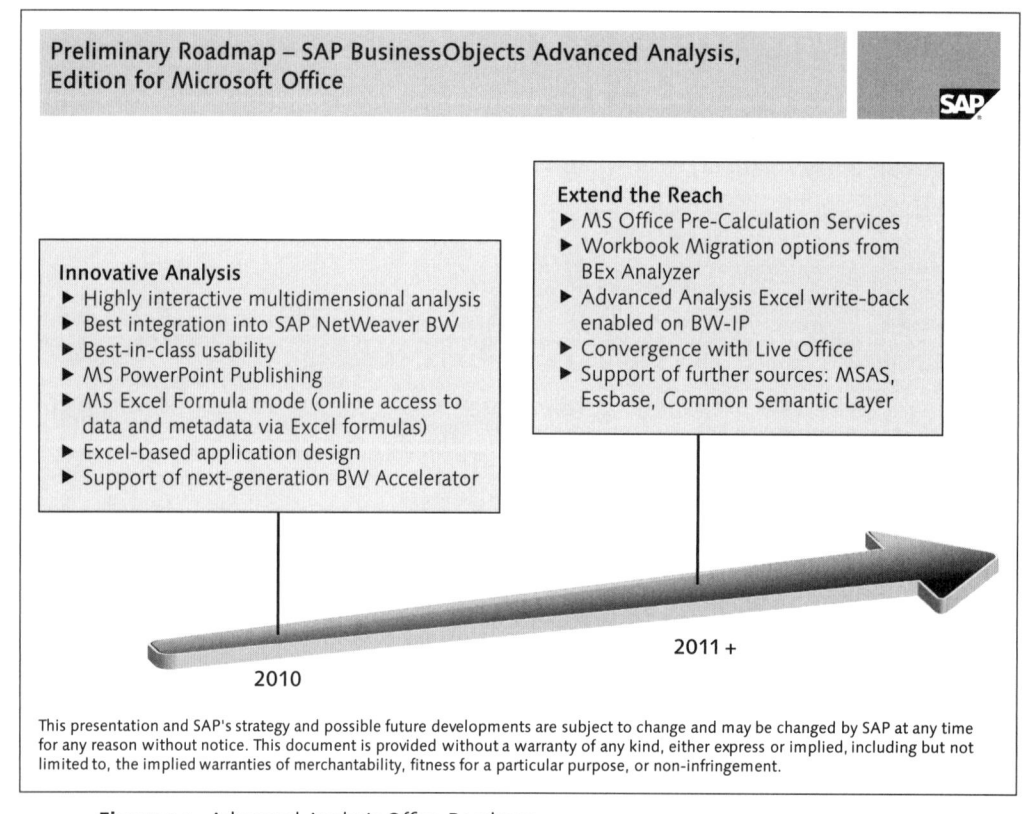

Innovative Analysis
- Highly interactive multidimensional analysis
- Best integration into SAP NetWeaver BW
- Best-in-class usability
- MS PowerPoint Publishing
- MS Excel Formula mode (online access to data and metadata via Excel formulas)
- Excel-based application design
- Support of next-generation BW Accelerator

Extend the Reach
- MS Office Pre-Calculation Services
- Workbook Migration options from BEx Analyzer
- Advanced Analysis Excel write-back enabled on BW-IP
- Convergence with Live Office
- Support of further sources: MSAS, Essbase, Common Semantic Layer

2010   2011 +

This presentation and SAP's strategy and possible future developments are subject to change and may be changed by SAP at any time for any reason without notice. This document is provided without a warranty of any kind, either express or implied, including but not limited to, the implied warranties of merchantability, fitness for a particular purpose, or non-infringement.

Figure 9.1 Advanced Analysis Office Roadmap

Figure 9.2 shows some important considerations for those waiting for an automatic migration of their BEx Analyzer workbooks to Advanced Analysis Office. Migrating BEx workbooks is planned for the second release of Advanced Analysis Office, but, as shown in Figure 9.2, there will be some limitations. Customers using workbooks with VBA code accessing the BEx Analyzer APIs, for example, should perform a manual migration or consider a re-creation of the workbooks in Advanced Analysis Office.

Migration from BEx Analyzer Workbooks to Advanced Analysis Workbooks

- Consideration of Workbook Migration*
  - Planned for version 2 of SAP BusinessObjects Advanced Analysis, edition for Microsoft Office
  - Planned scope of (semi-)automatic migration for BEx 3.5 & 7.0 Workbooks:
    - Workbooks without VBA programming
    - Standalone VBA code including result-set cell references
    - VBA code accessing BEx Analyzer APIs: conversion of callback macros in BEx 7.0 Workbooks (other API calls are not supported)
  - We recommend manual migration or new implementations
    - BEx 3.5 workbooks with VBA code accessing BEx Analyzer APIs
    - For complex workbooks
- SAP BusinessObjects Advanced Analysis, edition for Microsoft Office, substantially simplifies building of new reports
  - i.e., hidden sheets will typically not be needed any more
- Query Views based on BW InfoProviders & saved with SAP BusinessObjects Advanced Analysis, edition for Microsoft Office can be used by BEx tools

Please note: These are preliminary statements. The statements remain to be finalized once Advanced Analysis, edition for MS Office becomes available.

Figure 9.2 BEx Analyzer Workbook Migrations

In this section, we reviewed the roadmap for Advanced Analysis Office. In the next section we will move on to the upcoming release of Advanced Analysis, Web Edition.

9 | Advanced Analysis — Product Outlook

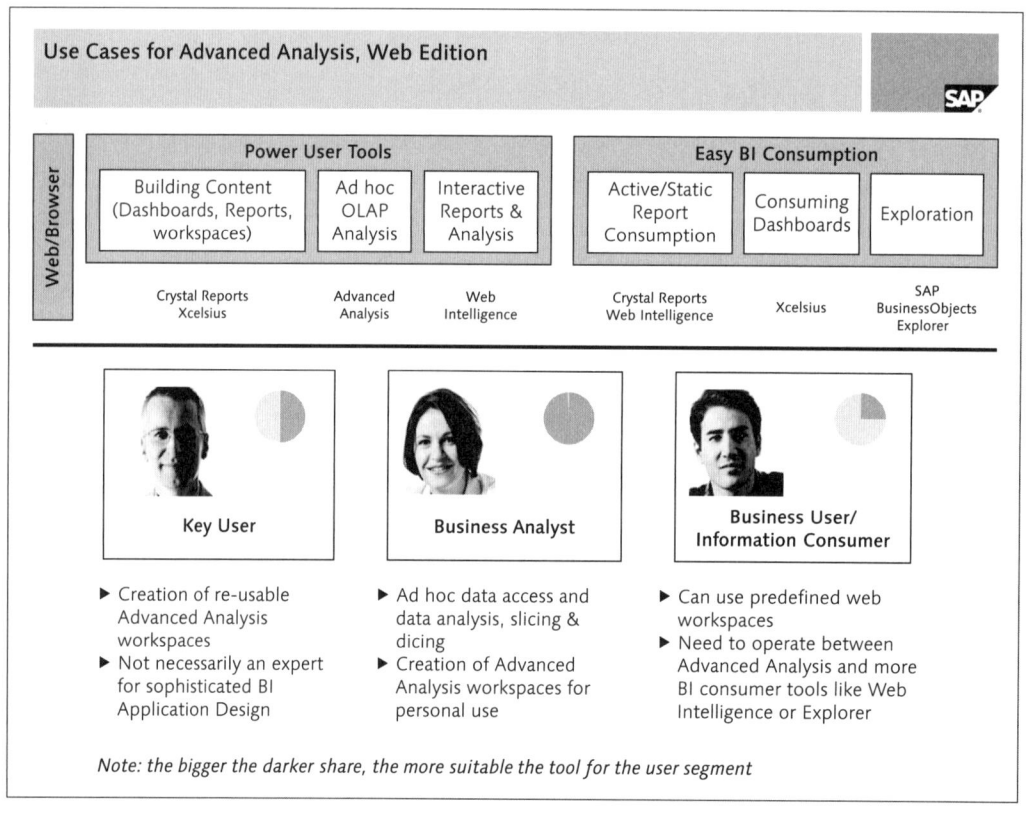

9.2 Advanced Analysis, Web Edition

In addition to the Microsoft Office Edition of Advanced Analysis, there is also a Web Edition of Advanced Analysis, so you can also replace BEx Web Reporting with Advanced Analysis and give your end users a consistent analysis tool.

It is very important to understand that Advanced Analysis Office and Advanced Analysis, Web Edition, target very different user groups. Whereas Advanced Analysis Office clearly targets the Business Analyst and the Information Consumer, you can see in Figure 9.3 that Advanced Analysis, Web Edition, also targets the Business Analyst but not so much the Information Consumer. Advanced Analysis, Web Edition, is designed for the classic Business Analyst and power user looking for typical analytical capabilities in the Business Intelligence (BI) client.

Figure 9.3 Advanced Analysis Web Edition

326

Figure 9.4 shows the roadmap for Advanced Analysis, Web Edition. The initial release of Advanced Analysis, Web Edition, is planned in conjunction with the release of SAP BusinessObjects XI 4.0 and will offer a very tight integration with SAP NetWeaver BW and provide a migration for those customers using Voyager. In addition to the support of SAP NetWeaver BW, Advanced Analysis, Web Edition, will also have support for Microsoft Analysis Services in the initial version. Figure 9.5 shows some of the advanced functionality Advanced Analysis, Web Edition, will deliver in its initial release, which will allow you to combine multiple data sources in a single workspace.

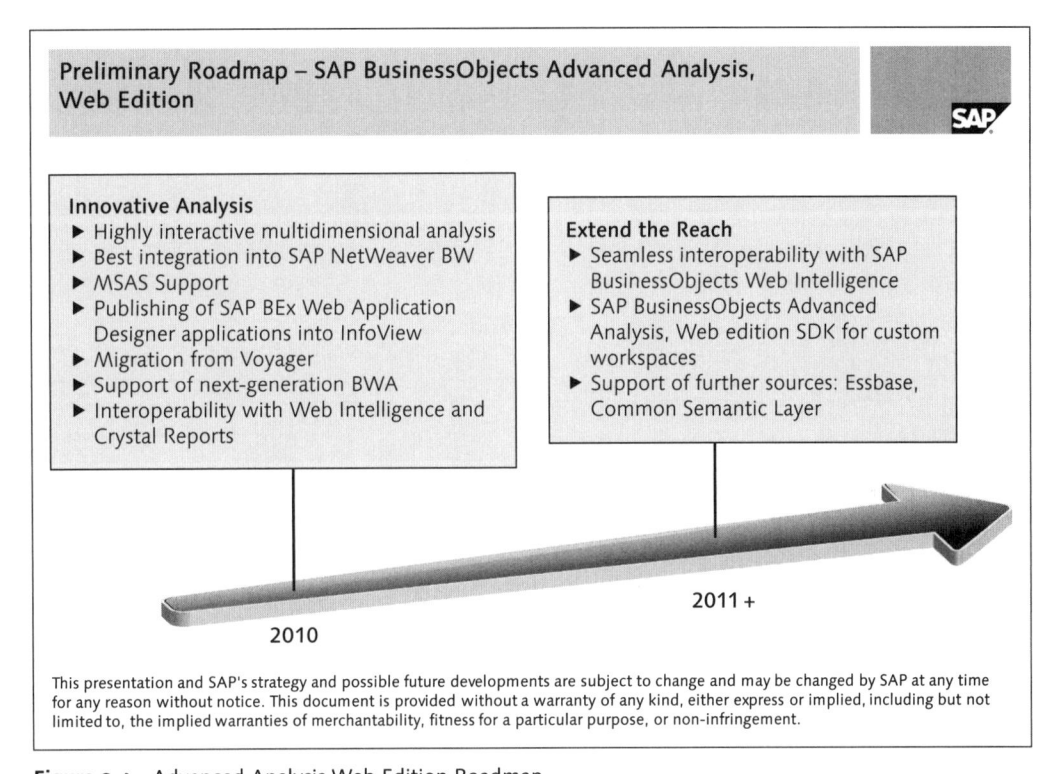

Preliminary Roadmap – SAP BusinessObjects Advanced Analysis, Web Edition

Innovative Analysis
- Highly interactive multidimensional analysis
- Best integration into SAP NetWeaver BW
- MSAS Support
- Publishing of SAP BEx Web Application Designer applications into InfoView
- Migration from Voyager
- Support of next-generation BWA
- Interoperability with Web Intelligence and Crystal Reports

Extend the Reach
- Seamless interoperability with SAP BusinessObjects Web Intelligence
- SAP BusinessObjects Advanced Analysis, Web edition SDK for custom workspaces
- Support of further sources: Essbase, Common Semantic Layer

2010
2011 +

This presentation and SAP's strategy and possible future developments are subject to change and may be changed by SAP at any time for any reason without notice. This document is provided without a warranty of any kind, either express or implied, including but not limited to, the implied warranties of merchantability, fitness for a particular purpose, or non-infringement.

Figure 9.4 Advanced Analysis Web Edition Roadmap

9 | Advanced Analysis — Product Outlook

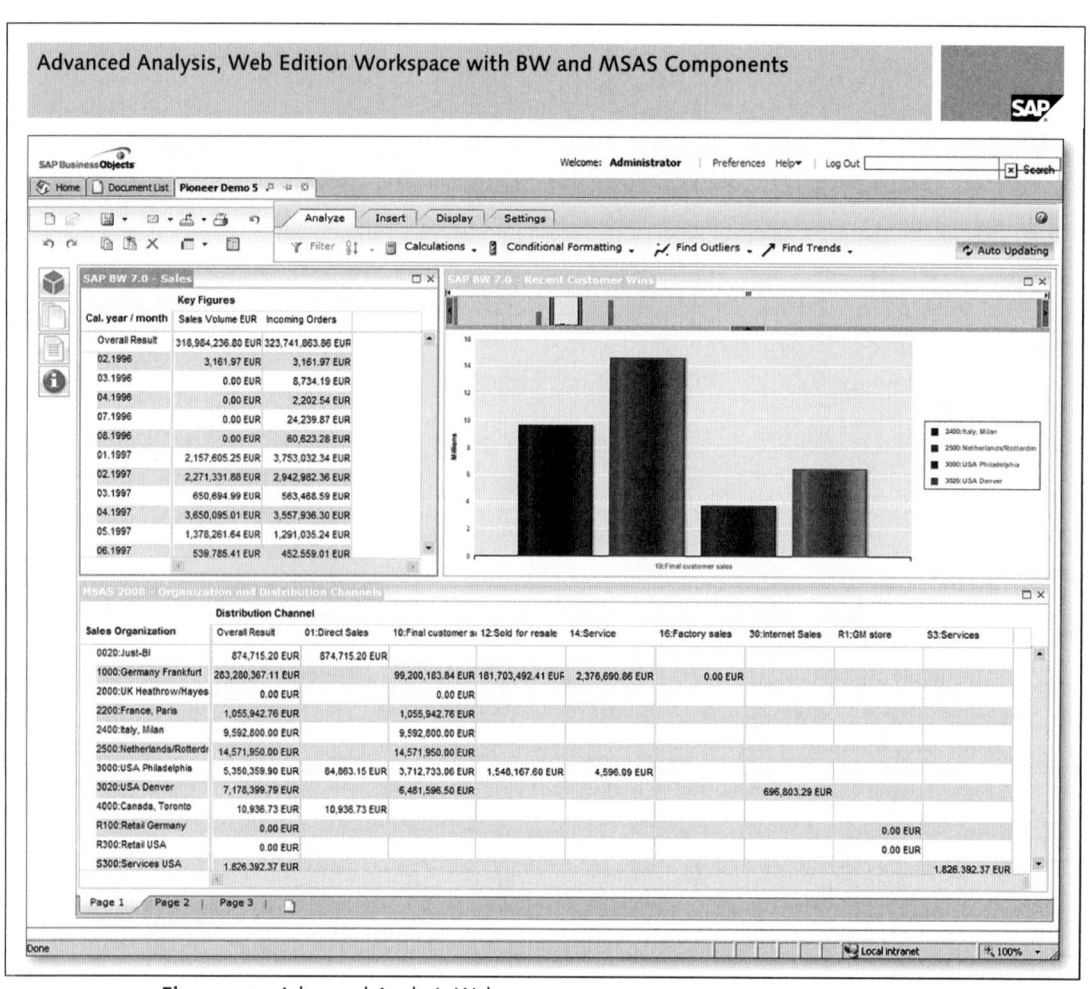

Figure 9.5 Advanced Analysis Web

Figure 9.6 shows the high-level architecture of Advanced Analysis, Web Edition, and you can see that Advanced Analysis, Web Edition, uses SAP BusinessObjects XI 4.0 for sharing connections, lifecycle management, and user authentication.

Advanced Analysis, Web Edition | 9.2

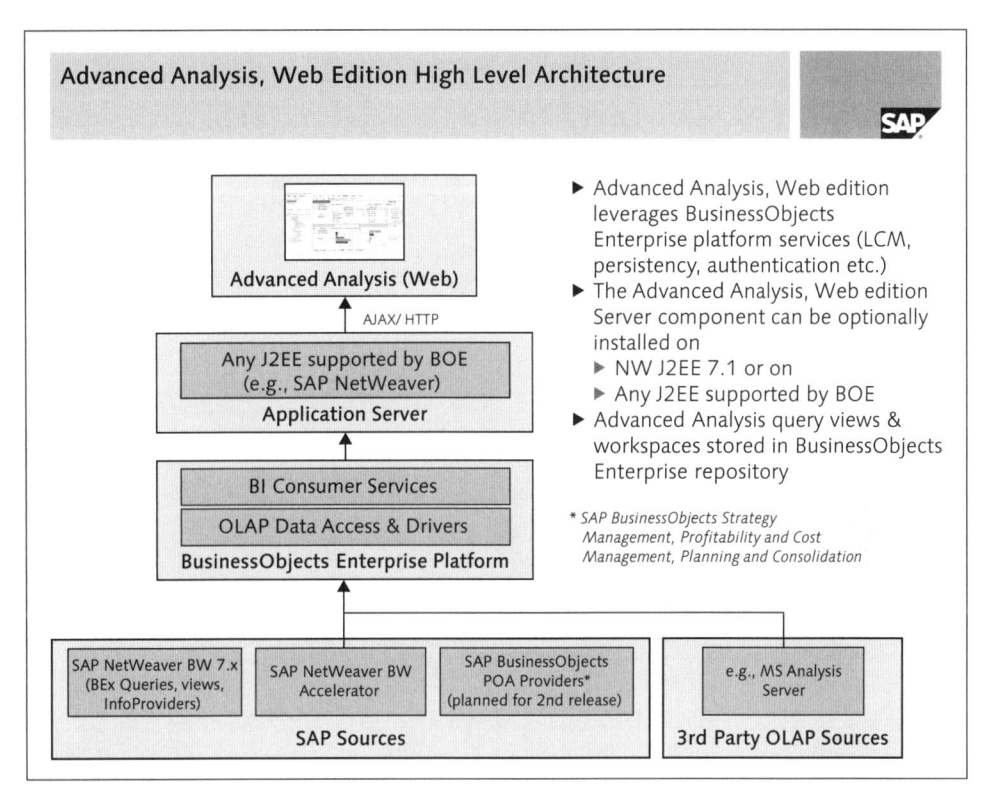

Figure 9.6 Advanced Analysis Architecture

Figure 9.7 is an overview of the plans for integrating BEx Web Application Designer (WAD) templates into SAP BusinessObjects Enterprise InfoView. The plan for this integration is to offer the option for integrating existing BEx WAD templates into SAP BusinessObjects XI 4.0 and leveraging the templates inside of InfoView and treat a BEx Web Application Designer template like any other content as part of your SAP BusinessObjects XI 4.0 platform. That way, you can consolidate all of your BI needs onto a single BI platform — SAP BusinessObjects XI 4.0.

In this section, we reviewed the roadmap for Advanced Analysis, Web Edition. In the next section, we will review the integration of Advanced Analysis Office and Advanced Analysis, Web Edition, with SAP BusinessObjects Enterprise XI 4.0.

9 | Advanced Analysis — Product Outlook

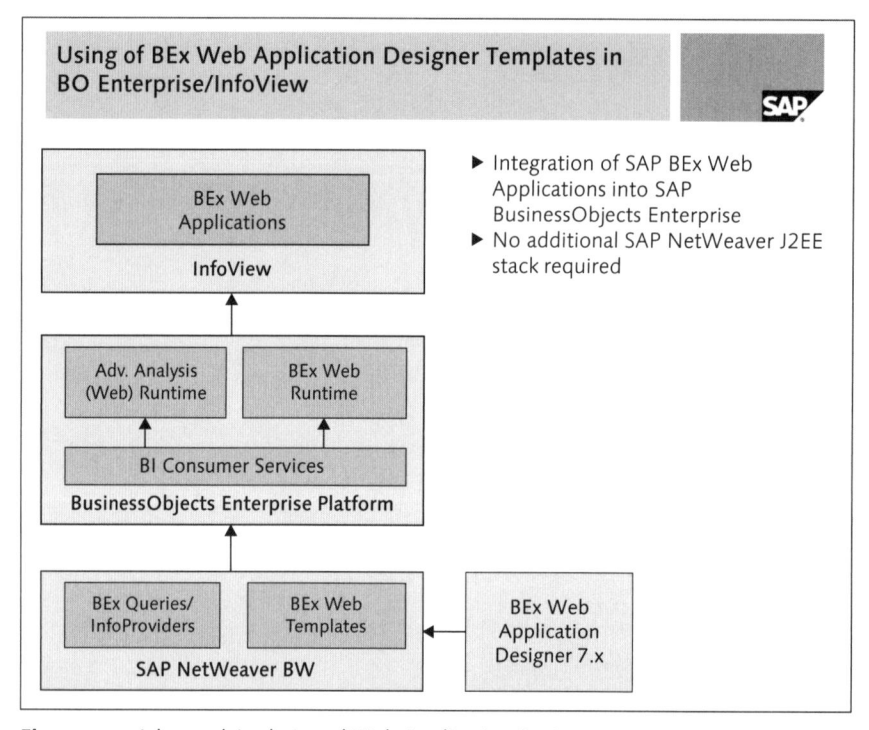

Figure 9.7 Advanced Analysis and Web Application Designer

9.3 Integration with SAP BusinessObjects XI 4.0

Advanced Analysis Office and Advanced Analysis, Web Edition, are both fully integrated with SAP BusinessObjects Enterprise. With the upcoming release of XI 4.0, the following is a list of enhancements that are planned for the integration between Advanced Analysis and SAP BusinessObjects Enterprise XI 4.0:

- SAP BusinessObjects Enterprise XI 4.0 will provide server-based and client-side SSO.

- Advanced Analysis Office and Advanced Analysis, Web Edition, will leverage the integration of SAP BusinessObjects Lifecycle Manager with the CTS+ transport mechanism, which is part of XI 4.0.

- Advanced Analysis will provide interoperability with other BI clients such as Crystal Reports and Web Intelligence.

Product interoperability of Advanced Analysis with other client tools (shown in Figure 9.8) is a great enhancement, where the user can leverage Advanced Analysis Office or Advanced Analysis, Web Edition, to start the analysis workflow and create a shared query definition. This shared query — also called Analysis View — can then be leveraged by Crystal Reports and Web Intelligence. The shared query will contain definitions, such as values for variables, filters, and the navigation status of the analysis, and each of the BI client tools — starting with Crystal Reports and Web Intelligence — will be able to leverage the shared query and provide a user experience best suited for the selected BI client.

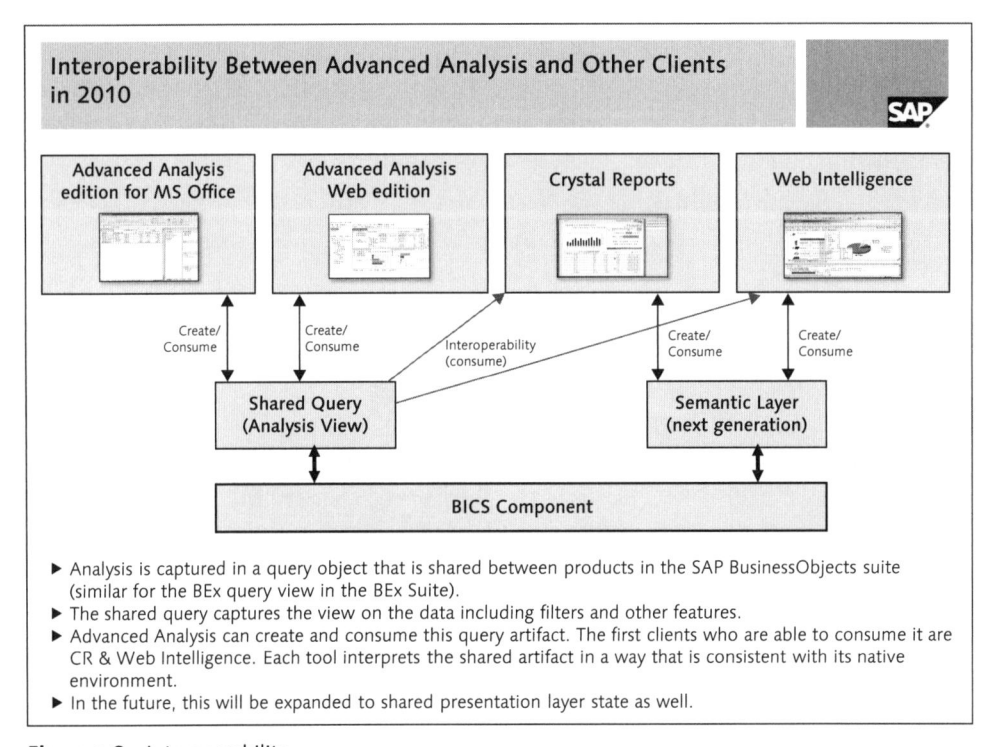

Figure 9.8 Interoperability

In this section, we reviewed the upcoming enhancements of the Advanced Analysis Office and Web Edition integration with SAP BusinessObjects Enterprise.

9.4 Beyond SAP BusinessObjects XI 4.0

In the previous sections we reviewed the product roadmap for Advanced Analysis Office and Advanced Analysis Web in combination with the upcoming release of SAP BusinessObjects XI 4.0. Now we will take a look even further into the future and review the plans beyond the XI 4.0 release in regards to the BI client portfolio.

Figure 9.9 shows the current portfolio of BI clients with analytical capabilities. On the far left you have the Web Application Designer (WAD) for creating custom BI applications. In addition you have Advanced Analysis Web Edition and Web Intelligence with the Business Analyst and Information Consumer as target audience, and on the far right you have SAP BusinessObjects Explorer as BI tool offering an exploration workflow. Advanced Analysis Office is seen as solution, which offers the functionality of Advanced Analysis Web, Web Intelligence, and some BI application building capabilities for the Microsoft environment. All of those BI clients are going to be available for the SAP BusinessObjects XI 4.0 platform.

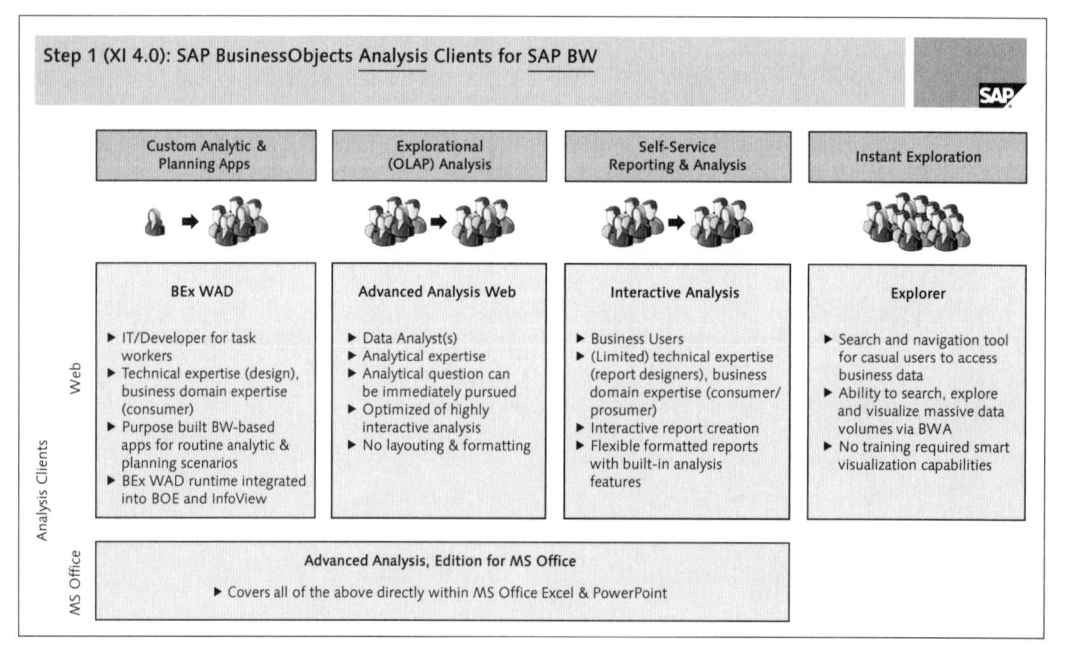

Figure 9.9 SAP BusinessObjects Analysis Clients

Figure 9.10 now shows the planned merging of functionality. You will notice two major changes. The first change being that the Web Application Designer (WAD) is being replaced with an Analytical Development Kit, which will provide you the capability to create BI applications including typical planning workflows and applications. The Analytical Development Kit is planned to be available as Eclipse Plug-In and will be integrated with other Software Development Kits (SDK) from the SAP BusinessObjects Enterprise platform.

The second major change is the merging of Advanced Analysis Web and Web Intelligence into a single BI client tool, which will provide interactive and advanced analysis functionality for the Business Analysis and the Information Consumer. In addition you can recognize that Advanced Analysis Office is not impacted by these changes.

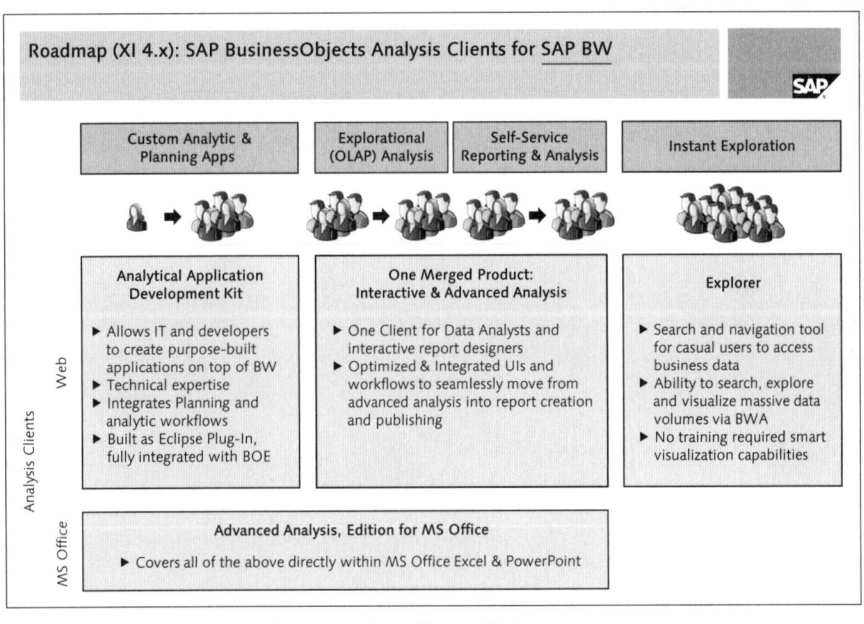

Figure 9.10 SAP BusinessObjects Analysis Clients XI 4.x

9.5 Summary

In this chapter, we reviewed the roadmap for Advanced Analysis Office and Advanced Analysis, Web Edition, and the integration capabilities of Advanced Analysis Office and Web Edition with SAP BusinessObjects.

The Author

Ingo Hilgefort started with Crystal Decisions in Frankfurt, Germany, in 1999 as a Trainer and Consultant for Crystal Reports and Crystal Enterprise. In 2001, he became part of a small team working at SAPs headquarters in Walldorf for Crystal Decisions as a Program Manager. During this time Ingo was working closely with the SAP BW development group and helped to design and shape the first integration of Crystal Reports with SAP BW, which then became an Original Equipment Manufacturer (OEM) relationship between SAP and Crystal Decisions. With the acquisition of Crystal Decisions by BusinessObjects, he then moved into Product Management for the integration between BusinessObjects and SAP. In 2004, Ingo moved to Vancouver, which is one of the main development sites for BusinessObjects.

In addition to his experience in Product Management and Engineering, Ingo has been involved in building and delivering BusinessObjects with SAP software for a number of worldwide customers. He has also been recognized by the SDN and BusinessObjects communities as a SDN Mentor for BusinessObjects and SAP integration–related topics.

Recently, Ingo has been working on BI End-to-End Solution Architecture, focusing on the SAP BusinessObjects BI portfolio and helping customers and partners successfully deploy this as part of their overall SAP landscape.

He is also the author of *Integrating BusinessObjects XI 3.1 BI Tools with SAP NetWeaver,* which focuses on the installation, deployment, and configuration of BusinessObjects software in an SAP landscape; *Reporting and Analytics with SAP BusinessObjects,* which focuses on selecting the right tools based on your requirements and how to best use them; and *Inside SAP BusinessObjects Explorer,* which focuses on using SAP BusinessObjects Explorer in combination with SAP NetWeaver BW Accelerator. All of these books are published by SAP PRESS.

Index

A

Abbreviate, 171, 248, 249, 251
Abbreviate table on this slide, 171, 174, 250
Access Level, 80, 82
Add Range, 136
Ad hoc, 25, 29
Administration services, 56
Adobe Flex, 34
Advanced, 80
Advanced Analysis, 15, 23, 24, 26, 31, 43, 44, 45, 54, 67, 323
Advanced Analysis, edition for Microsoft Office, 19
Advanced Analysis Office, 15, 26, 35, 36, 38, 39, 40, 43, 45, 46, 47, 49, 50, 53, 54, 55, 56, 57, 58, 59, 60, 66, 68, 70, 73, 75, 76, 83, 84, 85, 90, 187, 255, 261, 259, 266, 277, 279, 323, 324, 330
Advanced Analysis, Web Edition, 20, 25, 325, 327, 330
All dimensions Independently, 153, 156, 179
All Members and Total, 147
Allow External Access, 93
Apply Style Set, 243, 246
Apply Visualization to Another Measure, 148
Architecture, 54, 328
Attribute, 131
Attributes, 130, 135
Authentication, 64, 69, 83, 84, 108, 109, 261, 273, 274, 278, 279, 328
Authorization, 96, 257
Authorization Field, 77
Authorization Objects, 77
Authorizations, 58, 76, 77, 78
Authorization Value, 77
Authorization Variable, 96, 257

B

Background, 145
BEx, 19, 20, 21, 45, 73, 142, 187, 192, 234
BEx Analyzer, 19, 21, 23, 60, 73, 102, 142, 152, 255, 259, 323, 324
BEx Query, 85, 87
BEx Report Designer, 27
BEx text elements, 167
BEx Web Analyzer, 21, 23
BEx Web Application Designer, 329
BEx Web Reporting, 323, 325
BI, 25, 31
BI ABAP, 50
BIAR, 265
BI authorizations, 96
BI Java, 50
BOESettings.xml, 72
Break Hierarchies, 200
Business Analyst, 36, 39, 325, 326
Business Explorer Analyzer, 19, 31
Business Information Warehouse, 19, 50
BusinessObjects Lifecycle Manager, 262
BW, 15, 19, 21, 34, 38, 46, 50, 54, 56, 58, 60, 62, 64, 65, 68, 76, 85, 87, 89, 95, 96, 99, 101, 126, 130, 270, 273, 278, 323, 327
BW Accelerator, 35
BW documents, 258
BW-IP, 324
BW Query, 42, 65, 112
BW Query view, 112
By Data Source, 238, 241
By Sheet, 241

C

Calculated Key Figures, 94, 96, 256
Calculate Total AS, 163
Calculation, 41, 44, 173, 206, 207, 208, 210, 255, 259, 287, 289, 297, 308, 310, 318
Cell Editor, 256
Cell Styles, 244
Central Management Console, 62, 270
Central Management System, 69, 109
Characteristics, 87, 90, 93, 96, 112, 113, 216, 219, 256
Characteristic Values, 90
Characteristic Variables, 256
Chart, 140, 182, 295
Charting, 140, 142, 259
Client, 64
CMC, 62, 79, 82, 270, 271
CMS, 69, 109, 264
Column Headers, 148
COM Add-ins, 74
Compact display, 320
Compact Display in Rows, 204, 205
Components, 214, 215, 216, 237, 238, 240, 241
Compounded Characteristics, 256
Condition, 94, 96, 152, 161, 173, 255, 288, 289, 292
Conditional Formatting, 90, 142, 144, 149, 152, 173, 288, 289, 292, 309
Connection, 56, 57, 58, 59, 62, 63, 66, 68, 79, 82, 84, 89, 95, 102, 110, 111, 126, 206, 271, 273, 328
Connectivity, 85, 102
Constant Selection, 256
Contribution, 288, 292
Conversion Rates, 126
Convert to Formula, 213
Copy, 241
Create Slide, 232, 234, 320
Credentials, 84
Crosstab, 114

Crystal Analysis, 20
Crystal Reports, 26, 27, 28, 34, 38, 44, 45, 46, 60, 259, 330, 331
CTS, 330
Cube Browser, 65, 108, 273
Currency, 94, 96
Currency Conversion, 125, 255
Currency Conversion Type, 126
Custom Structures, 94, 96

D

Dashboard, 33, 45
Dashboarding, 33
Data Cells, 148, 150
Data Connectivity, 86
Data-Level Security, 270
Data Source, 218, 220, 224, 237
Data Source Name, 168, 226
Data Store Objects, 86
Decimal Places, 124, 178
Decimals, 93, 95
Decision tree, 40
Default area, 257
Defaults, 90
Default Values, 257
Delete Slides with Deleted Tables, 250
Deployment, 53, 55, 56, 57, 59, 60
Destination System, 265
Dimension, 90
Dimension Member, 218
Disable, 75
Disabling, 73
Discovery, 34
Display, 113, 135, 147, 176, 208, 214
Display as Hierarchy, 93, 95, 203
Display Attribute, 91, 93, 96, 130, 131, 256
Display settings, 93, 95
Display Symbols for Parent Members, 239
Distribution, 42, 45, 295

Index

Drill down, 290
DSO, 86, 87
Dynamic Calculation, 210, 289, 318

E

Effective Filters, 169
Element, 93
Enable, 75
Enabling, 73
Enterprise reporting, 27
ERP, 85
Exception aggregation, 255
Exceptions, 90, 94, 96, 142, 152, 256
EXIT, 257
Expand, 194
Expand to Level, 195, 197, 205
Expand Upwards (Rows), 197, 199
Exploration, 34
Export Style Sets, 246

F

Filter, 66, 86, 87, 93, 121, 126, 132, 134, 139, 173, 179, 228, 229, 256, 290, 306, 331
Filter by Measure, 132, 152, 153, 156, 161, 179, 181, 303, 304, 305, 312
Filter by Member, 132, 135, 143, 181, 201, 298
Filter Component, 230
Filter Members, 134
Filter Members and Swap With, 134
Filter Other Members, 134
Filtering, 126, 132, 134, 259
Flat Presentation, 120, 192, 303
Flat representation, 91
Folder, 82, 270
Force Prompts on Initial Refresh, 240
Format, 144
Formatting, 121, 125

Formula, 41, 44, 211, 213, 259
Formula Alias, 217, 238
Formula Variables, 256
Free Characteristics, 90
Functions, 216, 222, 223

G

General Format, 125
Guided navigations, 31

H

Hide Totals, 162, 179
Hide Totals for Single Members, 162
Hierarchical display, 193
Hierarchies, 41, 42, 44, 91, 94, 96, 120, 187, 188, 189, 190, 192, 204, 256, 257, 259, 299, 306
Hierarchy Level, 257
Hierarchy nodes, 299
Hierarchy Node Variables, 256
Hierarchy Variables, 256
Highlight, 292
Highlighting, 308

I

Import Style Sets, 246
InfoAreas, 104
InfoCubes, 86, 87
Info Fields, 226, 236, 295
InfoObject, 122
InfoProvider, 65, 85, 95, 96, 99, 105, 108, 112, 285
InfoProviderName, 226
InfoProviderTechName, 226
Information Consumer, 36, 39, 325
InfoSets, 85, 86, 87
InfoView, 261, 280, 281

Insert Component, 229
Insert Crosstab, 242
Insert Field, 168
Installation, 49, 52, 67
Integrated Planning, 324
Interoperability, 259, 330

K

Key, 93
Key Date, 96, 169, 226
Key Date Variables, 94, 96
Key Figures, 90, 93, 94, 96, 113, 122, 132, 216, 219, 256, 257
Key performance indicators, 43
KPI, 43, 47

L

Last Data Update, 168, 226, 235
Lean Deployment, 55, 56
Lifecycle Management, 261, 328
Lifecycle Manager, 58, 262, 266, 269, 330
Lifecycle mechanism, 56
Limitations, 324
Live Office, 34, 38
Load behavior, 75, 281
Log files, 67
Logon language, 76

M

Manage Dependencies, 267
Mandatory Variables, 165, 257
Maximum number of rows, 174, 233, 249
Measure, 90, 130, 131, 132, 220, 229
Measure Display, 125
Measure Format, 177
Member, 90, 147, 150

Member Combination, 220
Member Display, 122, 127, 176, 218, 219
Member Display Type, 130, 176
Metadata, 85, 87, 89, 90, 95, 256
Microsoft Analysis Services, 327
Microsoft Office, 41, 44
Microsoft Office 2007, 53
Migration, 259, 324, 325, 327
More Sort Options, 129, 176
Most Detailed Dimension in Columns, 154, 158
Most Detailed Dimension in Rows, 154, 157, 158
Multilingual, 75, 170
MultiProviders, 86, 87

N

Navigation, 86
Navigational Attributes, 94, 96, 256
NetWeaver Demo model, 99
Number Format, 124, 125, 177
Number of rows, 171

O

Object-Level Security, 270
Offline, 42, 46
OLAP, 31
OLAP Intelligence, 20
Open Workbook, 71, 110
Optimum Cell Width/Height, 239
Optional Variables, 165, 257
Options, 69

P

Parent Nodes, 257
Pause Refresh, 114
Percentage contribution, 210, 288, 292

Percentage share, 308
Personalization, 258
Personas, 38, 39
Pioneer, 23, 24, 26
Planning, 258
Precalculated, 42
Precalculating, 258
Principals, 79, 82
Product roadmap, 323
Profitability, 296, 300
Promotion Job, 263
Prompt, 90, 106, 166, 167
Prompting, 106, 164, 165
Properties, 216, 238
Provider, 64

Q

Query, 85, 86, 87, 88, 90, 91, 92, 93, 95, 96, 99, 126, 143, 164, 165, 187, 188, 192, 175, 234, 255, 273, 285, 300
Query as a web service, 34
QueryCreatedBy, 226
QueryLastChangedAt, 226
QueryLastChangedBy, 226
QueryTechName, 226
Query View, 86, 109, 274

R

Range, 239
Range Selection, 137
Ranking, 152, 306, 318
Refresh All, 252
Refresh Workbook on Opening, 240
Remote Cubes, 86
Repeat Members, 239
Replacement Paths, 257
Report Report Interface, 258
Repository, 56, 79, 110
Requirements, 25, 36, 40, 41, 42, 43, 44, 45, 46, 47

Restricted Key Figures, 94, 96, 256
Result, 162
Ribbon, 66, 68, 76, 103
Rights, 76, 81, 82
Roadmap, 323, 327
Row Headers, 148, 150
RRI, 258

S

SAPBorder, 246
SAP BusinessObjects Enterprise, 50, 54, 55, 57, 59, 60, 68, 72, 76, 78, 82, 83, 110, 261, 261, 270, 271, 277, 279, 330
SAP BusinessObjects Explorer, 34, 35, 60
SAPDataCell, 246
SAPDataTotalCell, 247
SAPDimensionCell, 245, 247
SAPEmphasized, 247
SAPExceptionLevel, 247
SAP Frontend, 55, 56, 58, 62, 102, 111
SAPGetData, 219
SAPGetDimensionDynamicFilter, 222
SAPGetDimensionEffectiveFilter, 222, 223, 224
SAPGetDimensionInfo, 222
SAPGetDimensionStaticFilter, 222
SAPGetDisplayedMeasures, 222, 225
SAPGetInfoLabel, 222, 226
SAPGetMeasureFilter, 222
SAPGetMember, 218, 221, 222
SAPGetSourceInfo, 223, 227
SAPGetVariable, 223
SAPGetWorkbookInfo, 223
SAPHierarchyCell, 247
SAPHierarchyOddCell, 247
SAPListOfEffectiveFilters, 223
SAPListOfVariables, 223
SAPMemberCell, 245, 247
SAPMemberTotalCell, 247
SAP NetWeaver BW, 16, 20, 55, 64, 65, 76, 85

341

SAP NetWeaver BW Accelerator, 35
SAP NetWeaver Demo Model, 99
SAP NetWeaver Frontend, 51
SAPSetFilterComponent, 223
Save Style Set, 245
Save Workbook, 71, 276
Saving workbooks, 110
Scaling Factor, 93, 95, 124, 178
Scenarios, 285
Scheduling, 258
Search, 136
Secure Network Communication, 278
Security, 79, 80, 82, 269
Select All Members, 139, 212
Select Data Source, 68, 103, 115, 191, 206, 211, 215, 236
Selection, 92, 146, 150
Self-service, 29
Semantic layer, 35, 324
Server-side trust, 278, 279
Server Type, 64
Settings, 66, 67
Shared connection, 107, 111
Shared query, 331
Sharing, 57, 59
Show Levels, 197, 205
Single Sign On, 59, 261
Slice-and-dice, 259
SNC, 60, 84, 278, 279, 280
SNC0, 278
Sort, 128, 129, 176
Sort Ascending, 127
Sort by, 199
Sorting, 126, 128
Sort options, 130, 176, 199
Source System, 263, 264
Split, 171, 248, 249, 251
Split table across multiple slides, 249, 251
SSO, 59, 60, 84, 108, 261, 274, 278, 279, 330
Status Symbol, 145

Store Prompts with Workbook, 240
Structure, 42, 44, 91, 93, 92, 93, 94, 95, 256
Structure elements, 93
Styles, 242, 245
Style Sets, 244, 246
SU01, 278
Subtotals, 161, 221
Supported Functionality, 255
Support Settings, 67
Suppress Zeros in Columns, 139
Suppress Zeros in Rows, 139
Swap, 290
Swap Axes, 119, 173
System, 64, 69, 226
System Number, 64

T

Table Layout, 176
Table Tools, 172
Target Currency, 126
Technical Prerequisites, 49
Temporal Hierarchy Join, 257
Terms, 90
Text, 93
Text Variables, 166, 256
Time dependency, 42, 44
Time-dependent, 43, 47, 96, 190
Top N, 154
Total, 147, 156, 161, 162
Total Columns Left of Members, 162
Total Rows above Members, 162
Transaction, 278
Transient Provider, 85
Transport, 330
Trend, 295
Trend Analysis, 259
Trend Ascending, 145
Trend Descending, 145, 149
Trend Grey, 145

U

Unit, 94, 96
Universe, 34
Use Data Source, 214, 215
User Authentication, 278
User management, 278
User Security, 79, 82
User Settings, 66

V

Value, 145
Variables, 90, 94, 96, 101, 106, 111, 164, 165, 169, 256, 331
Variants, 258
VBA, 260, 324
Virtual InfoCubes, 86
Visualization, 33
Voyager, 19, 20, 21, 23, 24, 31, 45, 62, 327
Voyager Connection, 62, 79, 82, 266, 272, 279, 280

W

WAD, 329
Web Application Designer, 21
Web Intelligence, 26, 29, 30, 31, 34, 35, 38, 44, 45, 50, 60, 259, 330, 331
Web Service URL, 69, 109
What-if analysis, 42, 45
Workbook, 86, 110, 235, 258, 270, 276, 277, 280, 295, 324
Wrap Headers, 239
Write-back, 324

X

Xcelsius, 26, 28, 33, 34, 45, 60
Xcelsius SDK, 34

Z

Zero suppression, 256

www.sap-press.com

Learn how to create effective reports for specific enterprise reporting needs using NetWeaver BW 7

Build composite reports using multiple BEx tools with ease, including report designer, Web analyzer, Excel analyzer, and Web application designer

Discover a plethora of hidden reporting functionality not available anywhere else

Jason Kraft

SAP NetWeaver BW 7 Reporting

This book provides a detailed, how-to guide for anyone using NetWeaver BW and the BEx tools to generate reports. It will teach how to design effective, good looking reports that meet business objectives and provide an up-to-date resource covering the latest version of NetWeaver BW 7.0.

approx. 480 pp., 79,95 Euro / US$ 79.95
ISBN 978-1-59229-357-5, Nov 2010

>> www.sap-press.com

SAP PRESS

www.sap-press.com

Discover how to develop and implement successful BW data models

Find complete explanations of key topics, including Architecture, Information Objects, Info Providers and SAP Business Content

Learn about Business Intelligence (BI) planning and related Business Object innovations

Frank K. Wolf, Stefan Yamada

Data Modeling in SAP NetWeaver BW

This book provides consultants, project/implementation teams, and IT staffs with clear guidance on how to develop, implement, maintain, and upgrade SAP data models. The book starts by explaining the entire data modeling process, from the logical design of a model through enterprise requirements, technical framework, and implementation requirements. It then moves into a more in-depth review of the technical/component requirements and maps the technologies to the specific business requirements outlined in the first chapter. The next several chapters focus on the primary foundations of a data model (i.e. Info Objects, Key Figures, Data Store Objects, etc.) and the principles of data modeling, including data architecture, data loading and transformation.

554 pp., 2010, 79,95 Euro / US$ 79.95
ISBN 978-1-59229-346-9

>> www.sap-press.com

www.sap-press.com

Explains what Explorer is and how it can be used in daily business activities

Details how to integrate and get Explorer up and running quickly

Uses real-world scenarios to show how it works in financials, HR, CRM, and retail

Ingo Hilgefort

Inside SAP BusinessObjects Explorer

With this book you'll learn what SAP BusinessObjects Explorer is, and find out how to install, deploy, and use it. Written for people who are interested in bringing Business Intelligence to business users, this book will teach you how to use it in your SAP environment and address specific questions about how it works with your existing SAP tools and data. After reading this book, you'll understand why and how to leverage Explorer to bring quick and easy access to data analysis to users throughout your company.

307 pp., 2010, 69,95 Euro / US$ 69.95
ISBN 978-1-59229-340-7

>> www.sap-press.com

SAP PRESS

www.sap-press.com

Explains how to use all of the features in Xcelsius

Teaches you how to build and customize interactive dashboards to effectively visualize your key business data

Provides guidance on using Xcelsius in an SAP environment

Ray Li, Evan Delodder

Creating Dashboards with Xcelsius - Practical Guide

Learn how to build your own Xcelsius dashboards, with this practical book. It explains how to use Xcelsius in an end-to-end, linear "common usage" manner, while highlighting typical scenarios where each feature can be used to solve business problems. It also gives you detailed, step-by-step guidance and best-practices for each feature, along with hands-on exercises that will help you begin creating dashboards and visualizations quickly. And if you're more advanced, you'll learn how to customize the Xcelsius components, themes, and data connections so you can use Xcelsius to the fullest extent.

approx. 587 pp., 49,95 Euro / US$ 49.95
ISBN 978-1-59229-335-3, Aug 2010

>> www.sap-press.com

SAP PRESS

www.sap-press.com

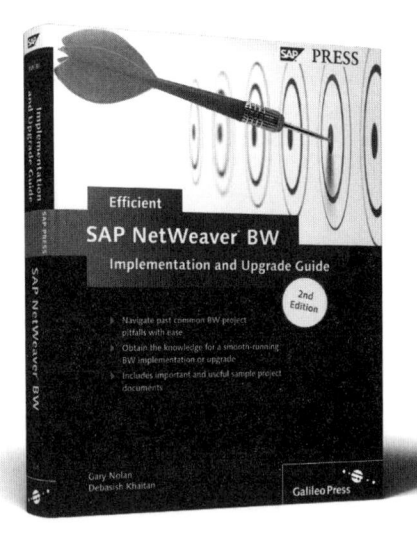

Explore the steps and components that ensure an efficient and smooth SAP BW implementation and upgrade

Learn about common practices and typical resource considerations for SAP BW projects

Leverage sample documents to help with your implementation/upgrade

Gary Nolan, Debasish Khaitan

Efficient SAP NetWeaver BW Implementation and Upgrade Guide

This book offers a clear and easy-to-follow path for efficient SAP BW implementations and upgrades. The book starts by defining a typical NetWeaver BW project lifecycle, followed by an examination of proper project management and upgrade strategies, including understanding common mistakes, resource requirements, and project planning and development. The topics are presented in a linear, intuitive, project-based scenario, to help you navigate easily through all stages of the project, including pre-project considerations, actual project guidance, as well as the Go-Live and Post-Live monitoring and maintenance considerations.

532 pp., 2. edition 2010, 79,95 Euro / US$ 79.95
ISBN 978-1-59229-336-0

>> www.sap-press.com

www.sap-press.com

Provides up-to-date, practical content for using Crystal Reports 2008.

Offers end-users and report designers targeted coverage for using Crystal Reports against SAP BW.

Written in an accessible, casual, very readable manner.

Mike Garrett

Using Crystal Reports with SAP

This book is a complete guide to the core functions of Crystal Reports, particularly as related to integration with other SAP data sources. The practical guidelines will give you the knowledge you need to create your own meaningful content using Crystal Reports with SAP BW as quickly as possible. And the end-of-chapter projects will help solidify and reinforce the reporting concepts presented and give you the foundation you need to begin creating your own formatted reports, sub-reports, alert reports, drill down reports, and more.

442 pp., 2010, 69,95 Euro / US$ 69.95
ISBN 978-1-59229-327-8

>> www.sap-press.com

www.sap-press.com

Provides a comprehensive guide to understanding Web Intelligence and its many functions.

Teaches how to integrate Web Intelligence with multiple data sources.

Shows how to customize and extend Web Intelligence using the SDK and Web Intelligence Extension Points.

Jim Brogden, Mac Holden, Heather Sinkwitz

SAP BusinessObjects Web Intelligence

With this complete guide to Web Intelligence, you'll learn what you need to know to generate your own queries and reports. For those of you who are new to the tool, the book begins with an overview of the fundamentals about what it is and then progresses through practical insights into the details of how to use it in your everyday work. And for those with more advanced knowledge, there is coverage of advanced topics and third party connectivity issues that will help you extend and maximize the usefulness of Web Intelligence.

583 pp., 2010, 79,95 Euro / US$ 79.95
ISBN 978-1-59229-322-3

>> www.sap-press.com

SAP PRESS

Interested in reading more?

Please visit our Web site for all
new book releases from SAP PRESS.

www.sap-press.com